OXFORD PHYSICS IN
THE THIRTEENTH CENTURY
(CA. 1250-1270)

STUDIEN UND TEXTE ZUR GEISTESGESCHICHTE DES MITTELALTERS

BEGRÜNDET VON

JOSEF KOCH

WEITERGEFÜHRT VON

PAUL WILPERT UND ALBERT ZIMMERMANN

HERAUSGEGEBEN VON

JAN A. AERTSEN

IN ZUSAMMENARBEIT MIT

TZOTCHO BOIADJIEV, KENT EMERY, JR.
UND ANDREAS SPEER (MANAGING EDITOR)

BAND LXXII

CECILIA TRIFOGLI

OXFORD PHYSICS IN
THE THIRTEENTH CENTURY
(CA. 1250-1270)

OXFORD PHYSICS IN THE THIRTEENTH CENTURY (CA. 1250-1270)

MOTION, INFINITY, PLACE AND TIME

BY

CECILIA TRIFOGLI

BRILL
LEIDEN · BOSTON · KÖLN
2000

This book is printed on acid-free paper.

Library of Congress Cataloging-in-Publication Data

Trifogli, Cecilia.
  Oxford physics in the thirteenth century (ca. 1250-1270) : motion, infinity, place, and time / by Cecilia Trifogli.
     p.   cm. — (Studien und Texte zur Geistesgeschichte des Mittelalters, ISSN 0169-8125 ; Bd. 72)
  Includes bibliographical references and index.
  ISBN 9004116575 (cloth : alk. paper)
     1. Aristotle. Physics. 2. Physics—Early works to 1800. 3. Physics—Study and teaching (Higher)—England—Oxford—History—To 1500. 4. Philosophy, Medieval.   I. Title.   II. Series.
  Q151 .T75   2000
  509'.42'09022—dc21
                                                                          00–029747
                                                                          CIP

Die Deutsche Bibliothek - CIP-Einheitsaufnahme

Cecilia Trifogli:
Oxford physics in the thirteenth century (ca. 1250-1270) / by Cecilia Trifogli. – Leiden ; Boston ; Köln : Brill, 2000
   (Studien und Texte zur Geistesgeschichte des Mittelalters ; Bd. 72)
   ISBN 90–04–11657–5

ISSN 0169-8125
ISBN 90 04 11657 5

PRINTED IN THE NETHERLANDS

CONTENTS

ACKNOWLEDGEMENTS

This book represents the first substantial result of my research about the English commentaries of the thirteenth century that I have carried out over the last ten years. I wish here to express my gratitude to all those who have contributed to its accomplishment.

First and foremost I want to thank the scientific director of my research, Prof. Francesco Del Punta, for suggesting the study of this topic to me, for his unfailing guide and constant support. I am also much grateful to Dr. Silvia Donati for her fruitful collaboration to the research-project about the English commentaries. Helpful comments and suggestions were made by Prof. Marilyn MacCord Adams, Prof. Stephen Dumont, and Prof. Richard Sorabji. I wish to thank William Duba for revising my English.

The De Wulf-Mansion Centrum of the University of Leuven and the Thomas-Institut of the University of Cologne provided a pleasant and stimulating environment to work in. Special thanks for their help and hospitality are due to Prof. Jozeph Brams, and Prof. Carlos Steel (University of Leuven), and to Prof. Andreas Speer, Prof. Albert Zimmermann, and Prof. Jan Aertsen (University of Cologne).

Materially, the research for this book has been financed by a variety of sources: the Fondazione "Ezio Franceschini", the Italian National Council for Research (CNR), the Italian Ministry of University and Scientific and Technological Research (MURST), the Alexander-von-Humboldt Stiftung, to which all my thanks go.

INTRODUCTION

1. *Content, Aim, and Limits of This Book*

This book offers an analysis of the reception of Aristotle's theories of motion, infinity, place, and time in a group of ten commentaries on the *Physics* that were most probably written in Oxford between 1250 and 1270, which is to say, before that of Aquinas. These "early English" commentaries, as we shall call them, are still unedited, preserved mostly in single manuscripts and, with a few exceptions, by unidentified authors.

In his book *Verzeichnis ungedruckter Kommentare zur Metaphysik und Physik des Aristoteles*, published in 1971, A. Zimmermann made the first systematic investigation into the early English tradition of commentaries on the *Physics*. Zimmermann examined some thirty manuscripts, mostly from Cambridge, Oxford and Paris libraries, gave a brief general description of the commentaries, and listed the questions in each. He further provided basic information concerning their structure, interrelations, and sources. More recently, our knowledge of the early English commentaries has grown considerably owing to the work of S. Donati. On the basis of complete transcriptions, Donati has developed a system of description that carefully records for each of these commentaries essential information concerning its extent, author, dating, style, and cross-references to other Aristotelian commentaries by the same author.[1]

Since the publication of Zimmermann's pioneering work some exegetical studies on specific commentaries or topics have indeed appeared;[2] yet, no significant attempt to compare a large number of

---

[1] See S. Donati, "Per lo studio dei commenti alla *Fisica* del XIII secolo. I: Commenti di probabile origine inglese degli anni 1250-1270 ca.", first part, *Documenti e studi sulla tradizione filosofica medievale*, 2 (1991), p. 361-441; second part, ibid., 4 (1993), p. 25-133.

[2] See H. Riggert, "Vier Fragen über die Zahl. Ein ungedruckter Text des Wilhelm von Clifford zu Arist. Phys. IV 14", in A. Zimmermann (ed.), *Aristotelisches Erbe im arabisch-lateinischen Mittelalter. Uebersetzungen, Kommentare, Interpretationen* (*Miscellanea Mediaevalia*, Bd. 18), De Gruyter, Berlin-New York 1986, p. 81-95; S. Donati, "Materie und räumliche Ausdehnung in einigen ungedruckten englischen Physikkommentaren aus der Zeit von etwa 1250-1270", in J. Aertsen, A. Speer (eds.), *Raum und Raumvorstellungen im Mittelalter* (*Miscellanea Mediaevalia*, Bd. 25), De Gruyter,

these early English commentaries on a variety of topics from Aristotle's *Physics* has so far been made. The present book is a first attempt in that direction. There are several objective reasons for choosing the topics of motion, infinity, place, and time: theoretically, they are basic notions of Aristotelian natural philosophy; historically, they tend to be the focus of the medieval debate, especially in the thirteenth century; practically, they are discussed in books III and IV of the *Physics*, which, for most of the commentaries considered here, include a complete set of questions, unlike the subsequent books (V-VIII).

We do not intend to give a complete account of all the topics discussed in the early English commentaries on *Physics* III and IV, but rather to concentrate only on those topics that are significant, either as expressions of the underlying ontological assumptions or for the assessment of our commentaries' position in the thirteenth-century tradition of Aristotle's *Physics*.[3] Our systematic approach is inspired by Anneliese Maier's *Studien zur Naturphilosophie der Spätscholastik*, published between 1949 and 1955. Indeed, the aim of our study is in effect to write the missing first chapter to the conceptual history of Aristotelian natural philosophy in the Middle Ages that Maier has so masterfully presented for the period from Aquinas onwards. As to a more comprehensive approach, this will be offered by a repertory of the questions on Books III and IV of the *Physics* in the early English commentaries that we are preparing and hope to publish soon.

The most obvious limitation to the present study is that our reconstruction of the early English interpretations of motion, infinity, place, and time is based exclusively on commentaries on the *Physics*,

---

Berlin-New York 1998, p. 17-51. Ead., "*Physica* I, 1: L'interpretazione dei commentatori inglesi della *Translatio Vetus* e la loro recezione del commento di Averroè", *Medioevo*, 21 (1995), p. 75-255. R. Plevano, "Richard Rufus of Cornwall and Geoffrey of Aspall. Two Questions on the Instant of Change", *Medioevo*, 19 (1993), p. 167-232. R. Wood, "Richard Rufus of Cornwall on Creation: The Reception of Aristotelian Physics in the West", *Medieval Philosophy and Theology*, 2 (1992), p. 1-30. Ead., "Richard Rufus of Cornwall and Aristotle's Physics", *Franciscan Studies*, 52 (1992), p. 247-279. Ead., "Richard Rufus: Physics at Paris before 1240", *Documenti e studi sulla tradizione filosofica medievale*, 5 (1994), p. 87-127. Rufus' *Physics* commentary was not known at the time of Zimmermann's book. It has recently been discovered by Rega Wood in an Erfurt manuscript. On Rufus' commentary, see below, p. 31-32.

[3] Most notably, the early English commentators' treatment of Aristotle's discussion of the void (*Physics* IV.6-9) has been left out of this study because it is not of major historical or philosophical interest. However, an analysis of some aspects of their treatment of the void can be found in C. Trifogli, "Le questioni sul libro IV della *Fisica* in alcuni commenti inglesi intorno alla metà del sec. XIII. Parte II", *Documenti e studi sulla tradizione filosofica medievale*, 9 (1998), p. 208-221.

whereas the treatment of these topics in theological sources, such as *Sentences* commentaries, is not taken into account. A major practical reason for this limit is that our actual knowledge of *Sentences* commentaries for this period, just as with *Physics* commentaries, is scanty and fragmentary: few are known at all and even fewer are edited. The edition of some important *Sentences* commentaries, such as that of Richard Fishacre,[4] is currently under way and will make possible a broader view of the early English tradition.

As to its structure, this study consists of four main chapters devoted respectively to motion (1), infinity (2), place (3), and time (4). Chapter 1, on motion, focuses on the debate over the ontological status of motion arising from Averroes' distinction between motion as an "incomplete form" (*forma incompleta*) and a "way towards form" (*via ad formam*). Averroes' distinction and its ontological implications are discussed throughout the thirteenth and fourteenth centuries. As will be made clear, the position of the early English commentators on this problem expresses realist assumptions about motion that are contrary to Averroes' own view. Chapter 2, on infinity, first presents some significant elements of the early English interpretation of Aristotle's theory of potential and actual infinites in continuous magnitudes and then analyzes the debate on the actual infinity of numbers, which is a distinctive aspect of our tradition. The first part of chapter 3, on place, investigates another distinctive and original aspect of this tradition: the theory of "immersive" place that arises as an attempt to combine Aristotle's views in the *Categories* and *Physics*. The second part examines the early English debate on two traditional difficulties in Aristotle's theory: the immobility of place and the place of the heavens. Chapter 4, on time, deals with three distinct topics of Aristotle's theory that were usually discussed by medieval commentators: the existence of time, its relation to the soul and to motion, and its unity. The treatment of the second of these topics given by the early English commentators is characterized by a realist approach very similar to that found in their discussion of the ontological status of motion. Finally, in the *Conclusion*, we point out some exegetical aspects of the early English reception of Aristotle's theory of motion,

---

[4] This is being edited by Prof. R. J. Long. Another important *Sentences* commentary is that by the Franciscan Master Richard Rufus of Cornwall, preserved in ms. Oxford, Balliol College, ms. 62. For an analysis of Rufus' views on creation in his *Physics* commentary and *Sentences* commentary, see Wood, "Richard Rufus of Cornwall on Creation", p. 7-16, 23-30.

infinity, place, and time, that allow us to give a general characterization of this tradition.

We turn now to a survey of Aristotle's theories of motion, infinity,
place, and time and a general description of the commentaries considered in this book.

2. *Aristotle's Theory of Motion, Infinity, Place, and Time*

Our four topics, together with the void, form the subject matter of
books III and IV of the *Physics*: book III.1-3 is concerned with
motion, book III.4-8 with infinity, book IV.1-5 with place, book
IV.6-9 with the void, and book IV.10-14 with time. While the
notions of infinity, place, and time are discussed systematically only in
these sections of the *Physics*, the notion of motion is, either directly or
indirectly, also the subject of books V-VIII. Roughly, book V deals
with the classification of the different species of motion and other
aspects of the classification and individuation of motion, book VI
with the continuity of motion, books VII and VIII with cosmological
issues, such as the causal chain of motion, the eternity of motion, and
the existence of an immobile mover. Yet, Aristotle's discussion of
motion in *Physics* III.1-3 has a very general and metaphysical character that does not appear in his treatment of this topic in books V-
VIII. Indeed, the metaphysical discussion of book III.1-3 is essentially
self-contained. And while, during the fourteenth century, Aristotle's
theory of continuity contained in book VI was increasingly used in
the interpretation of the metaphysics of motion, the early English
commentaries on book III.1-3 still preserve the self-contained metaphysical approach of Aristotle. Therefore, in the following sketch of
Aristotle's theory of motion, we shall concentrate exclusively on
Physics III.1-3.

At the beginning of *Physics* III, in announcing the program of
books III-IV, Aristotle points out the relevance of the study of
motion, infinity, place, the void, and time to natural philosophy:
these five concepts are all essentially connected with the concept of
nature, the central subject of the *Physics*. Indeed – Aristotle remarks –
the term "motion" appears in the very definition of nature as "the
principle of motion and change". In turn, the other four concepts are
all essentially involved in that of motion. For every motion is continuous and the infinite divisibility of the continuum is the primary

instance of infinity, while place, the void, and time are thought of as necessary conditions for the existence of motion.[5] With this introductory remark Aristotle suggests that the five topics of books III and IV are the most fundamental physical concepts; and, with the exception of the void, whose existence is radically denied, this suggestion is certainly confirmed throughout the rest of the *Physics*. He also suggests that the actual discussion of these topics in books III and IV has some intrinsic unity. Yet, he fails to give such a unity to this discussion. For example, according to Aristotle's initial remark, one would expect a significant part of his analysis of infinity in *Physics* III.4-8 to be devoted to the continuity of motion, but in fact the discussion of this topic is postponed until book VI. Similarly, place seems to be essential only to local motion and this connection is stressed by Aristotle throughout his discussion of place in *Physics* IV.1-5; yet, his discussion of motion in *Physics* III.1-3 does not specifically deal with local motion. More generally, the discussions of motion, infinity, place, and time in *Physics* III-IV are largely independent of one another. Thus, following a common practice, we shall introduce these four concepts separately.[6]

A short introduction to Aristotle's doctrine of motion, infinity, place, and time is also given at the beginning of each of the four chapters that form the bulk of this study; such treatments, however, are basically intended as an outline of the Aristotelian background to the thirteenth-century debate of these physical notions, particularly as seen by the early English commentators. Here, instead, we shall try to point out those aspects of Aristotle's doctrine that, besides being related in some way to the medieval debate, are currently of interest to Aristotelian scholars.

(a) *Motion*

Aristotle claims that the natural philosopher does not need to prove that motion or change exists, since this is the basic assumption of

---

[5] Aristotle, *Physics*, III.1, 200b12-25.

[6] In the presentation of these four concepts, we make implicit use of the following fundamental studies: *Aristotle's Physics*, a revised text with introduction and commentary by W. D. Ross, Clarendon Press, Oxford 1936 (repr. 1979); *Aristotle's Physics*, Books III and IV, Translated with Notes by Edward Hussey, Clarendon Press, Oxford 1983; F. Solmsen, *Aristotle's System of the Physical World. A comparison with his predecessors*, Cornell University Press, Ithaca (N. Y.) 1960.

natural philosophy.[7] But he thinks that the natural philosopher does
need to define motion. Indeed, Aristotle devotes a substantial part of
his metaphysical analysis of motion in *Physics* III.1-3 to its definition.
In the preliminary discussion leading to this definition,[8] he introduces the two main components of his metaphysics of motion: the
categories of being and the distinction between actuality and potentiality. In Aristotle's view, the sentence 'something changes' must
always be expanded to a sentence of the form 'something changes
from being not F to being F', where F stands for a predicate belonging to one of the ten categories. As Aristotle puts it, any motion or
change is with respect to substance, quantity, quality or place or one
of the other categories. The association of each motion with a category gives rise to the classification of the so-called species of motion,
each species corresponding to a category. These are substantial
motion (generation and corruption), qualitative motion, quantitative
motion (increase and decrease), locomotion and so on. Aristotle also
assumes a reverse correspondence, namely, that for each category
there is some motion with respect to it. On this point, he appeals to
the distinction between actuality and potentiality: any determination
of any category can exist either actually or potentially. For instance,
something can be potentially white or actually white, and therefore
it can change from being potentially so to being actually so. From
this, Aristotle infers the general definition of motion as "*the actuality of
what potentially is, as such*",[9] remarking that this general definition
applies to every species of motion.[10] He then illustrates this definition
with the example of the building of a house: when the buildable, qua
it is buildable, is in act, then it is being built, i.e., it is undergoing the
motion of being built.[11] Furthermore, he tries to explain the meaning of the qualification "as such" in his definition by referring to the
case of the bronze and its process of being transformed into a statue.
This process is not the actuality of the bronze insofar as it is bronze
(because this kind of actuality is the bronze itself and not the mak-

---

[7] Aristotle, *Physics*, I.2, 185a12-20. Following Kosman, among others, we translate
κίνησις as motion. See L. A. Kosman, "Aristotle's definition of motion", *Phronesis*, 14
(1969), p. 40-62. In the first four books of the *Physics*, Aristotle also uses μεταβολὴ,
which we translate as change, interchangeably with κίνησις.
[8] Aristotle, *Physics*, III.1, 200b26-201a9.
[9] Ibid., 201a10-11.
[10] Ibid., 201a11-15.
[11] Ibid., 201a15-18.

ing), but rather the actuality of the bronze insofar as it is potentially a statue.[12]

Despite Aristotle's efforts to illustrate his definition of motion with examples, it remains very abstract and obscure and is still a matter of contention among scholars. An extreme position in the modern debate regards Aristotle's attempt at a general definition of motion as a mistake. Since motion is one of the fundamental concepts in natural philosophy, it cannot be defined in terms of something more fundamental and therefore does not need a definition.[13] This extreme position is generally rejected on the grounds that it misconceives the aim of Aristotle's definition, which is not to explain motion in terms of more fundamental *physical* notions, but to relate it to more basic *metaphysical* structures of the universe, such as actuality and potentiality.[14] There is, however, no universal agreement among scholars on the interpretation of Aristotle's "metaphysics" of motion as it is expressed by its definition. The main point of divergence is the meaning of the term ἐντελέχεια. The two major conflicting positions on this point have been labelled the process-view and the actuality-view.[15] In the process-view, the term ἐντελέχεια means actualization, and accordingly motion is defined as the actualization of a potentiality, in the sense of the process of actualizing a potentiality. In the actuality-view, ἐντελέχεια must be understood as actuality, hence expressing the state of being actual and not the process of actualization; accordingly, motion is defined as the actuality of a potentiality.

In a very influential paper, published in 1969, Kosman was the first to distinguish neatly between the process and actuality views of motion.[16] He points out that each of these views involves a major conceptual problem. The problem with the process-view is that it makes Aristotle's definition of motion circular and vacuous, since an actualization or an actualizing is just a process or motion. To reinforce this objection, Kosman also mentions Aquinas' warning against those who define motion as *exitus de potentia in actum non subito*. This,

---

[12] Ibid., 201a29-34.

[13] David Bostock is an authoritative exponent of this extreme position. See Aristotle, *Physics*, translated by Robin Waterfield, Introduction and notes by David Bostock, Oxford University Press, Oxford 1996, Introduction, p. xxxi-xxxii.

[14] This is, for example, Hussey's view. See Hussey, *Aristotle's Physics*, Introduction, p. xiii.

[15] See, for example, J. Kostman, "Aristotle's Definition of Change", *History of Philosophy Quarterly*, 4 (1987), p. 3.

[16] Kosman, "Aristotle's definition of motion".

according to Aquinas, is logically mistaken because *exitus* itself is a species of motion.[17] The problem with the actuality-view is that defining motion as the actuality of a potentiality apparently yields the final state of motion rather than motion itself. To use one of Aristotle's examples, the actuality of the bricks and stones (i. e., of the buildable) insofar as they are potentially a house is apparently the house and not the building of the house.[18] Kosman thinks that the process-view must be rejected and supports the actuality-view, taking great care to solve the problem just mentioned. He acknowledges that the notion of the actuality of a potentiality is too general and can accomodate both motion and the product of motion. Accordingly, he introduces a distinction between the "deprivative" and the "constitutive" actuality of a potentiality. As these qualifications suggest, a deprivative actuality of a potentiality implies the destruction of the potentiality itself, so that when the potentiality is actualized in this deprivative sense it no longer exists; on the other hand, a constitutive actuality of a potentiality, far from destroying the potentiality, is this potentiality in its full manifestation. The product of motion – Kosman argues – is a deprivative actuality of a potentiality, whereas motion itself is a constitutive actuality of a potentiality. For instance, the deprivative actuality of the potentiality of bricks and stones to be a house is the house itself, since this actuality occurs when the potentiality of the bricks and stones to be a house disappears. The constitutive actuality of this potentiality is the building of the house, because the building is the full manifestation of this potentiality. Although the distinction between deprivative and constitutive actuality is never explicitly formulated in the *Physics*, Kosman argues that Aristotle is trying to denote the latter type of actuality by using the qualification "as such" in the definition of motion.[19]

Kosman's pioneering discussion of the actuality-view and the process-view is very influential for the subsequent debate on Aristotle's definition of motion, and current literature regards the actuality-view defended by Kosman as "orthodox".[20] A major reason for its fortune

---

[17] Ibid., p. 41 and note 6.

[18] Ibid., p. 43-46.

[19] Ibid., p. 46-54.

[20] This view is supported, for example, in Hussey, *Aristotle's Physics*, p. 58-60; M. L. Gill, "Aristotle's Theory of Causal Action in *Physics* III 3", *Phronesis*, 25 (1980), p. 130-133; S. Waterlow, *Nature, Change and Agency in Aristotle's Physics, A philosophical study*, Clarendon Press, Oxford 1982, p. 112-114. The process-view has been recently

is that it avoids the circularity of the process-view, that is, it succeeds in showing that motion, although a fundamental physical notion, can be defined in terms of more fundamental, non-kinetic metaphysical notions. Yet, the requirement that the definition of motion be non-circular has recently been questioned by White on ontological grounds. White argues that if motion is regarded as "a fundamental metaphysical kind or category", then it is impossible to avoid circularity in its definition completely, i. e., to give a "reductive" definition which reduces motion to non-kinetic concepts. In short, White's point is that a non-reductive ontology of motion is committed to a definition of motion that is not reductive, but simply explicative, that is, it describes motion in terms of more familiar notions of Aristotle's metaphysics.[21] The relevance of White's discussion in this context is that it introduces the problem of the ontological status of motion into the modern debate about Aristotle's definition of motion, where it is usually ignored.[22] As we shall see in chapter 1, however, the problem of the ontological status of motion dominates the discussion of Aristotle's doctrine of motion in the medieval tradition. Put abstractly, the central question in the medieval debate is whether successive entities, and above all motion, form an ontological kind distinct from permanent entities, such as substances and their non-kinetic determinations, or are reducible to permanent entities. More specifically, in the case of motion, the question is whether it is a *res* in itself distinct from the form that represents its *terminus ad quem*. White explicitly refers to the medieval debate on the ontological status of motion. He also thinks that the realist and non-reductionist position in this debate according to which motion is a *res* distinct from any permanent entity better reflects the non-reductive ontology of motion that he ascribes to Aristotle.[23] In chapter 1, we shall see that the early English commentators support the realist position on the ontology of motion and examine the peculiar form their solution takes in finding a "non-reductive" interpretation of Aristotle's definition of motion.

---

defended in Kostman, "Aristotle's Definition of Change". A critique of Kosman's interpretation is also found in D. W. Graham, "Aristotle's Definition of Motion", *Ancient Philosophy*, 8 (1988), p. 209-215.

[21] See M. J. White, *The Continuous and the Discrete. Ancient Physical Theories from a Contemporary Perspective*, Clarendon Press, Oxford 1992, p. 99-100.

[22] The problem of the ontological status of motion is also touched upon by S. Waterlow, in *Nature, Change and Agency*, p. 111. See also below p. 39, n. 8.

[23] See White, *The Continuous and the Discrete*, p. 113-115.

(b) *Infinity*

Contrary to the introductory passage at the beginning of book III, Aristotle's treatment of infinity in *Physics* III.4-8 is not focused on the infinite divisibility of the continuum, but is much more general. Indeed, a significant part of Aristotle's discussion is devoted to the major cosmological issue of whether an infinitely extended body exists.[24] Deciding this question is – Aristotle claims – the primary task of the physical analysis of infinity. Aristotle radically rejects the existence of an infinite body, thereby implying that the physical universe as a whole and each of the bodies contained in it are finite. Despite the importance of this cosmological topic, Aristotle's actual treatment of it is relatively uninteresting and disappointing. And it is so because Aristotle's arguments against an infinite body rely on theories, most notably those of natural places and motions, which would not at all be accepted by his predecessors who posit an infinite universe.[25] Much more interesting is the "positive" part of Aristotle's discussion, in which he deals with the problem of the admissible forms of infinity. Here Aristotle introduces his distinction between the potential and actual infinite. This is the fundamental and most controversial aspect of his general theory of infinity, and we shall concentrate on it.

Having argued against the existence of an infinitely extended body, Aristotle opens his positive discussion by claiming that the existence of the infinite in the physical world cannot be absolutely denied. He points out three basic physical structures which show some form of infinity: time has neither beginning nor end, continuous quantities are divisible into parts *ad infinitum*, and number is infinite.[26] Aristotle then turns to the general question of determining which kinds of infinites are admissible. His view on this point is usually summarized by the statement that the infinite exists potentially and not actually. Indeed, (i) he starts by drawing a distinction between two ways of being: being in potency and being in act. He recalls that magnitude is not actually infinite in the sense that it is not infinitely extended, but is infinite by division. From this he infers that the infi-

---

[24] Aristotle, *Physics*, III.5, 204b34-206a8.
[25] On this point, see, for example, Solmsen, *Aristotle's System of the Physical World*, p. 167; Hussey, *Aristotle's Physics*, Introduction, p. xxxiii-xxxiv; Bostock, *Aristotle, Physics*, Introduction, p. xxxiii-xxxiv.
[26] Aristotle, *Physics*, III.6, 206a9-14.

nite exists in potency, thereby implying that the infinite divisibility of the continuum is a potential infinite. (ii) He next specifies that the infinite is not said to exist potentially in the sense in which something is potentially a statue, because, unlike that which is potentially a statue, that which is potentially infinite will not also be actually infinite at some time. (iii) He apparently illustrates the special sense in which the infinite exists potentially distinguishing between the way in which substances, like a man or a house, and processes, like a day or an athletic contest, have being. He claims that the infinite is analogous to a process, noting that the distinction between being in potency and being in act also applies to processes. An athletic contest, for instance, exists in potency if it might occur, and exists in act if it is actually occurring.[27] These are the three main points of Aristotle's general theory of actual and potential infinites in *Physics* III.6.

Aristotle's discussion is extremely compressed and ambiguous. Even the apparently uncontroversial claim that for Aristotle the infinite exists only potentially and never actually has been rejected by some scholars. The controversy on this central issue is connected in some way with the interpretation of point (ii) above concerning the sense in which the infinite exists potentially. It seems clear that in (ii) Aristotle introduces a deviant sense of "potentially" that applies to the infinite, the standard sense being that in which we say that something is potentially a statue and can also be actually a statue. Yet, when also point (iii) is taken into account, it is no longer so clear that Aristotle has in mind so much a deviant sense of "potentially" as a deviant sense of "being". Indeed, in (ii) the apparently deviant sense of potentiality is contrasted with the case of substances, but in (iii) substances, or more generally objects, are distinguished from processes, which, unlike substances, have a successive and not permanent kind of being. The infinite is then said to be a process. Accordingly, it might be suggested that in (ii) Aristotle introduces for the infinite not a deviant or unusual sense of potentiality, but of being: for the usual sense of being is that of substances, while the infinite exists, instead, as a process.

This suggestion is followed by J. Hintikka and D. Bostock, among others. The main aim of Hintikka's discussion is to show that Aristotle's theory of infinity does not constitute a counterexample to the so-

---

[27] Ibid., 206a14-25.

called principle of plenitude, according to which every genuine possibility is at some time actualized. If this principle is valid, then, since Aristotle denies that the infinite exists actually, he should also deny that the infinite exists potentially. This is in fact the view that Hintikka ascribes to Aristotle.[28] But then Hintikka has to explain Aristotle's opposing claim that the infinite exists potentially. Hintikka's position is that Aristotle here uses the term "potentially" in an inappropriate and misleading sense to express the fact that the infinite has the type of being of a day and an athletic contest, that is, of a process, and when an "infinite" process occurs, the infinite exists actually. Thus, in Hintikka's view, there is strictly speaking no distinction between the potential and actual infinite in Aristotle's theory.[29] Hintikka's interpretation is not regarded as sound and has been strongly criticized.[30] A more accurate version of the process-view of Aristotle's notion of infinity is proposed by Bostock. He maintains that in Aristotle's theory a process (a series of occurrences that take place one after the other) is the only sort of thing that can be infinite. Examples of infinite processes are the (theoretical) division of a continuous magnitude and the flow of time. But since these infinite processes do or can actually occur, one may still ask in what sense Aristotle claims that the infinite exists only potentially. Bostock's answer is that Aristotle means that these infinite processes are endless and cannot be completed. In this sense the being of the infinite differs from that of a substance. While it is never the case that a continuous magnitude, for example, can actually be infinitely divided, a lump of bronze can become a statue. Conversely, on this interpretation, the type of infinity that is not admissible for Aristotle is that of an infinite totality of simultaneously existing things.[31] Roughly speaking, Bostock's interpretation of Aristotle's distinction between the "potential" infinite, as the admissible

---

[28] See J. Hintikka, "Aristotelian Infinity", *Philosophical Review*, 75 (1966), p. 197-198.

[29] Ibid., 199-200.

[30] See, for example, J. Lear, "Aristotelian Infinity", *Proceedings of the Aristotelian Society*, 80 (1979-80), p. 189-193.

[31] See D. Bostock, "Aristotle, Zeno and the Potential Infinite", *Proceedings of the Aristotelian Society*, 73 (1972-73), p. 37-40; Id., *Aristotle, Physics*, Introduction, p. xxxiv-xxxv. Against Bostock's analysis, Prof. Richard Sorabji points out that Aristotle would not be happy with a more than finite number of successive entities, given that *Physics* III.5, 204a20-26 objects to an infinity whose parts are infinite. On Sorabji's interpretation of Aristotle's theory of infinity and the implications of a beginningless universe for this theory, see R. Sorabji, *Time, Creation and the Continuum, theories in antiquity and the early middle ages*, Duckworth, London 1983, especially p. 210-216.

type of infinity, and the "actual" infinite, as the non-admissible type of infinity, can be formulated as follows: the former consists of a series of events or things that occur one after the other in time endlessly, whereas the latter consists of collections of infinitely many things that exist at the same time. Bostock's interpretation is often found both in Greek and thirteenth-century commentaries.

An alternative interpretation to the process-view is proposed by J. Lear and W. Charlton. In particular, Lear insists that Aristotle's potential infinite is primarily connected with the structure itself of certain quantities and not with the processes that these quantities can undergo. For instance, continuous magnitude is potentially infinite insofar as it is continuous and not because it is actually divided.[32] Contrary to Hintikka, Lear points out that the deviant sense of "potentiality" of the infinite is that according to which there will always be possibilities that remain unactualized. Thus, number is potentially infinite in the sense that, given any number, a greater number could still be found. Similarly, magnitude is potentially infinite in the sense that no matter how many parts have been divided from it, another part could still be divided. Lear specifies that, in these sentences, "could" is not tied to our ability to carry out a process (of counting or dividing), but expresses a logical possibility that is guaranteed by the structure of numbers and continuous magnitudes.[33] Lear's idea of expressing Aristotle's notion of potential infinite by means of the modal notion of possibility is developed systematically by Charlton, who gives an accurate logical formulation of potential and actual infinites in which modality has an essential role. For example, the claim that the series of numbers is potentially infinite is equivalent to a sentence of the form (i) "for every finite number x, there *could exist* a finite number y greater than x", whereas the claim that the series of numbers is actually infinite is equivalent to the sentence (ii) "for every finite number x, *there exists* a finite number y greater than x".[34] This formulation is very elegant and powerful. In particular, it gives a precise logical meaning to the notion of the actual infinite, a notion for which the process-view does not even provide a general definition. Furthermore, as we shall see in chapter 2, it is

<hr />

[32] See Lear, "Aristotelian Infinity", p. 193.
[33] Ibid., 193-198.
[34] See W. Charlton, "Aristotle's Potential Infinites", in L. Judson (ed.), *Aristotle's Physics: A Collection of Essays*, Clarendon Press, Oxford 1991, p. 141-142.

very useful in the analysis of some aspects of Aristotle's discussion of the infinite in magnitude and was, in fact, used for this purpose by some fourteenth-century commentators.[35] Nevertheless, it seems too restrictive in its definition of the potential infinite. For there are series of events that Aristotle is apparently willing to regard as forms of potential infinites, which, nevertheless, turn out to be actual infinites according to Charlton's formulation. These are basically infinite series of past events or objects. Indeed, the infinity of any of these series is better expressed by sentences of type (ii) rather than type (i). For example, Aristotle seems to hold that, for every sidereal revolution, there actually has been, and not merely could have been, an earlier one.[36] For these cosmological cases, Bostock's version of the process-view seems to capture better Aristotle's intention, since on this interpretation such series are in fact potential infinites, comprising a succession of things that exist one after the other in time.

In conclusion, the process-view and the "modal"-view (i.e., that of Lear and Charlton) represent the two main interpretations of Aristotle's ambiguous notion of infinity. Since neither is without its problems, it seems difficult to provide a coherent account of all aspects of Aristotle's theory. As we shall see in chapter 2, the early English commentators found this theory obscure. Indeed, they do not even reach a clear understanding of the ambiguities and inconsistencies involved in Aristotle's distinction between the potential and actual infinites. They implicitly use, in different contexts and sometimes without much consistency, both the process-view and the "modal"-view.

(c) *Place*

In his introduction to Book III, Aristotle says that the motivation for studying place is that it is a necessary condition of motion. At the outset of his discussion of place, he clarifies this point, claiming that place is intrinsically involved in just one type of motion, local motion,

---

[35] See below, p. 108-111.

[36] Lear, Charlton and also Hussey are aware that the "modal"-view of Aristotle's infinity creates problems in the case of time. Lear and Hussey, for instance, point out that, if the series of past events (or, in general, time) is a potential infinite in the "modal" interpretation, then the reality of the past (or of time in general) cannot be maintained. See Lear, "Aristotelian Infinity", p. 202-208; Hussey, *Aristotle's Physics*, Introduction, p. xxv. See also Charlton, "Aristotle's Potential Infinites", p. 143-149.

which is, however, the most universal and primary species of motion.[37] The intrinsic connection between place and local motion comes out repeatedly in Aristotle's subsequent treatment. For example, the existence of local motion provides a prima facie argument for the existence of place: we must suppose the existence of place, because we see that different bodies come to occupy the same place successively.[38] Furthermore, many important properties that Aristotle ascribes to place derive from local motion. Yet, there is also a more general motivation for the study of place, namely, to establish how we locate things, and more specifically how, in the case of a sensible body, we should answer the question, "Where is it?".[39] This type of question has a metaphysical meaning, for Aristotle, since "to exist somewhere" is one of the categories of being. And in his discussion of place Aristotle is primarily concerned with just such a question.

Aristotle considers two main ways of thinking about location. Place can be viewed either as something containing a thing, viz. surrounding it, or as something coextensive with it. These two views are embodied in the list of four candidates for place explicitly discussed by Aristotle: the form of the located body, its matter, the extension between the extremes of the surrounding body, and these extremes themselves.[40] The form of the located body and the extremes of the body surrounding it express the container-view of place, while the matter of the located body and the extension between the extremes of the surrounding body express the view of place as something coextensive with what is in a place. In this context, form is understood as the shape of the located body;[41] matter, instead, tends to be identified with the three-dimensional extension of this body, when this extension is thought of as devoid of any formal determination, indefinite in itself and formally delimited and contained by the form of the located body.[42]

It seems to us rather odd that form and matter could possibly have any role in answering the question of where a body is. Aristotle brings them up here, because he needs them to distinguish the two competing models, that is, the "container" and the "coextensive" views of place. In any case, Aristotle takes seriously the suggestion that either

---

[37] Aristotle, *Physics*, IV.1, 208a31-32.
[38] Ibid., 208b1-8.
[39] Ibid., 208a29-31.
[40] Ibid., IV.4, 211b5-10.
[41] Ibid., IV.2, 209b1-6; 4, 211b10-14.
[42] Ibid., IV.2, 209b6-11.

matter or form is the place of a body and formulates a number of arguments to reject each idea. His main point is that neither matter nor form satisfies the basic requirement that place must be physically separated from the located body. Indeed, Aristotle assumes that the located body can leave its former place and come to be in a new one without any change in its matter or form.[43]

The other two candidates for place, the extension between the extremes of the containing body and the extremes themselves of this body, can be regarded as the physical counterparts of matter and form respectively. Besides representing different views on location, they involve a crucial ontological difference. If the place of a body is the limit (i.e., the extremes) of the body that immediately surrounds it, then in order to account for location it is not necessary to posit anything else apart from bodies. This is not so on the other view that place is the extension between the sides of the containing body, because such an extension must be self-subsistent, that is, not inhering in any body. Bodies alone will then not be sufficient to account for location. In short, this latter view of place is committed to positing a three-dimensional incorporeal extension, i.e., space. Yet, Aristotle absolutely denies the existence of space.[44] Thus, he identifies place with the limit of the containing body that is in contact with the located body. The requirement of contact between place and the located body is needed to distinguish its proper and common places, i.e., the place that contains only this body as distinct from all those places that also contain other bodies.[45] In his final definition of place, Aristotle further stipulates that the limit of the containing body must be immobile in order to be strictly speaking a place. As he puts it, a mobile container is a vessel rather than a place.[46]

Aristotle's discussion of place, although more accessible than his account of motion and infinity, contains two main internal inconsistencies. The first arises in connection with his further stipulation that place be immobile. Indeed, this seems to be opposed to the require-

---

[43] Ibid., IV.2, 209b21-210a13.

[44] Aristotle's arguments against the existence of an extension between the sides of the containing body (*Physics*, IV.4, 211b19-29) are rather obscure. They are apparently based on the assumption that this extension changes place when the containing body undergoes local motion. On these arguments, see especially, Hussey, *Aristotle's Physics*, p. 115-116; Bostock, *Aristotle, Physics*, Introduction, p. xxxviii-xxxix. Aristotle's attack on more general theories of space is postponed until the discussion of the void in *Physics* IV.6-9.

[45] Aristotle, *Physics*, IV.2, 209a31-b1; 4, 212a2-6a.

[46] Ibid., IV.4, 212a14-21.

ment for proper place. To use Aristotle's example, when a ship is in a river, the surface of water in contact with this ship is the proper place of the ship; water and its surface, however, are not immobile. On the other hand, the banks of the river are immobile and surround the ship, but they are not in contact with the ship. More generally, the immobility of place conflicts with the ontological status of place as the limit of a sensible and hence mobile body. Aristotle, however, does not notice these difficulties.

The second inconsistency in Aristotle's account arises in connection with the heavens and, in particular, with the outermost celestial sphere or the sphere of the fixed stars. This sphere is subject to rotation, which is a species of locomotion; hence, it should have a place. Yet, since it is the extreme boundary of the physical universe, it has no external container and therefore, according to Aristotle's definition, no place. Aristotle is fully aware of this problem and attempts a solution, which is nevertheless unsatisfactory in many respects.[47]

We shall see in chapter 3 that medieval commentators discuss at length both of these problems and their attempted solutions represent their most original contribution to Aristotle's doctrine of place. In particular, in dealing with the immobility of place, they introduce the innovation that the place of a body must be defined not only with respect to its immediate surroundings, but also with respect to its distance from the "fixed points" of the physical universe, namely, the earth and celestial region. Thus, in their view, Aristotle's definition of place must be expanded to state that place is the limit of the containing body insofar as this body has a definite distance from the fixed points of the cosmos. This notion of distance represents a new conceptual element, which is neglected by Aristotle, but turns out to be extremely important in the description of local motion and rest.[48]

There is also an "external" incoherence in Aristotle's doctrine that emerges when his depiction of place in the *Physics* as the limit of the containing body is compared with that in the *Categories*, where place seems rather to be identified with incorporeal, three-dimensional extension.[49] This conflict will also be examined in detail in chapter 3,

---

[47] Ibid., IV.5, 212a31-b22. On Aristotle's attempted solution, see below, p. 188-189.

[48] More generally, the importance of the notion of the distance from a given thing in an Aristotelian account of location has recently been emphasized by D. Bostock. See Bostock, *Aristotle, Physics*, Introduction, p. lx.

[49] See below, p. 134-137.

where we establish that a distinctive doctrine of the early English commentators arises out of their attempt to reconcile Aristotle's views of place in the *Physics* and the *Categories*.

(d) *Time*

Aristotle's discussion of time is strictly physical. Departing from the Platonic tradition, Aristotle assumes that the nature of time can be fully understood without any reference to eternity.[50] Furthermore, he assumes that time is intrinsically connected with motion, the basic component of the physical world.[51] The relation of time to motion is the dominant topic of *Physics* IV.10-14. Yet the metaphysical definition of motion of *Physics* III.1 does not play a significant role in Aristotle's account of time. Here, it is some of the quantitative and logical properties of motion, such as its continuity and ordered structure, that are important.

Generally speaking, while Aristotle admits that every motion is in time, and hence that motion is inseparable from time, he also regards motion as the more fundamental entity. In Aristotle's view, time depends ontologically on motion in the sense that it is an aspect of motion. Although motion is not a substance, it is regarded as the subject of time. Aristotle's most explicit argument for the ontological dependence of time on motion is "phenomenological". When we do not perceive change, we do not perceive time; conversely, as soon as we perceive change, we perceive time.[52] This argument seems inadequate to conclude, as Aristotle does, that time cannot exist without change and even more specifically that time is an attribute of motion.[53] Yet, Aristotle apparently regards it as sufficient for this ontological conclusion. What is more, he analyzes the way in which our perception of time derives from that of motion in order to establish what kind of attribute of motion time is.[54] The nature time has as an attribute is

---

[50] On this point, see especially Solmsen, *Aristotle's System of the Physical World*, p. 144-145.

[51] Aristotle's physical perspective is considerably broadened in the Middle Ages to include, for example, the duration of separate substances. For a comprehensive study of this topic, see P. Porro, *Forme e modelli di durata nel pensiero medievale. L'aevum, il tempo discreto, la categoria "quando"*, Leuven University Press, Leuven 1996.

[52] Aristotle, *Physics*, IV.11, 218b21-219a10.

[53] A major defence of this argument is discussed in Sorabji, *Time, Creation and the Continuum*, p. 74-78.

[54] Ibid., 219a22-b1.

finally specified in Aristotle's famous definition: time is the number of motion in respect of before and after.[55] Since number is a kind of quantity, this definition implies that time is a quantity of motion, but the identification of time with some kind of number of motion remains obscure. Aristotle tries to explain it by appealing to the following analogy: we discern the greater and the lesser by number; since we perceive greater and less change by time, time is a kind of number.[56] With this argument Aristotle suggests that the notion of number when applied to time means essentially a measure, so that time reflects a metrical property of motion. This suggestion is confirmed by the fact that Aristotle tends to describe time indifferently as either a number or a measure of motion. Thus, Aristotle's definition can be very roughly understood as stating that time is a measurable quantity of motion, i.e., its duration.[57] As to the operational aspects of time-measurement, Aristotle's "universal clock" is given by the uniform motion of the sphere of the fixed stars. This motion provides us with the units of time, such as hours, days, years, that we use in the measurement of the duration of each motion.[58]

The interpretation of the definition of time in terms of measure leads naturally to the question of whether time exists as an attribute of motion independently of our activity of measuring the duration of motion. Aristotle himself asks this question and his answer is negative. More accurately, Aristotle asks whether there would be time if there were no soul.[59] He argues that the existence of number depends on that which counts, and only the soul can count. Since time is a kind of number, time too depends on the soul. Some Aristotelian scholars have pointed out that Aristotle's assumption of the dependence of time on the soul does not reflect a radically subjective view of time according to which the existence of time depends on our perception of temporal events, but rather Aristotle's deliberate application to time of an anti-Platonist theory of number and counting.[60] The crucial idea of Aristotle's anti-Platonism about numbers, as J. Annas puts it, is that numbers do not exist over and above collections of num-

---

[55] Ibid., 219b1-2.

[56] Ibid., 219b3-5.

[57] A rival view is supported by R. Sorabji, who maintains that 'number' is not interchangeable with 'measure'. See Sorabji, *Time, Creation and the Continuum*, p. 84-89.

[58] Ibid., IV.14, 223b12-224a2.

[59] Ibid., 223a21-29.

[60] See J. Annas, "Aristotle, Number and Time", *The Philosophical Quarterly*, 25 (1975), p. 101; Hussey, *Aristotle's Physics*, p. 172-173.

bered things. When we say that a collection of things has a certain
number, we are simply expressing the result of our counting the
members of this collection. When applied to time, the idea is that in
the physical universe only motions exist and not time over and above
motions. Our reference to the time taken by a motion can be fully
understood in terms of the measurement of its duration. More generally, Annas argues that Aristotle's description of time as a kind of
number is an attempt to produce an anti-Platonist theory of time that
ties time to our activity of timing things.[61]

Annas' interpretation of Aristotle's doctrine of time is very illuminating and attractive. As we shall see in chapter 4, Averroes expresses
a similar reductionist view on the ontological status of time, claiming
that only motions and not also time exist in extra-mental reality. We
shall also see, however, that a number of Greek and medieval commentators reject such a view and maintain that time is an extramental property of motion, really distinct from motion itself. The early
English commentators, in particular, argue for the extra-mental reality of both number and time.

The analysis of time in terms of number and measure pertains to
the "metrical" component of Aristotle's conception of time. But there
is also a "topological" component, namely, time as a continuous, unidimensional extension.[62] These two components are not clearly distinguished or well integrated in Aristotle's discussion. For instance,
although the metrical interpretation of time seems to capture the
main idea of Aristotle's definition, it does not account for all its
aspects. Indeed, the clause "in respect of the before and after", with
which Aristotle qualifies the sense in which time is a number of
motion, expresses the ordered structure of the temporal continuum.
This is a topological property of time, however, and is not essentially
connected with the metrical component.[63] A further complication
arises from the fact that the topological component seems to contain

---

[61] Annas, "Aristotle, Number and Time", esp. p. 100. See also Hussey, *Aristotle's
Physics*, Introduction, p. xxxviii-xl.

[62] The distinction between a "metrical" component and a "topological" component of Aristotle's conception of time has been pointed out by M. J. White in *The
Continuous and the Discrete*, p. 74. It is, however, also assumed by other scholars. See,
for example, Annas, "Aristotle, Number and Time", p. 107-113.

[63] See, for example, Hussey, *Aristotle's Physics*, Introduction, p. xxxviii. Other major
conflicting aspects of the metrical and topological components have been pointed out
by J. Annas. See reference in the preceding note.

two different views of the temporal continuum: roughly speaking, a static view and a dynamic view.[64] An intuitive model of the static view would portray time as a geometrical line, and the instant of time as analogous to the point of a line. If, on the other hand, a line is thought of as produced by the flow of a point, as when we actually draw a line, we have an intuitive picture of the dynamic view of the temporal continuum. In this case, the instant of time is thought of, in medieval terms, as a *nunc fluens* and its being present, as opposed to being past or future, is emphasized. While the static and geometrical view of time is used throughout Aristotle's discussion of continuity in *Physics* VI, the dynamic view, according to which time flows from the future through the present into the past, is dominant in his treatment of time in *Physics* IV.10-14.[65] Moreover, in the latter discussion, there are a number of characteristic doctrines and problems related to each of the two views.

A distinctive doctrine primarily connected with the static view appears in Aristotle's analysis of the relation between the topological structures of spatial magnitude, motion, and time. Aristotle claims that the continuity and order of "before and after" in time derive from the continuity and order of before and after in motion, and these in turn derive from those in magnitude.[66] This means that the statements that time is continuous and linearly ordered in earlier and later phases can be fully understood only by reference to the corresponding properties of magnitude and motion. As we shall see in chapter 4, some details of Aristotle's attempted derivation of the topological structure of time from magnitude and motion are problematic. But even apart from the understanding of such details, it is clear that the derivative character of the structure of time expresses, at the topological level, the same reductionist attitude towards the ontological status of time as appears in Aristotle's analysis of the relation between time and the soul.[67] Thus, it is not surprising that many Aristotelian commentators who advocate a realist view of time,

---

[64] On these two views, see especially F. D. Miller, "Aristotle on the Reality of Time", *Archiv für Geschichte der Philosophie*, 56 (1974), p. 141-155.

[65] A different opinion is expressed by N. Kretzmann, who holds that Aristotle takes time as essentially static. See N. Kretzmann, "Aristotle on the Instant of Change", *Proceedings of the Aristotelian Society*, Suppl. vol. 50 (1976), p. 107-110.

[66] Ibid., IV.11, 219a10-19.

[67] On Aristotle's programme of reduction of the topological structure of time to the structures of motion and magnitude, see especially Hussey, *Aristotle's Physics*, Introduction, p. xlii-xliii.

according to which time is really distinct from motion, do not follow Aristotle's doctrine of the derivative character of the topological structure of time. Indeed, they feel that this doctrine must be rejected if their realist position is not simply to consist in positing time as a sort of duplicate of motion. We shall see, however, that the early English commentators fail to see this point and accept Aristotle's doctrine. Accordingly, they do not succeed in giving a satisfactory account of why time must be a distinct entity in addition to motion.

The most notable problem arising from the dynamic view of time is the reality of time. In *Physics* IV.10, Aristotle presents some objections to the reality of time based on the non-reality of the past and future.[68] These objections are generally thought of as connected with the dynamic view of time, since the distinction between past, present, and future is an essential ingredient of such a view. Specifically, Aristotle argues that time is composed of the past and the future. But neither of them exists, for the past no longer is and the future is not yet. The present, on the other hand, does exist, but is not a part of time, since it has no temporal extension. It is clear that Aristotle's argument relies on the fact that the verb 'to be' is essentially tensed in Greek, so that 'something is' means 'something is now' and is contrasted with 'something was' and 'something will be'. According to one contemporary interpretation, the solution of Aristotle's argument requires a tenseless sense of 'to be', which allows one to say that something exists without implying that it exists right now, so that past and future events can be said to exist in a tenseless way.[69] Yet, in *Physics* IV.10-14 there are no explicit indications for this kind of solution, which is in fact neglected in the Greek and medieval debate on the reality of time arising from the argument of *Physics* IV.10. As we shall see in chapter 4, Aristotelian commentators, relying on different suggestions by Aristotle, propose a variety of alternative solutions to this problem. In particular, the early English commentators assume that this problem can be solved by introducing a sense of 'to be' that applies specifically to successive entities as distinct from permanent ones.

---

[68] Aristotle, *Physics*, IV.10, 217b32-218a8.

[69] See Miller, "Aristotle on the Reality of Time", p. 135-136; Sorabji, *Time, Creation and the Continuum*, p. 13. Some objections against this interpretation have been recently raised by M. Inwood, "Aristotle on the Reality of Time", in Judson (ed.), *Aristotle's Physics*, p. 155-157.

3. *The Early English Commentaries*

In this general presentation of the early English commentaries, we shall (a) list the commentaries to be treated and (b) briefly discuss the problems of authorship and dating, after which we shall (c) focus on our main argument for assigning all these commentaries to the Oxford Faculty of Arts in the years 1250-1270, namely, their exegetical unity and their interrelations.[70] Finally, we shall (d) consider some earlier commentaries on the *Physics* that are likely sources for our group of commentaries.

(a) *List of the Commentaries*

The early English commentaries on *Physics* III and IV systematically considered in this book are, in probable chronological order, the following:

S =   Anonymus, *Quaestiones super Physicam*, Books I-VIII.
       Ms.: Siena, Biblioteca Comunale degli Intronati, ms. L. III. 21, ff. 1ra-92ra. (*SiLIII21*).[71]
       Books III-IV: ff. 39vb, lin. 27-64ra, lin. 9.

P =   Guillelmus de Clifford, *Compilationes super librum Physicorum Aristotelis*, Books I-V, 4; VII.
       Ms.: Cambridge, Peterhouse, ms. 157, I, ff. 43ra-104va. (*Pe157*).
       Books III-IV: ff. 65rb, lin. 1-96vb, lin. 1 ab imo.

M¹ = Galfridus de Aspall, *Quaestiones super Physicam*, Books I-IV (fragm.), VIII.
       Ms.: Oxford, Merton College, ms. 272, ff. 88ra-118vb. (*Me272(1)*).[72]
       Books III-IV: ff. 108vb, lin. 1-112vb, lin. 1 ab imo.

---

[70] Sections (a)-(c) present a synthesis of the main results of S. Donati's and my own preliminary research for the critical editions of these commentaries as published in Donati, "Per lo studio dei commenti alla *Fisica* del XIII secolo. I: Commenti di probabile origine inglese degli anni 1250-1270 ca." and C. Trifogli, "Le questioni sul libro III della *Fisica* in alcuni commenti inglesi intorno alla metà del sec. XIII", first part, *Documenti e studi sulla tradizione filosofica medievale*, 2 (1991) 2, p. 443-466; Ead., "Le questioni sul libro IV della *Fisica* in alcuni commenti inglesi intorno alla metà del sec. XIII. Parte I", *Documenti e studi sulla tradizione filosofica medievale*, 7 (1996), p. 39-77.

[71] Another (incomplete) copy of this set of questions is contained in ms. Cambridge, Gonville and Caius College, ms. 509, ff. 1ra-51rb, Books I-VI (*GC509(1)*).

[72] Other manuscripts containing Aspall's questions are: Cambridge, Gonville and

T =   Anonymus, *Quaestiones super Physicam*, Books IV, V.
       Ms.: Todi, Biblioteca Comunale, ms. 23, ff. 39vb, lin. 7-59va,
       lin. 9 ab imo (*To23(2)*).
       Book IV: ff. 39vb, lin. 7-57rb, lin. 40.

G¹ =   Anonymus, *Quaestiones super Physicam*, Books I-IV.
       Ms.: Cambridge, Gonville and Caius College, ms. 367, ff.
       120ra-125vb, 136ra-151vb (*GC367(1)*).
       Books III-IV: ff. 139rb, lin. 18-151vb, lin. 1 ab imo.

M³ =   Anonymus, *Quaestiones super Physicam*, Books I-V (fragm.).
       Ms.: Oxford, Merton College, ms. 272, ff. 136ra-174Brb
       (*Me272(3)*).
       Books III-IV: ff. 152rb, lin. 4-173rb, lin. 42.

G³ =   Anonymus, *Quaestiones super Physicam*, Books IV, VI-VIII.
       Ms.: Cambridge, Gonville and Caius College, ms. 509, ff.
       155va-206vb (*GC509(3)*).
       Book IV: ff. 155va, lin. 1-180ra, lin. 8.

N =   Anonymus, *Quaestiones super Physicam*, Books I (fragm.)-IV, VI
       (fragm.).
       Ms.: Oxford, New College, ms. 285, ff. 118ra-162ra (*NC285(2)*).
       Books III-IV: ff. 132ra, lin. 12-161rb, lin. 30.

M² =   Anonymus, *Quaestiones super Physicam*, Books I, III, 1-3, IV, 10-
       14.[73]
       Ms.: Oxford, Merton College, ms. 272, ff. 119ra-135Crb
       (*Me272(2)*).
       Books III-IV: ff. 125ra, lin. 8-135Crb, lin. 24.

W =   Anonymus, *Quaestiones super Physicam*, Books I,2-III.
       Ms.: London, Wellcome Historical Medical Library, ms. 333,
       ff. 8ra-68vb (*Well333(2)*).

Caius College, ms. 509, ff. 124ra-155rb, Books I-IV (fragm.) (*GC509(2)*); Oxford, New College, ms. 285, ff. 114ra-115vb, Book I (excerpta) (*NC285(1)*); Todi, Biblioteca Comunale, ms. 23, ff. 1ra-39vb, lin. 7, Books I-III (*To23(1)*); Todi, Biblioteca Comunale, ms. 23, ff. 74rb-82vb, Book VIII (*To23(4)*); London, Wellcome Historical Medical Library, ms. 333, ff. 98ra, lin. 21-105va, lin. 23, Book VIII (*Well333(6)*). Also the set of questions on Book VI contained in the two following manuscripts is probably to be ascribed to Aspall: Todi, Biblioteca Comunale, ms. 23, ff. 59va, lin. 8 ab imo-74ra, (*To23(3)*); London, Wellcome Historical Medical Library, ms. 333, ff. 81ra-92ra, (*Well333(4)*). On the manuscripts containing Aspall's questions, cf. Donati, "Per lo studio dei commenti alla *Fisica*", first part, p. 421-432.

[73] That is, for books III and IV, M² contains only the questions on motion (III.1-3) and the questions on time (IV.10-14). The questions on infinity (III.4-8), place (IV.1-5), the void (IV.6-9) seem to have been deliberately omitted by this commentator. See Donati, "Per lo studio dei commenti alla *Fisica*", second part, p. 47-48.

Book III: ff. 52ra, lin. 5-68vb, lin. 1 ab imo.

For the sake of brevity, we shall use the sigla that appear at the beginning of each item on the list.[74]

All ten commentaries in this list are *per modum quaestionis*.[75] Only S, however, contains a complete set of questions on the eight books of the *Physics*. As to books III and IV, S, P, G[1], M[3], N, M[2] contain questions on both these books, whereas M[1] and W contain questions only on Book III and T and G[3] only on book IV.[76]

(b) *Authors and Dating of the Commentaries*

We know the authors of P, William of Clifford, and of M[1], Geoffrey of Aspall. The authors of the other eight commentaries have not yet been identified.

Oxford master of Arts by 1262, Aspall (died 1287) is the author of commentaries on several Aristotelian works. He is regarded as one of the most prominent figures in the introduction of Aristotelian natural philosophy to Oxford and specifically one of the first Oxford masters who wrote commentaries *per modum quaestionis*.[77] His activity as Aristotelian commentator and the style of his commentaries have been extensively investigated by E. Macrae and recently by S. Donati.[78] His questions on the *Physics*, in particular, were most probably written between 1255 and 1265.

William of Clifford (died 1306) was Arts master at Oxford by 1265. Although his activity as a commentator is much less known than

---

[74] The sigla in italics within parentheses, instead, are those used in Donati's and Trifogli's works mentioned in note 70.

[75] Only P contains in addition a systematic exposition of Aristotle's text. I am grateful to Dr. H. Riggert for having made available to me his transcription of this commentary.

[76] In fact, M[1] contains a fragment of Book IV that consists of seven questions on place. The list of these questions is given in Trifogli, "Le questioni sul libro IV della *Fisica*". Parte I, p. 68.

[77] For instance, in his fundamental work on the *Introduction of Aristotelian Learning to Oxford*, Callus mentions an anonymous set of questions on *De anima* contained in ms. Merton College, 272, as one of the earliest examples of Oxford commentaries *per modum questionis*. This set of questions was later ascribed to Aspall by Macrae. See D. A. Callus, "Introduction of Aristotelian Learning to Oxford", *Proceedings of the British Academy*, 29 (1943), p. 271-272, and E. Macrae, "Geoffrey of Aspall's Commentaries on Aristotle", *Mediaeval and Renaissance Studies*, 6 (1968), p. 103-107.

[78] See Macrae, "Geoffrey of Aspall's Commentaries", and Donati, "Per lo studio dei commenti alla *Fisica*", first part, p. 421-432.

Aspall's, he seems to have commented on a number of Aristotelian works. For instance, his questions on the *Physics* contain references to his commentaries on *De Interpretatione, Prior Analytics, Posterior Analytics, Topics, De Generatione* and *De Anima*. Moreover, Donati has identified Clifford as the author of the commentaries on *De Anima, De Generatione, Meteora I* and *De Somno et vigilia* preserved anonymously in ms. Cambridge, Peterhouse 157. His questions on the *Physics* were most probably written in the period 1250-1260.[79]

As to the anonymous authors, the evidence for identifying them as Oxford masters of Arts derives from a variety of considerations: the tendency to distinguish their positions from those of the theologians, the English origin of the manuscripts in which their questions are contained, the fact that these manuscripts also contain works of certain English origin, and a few geographical examples. Several data point to dating these commentaries to the years 1250-1270: the opinions discussed, references to dated works, the numbering of the books of the *Metaphysics* used in them, the use of the *Translatio Vetus* of the *Physics*. Most important for the *terminus ante quem*, however, is the fact that none of these commentaries show even a trace of Aquinas' commentary on the *Physics*, written in 1269/70. Aquinas' commentary was so influential, not only for the continental but also for the English tradition of the late thirteenth century,[80] that we can be fairly confident about making ca.1270 the *terminus ante quem* of our commentaries.[81] But, in our view, the most general and convincing argument that all ten commentaries derive from the Oxford Faculty of Arts of the years 1250-1270 is based on their exegetical homogeneity and the complex framework of relations among them.

---

[79] See Donati, "Per lo studio dei commenti alla *Fisica*", first part, p. 409-421.

[80] For an example of the influence of Aquinas' *Physics* commentary in the late thirteenth-century English tradition, see C. Trifogli, "An Anonymous Question on the Immobility of Place from the End of the XIIIth Century", in A. Speer (ed.), *Raum und Raumvorstellungen im Mittelalter*, p. 147-167.

[81] The data concerning the origin and the dating of the commentaries have carefully been collected by Donati in the sections "Autore" and "Elementi di datazione" of her description of these commentaries in "Per lo studio dei commenti alla *Fisica*".

(c) *Homogeneity of the Tradition and Relations among the Commentaries*

A comparative analysis of the early English commentaries reveals, on one hand, some structural differences,[82] but, on the other, a deeper unity in their exegetical content. The unity of our tradition is clear from a marked similarity in:

(1) the topics of the questions;
(2) the doctrinal concerns raised;
(3) the positions taken on important issues;
(4) the opinions reported;
(5) and from a relevant number of parallel passages (i.e., arguments or series of arguments) in corresponding questions of different commentaries.

The following chapters of this study will offer a great variety of instances of points (2)-(4).[83] As to point (2), for example, two doctrinal issues that seem characteristic of our tradition are the debate on the actual infinity of numbers and the theory of immersive place.[84] As to (3), we shall see that all our commentators agree on certain major doctrinal issues, such as the ontological status of motion and time.[85] Point (4) will be evident in the discussion of the traditional problems of *Physics* III-IV, such as the immobility of place, the place of the heavens, and the unity of time.[86] Point (5) will be fully documented in our forthcoming repertory of the questions on books III and IV in the English commentaries. In this study, however, some significant indi-

---

[82] These appear mainly in the length and complexity of the questions. For instance, S and P are formed by short and simple questions, whereas in G^1 and M^3 questions become longer and more articulated; even longer are the questions of M^2 and W. On the structure of the questions in each of our commentaries, see the section on "Stile" of Donati's descriptions in "Per lo studio dei commenti alla *Fisica*".

[83] On point (1), we refer the reader to the list of questions on Books III-IV in our commentaries published in Trifogli, "Le questioni sul libro III della *Fisica*", first part, p. 490-501; second part, p. 166-178; Ead., "Le questioni sul libro IV della *Fisica*. Parte I", p. 78-114. On point (5), the frequency of parallel passages in the questions on motion and on time is recorded in F. Del Punta, S. Donati, C. Trifogli, "Commentaries on Aristotle's *Physics* in Britain, ca. 1250-1270", in J. Marenbon (ed.), *Aristotle in Britain during the Middle Ages*, Proceedings of the international conference at Cambridge 8-11 April 1994 organized by the Société Internationale pour l'Etude de la Philosophie Médiévale, Brepols, Turnhout 1996, p. 272.

[84] See below, p. 114-132 and 141-159.

[85] See below, p. 51-59 and 221-230.

[86] See below, p. 164-202 and 238-261.

cations of the frequent occurrences of parallel passages can be found in the documentation of the following chapters. It should be noticed that such occurrences reveal not only the unity of our tradition, but more specifically the methodological attitude common to our commentators of using other commentaries extensively without being very concerned about originality.

Besides the exegetical unity of our tradition as a whole, some individual commentaries are even more closely related. This makes it possible to articulate this tradition into smaller groups formed by two commentaries, i.e., "couples" of commentaries. Roughly speaking, we say that two commentaries form a couple if they have homogeneous structures, that is, questions of almost the same length and complexity and presenting the same degree of elaboration in the treatment of exegetical issues; and if they contain a high number of strictly parallel passages or common questions, that is, questions with only slight differences in their content. Concretely, when two commentaries form a couple, it is believed that one of them is the main source of the other. We have identified four such couples of commentaries.

The first couple is formed by S and P. These two commentaries have a high degree of unity in the questions on Book III and the first five chapters of Book IV (questions on place). For example, the set of questions on place in S is included in the set of questions on place in P. This strong degree of unity gradually tends to diminish in the course of the subsequent chapters of Book IV. In the questions on the void (IV.6-9) there are still many parallel passages, but some topics are dealt with differently in the two commentaries. In the questions on time (IV.10-14), they no longer have common questions or present a significant number of parallel passages. Since there is evidence that P is posterior to S, we can conclude that S is the main source of P for Book III, for the first five chapters of Book IV, and still to some extent for chapters 6-9 , but no longer for chapters 10-14.[87]

G^1 and M^3 form a second couple for the questions on both books III and IV. The strong unity of G^1 and M^3 was noticed by Prof. Zimmermann, who raised the question whether these two commentaries are just two different redactions by the same author.[88] Our analysis

---

[87] See Trifogli, "Le questioni sul libro III della *Fisica*", first part, p. 445-448; Ead., "Le questioni sul libro IV della *Fisica*. Parte I", p. 44-48.

[88] Zimmermann, *Verzeichnis ungedruckter Kommentare*, p. 10.

has established that G^1 and M^3 cannot be ascribed to the same author, since they treat some exegetical issues differently. For instance, discussing the ontological status of motion, G^1 tries to defend Averroes' position, while M^3 argues explicitly against it. Similarly, in the case of the unity of time, G^1 tries to defend Bonaventure's opinion, but M^3 does not even mention it. There is little doubt, however, that G^1 is the main source of M^3. A secondary source of M^3 is M^1, that is, Aspall's commentary.[89]

The third couple is formed by M^2 and W for the questions on motion (*Physics* III.1-3).[90] The exegetical content of these two commentaries is substantially the same, but W contains a much more analytical and expanded form. Furthermore, M^2 and W are the only commentaries that use Albert the Great's paraphrase of the *Physics* for certain points, as for example in a historical digression on the categorical classification of motion. M^2 is very probably the main source of W.[91]

The fourth couple is formed by G^3 and N for the questions on book IV.[92] G^3 and N contain substantially the same set of questions, with only slight differences in their content. Furthermore, there is no exegetical contrast between the two commentaries. These are certainly strong arguments in favour of the conjecture that for questions on Book IV G^3 and N are two redactions by the same author. The stylistic differences between the two commentaries, however, argue against this conjecture. Although these differences tend to disappear in the questions on time, it seems safe nevertheless to regard G^3 and N as two distinct works. In any case, N is very probably posterior to G^3. One also is left with the impression that G^3 and N are not very original. Rather, it seems that they represent largely a reorganization of the exegetical material contained in G^1 and P.[93]

Finally, we can add that M^1, i.e., Aspall's commentary, and T have some kind of close relationship. Strictly speaking, they do not form a couple, because they transmit questions on complementary portions of Aristotle's text. M^1 contains only Aspall's questions on book III and just

---

[89] See Trifogli, "Le questioni sul libro III della *Fisica*", first part, p. 448-453; Ead., "Le questioni sul libro IV della *Fisica*. Parte I", p. 48-54.

[90] This is, in fact, the only portion of Aristotle's *Physics* III and IV on which there are questions in both commentaries.

[91] See Trifogli, "Le questioni sul libro III della *Fisica*", first part, p. 453-457.

[92] G^3 has no questions on book III.

[93] See Trifogli, "Le questioni sul libro IV della *Fisica*. Parte I", p. 54-67.

a fragment of book IV, whereas T contains only questions on book IV. Furthermore, the comparison of the two commentaries on the common fragment of book IV strongly suggests that T cannot be ascribed to Aspall. Yet, the two commentaries share some significant exegetical features that show that T is very close to Aspall's commentary.[94] Thus, it may be helpful for the reader to regard T as a virtual approximation of Aspall's questions on book IV that have not yet been found.

In conclusion, our group of ten commentaries is subdivided in five couples: S-P, G^1-M^3, G^3-N, M^2-W, M^1-T (in the sense just specified). There are also secondary relations among some of these couples. Most notably, the couple G^3-N is largely dependent on S-P and G^1-M^3. As to the relative chronology of the ten commentaries examined, our conjecture is that S is the earliest and the other commentaries follow in this order: P, M^1, T, G^1, M^3, G^3, N, M^2, W. We have textual evidence for some steps of this ordering. In the other cases, we have assumed that a more complex structure of the questions, a more articulated and sophisticated treatment of the exegetical points, and a deeper understanding of the philosophical issues are marks of a posterior commentary. Since we are dealing with an early and still developing stage of the reception of Aristotle's *Physics*, we think that our assumption is reasonably well founded.

(d) *Earlier commentaries*

Although the commentaries considered in this study reflect an early stage of the reception of Aristotle's *Physics* both chronologically and conceptually, they are not really the first. The very first Latin commentary on the *Physics* is Robert Grosseteste's paraphrase, written in the period 1228-1232.[95] There is no trace, however, of any influence of Grosseteste's work on our commentaries. In fact, it seems that this work was unknown for nearly fifty years after Grosseteste's death in 1253.[96] Soon after Grosseteste's paraphrase, Averroes' commentary on the *Physics* was translated into Latin[97] and exerted an enormous

---

[94] Ibid., p. 67-74.
[95] See *Roberti Grosseteste Episcopi Lincolniensis Commentarius in VIII libros Physicorum Aristotelis*, ed. R. C. Dales, University of Colorado Press, Boulder (Colorado) 1963.
[96] See R. Dales' introduction to the edition of Grosseteste's commentary, p. xxi-xxiii.
[97] See Averroes Cordubensis, *Aristotelis de Physico Auditu* (*Aristotelis Opera cum Averrois Commentariis*, IV), Venetiis apud Junctas 1562, repr. Minerva, Frankfurt 1962. Averroes' commentaries were translated around 1230.

influence on our commentators. It is clear that they rely on Averroes' commentary for an understanding not only of Aristotle's text, but also of the philosophical issues arising from it. Yet, their general attitude towards Averroes is very critical. The "anti-Averroism" of our tradition in its several manifestations is one of the major topics of this study and will be analyzed in detail in the following chapters. In this context, we wish to point out three other commentaries on the *Physics* that apparently circulated in Oxford around the middle of the thirteenth century and that show some connection with our tradition. These are commentaries by Richard Rufus of Cornwall, Roger Bacon and an unknown author in ms. Oxford, Bodleian Library, lat. misc. C.69, henceforth B.

Richard Rufus of Cornwall probably wrote his commentary *per modum quaestionis* on the *Physics* as a master of Arts in Paris around 1235, before going back to Oxford to join the Franciscan Order in 1238. The Parisian origin and early dating have been argued for by R. Wood, who some years ago discovered Rufus' work in an Erfurt manuscript.[98] Even apart from chronological considerations, it is clear that Rufus' questions on the *Physics* do not belong to our tradition but to an earlier stage. A comparative analysis shows that the structure of Rufus' questions is much more "archaic" than that of our commentaries. Indeed, Rufus' questions are very short and have a barely articulated structure. Furthermore, many of them are "exegetical", in the sense that they arise from some specific claim by Aristotle and tend simply to remove an immediate obstacle to its understanding. In effect, they look like glosses to Aristotle's text. Consequently, the philosophical content of Rufus' questions is comparatively scanty. For example, Rufus does not even mention the problem of the ontological status of motion, one of the "great" topics of Book III. Similarly, he raises no objections against Aristotle's view of place as the surface of the containing body, a major issue raised by our commentators from which their theory of "immersive place" derives. Finally, there are no questions on the existence of time, a problem left open by Aristotle and constantly discussed in the Aristotelian tradition. Yet, there are some significant doxographical and doctrinal aspects common to Rufus and our commentators. For instance, one of the doxographical points of contact occurs in the discussion of the immo-

---

[98] See R. Wood's studies quoted in note 2 above.

bility of place. Our commentators discuss and accept an opinion according to which place is immobile in virtue of the identity of its spatial relation (*respectus*) to the fixed points of the universe. This opinion reflects Rufus' explanation of the immobility of place. A second opinion on this issue, according to which place is immobile in virtue of a celestial nature, is also discussed and rejected both by Rufus and our commentators.[99] Similarly, on the topic of the place of the heavens, both Rufus and our commentators reject Averroes' influential opinion that the heavens are in a place because of the earth.[100] Finally, a version of Rufus' solution to the problem of the unity of time is quoted and accepted by a number of our commentators.[101] As to the doctrine, Rufus, like our commentators, supports the extra-mental reality of time against Averroes' contrary view that time depends on the soul.[102] Furthermore, some of the origins of our commentators' debate on the actual infinity in numbers can be found in Rufus.[103] Finally, G[1] and M[3] show first-hand knowledge of Rufus' commentary. Indeed, in both these commentaries there is a high number of passages that appear almost *verbatim* in Rufus' questions.

The doxographical and doctrinal elements common to Rufus and our commentators can also be found (with a few exceptions) in a more mature and expanded form, in Roger Bacon's questions on the *Physics*, discussed in Paris in the 1240s.[104] Furthermore, Bacon is apparently a major source for our commentators' doctrine of "immersive" place. Indeed, in Bacon's treatment of this doctrine, which does not appear in Rufus, all the elements that characterize our commentators' discussion are already present, although sometimes in an inchoate form. This doctrine can be regarded as the most characteristic connection between Bacon and our tradition.[105] Furthermore, Bacon's questions

---

[99] See below, p. 171-186.

[100] See below, p. 192-197.

[101] See below, p. 246-256.

[102] See below, p. 219-230.

[103] See below, p. 114-125.

[104] Bacon wrote two sets of questions on the *Physics*, that are indicated by their editors as *Questiones prime* and *Questiones altere*. See *Opera hactenus inedita Rogeri Baconi*, Fasc. VIII, *Questiones supra libros quatuor Physicorum Aristotelis* (*Questiones prime*), ed. F.M. Delorme with the collaboration of R. Steele, Clarendon Press, Oxford 1928. Fasc. XIII, *Questiones supra libros octo Physicorum Aristotelis* (*Questiones altere*), ed. F.M. Delorme with the collaboration of R. Steele, Clarendon Press, Oxford 1935. Throughout this study we refer exclusively to Bacon's *Questiones altere*, since there is no trace of any influence of the *Questiones prime* on our commentators.

[105] See below, p. 140-141.

are a direct source of S and P, since there is a number of questions in S and P that can also be found in Bacon.

We can conclude that there is a significant continuity between the earlier commentaries by Rufus and Bacon, on one hand, and our commentaries, on the other. In summary, this continuity manifests itself in the treatment of the traditional problems of *Physics* IV, such as the immobility of place, the place of the heavens and the unity of time, in the realist approach to the problem of the extra-mental reality of time, and to a lesser degree in the two distinctive doctrines of our tradition: the discussion of the actual infinity of numbers and the theory of immersive place.

This conclusion is not, however, valid for the third commentary mentioned above, the anonymous commentary B. B is basically an exposition of Aristotle's text, i.e., a commentary *per modum commenti*, with some questions. For book III, there are very few questions. Book IV contains a greater number of questions, but still far fewer than in our commentaries.[106] The literal exposition of B is extremely close to Adam of Bocfeld's commentary. In fact, B was traditionally regarded as a copy of Bocfeld's work. Donati has recently shown that B probably cannot be ascribed to Bocfeld. It remains true, however, that it belongs to Bocfeld's school and hence should have been written around the middle of the thirteenth century, perhaps slightly earlier than our commentaries.[107] Apart from the structural dissimilarities, a more intrinsic difference that marks the lack of continuity between B and our commentaries is their attitudes towards Averroes. While our commentaries tend to criticize Averroes systematically, B follows him very closely. In significant cases, the content of the questions in B is a repetition or a reformulation of Averroes' discussion, as in the cases of the relation between the different types of infinity in continuous magnitudes and numbers[108] and the place of the heavens.[109] Furthermore, B accepts Averroes' view on the ontological status of time, which is rejected by all our commentators.[110] On the other hand,

---

[106] The list of the questions of B is published in Zimmermann, *Verzeichnis ungedruckter Kommentare*, p. 146-152 (on p. 146 read "Oxford, Bodleian Library, Cod. lat. misc. C. 69, 1ra-55rb" instead of "Cambridge, Gonville and Caius College, Cod. 367, 126ra-135vb, 152ra-163va).

[107] See Donati, "Per lo studio dei commenti alla *Fisica*", first part, p. 386-396.

[108] See below, p. 104-105, n. 50; p. 107, n. 56.

[109] See below, p. 196, n. 157.

[110] See below, p. 223, n. 60.

they have some common attitudes towards Averroes. Like our commentators, B rejects Averroes' view on the ontological status of motion, according to which motion does not differ essentially from the final form acquired through motion, and follows, instead, the *via*-theory of motion.[111] This is certainly the most significant link between B and our tradition.

In concluding this introduction, let us just mention the problem of the "later commentaries". We know of the existence of a number of thirteenth-century commentaries of English origin written after Thomas Aquinas' commentary on the *Physics*, that is, in the thirty years after our "early" English period.[112] However, these commentaries remain unpublished and have yet to be studied. The present book therefore contains no systematic references to works on the *Physics* in the Oxford Faculty of Arts in the late thirteenth century. On some crucial points, however, reference will be made to two early fourteenth-century English commentators, Thomas Wylton and Walter Burley. The relevance of Wylton and Burley derives essentially from the ontological realism of their positions in natural philosophy, which they share with our early tradition. Comparison with these fourteenth-century commentators helps, on one hand, to clarify aspects of the ontological presuppositions of their earlier counterparts and, on the other, makes it possible to trace, though in a general way, the evolution of the realist approach to Aristotle's natural philosophy.

***

For convenience of the reader, we collect here the sigla for the English commentaries introduced above and that will be used throughout the subsequent chapters:

B =   Anonymus, *Notulae super libris Physicorum*, ms. Oxford, Bodleian Library, lat. misc. C.69; Books III-IV: ff. 14va, lin. 37-33ra, lin. 15.

G¹ =   Anonymus, *Quaestiones super Physicam*, ms. Cambridge, Gonville and Caius College, 367; Books III-IV: ff. 139rb, lin. 18-151vb, lin. 1 ab imo.

---

[111] See below, p. 59.

[112] A list of these commentaries can be found in Donati, "Per lo studio dei commenti alla *Fisica*", first part, p. 369-373.

G³ = Anonymus, *Quaestiones super Physicam*, ms. Cambridge, Gonville and Caius, 509; Book IV: ff. 155va, lin. 1-180ra, lin. 8.

M¹ = Galfridus de Aspall, *Quaestiones super Physicam*, ms. Oxford, Merton College, 272; Books III-IV: ff. 108vb, lin. 1-112vb, lin. 1 ab imo.

M² = Anonymus, *Quaestiones super Physicam*, ms. Oxford, Merton College, 272; Books III-IV: ff. 125ra, lin. 8-135Crb, lin. 24.

M³ = Anonymus, *Quaestiones super Physicam*, ms. Oxford, Merton College, 272; Books III-IV: ff. 152rb, lin. 4-173rb, lin. 42.

N = Anonymus, *Quaestiones super Physicam*, ms. Oxford, New College, 285; Books III-IV: ff. 132ra, lin. 12-161rb, lin. 30.

P = Guillelmus de Clifford, *Compilationes super librum Physicorum Aristotelis*, ms. Cambridge, Peterhouse, 157; Books III-IV: ff. 65rb, lin. 1-96, lin. 1 ab imo.

S = Anonymus, *Quaestiones super Physicam*, ms. Siena, Biblioteca Comunale degli Intronati, L. III. 21; Books III-IV: ff. 39vb, lin. 27-64ra, lin. 9.

T = Anonymus, *Quaestiones super Physicam*, ms. Todi, Biblioteca Comunale, 23; Book IV: ff. 39vb, lin. 7-57rb, lin. 40.

W = Anonymus, *Quaestiones super Physicam*, ms. London, Wellcome Historical Medical Library, 333; Book III: ff. 52ra, lin. 5-68vb, lin. 1 ab imo.

As to the other Greek and Latin works, we refer to them in an abbreviated form in the footnotes to the subsequent chapters and we give the complete references in the Bibliography. Here we recall that all references to Roger Bacon's Commentary on the *Physics* are to the *Questiones altere* (*Opera hactenus inedita*, Fasc. XIII).

CHAPTER ONE

MOTION: ITS ONTOLOGICAL STATUS

Introduction: The Aristotelian Background

In Aristotle's view, the nature of motion is that of being the actuality of what is potentially, insofar as it is potentially, as the well-known definition of *Physics* III.1 states.[1] For instance, the process of becoming white (a qualitative change) is the actuality of a substance which is potentially white, insofar as it is potentially white, i.e., as long as it is not yet white. Clearly, in this definition Aristotle's main point is that motion can be understood only against the metaphysical background of his theory of actuality and potentiality. Indeed, he devotes a substantial part of his treatment of motion in *Physics* III.1-3 to specifying exactly what kind of potentiality and actuality motion involves. Despite Aristotle's effort to clarify what he meant, his medieval commentators found it difficult to derive from his definition a clear position on the ontological status of motion. A sign of this is that although Aristotle's definition was generally accepted in the medieval tradition, opposing interpretations of the ontological status of motion soon arose. Furthermore, generally speaking, the different positions in the medieval debate on the ontological status of motion did not arise from different interpretations of Aristotle's definition. Rather, the opposite was true. A commentator would develop his own view on the ontological status of motion independently of Aristotle's definition and then subsequently apply this view to his interpretation of Aristotle's definition.

Although the definition of motion plays no important role in the medieval debate on its ontological status, there is, nevertheless, an Aristotelian background for this debate. It can be found in a passage of *Physics* III.1, leading to the definition of motion, in which Aristotle relates motion to his system of categories. There Aristotle claims that:

---

[1] Aristotle, *Physics*, III.1, 201a10-11.

(I) There is no motion apart from actual things.[2]

The things in question are those belonging to the categories of the initial state and of the final state of a motion, as is clear from what he adds immediately afterward:

> (II) For whatever changes always does so in respect either of substance or of quantity or of quality or of place, and there is, as we assert, nothing to be found as a common item superior to these, which is neither a "this" nor a quantity nor a qualification nor any of the other occupants of categories; and so there is nothing apart from the things mentioned, because nothing is, apart from the things mentioned.[3]

And from this he concludes:

> (III) So that there are just as many species of motion and change as of that-which-is.[4]

The passages just quoted are the *locus classicus* for the medieval debate. The commentaries generally raise the question of what kind of entity motion is in the section devoted to these passages. Indeed, so far as the ontological status of motion is concerned these passages are certainly more explicit and less vague than those that can be derived from Aristotle's much more extensive treatment of the definition of motion. Furthermore, as we shall see, passages (I)-(III) also establish the common terms in which medieval commentaries discussed the question of the ontological status of motion. Yet, Aristotle's remarks here provide no explicit answer to the question. In (II) Aristotle implicitly appeals to the metaphysical description of change he has worked out in Book I: in any change there is a subject of change which passes from being not F to being F.[5] What he does stress in (II) is that the term 'F' stands for a category-occupant. This only leads, however, to an exhaustive classification of the species of motion or change, which is, in fact, the conclusion drawn in passage (III).

Aristotle's principle that motion does not exist over and above actual things, in the sense that every motion is in respect of something

---

² Ibid., 200b32-33. In the quotations of passages from Books III and IV of Aristotle's *Physics*. I use an adopted version of Hussey's translation found in *Aristotle's Physics*, Books III and IV, translated with Notes by Edward Hussey, Clarendon Press, Oxford 1983.
³ Ibid., 200b32-201a3.
⁴ Ibid., 201a8-9.
⁵ Ibid., I.7, 189b30-191a22.

belonging to a category, is commonly accepted in the Aristotelian tradition. The restriction of the essential species of change to four categories is also rather uncontroversial, at least for medieval commentators. Yet, the implicit ontological commitments of Aristotle's principle are much debated by them. Indeed, Aristotle does not clarify how the ontological relationship between motion and the entities that represent its initial and final state is to be understood. He does claim that motion has a privileged relationship with its final state. For instance, motions are denominated by their final states.[6] One might, however, still ask whether a motion, such as becoming white, is essentially the same thing as its final state of whiteness[7] and, if it is something else, what kind of thing it is.[8] More generally, one might ask whether motion is a *res* distinct from the mobile substance and the formal determinations taken on successively by this substance during that motion. Questions such as these are precisely the ones that characterize the medieval debate on the ontological status of motion.[9]

The main concern of this chapter is to establish the position of the early English commentators in the medieval debate on the ontological status of motion. This will be done in sections 3-6. In order to get a synthetic view of the reception of the doctrine of motion in the Aris-

---

[6] Aristotle, *Physics*, V.1, 224b7-10; 5, 229a25-27.

[7] In fact, in *Physics* V.1 Aristotle claims that becoming white and not whiteness is a motion (224b15-16). But the point of his claim is to establish that the final state of a motion is not itself a motion.

[8] On the problem of determining to what category does motion belong, S. Waterlow suggests the category of relation, since the only alternatives left for Aristotle are denying that motion is strictly real or admitting realities not covered by any category. See Waterlow, *Nature, Change and Agency*, p. 111. There is, however, no positive evidence in support of S. Waterlow's suggestion. For other suggestions offered by Aristotle himself which are taken into account by medieval authors, see below p. 75-86.

[9] The most comprehensive and systematic account of this debate is given by A. Maier in *Zwischen Philosophie und Mechanik*, (*Studien zur Naturphilosophie der Spätscholastik*, Bd. V), Edizioni di storia e letteratura, Roma 1958, p. 59-143. Since Maier's study, the investigation of this debate has focused on the positions held by specific authors. See, for instance, E.J. McCullough, "St. Albert on Motion as *Forma fluens* and *Fluxus formae*", in J. A. Weisheipl (ed.), *Albertus Magnus and the Sciences, Commemorative Essays 1980*, Pontifical Institute of Mediaeval Studies, Toronto 1980, p.129-153; G. Meyer, "Die Bewegungslehre des Thomas von Aquin im Kommentar zum 3. Buch der Aristotelischen Physik", in L. Elders (ed.), *La philosophie de la nature de Saint Thomas d'Aquin*, Actes du Symposium sur la pensée de Saint Thomas tenu à Rolduc, les 7 et 8 Nov. 1981, Libreria editrice Vaticana, Città del Vaticano 1982, p. 45-65; M. McCord Adams,*William Ockham*, University of Notre Dame Press, Notre Dame, Indiana 1987, vol. II, p. 799-827; S. Caroti, "Oresme on Motion (Quaestiones super Physicam, III, 1-8)", *Vivarium*, 31 (1993) 1, p. 8-36; C. Trifogli, "Thomas Wylton on Motion", *Archiv für Geschichte der Philosophie*, 77 (1995), p. 135-154.

totelian tradition, we shall first outline the discussion of this doctrine in Simplicius' *Physics* commentary. Indeed, passages (I)-(III) quoted above also caused debate in the Greek exegetical tradition. Although a relevant discussion is found only in Simplicius, his quotations of lost commentaries by Alexander of Aphrodisia, Theophrastus and Eudemus suggest that his concern with these passages was shared to some degree by a larger group of early Greek commentators. The comparison of Simplicius' discussion to Averroes' position, which determined the thirteenth-century approach to the problem of the ontology of motion, will make clear the lack of continuity between the Greek and the medieval traditions. As we shall see, although both the Greek and the medieval debates on Aristotle's doctrine of motion arise from the same section of Aristotle's text, they address in fact two different problems.

1. *Simplicius' Position*

Like the medieval commentators, Simplicius does not question Aristotle's main ontological claim in the passage of *Physics* III.1 quoted above, namely, that motion is always in respect of something that belongs to a category.[10] Like Aristotle and unlike the medieval tradition, he does not even work out the possible interpretations and consequences of this point. In fact, Simplicius' discussion aims at the classification of motion in Aristotle's categorical system rather than the ontology of motion. Indeed, the point of departure for his discussion is the conclusion drawn by Aristotle in passage (III) above, according to which there are as many species of motion and change as there are species of being. Here Aristotle establishes a one-one correspondence, which, as such, contains two sides:

(i) each species of motion is associated with a category, namely, that to which the initial and the final states of this species of motion belong (e. g., alteration is associated with quality);

(ii) each category is associated with some motion, i.e., given a determination belonging to any category whatsoever, there is a species of motion leading to the acquisition of such a determination. In

---

[10] See Simplicius, *In Physicam*, III, p. 402, lin. 9-406, lin. 16.

other words, things can change or move with respect to each category.

While (i) expresses Aristotle's ontological commitment that motion is always with respect to some category, (ii) is a claim about the scope of such a commitment. Simplicius' discussion focuses precisely on the issue addressed in (ii).

In order to understand the main points of Simplicius' discussion, it is necessary to introduce some other aspects of Aristotle's treatment of the classification of motion. While in passage (III) from *Physics* III.1 Aristotle's claim is apparently that motion (or change) can exist in each category (i.e., something can change with respect to a determination of whatsoever category), he qualifies this claim in *Physics* V.2, where he deals more accurately with the problem of classification. There he draws a distinction between essential (*per se*) and accidental change, according to which an essential change is a basic and primary change, whereas an accidental change is a change that is secondary to and dependent on some basic change. He holds that some categories yield changes that are accidental, viz., dependent on changes in other categories. He argues explicitly against the existence of essential change in the categories of relation, action and passion.[11] He concludes that, in fact, essential change exists in only four categories, namely, substance, quality, quantity, and being somewhere. In another formulation, Aristotle's final position on the problem of classification is that there are only four species of essential change: generation and corruption, qualitative change, quantitative change, and local motion.[12]

In the medieval exegetical tradition, this more restrictive view is regarded as reflecting Aristotle's definitive position. This is acknowledged by Simplicius as well. Thus, in his literal exegesis of *Physics* V.2,

---

[11] Ibid., V.2, 225b11-226a23.

[12] See Aristotle, *Physics*, V.2, 226a23-26. A more accurate formulation of Aristotle's conclusion is that there are three types of *per se* motion (κίνησις), namely, alteration, quantitative motion, and local motion, and one type of *per se* change (μεταβολή), namely, generation and corruption. For Aristotle distinguishes in this context between κίνησις and μεταβολή and reserves the term κίνησις for those changes in which there is a persisting actual substrate, to the effect that generation and corruption are not κινήσεις, but μεταβολαί. See Aristotle, *Physics*, V.1, 224b35-225b9. Since the distinction between κινησις and μεταβολὴ is not very relevant to our discussion, we tend to use the two terms interchangeably, as Aristotle himself does in Books III and IV.

he explains that Aristotle's view as expressed there need not be construed as in conflict with his position in *Physics* III.1, that there are as many species of change as there are of being. In fact, by "species of being" Aristotle means the species of being subject to motion and change, and these are only the four species of being that Aristotle identifies in *Physics* V.1-2 as those which can undergo a *per se* change.[13] In conclusion, both medieval commentators and Simplicius agree that Aristotle's final position on the problem of classification is that of *Physics* V.2, which limits change to four categories. There is, however, a major difference in the reception of Aristotle's position. While, in the medieval commentaries, Aristotle's restriction of motion to four categories is commonly accepted and never becomes matter of debate, Simplicius discusses it at length and is not willing to accept it as it stands.

At the end of the literal exegesis of passage (III), Simplicius opens his discussion of the problem of classification by raising an objection against Aristotle's restriction of motion to four categories:

> (1) Since that which is in potency and that which is in act are in all genera of being and since motion is an act of that which is in potency insofar as it is in potency, it is worth investigating why motion exists only in four genera of being, namely, in substance, in quality, in quantity, and in "being somewhere" (as Aristotle divides motion in the *Categories* and will take care to prove in the fifth book of this treatise), but not also in the other genera, despite the fact that in all these genera there is the act of what is in potency while it is in potency. (2) Indeed, also the change to being on the left of that which in on the right but is apt by nature to be on the left is an act of that which is in potency and remains in potency as long as it changes. And someone who is sitting but is apt by nature to stand and changes from one of these two positions to the other, since during this change the potential aspect persists, he falls under the definition of motion with respect to such a change of position. Similarly, in the case of the other categories, we shall be able to include the changes with respect to the different species of that genus under the definition of motion.[14]

---

[13] See Simplicius, *In Physicam*, III, p. 408, lin. 5-14.

[14] Ibid., p. 408, lin. 15-27: "Ἀλλ᾽ ἄξιον ζητεῖν, διὰ τί τοῦ δυνάμει καὶ ἐντελεχείᾳ ἐν πᾶσιν ὄντος τοῖς γένεσι τοῦ ὄντος, καὶ τῆς κινήσεως οὔσης ἐνεργείας τοῦ δυνάμει ᾗ τοιοῦτόν ἐστιν, ἐν τέτρασι μόνοις γένεσι τοῦ ὄντος τῇ οὐσίᾳ καὶ τῷ ποιῷ καὶ τῷ ποσῷ καὶ τῷ ποῦ ἐστιν ἡ κίνησις (ὡς καὶ ἐν Κατηγορίαις διῄρηται καὶ ἐν τῷ πέμπτῳ ταύτης τῆς πραγματείας σπουδάσει δεῖξαι), ἐν δὲ τοῖς ἄλλοις οὐκέτι, καίτοι ἐν πᾶσίν ἐστιν ἡ τοῦ δυνάμει ἐνέργεια

The general objection raised in part (1) of this passage is that Aristotle's restriction of motion to four categories is to some extent in conflict with the definition of motion, which seems general enough to apply to all categories of being. In (2) this point is illustrated with the case of a change in the category of relation (passage from left to right) and of a change in the category of position (passage from sitting to standing).

The contrast between Aristotle's definition of motion and the restriction of motion to four categories is not so radical as Simplicius wants us to believe in the passage quoted, since Aristotle does not deny the other categories any form of motion but only motion in the strict sense (*per se*). For instance, in the example of the passage from being on the left to being on the right quoted by Simplicius, Aristotle's view is that this passage does involve an actualization of a potency and in this sense falls under the definition of motion to some extent. Yet, it is only an accidental or secondary kind of motion, since it presupposes local motion as a more basic kind of motion from which it derives. Similarly, the change in any kind of relation can be reduced to a *per se* change with respect to one of the four categories of substance, quality, quantity or place.

Simplicius seems to be aware of the fact that the argument from the definition of motion is not conclusive against Aristotle's restriction of *per se* motion to four categories. He insists, however, that there is also a *per se* motion in the other categories. In particular, he replies to Aristotle's arguments against *per se* motion in the categories of relation and of action and passion and formulates his own arguments for *per se* motion in the categories not mentioned by Aristotle ("when", position, "habit").[15] The conflict between Aristotle and Simplicius on this

---

μένοντος δυνάμει· καὶ γὰρ ἡ τοῦ δεξιοῦ πεφυκότος δὲ ἀριστεροῦ γίνεσθαι ἐπὶ τὸ ἀριστερὸν μεταβολὴ τοῦ δυνάμει ἐστὶν ἐνέργεια μένοντος δυνάμει, ἕως ὅτε μεταβάλλει. καὶ ὁ καθήμενος πεφυκὼς δὲ καὶ ἀνακλίνεσθαι καὶ μεταβάλλων ἀπὸ θατέρου ἐπὶ θάτερον μένοντος τοῦ δυνάμει ἐν τῇ μεταβολῇ ὑποπίπτει τῷ ὁρισμῷ τῆς κινήσεως κατὰ τὴν τοιαύτην μεταβολήν". The same objection is raised at p. 412, lin. 20-28.

[15] For the category of relation, see Simplicius, *In Physicam*, III, p. 409, lin. 13-32 (at lin. 27-32, he quotes Alexander in support of his thesis of a *per se* motion in the relation); V, p. 834, lin. 22-837, lin. 18 (at the end of this passage, however, Simplicius seems to concede to Aristotle that motion in the relatives is only accidental); V, p. 858, lin. 15-25. For the category of action and passion, see ibid., III, p. 410, lin. 1-32; V, p. 850, lin. 30-852, lin. 25; V, p. 858, lin. 25-859, lin. 4. For the category of "when", see ibid., III, p. 410, lin. 33-411, lin. 28 (at lin. 17-18 he quotes Eudemus in support of his thesis); V, p. 830, lin. 5-832, lin. 3 (he discusses and replies to Alexander's arguments against the existence of motion in this category); V, p. 859, lin. 5-7.

point can be illustrated with the case of motion in the category of relation. Aristotle's short argument against *per se* motion in this category goes as follows: a change with respect to a relation can take place even when only one of the two relatives in fact changes.[16] For instance, to use Simplicius' example, if A is to the right of B and B moves to the right of A, then A comes to be on the left of B; but since A has not moved locally, the change of A to the left is in fact "parasitic" on that of B's moving to the right of A. Simplicius replies that this argument is not conclusive against a *per se* motion in the category of relation:

> ... Indeed, even if, when that which is on the right moves <to the left>, that which first was on the left comes to be on the right, without having undergone a change, and in this sense it changes accidentally, nevertheless, (1) first, that which was first on the right and has moved, since it comes to be on the left, changes essentially, not accidentally, with respect to the relation of being on the right as well as with respect to its place. (2) And since the relation does not inhere in just one of the two relatives but in both, the relation has changed *per se* and not accidentally in the relative that has not moved as well as in the relative that has undergone local motion.[17]

In (1) Simplicius points out that the relative that moves locally from right to left does in fact change *per se* not only with respect to place

---

For the category of position, see ibid., III, p. 411, lin. 29-33; V, p. 859, lin. 7-10. For the category of "habit", see ibid., III, p. 411, lin. 33-412, lin. 8; V, p. 859, lin. 10-15. Finally, in Book III, p. 413, lin. 1-9, Simplicius quotes Theophrastus in support of the thesis of the existence of motion in all categories. It should be remarked, however, the Simplicius' quotations of other Greek commentators do not provide strong evidence in favour of his main thesis on the existence of a *per se* motion in each category. It must also be remarked that in the other two surviving Greek commentaries on the *Physics*, namely, Themistius' paraphrasis and Philoponus' commentary, Aristotle's position on the classification problem is accepted without significant objections.

[16] Aristotle, *Physics*, V.2, 225b11-13.

[17] Simplicius, *In Physicam*, III, p. 409, lin. 15-22: "κἂν γὰρ τοῦ δεξιοῦ κινηθέντος ὁ πρότερον ἀριστερὸς ὢν μὴ κινηθεὶς αὐτὸς γίνηται δεξιὸς καὶ διὰ τοῦτο κατὰ συμβεβηκὸς μεταβάλλῃ, ἀλλὰ πρῶτον μὲν ὁ δεξιὸς πρότερον ἑστὼς καὶ κινηθεὶς οὐ κατὰ συμβεβηκὸς ἀλλὰ καθ'αὑτὸν μετέβαλε μετὰ τοῦ τόπου καὶ τὴν τοῦ δεξιοῦ σχέσιν ἀριστερὸς γενόμενος. καὶ ὁ μὴ κινηθεὶς δέ, ἐπειδὴ ἡ σχέσις οὐκ ἐν τῷ ἑνί ἐστιν ἀλλ'ἐν ἀμφοτέροις, τὴν ἐν αὐτῷ σχέσιν οὐ κατὰ συμβεβηκὸς ἀλλὰ καθ'αὑτὸ συγκινουμένην ἔσχε τῇ τοῦ μεταβεβηκότος". Simplicius' discussion of motion in the category of relation has been analysed in detail in C. Luna, "La relation chez Simplicius", in I. Hadot (ed.), *Simplicius. Sa vie, son oeuvre, sa survie*. Actes du colloque international de Paris (28 Sept.-1er Oct. 1985), De Gruyter, Berlin-New York 1987, p. 140-145, and I. Croese, *Simplicius on Continuous and Instantaneous Change*, Zeno Institute of Philosophy, The Leiden-Utrecht Research Institute, Utrecht 1998, p. 151-167.

but also with respect to its relation of being on the right. In (2) he points out that even the relative that has not moved locally has nevertheless changed its relation. Accordingly, Aristotle and Simplicius agree that there is a change of relation and that this involves both relatives. The controversial point is whether to regard this change as only accidental, as Aristotle maintains, or as "essential", as Simplicius does. This point comes out repeatedly in Simplicius' discussion, but it is simply asserted and not explained.

Some light on this controversy is shed by a few remarks made by Simplicius in his commentary on Book V, where, showing a more exegetical attitude, he tries to find the motivation for Aristotle's restriction of *per se* change to four categories. He explains that in Aristotle's view a *per se* change is that in which the subject of change acquires some stable intrinsic disposition. There are, however, only four kinds of such dispositions, namely, substance, quality, quantity, and being in a place, and these four kinds of dispositions determine the four kinds of *per se* change in Aristotle's sense.[18] Thus, in Simplicius' interpretation, Aristotle's distinction between *per se* and accidental changes ultimately relies on a hierarchy between the different types of categorical being. Just as there are stronger and weaker types of categorical being, so correspondingly there are motions in a strict sense (*per se*) and in a weaker or accidental sense. Certainly, Simplicius' interpretation sounds very Aristotelian. For instance, it is a good explanation of why Aristotle denies that the passage from being on the right to being on the left is a motion in the strict sense, since it is clear that such a change does not produce any intrinsic and stable modification in the subject undergoing it. More generally, the principle that the hierarchy of the different types of being determines a hierarchy of their corresponding motions ties in well with Aristotle's ontological claim in *Physics* III.1 according to which motion is always with respect to some categorical being.

Simplicius himself admits that Aristotle's restrictive view on the types of *per se* changes has some plausibility when interpreted in this way. Yet, he seems unwilling to adhere to it completely. More precisely, while he acknowledges that there is a hierarchy among the different types of categorical being, he is reluctant to admit that such a hierarchy passes over to motion or change.[19] In particular, he dis-

---

[18] See Simplicius, *In Physicam*, V, p. 859, lin. 16-860, lin. 2.
[19] See, for instance, ibid., V, p. 860, lin. 28-861, lin. 4.

putes Aristotle's relegation of motions with respect to the "secondary" categories of being to the realm of the accidental. Rather, he emphasizes that these are also motions in their own right, though different from those in the "primary" categories of being. He also suggests that motions corresponding to the different kinds of categorical being should not be divided into *per se* and accidental, as Aristotle does, but into motions that lead to a disposition (κατὰ διάθεσιν) (or to a substance) and relative motions (κατὰ σχέσιν), namely, those that lead to a determination of any other "secondary" category.[20] In short, Simplicius insists that in each category there is a specific type of change unique to it, which is to some extent unaffected by the weaker or stronger type of being represented by that category.

It is not easy to determine with precision the ultimate reasons for Simplicius' insistence on this point, but nevertheless some general and partial suggestions can be attempted. A passage from his commentary on Book III offers a glimpse of his motivation:

> In general, it is worth remarking that all the categories, since they are considered *in becoming* (ἐν τῇ γενέσει) and subsist in particulars, are subject to change. Indeed, as the substance *of this world* (ἡ οὐσία ... ἡ ἐνταῦθα) is generable and corruptible, the same is true for qualities, for quantities and for all the other categories.[21]

This passage contains one of Simplicius' several arguments for the existence of change in each category. While the argument itself is not so interesting, its language is. Terms like "becoming" (γένεσις) and "of this world" (ἐνταῦθα) seem to point to a Platonic/Neoplatonic metaphysical background rather than a genuinely Aristotelian one. Although it is true that Aristotle uses the term γένεσις not only in the technical sense of change in the category of substance, but also in a

---

[20] See ibid., p. 861, lin. 9-19. Note, however, that immediately after at lin. 19-28, at the very end of his discussion of the classification problem, Simplicius remarks that Aristotle would deny that "relative" motions are per se motions. This and other cases show that in Simplicius' discussion there is a latent conflict between the demands of fidelity to Aristotle's thought and the expression of his own personal view. We agree, however, with Croese who maintains that in conceding that relational changes are only accidental Simplicius means that they are changes with respect to "weak" categories and not that they are not per se changes in Aristotle's sense. On this point, see Croese, *Simplicius on Continuous and Instantaneous Change*, p. 163-166.

[21] Simplicius, *In Physicam*, III, p. 412, lin. 9-12: "Κοινῶς δὲ ἐπιστῆσαι ἄξιον, ὅτι πᾶσαι αἱ κατηγορίαι ἐν τῇ γενέσει θεωρούμεναι καὶ ἐν τοῖς καθ᾽ ἕκαστα ὑφεστηκυῖαι μεταβολὴν ὑπομένουσιν. ὡς γὰρ ἡ οὐσία γενητὴ καὶ φθαρτή ἐστιν ἡ ἐνταῦθα, οὕτως καὶ ποιότητες καὶ ποσότητες καὶ αἱ ἄλλαι κατηγορίαι".

much more general sense to indicate any type of change or event, in Simplicius' passage this term is correlated with the expression ἐνταῦθα, and this connection does not sound Aristotelian.[22] Indeed, here Simplicius seems tacitly to assume the Platonic/Neoplatonic dualism between sensible world and intelligible world. If this is the case, Simplicius' polemic against Aristotle becomes more understandable. Indeed, from a "Platonic" perspective, change or motion is the distinctive feature of the sensible as opposed to the intelligible universe, and, as Simplicius assumes, since the categories form the basic structure of the sensible world, change is an intrinsic and essential aspect of each of them. On the other hand, Aristotle seems to weaken this intrinsic connection between the categories of the sensible world and the notion of becoming by restricting *per se* motion to just four categories. If our suggestion that a Platonic/Neoplatonic metaphysical background at least partially motivated Simplicius' concern with Aristotle's position on the classification problem is right, then it might also help to explain why medieval commentators, starting from a more Aristotelian perspective, did not find serious problems in Aristotle's restrictive view on the types of *per se* changes.

2. *Averroes' Position*

In the last section, the one-one correspondence between the species of categorical being and the species of motion established by Aristotle in *Physics* III.1 was seen to involve (i) an ontological commitment (motion is always with respect to some categorical being) and (ii) the scope of such a commitment (for each type of categorical being there is a motion with respect to this being). It has been pointed out that Simplicius' discussion targets the scope of Aristotle's ontological commitment. In contrast, the thirteenth-century debate on Aristotle's

---

[22] Indeed, in the *Physics*, Aristotle uses γένεσις in its more general sense to describe the type of being of events as opposed to the permanent type of being of substances. See, for instance, his introductory remarks on the type of being of the infinite at III.6, 206a21-25, 29a-33. In support of our suggestion of a Neoplatonic origin of Simplicius' defence of a per se motion in each category, we can mention Croese's view according to which, in the particular case of motion in the category of relation, Simplicius' claim that such a motion is per se derives from a Neoplatonic interpretation of the category of relation. See Croese, *Simplicius on Continuous and Instantaneous Change*, p. 153-158.

doctrine of motion arises from the ontological commitment itself. In brief, the central question of the thirteenth-century debate is the following: assuming that in each motion the mobile substance changes with respect to some category, what is the ontological relation between motion itself and the category-occupant of its final state? The most significant origin of this question lies in Averroes.

In t.c. 4 of his commentary on *Physics* III, at the end of his literal exegesis of passages (I)-(III) quoted above, Averroes raises a difficulty against Aristotle's conclusion that motion exists in the four categories of its *per se* termini. This conclusion seems to conflict with some of Aristotle's suggestions in the *Categories*, such as being heated and being cooled as examples of passions.[23] Since these processes are also species of motion, Aristotle's examples seem to imply that motion belongs to the category of passion. This difficulty, as it stands, pertains to the classificatory level of Aristotle's doctrine. Yet, the solution given by Averroes goes far beyond that. In fact, it contains a definite answer to the ontological question of the relation between motion and its final state. In trying to reconcile Aristotle's conflicting views, Averroes introduces a distinction between two ways of regarding motion:

> ... insofar as motion does not differ from the perfection to which it goes except according to more or less, it must exist in the genus of that perfection. For motion is nothing but the generation of one part after another of the perfection to which motion is directed until it is perfected and exists in act. Thus, it is necessary that the motion that is in substance is found in the genus of substance, and the motion that is in quantity in the genus of quantity and likewise for motion in place and quality. But insofar as motion is the way to that perfection, where the way is other than the perfection, it must be a genus through itself. For the way to a thing is different from the thing, and to that extent, it was assumed [to be] a category through itself. And the latter way is the more famous, but the former is the truer. Therefore, Aristotle introduces the more famous way in the *Categories* and the true way in this book.[24]

---

[23] Aristotle, *Categories*, 9, 11b1-8. Yet, Aristotle's view in the *Categories* that motion is a passion does not necessarily contradict his claim that motion can occur in respect of substance, quantity, quality, and place, if this claim is understood in the sense that the initial and final states of motion belong to these categories and not in the sense that motion itself belongs to them. I owe this remark to Prof. Richard Sorabji.

[24] Averroes, *In Physicam*, III, t.c. 4, f. 87raC-rbE: "... motus secundum quod non

In short, Averroes' solution is that motion must be classified in the category of its final state, when it is regarded as something that differs only in degree from that state, whereas it must posited as a determination of the category of passion when it is regarded as the process (*via*) which leads to its final state. He also adds that the former type of classification, namely, that of the *Physics*, is the "true" one, while the latter, namely, that of the *Categories*, is simply "famous".

Averroes' solution has clear ontological implications. Indeed, a sign of this is that his solution provides Aristotle's classification of the species of motion in the *Physics* with a much more solid ontological foundation than that given by Aristotle himself. For Averroes' solution implies that motion belongs to the four categories of substance, quality, quantity, and *ubi*, not only because motion is with respect to entities belonging to these categories, but also because in itself motion differs only in degrees and not in essence from these entities and, in particular, from the entity represented by its final state. Furthermore, it is also clear that the distinction between the classifications of the *Physics* and of the *Categories*, which Averroes apparently regards as being between two ways of considering motion, in fact reflects two irreducible ontologies of motion. In the first sense, that is, motion "regarded" as essentially the same as its final state, only two *res* are necessary to account for a substance's becoming white: the mobile substance and whiteness, since becoming white is nothing other than whiteness in a "less intense" degree or, as the early English commentators often put it, whiteness in a state of incompletion (*forma incompleta*). According to the second way, that is, motion "regarded" as *via*, it

---

differt a perfectione ad quam vadit nisi secundum magis et minus, necesse est ut sit de genere illius perfectionis. Motus enim nihil aliud est quam generatio partis post aliam illius perfectionis ad quam intendit motus, donec perficiatur et fit in actu. Unde necesse est ut motus qui est in substantia inveniatur in genere substantiae, et motus qui est in quantitate in genere quantitatis et similiter qui est in ubi et qualitate. Secundum autem quod est via ad perfectionem, quae est alia ab ipsa perfectione, necesse est ut sit genus per se. Via enim ad rem est aliud ab ipsa re, et secundum hoc fuit positum praedicamentum per se. Et iste modus est famosior, ille autem est verior. Et ideo Aristoteles induxit illum modum famosum in *Praedicamentis* et istum modum verum in hoc libro". The English translation of this passage is that given by McCord Adams in *William Ockham*, II, p. 802-803. Averroes raises again the question of the two different categorical classifications of motion in t. c. 9 of his comment on Book V at ff. 214vbK-215raC. He also offers a solution, which is similar, but not exactly the same as that of t. c. 4 of Book III. For a detailed exposition of both of Averroes' solutions, see Maier, *Zwischen Philosophie und Mechanik*, p. 62-67. However, our commentators' discussion focuses on the solution of t. c. 4 of Book III.

is necessary to postulate motion as a *res* distinct from both the mobile substance and whiteness, since it is the *via* through which whiteness is acquired by the mobile substance.

This remark on the ontological implications of Averroes' distinction was most explicitly made by Ockham:

> Thus, it must first be known that when the Commentator makes distinctions about motion in that passage, he does not mean that motion could be truly taken in two ways, so far as the truth of the matter is concerned, so that evidently one way it is the term to which and another way it is the way that differs from the term of the motion and from the mobile object. For no motion is any such distinct thing. Rather he intends to say that there are two opinions about motion, of which the one, viz., the famous one, is false and the other true.[25]

The ontological commitments of Averroes' solution of the classification problem were generally perceived by the thirteenth- and fourteenth-century commentators. Accordingly, the passage from t.c.4 of Book III quoted above became the *locus classicus* for raising the question about the ontological status of motion.[26] For the early English commentaries in particular, this question originates exclusively from Averroes' passage, the only exceptions being M[2] and W. These two commentaries give a more comprehensive review of opinions about the problem of the categorical classification of motion, in which Avi-

---

[25] Ockham, *In Physicam*, III, cap. 2, § 7, p. 436, lin. 5-10: "Unde sciendum est primo quod Commentator ibi distinguens de motu non intendit quod veraciter 'motus' possit duobus modis accipi, videlicet quod realiter motus, uno modo accepto motu, sit terminus ad quem, et alio modo sit via differens a termino et a mobili, quia nullus motus est talis res alia, sed intendit ibi duas opiniones de motu, quarum una, scilicet famosa, est falsa et alia opinio est vera". I have used McCord Adams' translation of the corresponding passage from the *Tractatus de successivis*. See Mc Cords Adams, *William Ockham*, II, p. 803-804.

[26] Following Avicenna's terminology, however, many medieval authors use the distinction between motion as *forma fluens* and motion as *fluxus formae*, which is not completely equivalent to Averroes' distinction between motion as *forma incompleta* and motion as *via ad formam*, but has the same ontological implications. Avicenna deals with the problem of the categorical classification of motion in the *Sufficientia*, II, cap. 2, ff. 24vb-25va. On Avicenna's position, see Maier, *Zwischen Philosophie und Mechanik*, p. 68-73. A. Hasnawi remarks that a Greek origin of the distinction between motion as *forma fluens* and motion as *fluxus formae* is to be found in Themistius', Philoponus' and Simplicius' discussion on the homonymy of the term 'motion'. See A. Hasnawi, "Alexandre d'Aphrodise vs Jean Philopon: Notes sur quelques traités d'Alexandre "perdus" en Grec, conservés en Arabe", *Arabic Sciences and Philosophy*, 4 (1994), p. 67. I am grateful to dr. J. Janssen for drawing my attention to Hasnawi's paper.

cenna's position is also presented.[27] This review, however, is substantially a reformulation of the doxographical digression on the topic offered by Albert the Great in his commentary on the *Physics*.[28] Furthermore, it makes no significant contribution to the doctrinal aspects of the debate. Indeed, from a doctrinal point of view, the question on the ontological status of motion in all our commentaries focuses on Averroes' alternatives of motion as *forma incompleta* and motion as *via ad formam* really distinct from this form. For the sake of brevity, we shall henceforth refer to the first alternative as the *forma*-theory of motion and to the second one as the *via*-theory.

In section 3, the reaction of the early English commentators against Averroes is analysed. It will be made clear that these commentators hold a realist position on the ontological status of motion according to which motion is a *via ad formam* essentially distinct from the form to which it is directed. In section 4, we shall see that the discussion of Averroes' position also exerted a strong influence on the exegesis of Aristotle's definition of motion given by our commentators. Finally, in section 5, we shall present the answer of our commentators to the problem of the classification of motion in Aristotle's system of categories.

3. *The Rejection of Averroes' Position*

The early English commentators depart from Averroes' *forma*-theory of motion and follow a *via*-theory. As to the exegesis of Averroes' discussion, almost all our commentators assume that with the distinction between the true way and the famous way of "regarding" motion, Averroes in fact rules out the *via*-theory of motion. Accordingly, they react explicitly against Averroes and formulate a number of arguments to show that the *forma*-theory of motion cannot be maintained. These arguments will be analysed in section 3.2. To point out the peculiarity of the refutation of Averroes' position in the early English tradition, we shall then discuss in section 3.3 an alternative approach,

---

[27] M², III, q. 4, ff. 125va, lin. 42-126ra, lin.9; W, III, q. 3, ff. 53rb, lin. 8-54rb, lin. 7.
[28] Albert the Great, *In Physicam*, III, tract. 1, cap. 3, p. 150b, lin. 46-156b, lin. 74. For Albert's treatment of the problem of the categorical classification of motion and its relation to Avicenna's and Averroes' discussions see Maier, *Zwischen Philosophie und Mechanik*, p. 73-76; McCullough, "St. Albert on Motion", p. 132-145, 149-153.

based on a physical analysis of motion, which will become increasingly widespread in the later thirteenth and early fourteenth centuries. While in general the discussion of the early English commentators about the problem of the ontological status of motion is characterized by open critique of Averroes, exceptions do exist, and it is those that we shall presently consider.

3.1. *The Exegesis of Averroes' Distinction Between the True Way and the Famous Way of Regarding Motion*

Our commentators do not give a detailed exegesis of the passage from t.c. 4 of Averroes' commentary on Book III, quoted in section 2. Rather, they tend to quote it in an abridged form without further analysis. Nevertheless, two of our commentators, namely, G[1] and the largely derivative N, investigate more closely the meaning of Averroes' distinction between the two ways of regarding motion (*forma incompleta* and *via ad formam*). In particular, G[1] devotes the following question to the topic:

> But since motion is said of these two things <i.e., of the form and of the way to the form>, it is then asked of which of these it is said more truly.[29]

It is clear from other passages that G[1] holds a *via*-theory of motion. For instance, in his solution to the question on the existence of motion he claims:

> It can be said that, if we extend the name of being to that which is being in the true sense, as substance, and to the passion of being, as accident, and to the intermediate way which leads to being, in this last sense motion can be called a being. For motion is the intermediate way through which the mobile thing acquires its form.[30]

---

[29] G[1], III, q. 6, f. 140ra, lin. 25-26: "Sed tunc quaeritur, cum motus dicitur de istis duobus, de quo istorum (aliorum *ms.*) dicitur verius". G[1] reports Averroes' opinion with some slight modifications in III, q. 5, f. 140ra, lin. 15-23. In the footnotes to this chapter we use the numbering of the questions on *Physics* III.1-3 in our commentaries that appear in the list of these questions published in Trifogli, "Le questioni sul libro III della *Fisica*", p. 490-501.

[30] G[1], III, q. 1, f. 139rb, lin. 56-62: "Potest dici quod extendendo nomen entis ad illud quod est vere ens, ut substantia, et ad passionem entis, ut accidens, et ad viam mediam deveniendi ad ens, sic[ut] potest dici ens. Est enim via media per quam mobile acquirit suam formam".

Here motion is explicitly identified with the *via ad formam*. Therefore, one should expect that, in answering the question about Averroes' distinction, G¹ takes a position openly against the *Commentator*. In fact, this is not the case. Instead, G¹ tends to show that the *via*-theory of motion can be reconciled with Averroes' view in the passage of t.c. 4. Indeed, he replies:

> It can be said that the sense in which motion is called an intermediate way is truer in one way and not in another. It is truer, since it is more properly called motion in that sense <i.e., as a way> than in the other. It is less true, since motion insofar as it names a way has a less true kind of reality than insofar as it names the perfection itself. And this makes clear the meaning of the *Commentator*'s assertion.[31]

Thus, in the interpretation of Averroes' distinction given by G¹, the *via*-theory also becomes to some extent legitimate, since it turns out that it is in some sense truer than the *forma*-theory.

It is clear that attempt of G¹ to reconcile the *via*-theory with Averroes' view rests on an unfaithful interpretation of Averroes' distinction. First of all, the *via*-theory of motion is not called "famous", as in Averroes, but simply in a sense less true. Furthermore, in the two propositions (i) "motion is said more truly of the way than of the perfection" and (ii) "motion is said less truly of the way than of the perfection" "truly" is taken in two quite distinct senses. In (i) it refers to the proper meaning of the term "motion", whereas in (ii) "truly" is taken in the metaphysical sense of "existing in reality". Indeed, in (ii) G¹ appeals implicitly to the common presupposition that successive things have an inferior degree of reality than permanent things, and motion regarded as a *via* is a successive thing, whereas the form acquired by the substance through motion is a permanent one.[32] Accordingly, the interpretation of G¹ radically changes the original meaning of Averroes' distinction, to the effect that the *via*-theory turns out to be the "truer" one.

Yet, the interpretation of G¹, however odd and unfaithful it might

---

[31] G¹, III, q. 6, f. 140ra, lin. 33-36: "Potest dici quod ille modus quo motus dicitur via media uno modo est verior et alio modo non. Verior est, quia magis proprie dicitur motus de illo modo quam de alio; minus vere, quia motus prout nominat viam minus vere habet entitatem quam prout nominat ipsam perfectionem. Et sic patet intellectus dicti Commentatoris". See also N, III, q. 6, f. 133rb, lin. 42-45.

[32] For permanent things are primarily substances, whereas successive things are processes. On this point, see below in section 3.2.

appear, turns out to be important in the history of the reception of Averroes' position. Indeed, in the fourteenth century, Walter Burley will give a very similar interpretation. In his last commentary on the *Physics*, Burley's polemical target in the discussion on the ontological status of motion is William of Ockham. Burley argues against Ockham that motion is a *res* distinct from the mobile substance and the form acquired by it during motion.[33] Clearly, this is in conflict with Averroes' *forma*-theory of motion, and thus one would expect to see Burley raise this conflict explicitly when he comments on Averroes' distinction between the famous and the true ways of regarding motion. Yet, on that occasion Burley takes the same conciliatory attitude found in G[1]. He explains:

> One way of regarding motion being truer than the other can be understood in two ways, namely, with respect to the reality of the thing or with respect to the signification of the name. And then I say that the way of taking motion as the diminished form is truer with respect to the being of the thing, because motion regarded as a diminished form is a more perfect kind of being than the motion which belongs to the category of passion, since the former belongs to a more perfect genre. Yet, the way of taking motion as a successive transmutation is truer with respect to the signification of the name, because the term "motion" primarily signifies a successive transmutation rather than a diminished form. [34]

The expression "successive transmutation" (*transmutatio successiva*) employed by Burley in this passage (instead of *via ad formam*) derives from Averroes' second digression on the problem of classification in his commentary on Book V, where he claims that motion considered as a *transmutatio coniucta cum tempore* is in the category of passion.[35] Apart from this linguistic difference, however, Burley's "defence" of Averroes' distinction has striking similarities with that found in G[1]. In particular, the common strategy of these two commentators is to

---

[33] Burley, *In Physicam*, III, ff. 64rb-65vb.

[34] Ibid., f. 62va: "... unum modum accipiendi motum esse veriorem alio potest intelligi dupliciter, scilicet vel quantum ad entitatem rei vel quantum ad significationem nominis. Et tunc dico quod modus accipiendi motum pro forma diminuta est verior quantum ad entitatem rei, quoniam motus acceptus pro forma diminuta est perfectius ens, cum sit perfectioris generis, quam motus de genere passionis. Sed modus accipiendi motum pro transmutatione successiva est verior quantum ad significationem nominis, quia hoc nomen 'motus' per prius significat transmutationem successivam quam formam diminutam".

[35] Cfr. Averroes, *In Physicam*, V, t.c. 9, f. 215raB.

neglect in this context the adjective "famosa" with which Averroes refers to the *via*-theory and to replace it with the adjective "less true" in the ontological sense of something having a weaker kind of reality.

3.2 *The Arguments Against Averroes' Position*

Apart from G¹, the other commentators react explicitly against the *forma*-theory of motion supported by Averroes. In presenting their reaction, it is useful to distinguish two aspects of Averroes' theory: (1) the assumption that motion is essentially the same as the form acquired through it and is this same form in an incomplete state (*forma incompleta*); (2) the reductionist ontology of motion entailed by (1), namely, that to account for processes like a substance's becoming white it is not necessary to postulate motion as a *res* over and above the mobile substance and whiteness.

The arguments of our commentators against Averroes' *forma*-theory of motion are directed at both of these aspects.

The main conceptual tool used by our commentators against (1) is the distinction between *permanentia* and *successiva*. In most general terms, permanent things and successive things correspond to objects and processes respectively. The *locus classicus* for this distinction is a passage of *Physics* III.6, where Aristotle contrasts the mode of being of a house and a man with that of a day and an athletic contest.³⁶ But this general distinction becomes most relevant to the debate on the ontological status of motion in its specific application to the parts of divisible things. Any part of a permanent thing can exist in an instant, i.e., in a durationless temporal point, but no part of a process can exist in an instant. For instance, any phase of a motion takes time, i.e., it does not occur in an instant. Furthermore, all the parts of a permanent thing can exist in the same instant, as is clear for the physical parts of an object. As medieval commentators put it, the parts of a permanent thing can exist *simul*. The parts of a successive thing, on the contrary, cannot exist *simul*, but only one after the other.

In the Aristotelian tradition, the existence of successive things is more controversial than that of permanent things. While it is true that Aristotle is always confident that motion exists,³⁷ he casts doubts on the existence of time, and his main argument against its existence

---

³⁶ Cfr. Aristotle, *Physics*, III.6, 206a29a-33.
³⁷ Cfr., for instance, ibid., VIII.3, 253a32-b6.

is based exactly on the principle that no part of time exists "now", i.e., in the present instant.[38] But, as we have just seen, this same principle holds for any successive thing. Aristotle provides no explicit answer to the arguments against the existence of time, and different ways of legitimizing the existence of the *successiva* were proposed by Aristotelian commentators. We shall postpone until chapter 4 the examination of our commentators' treatment of this topic. In this context what is important is that, as soon as one assumes the existence of successive things, their ontological status is apparently determined. Since the parts of permanent things can exist simultaneously, whereas those of successive things cannot, then, so it seems, successive things must be distinct from any permanent thing.[39] In particular, since motion is a successive thing and the form generated through it is a permanent thing, motion is something distinct from this form. Indeed, this is the kind of reasoning most frequently deployed by our commentators against Averroes' position. It is clearly illustrated in the following argument proposed by M[2]:

> According to the Commentator and Aristotle, the form to which motion is directed is acquired part by part continuously, until that form is completely induced, such that each part receives in itself another part, and finally, when this form attains its completion, it exists all at once. Therefore, if motion is nothing else than this form insofar as it is flowing, motion will finally exist all at once, which is impossible.[40]

---

[38] Cfr. ibid., IV.10, 218a3-6.

[39] This kind of reasoning is also proposed by Ockham as one of the main arguments against his position that successive things and in particular motion are not something over and above permanent things: "Unde p r i m o videtur quod motus sit alia res a rebus permanentibus. P r i m o, quia quando aliqua sic se habent quod unum est habens omnes partes suas simul et aliud non est habens omnes partes suas simul, illa distinguuntur; sed omnes res permanentes quae habent partes, habent omnes partes simul et motus non habet omnes partes simul; ergo motus et res permanentes distinguuntur realiter" (Ockham, *In Physicam*, III, cap. 2, p. 440, lin. 5-10).

[40] M[2], III, q. 4, f. 125vb, lin. 18 ab imo-13 ab imo: "Secundum Commentatorem et Aristotelem, de forma ad quam est motus continue acquiritur pars post partem quousque tandem ipsa complete sit inducta, ita quod quaelibet pars accipit supra se aliam partem et in fine, cum completur, manet forma simul tota; ergo si motus non sit aliud quam haec forma ut est fluens, in fine erit totus motus simul, quod est impossibile". Note that in this passage M[2] uses the expression "forma fluens" to refer to Averroes' *forma*-theory. This usage derives from Albert the Great. See, for instance, Albertus Magnus, *In Physicam*, III, tract. 1, cap. 3, p. 153, lin. 22-36. For similar arguments based on the *permanentia-successiva* distinction, see also M[1], III, q. 5, f. 109rb, lin. 26-30; M[3], III, q. 5, f. 153ra, lin. 4-5; N, III, q. 6, f. 133va, lin. 5-9; W, III, q. 3, f. 54ra, lin. 8-14.

One might reply to this argument that motion is the form eventually acquired by the mobile substance, but only insofar as this form is still incomplete or under generation. In other words, motion is the mode of being that characterizes the form while it is still under generation. More generally, one might object that the argument taken from the *permanentia-successiva* distinction is not conclusive, since this distinction is not as radical as the argument pretends. Although the "parts" of an incomplete form exist simultaneously at the end of a motion, they are, after all, acquired successively. Accordingly it seems that the successive character of motion can be accounted for by the permanent forms taken on successively by the mobile substance during motion, so that it is not necessary to postulate motion as a *res* distinct from the permanent ones. But this line of reasoning is completely extraneous to the approach of our commentators.[41] In their view, the crucial question is not whether the various stages of incompleteness of a form can account for the successive character of motion, but whether these stages can account for the fact that this form becomes complete. The answer of our commentators to this latter question is negative. They assume that, whatever may be the incomplete mode of being of a form, the passage from an incomplete form to a complete one, or more generally from one form to another, can only be accounted for by motion conceived of as something distinct from any form acquired by the mobile substance. In other words, our commentators reject the reductionist ontology of motion contained in aspect (2) of the *forma*-theory mentioned above.

Against (2) Geoffrey of Aspall (M[1]) argues:

> Furthermore, if it were as the Commentator says, then (i) since form is produced in act from that incomplete being and not through it, so too in motion as (ii) form is produced from that motion and not through that motion, which we know to be false, because (iii) form is acquired through motion.[42]

---

[41] It is, however, approximately the one followed by Ockham in his reply to the argument based on the *permanentia-successiva* distinction quoted in note 39. He introduces this reply with the following remark: "Ad p r i m u m istorum dicendum est quod ad omnem non simultatem partium motus sufficit non simultas partium rei permanentis. Nisi enim in re permanente una pars esset ante aliam vel nisi mobile prius esset in una parte loci quam in alia, nullo modo essent plures partes motus non simul existentes. Et talis non simultas plurium rerum permanentium praeter omnem rem aliam sufficit ad hoc quod partes motus non sint simul, et ita propter non simultatem partium motus non oportet ponere aliam rem a rebus permanentibus" (Ockham, *In Physicam*, III, cap. 2, p. 441, lin. 36-43).

[42] M[1], III, q. 5, f. 109rb, lin. 31-34: "Item, si ita esset ut dicit Commentator, tunc,

As to the logical structure of this argument, (ii) is obtained from (i) by substituting "incomplete thing" with "motion". Then the crucial assumption in (i) and (iii) is that any incomplete form becomes complete through motion conceived of as something distinct from that incomplete form. The argument, however, does not seem altogether sound. Since (ii) refers to a particular motion, it does also not follow universally that there is no motion through which that incomplete form becomes complete, as assumed in (iii). The alternative that there might be another motion through which the incomplete form becomes complete is implicitly ruled out by M^1, since it would involve an infinite regress, for this other motion would be an incomplete form which becomes complete, in Averroes' view. This kind of reasoning is used in the following argument by M^3, which assumes in the proof of the minor premise that any form becomes complete through motion conceived of as something distinct from that form and hence implies that the essential identity between motion and its final form would involve an infinite regress:

> ...the only thing which does not differ from a form or a perfection is that which acquires one part after another of this perfection; but motion cannot acquire one part after another of a given perfection; therefore, etc. The minor premise of this argument is proved by the fact that the acquisition of one part after another takes place through motion. Consequently <if a motion acquires one part after another of a certain perfection> there will be a motion of the motion and so on to infinity. Therefore, motion is not indistinct from the form to which it is directed solely according to more and less....[43]

A possible reply to the arguments against (2) quoted from M^1 and M^3 might run as follows. It is true that the form alone cannot account for its passage from an incomplete state to a complete one. Indeed, what is needed is an efficient cause of this passage, that is, the agent of change, but, in addition to the agent, it does not seem necessary to postulate the passage of the form (i.e., motion) as a *res* distinct from

---

cum ex illo incompleto fiat forma in actu et non per illud incompletum, ita erit in motu quod ex illo motu fiet forma et non per illum motum, quod scimus esse falsum, quia per motum acquiritur forma".

[43] M^3, III, q. 5, f. 153ra, lin. 42-46: "... illud solum est indifferens a forma et perfectione quod acquirit partem post partem illius perfectionis; sed motus non potest acquirere partem post partem alicuius perfectionis; quare etc. Probatio minoris est, quia acquisitio partis post partem est per motum, et ita motus erit motus, et ita in infinitum. Quare motus non est solum indifferens a forma ad quam est secundum plus et minus...".

the form.[44] However, this kind of reply is never considered by our commentators.

The arguments considered so far shed light on the type of critique that our commentators raise against Averroes' *forma*-theory of motion. This critique can be defined as metaphysical or ontological as opposed to physical, for it appeals exclusively to some general or metaphysical assumptions, such as the real distinction between *permanentia* and *successiva* or the characterization of motion as something through which a form comes to inhere in a substance. But, as we have seen, appeals to these kinds of assumptions are more or less different ways of expressing a realist position on the ontological status of motion. Moreover, this metaphysical approach seems to reflect an early stage of the debate about Averroes' *forma*-theory in the English tradition. It is also found, for instance, in B, the set of questions on the *Physics* very close to Adam of Bocfeld's commentary. B formulates two short arguments against Averroes' claim that motion differs only in degrees (*secundum magis et minus*) from its final terminus. Like most of the arguments by our group of commentators presented in this section, they are based respectively on (a) the assumption that any perfection is acquired through motion as something distinct from that perfection and (b) on the *permanentia-successiva* distinction.[45] Later commentators, however, tend to develop a different, physical approach to Averroes' position.

---

[44] As Prof. Marilyn McCord Adams remarks, this kind of reply is based on an Ockham-like move: to let an efficient cause do the work of a putative additional formal cause.

[45] B, III, q. 2, f. 15vb, lin. 26-37: "Sed super hoc dubitatur qualiter motus non differt a perfectione ad quam vadit nisi secundum magis et minus. Videtur enim hoc esse impossibile sic: (a) dum res est in motu ad perfectionem et circa (*pro citra?*) perfectionem, successive recipitur aliquid de perfectione, et hoc per motum; quare illud aliquid quod recipitur de perfectione per motum non est motus. Per motum enim recipitur. Si ergo illud tantum quod recipitur quod vadit ad perfectionem differt a perfectione secundum magis et minus, et motus non sit illud quod recipitur de perfectione, ergo motus non differt a perfectione secundum magis et minus. (b) Ad idem, si motus non differret a perfectione ad quam vadit nisi secundum magis et minus, non differret a perfectione nisi sicut imperfectum differt a perfecto; sed imperfectum, cum venit ad perfectionem (ad perfectionem *ante* cum *ms.*), tunc maxime est; ergo motus, cum veniet ad ipsam perfectionem propter quam fuit motus, tunc maxime esset; sed (ad *ms.*) hoc falsum. Tunc enim cessat esse; ergo illud ex quo sequitur est falsum". The numbering of the questions in B is that given by A. Zimmermann in *Verzeichnis ungedruckter Kommentare*, p. 146-152.

3.3 *The Physical Approach to Averroes' Position*

Although our commentators do not submit the *forma*-theory to a systematic physical examination, they do occasionally propose some counterexamples. For instance, they do not specify precisely how Averroes' incomplete form is to be understood in each concrete species of motion, but some of them point to substantial motion as a species in which no incomplete form intervenes in any immediate sense of "incomplete form". So, for example, relying on the Aristotelian principle that substantial forms do not admit of degrees, M³ argues that the *forma*-theory would deny substantial motion:

> ... if motion directed to a substantial form differs from this form only according to more and less, since there is no succession of parts in the acquisition of this form, but it is acquired all at once, then there would be no motion in the category of substance.[46]

Another physical counterexample to the *forma*-theory is the case of local motion. For instance, S remarks that this theory turns out to be quite implausible when applied to local motion, since it implies that local motion is essentially the same as the space along which this motion takes place.[47] The case of local motion is also adduced by M², who argues that according to the *forma*-theory:

> ... the motion of the light body above would be the upper place, which exists below and flows above, which is most absurd.[48]

These physical objections against Averroes' *forma*-theory play a very marginal role in the discussion of our commentators. Nevertheless, they are historically important, since they indicate the direction in which the examination of this theory will be developed later in the thirteenth and fourteenth centuries.

---

[46] M³, III, q. 5, f. 153ra, lin. 1-4: "... si motus ad formam substantialem differt a forma ad quam est solum secundum plus et minus, tunc, cum in forma substantiali generanda non sit successio in acquirendo partem post partem, sed simul tota acquiritur, tunc non esset motus in praedicamento substantiae". See also N, III, q. 6, f. 133rb, lin. 46-va, lin. 1.

[47] S, III, q. 8, f. 41rb, lin. 38-41: "... quare similiter non potest dici quod spatium super quod fit motus localis non diceretur motus, spatium dico inter terminum a quo et terminum ad quem? Non enim, ut videtur, est ratio".

[48] M², III, q. 4, f. 125vb, lin. 2 ab imo-1 ab imo: "... motus levis sursum esset locus sursum existens deorsum fluens sursum, quod nimis videtur absurdum". See also W, q. 3, f. 54ra, lin. 21-29.

Soon after our group of English commentators, an important instance of the physical approach to Averroes' theory is found in Thomas Aquinas' commentary on the *Physics*. To be precise, Aquinas' remarks on the physical nature of motion are not directly concerned with Averroes' position. In fact, Aquinas does not explicitly discuss Averroes' famous passage from t.c. 4. Yet, the relevance of Aquinas' remarks to Averroes' *forma*-theory of motion is evident, as will be made explicit by, among others, Giles of Rome, who inserts Aquinas' view on motion in his answer to the question "Whether motion is the same as an incomplete form".[49] The immediate context of Aquinas' remarks is Aristotle's definition of motion as "the act of what is potentially insofar as it is potentially". Aquinas explains this definition with the example of water's being heated (*calefactio*):

> ... for when water is hot only in potentiality, it is not yet moved; when it has already been heated the heating motion has been completed; but when it shares in heat to some degree, but incompletely, it is being moved (*movetur*) toward heat, for what becomes hot shares in heat gradually by degrees. Therefore, the incomplete actuality of heat existing in the heatable thing is itself motion (*motus*), not, indeed, insofar as it is in actuality alone, but insofar as what already exists in actuality is ordered toward further actuality. For if one were to take away its being ordered toward further actuality, the actuality itself (however imperfect) would be the terminus of motion and not motion, as happens when something heats partially...[50]

This passage almost exhausts Aquinas' original remarks on the ontological status of motion. It is extremely contracted but also extremely rich and complex. It contains (a) a physical analysis of Aristotle's definition of motion; (b) an implicit criticism of Averroes' *forma*-theory; and (c) the formulation of an alternative view on the ontological status of motion. What is relevant for our purpose is that the ontological aspects involved in (b) and (c) are derived from the analysis of the physical case of water's being heated. Aquinas remarks that, as long as water undergoes the process of being heated, it is not yet completely hot, but has only some intermediate and incomplete degree of heat; for instance, it is temperate. Thus, one might be tempted to

---

[49] Giles of Rome, *In Physicam*, III, lectio 3, f. 54ra.
[50] Thomas Aquinas, *In Physicam*, III, lectio 3, p. 145 (The English translation is that found in S. MacDonald, "Aquinas's Parasitic Cosmological Argument", *Medieval Philosophy and Theology*, 1 (1991), p. 125).

identify the process itself of being heated with the incomplete actuality of heat, namely, the temperate itself. Indeed, this reflects Averroes'
view. Yet, Aquinas argues that this view is not sound and requires
qualification. If the process of being heated were simply identified
with the temperate, then being heated or, more generally, any
motion could not be distinguished from its final terminus. A counterexample is suggested at the very end of the quoted passage: if
water starts being heated, but the process stops abruptly before the
water is completely hot, the final terminus of this motion is being
temperate. Hence, from the case of being heated it is implied that
motion cannot be simply an incomplete form, as Averroes believes.
In Aquinas' view, what needs to be added to the incomplete form to
distinguish motion from its final terminus is an "order toward a further actuality". As Giles of Rome formulates this point, motion is a
forma incompleta cum actuali ordine ad complementum.[51] Thus, being heated
is the same as the temperate only when the temperate is regarded not
only as an incomplete degree of heat, but also as directed towards a
more complete degree of heat.[52]

Methodologically, Aquinas' discussion is very important because it
combines the "physical" (i.e., based on the physical analysis of
change) and "ontological" approaches to Averroes' theory. The integration of these two approaches is apparent in the case of a process of
being heated interrupted before its natural end. This case clearly pertains to the physical analysis of motion. Yet, the objection against
Averroes conveyed by this example is still fundamentally metaphysical, since it derives from the ontological assumption that motion must
be distinguishable from its final terminus. This assumption, in turn, is
ultimately related to the *permanentia-successiva* distinction, explicitly
used against Averroes by the early English commentators. Indeed,
the notion of "ordo ad ulteriorem complementum" with which
Aquinas qualifies Averroes' original identification of motion with an
incomplete form is needed to distinguish motion from permanent
entities. Moreover, the physical case of a process of being heated
interrupted before its natural end also suggests a more purely physical
line of attack to Averroes' position. If a motion directed toward hot as

---

[51] Giles of Rome, *In Physicam*, III, lectio 3, f. 54ra.
[52] For a more detailed analysis of the ontological aspects of Aquinas' position, see
Trifogli, "Thomas Wylton on Motion", p. 147-151. On Aquinas' doctrine of motion,
see also Meyer, "Die Bewegungslehre des Thomas von Aquin", p. 45-65.

its final terminus passes through temperate, as this case points out, then one might argue against Averroes that it is not true universally that motion does not differ essentially from its final terminus, because temperate seems to be a form essentially distinct from hot. More generally, one might argue that, as long as a motion continues, the form represented by the final terminus of this motion does not inhere, even in an incomplete state, in the mobile substance, so that motion cannot plausibly be identified with an incomplete state of its final form, as Averroes pretends.

A significant instance of this sort of criticism of Averroes' theory occurs in the *Quaestiones super Physicam*, probably to be ascribed to William of Bonkes, an Oxford master of Arts of the 1290s.[53] Bonkes is heavily influenced by Aquinas' short discussion on motion. In particular, he repeats Aquinas' example of water being heated. Furthermore, he maintains that the process of being heated (*calefactio*) cannot simply be identified with the temperate; rather it is the temperate insofar as the temperate is ordered to hot. As Bonkes puts it, the temperate represents only "illud quod est in rerum natura de motu" or "res illa quae motus est", but is formally motion (of being heated, in this case) when regarded as having an order to hot.[54] This is substantially Aquinas' view on the ontological status of motion. Bonkes, however, also discusses the question, "An motus sit eiusdem essentiae cum termino motus", which is devoted specifically to Averroes' position. To this question, he replies that:

> ... (i) motion and the final state of motion do not have formally the same essence, but (ii) that thing which motion is sometimes has the same essence as the final state of motion, sometimes has an essence different from it in species and sometimes in genre.[55]

---

[53] This set of questions covers all eight books of Aristotle's *Physics*. It is preserved in ms. Cambridge, Peterhouse, ms. 192, ff. 37ra-119vb. For the attribution of this work to Guillelmus de Bonkes, cf. S. Donati, "Per lo studio dei commenti alla *Fisica*", first part, p. 371-372.

[54] Bonkes' Thomistic view on the ontological status of motion especially appears in the following passage, where in reference to the *res* representing "illud quod in rerum natura est de motu" he claims: "... illa res potest considerari dupliciter: vel in se vel in quantum est ordinabilis ad aliud, sicut tepidum est quaedam species media inter frigidum et calidum, formaliter distincta ab utroque, ut in se consideratur, et tamen manifestum est quod, si motus sit a frigido in calidum, oportet ipsum esse per tepidum; ideo tepidum praeter id quod in se consideratur oportet considerari ut ordinem habet ad calidum, et sic ut ordinem habet ad calidum est calefactio illius quod ad calidum movetur" (Bonkes, *In Physicam*, f. 64vb, lin. 25-31).

[55] Bonkes, *In Physicam*, III, f. 67ra, lin. 17-19: "... motus et terminus motus non sunt

Point (i) of Bonkes' answer is a direct consequence of the introduction of the notion of order, which formally characterizes motion and distinguishes it from any permanent form involved in motion itself. Point (ii) is the one that interests us here. It contains the attack of Averroes' position on physical grounds alluded to above. Here by "that thing which motion is" (*res illa quae motus est*) Bonkes means any form that inheres in the mobile substance during motion. Thus, the claim in (ii) is that it is not universally true that the forms inhering in the mobile substance during motion have specifically the same essence as the final form acquired by this substance at the end of a motion. In fact, as Bonkes remarks, this is true only in a very restricted type of motion, namely, the "intension and remission" (in technical terms) of a given quality, for instance, the passage from a less intense to a more intense degree of whiteness.[56] Yet, it is not true of the motion from being black to being white, because, as Bonkes argues:

> ... if the mobile thing comes to rest in the middle of that motion, it would be at rest under a species opposed to whiteness; and it is evident that the form that one finds at that state of rest is the same as the one that one would find if the mobile thing were to move continuously towards whiteness.[57]

Here we meet again Aquinas' case of an interrupted motion, but it is adapted this time to provide a physical objection against Averroes' theory, which can be expanded as follows. A form remains the same species whether at rest or in motion. If Averroes is right in claiming that motion does not differ essentially from its final terminus, then, if a motion is stopped abruptly before its natural end, one should find the same form inhering in the mobile substance as one would find at the natural end of that motion. This, however, is not the case in the

---

eiusdem essentiae formaliter, sed res illa quae motus est quandoque est eiusdem essentiae cum termino, quandoque diversa secundum speciem et quandoque secundum genus".

[56] Ibid., f. 67ra, lin. 33-37: "... sed tamen si fit motus in eadem specie, ut in albedine, quia idem subiectum nunc est minus album et nunc magis, et hoc manente eadem specie coloris, quia comparatio secundum magis et minus debet esse in eadem specie, per Philosophum VII huius, ideo [quandoque] res <quae est> motus quandoque est eiusdem essentiae cum termino motus...".

[57] Ibid., f. 67ra, lin. 27-29: "... si quiescat mobile in medio motus, quiescet sub specie opposita respectu albedinis, et manifestum est quod eadem res est sub illa quiete et non alia quam esset si continue moveretur ad albedinem".

passage from black to white, since what one finds when this motion is interrupted is some intermediate form between black and white, such as greyness, which is specifically distinct from both.

A further step in the evolution of the physical investigation of Averroes' position is taken by Thomas Wylton, an English commentator and theologian who wrote an extensive set of questions on the *Physics*, probably as a master of Arts at Oxford University at the turn of the thirteenth century. As to the ontology of motion, Wylton's position is very similar to that of the early English commentators examined in Section 3.2, according to which motion is a *res* distinct from any form involved in motion. In particular, Wylton completely rejects Averroes' *forma*-theory of motion. Yet, he departs from the early English commentators, and at least partially from Aquinas and Bonkes, when he presents a purely physical rejection of Averroes' theory. Furthermore, although the general point of Wylton's physical arguments against Averroes is the same as that expressed by Bonkes in the passage quoted above, that is, that during motion the forms successively inhering in the mobile substance are specifically different from the final form, Wylton formulates this line of reasoning by means of a sophisticated physical theory, which will be increasingly refined and applied in the course of the fourteenth century, namely, the theory of the latitude of forms (*latitudo formarum*).[58]

Finally, as a sign of the increasing attention in the fourteenth century to the physical aspects of Averroes' *forma*-theory, the case of Walter Burley is worth mentioning. In Section 3.1, we have seen that, while holding a realist position on the ontological status of motion, Burley is willing to defend Averroes' position, in the sense that he tries to show that, in Averroes' view, not only the *forma*-theory but also the *via*-theory of motion is in some sense true. Yet, from other passages of his discussion, it appears that he is also fully aware of the physical objections that apparently disprove the *forma*-theory, at least as a general theory of motion. For instance, he presents the following objection: since, in this theory, motion differs from the final form only by degree, according to this view, motion is apparently possible only in respect of those forms that admit of degrees. But there are few such motions. In fact, only the processes of intension and remission of a given quality admit of degrees, as Bonkes and Wylton had already

---

[58] For Wylton's position on the ontological status of motion and his consequent rejection of Averroes' theory, see Trifogli, "Thomas Wylton on Motion", p. 137-154.

remarked. Hence, three out of four of the Aristotelian species of motion seem to be excluded from Averroes' *forma*-theory. That is, the theory excludes substantial, quantitative, and local motion, since there are no "diminished" or incomplete forms in the categories of substance, quantity, and "being somewhere".[59] Burley tries to solve this objection by distinguishing two possible meanings of the expression "diminished form":

> ... by diminished form we can understand two things: (i) either a remitted form or (ii) a form in potency, taking potency as opposed to the act of rest. Indeed, a form under which the mobile is at rest is said to be a form in act and a form under which the mobile is not at rest is said to be a form in potency as potency is opposed to the act of rest... Therefore, I say that by diminished form the Commentator does not mean a form in a remitted degree; instead he means by diminished form a form in transition and in becoming under which the mobile is not at rest. And this latter kind of diminished form is found in four genera <i.e., substance, quality, quantity, and "being somewhere">.[60]

This passage shows that Burley takes very seriously the physical objections against Averroes' *forma*-theory. It also shows that he is aware that these objections cannot be solved if "diminished form" is construed in the physical and technical sense of form in a remitted degree. Indeed, in order to save Averroes' *forma*-theory Burley is led to introduce a non-technical sense of diminished form, namely, any form inhering in the mobile substance during motion. Thus, Burley's interpretation apparently solves some of the physical objections, but at the price that Averroes' original theory is devoid of any specifically physical meaning. In this regard, it should be noted that, while Burley's interpretation can accomodate the reductionist ontology of motion implicit in Averroes' original view, it leaves unexplained the more physical part of Averroes' theory, in particular the claim that motion as incomplete form differs only in degree from the form that obtains at the end of motion.

---

[59] See Burley, *In Physicam*, III, f. 62ra.

[60] Ibid., f. 62rb: "... per formam diminutam possumus duo intelligere, scilicet vel formam remissam vel formam in potentia, accipiendo potentiam prout opponitur actui quietationis. Forma enim sub qua mobile quiescit dicitur esse forma in actu, et forma sub qua mobile non quiescit dicitur esse forma in potentia opposita actui quietationis, ut patet VI et VIII huius. Dico igitur quod Commentator non intelligit per formam diminutam formam sub gradu remisso, sed intelligit per formam diminutam <formam> in transitu et in fieri sub qua mobile non quiescit. Et talis forma diminuta reperitur in quattuor generibus".

4. *The Exegesis of the Definition of Motion*

As we have seen in § 2, Averroes claims, at the end of his solution to
the classification problem in t.c. 4 of Book III, that Aristotle introduces
the true way of regarding motion, i.e., the *forma*-theory of motion, in
the *Physics*.[61] In *Physics* III.1, however, Aristotle explicitly defines
motion as the actuality of that which is potentially insofar as it is
potentially (*actus entis in potentia secundum quod in potentia*).[62] Now it is not
at all clear that this definition implies that motion is the incomplete
state of the final form acquired by the mobile substance, as Averroes'
forma-theory states. Consequently, one would expect to find Averroes
giving some explanation of this point in his exegesis of Aristotle's definition. Yet, this is not the case. Rather, he simply gives a literal exposition of Aristotle's text.[63] Furthermore, Averroes never appeals again to
the *forma*-theory in his commentary on *Physics* III.1-3.

Although the exegesis of the definition of motion given by the early
English commentators adds no new philosophical elements to the
debate over its ontological status, nevertheless, it is not so indifferent
to the issue as that given by Averroes. On the contrary, their exegesis
of Aristotle's definition is heavily influenced by Averroes' *forma-via*
distinction and openly reflects their view on it. For, as we shall see,
our commentators want both (1) to prevent a reading of Aristotle's
definition that supports the *forma*-theory, and (2) to use the *via*-theory
as an exegetical tool in order to make this definition more intelligible.

(1) Despite Averroes' silence, the early English commentators seem
to realize that Aristotle's definition, as it stands, can also accommo-
date a *forma*-theory of motion. One of their major concerns in the
questions devoted to the definition of motion is precisely to prevent
such an interpretation of Aristotle's formula *motus est actus entis in potentia secundum quod in potentia*. This concern appears principally in their
analysis of the first part of this formula, namely, *motus est actus*,[64] to
which they devote a special question.

---

[61] See above, p. 48.

[62] Aristotle, *Physics*, III.1, 201a10-11. On the current debate on Aristotle's definition of motion, see Introduction, p. 5-9.

[63] Averroes, *In Physicam*, III, t. c. 6-7, f. 88raA-vaG. Averroes' exegesis of Aristotle's
definition of motion has been analysed by A. Maier in *Zwischen Philosophie und
Mechanik*, p. 20-23.

[64] The commentators assume that Aristotle's definition of motion contains two *particulae*: the first one is *motus est actus*, the second one is *entis in potentia secundum quod
huiusmodi*. They discuss these two *particulae* in distinct questions. The division of Aris-

As is especially clear in M¹, G¹, and M³, most of the *contra*-argu-
ments of the question "Utrum motus est actus" show that any act is a
form and then conclude that motion is not an act, since it is not a
form.[65] One of these arguments in particular deserves attention,
because it is found in all our commentaries. Geoffrey of Aspall (M¹)
formulates it as follows:

> (C1) And it seems that motion is not an act, (i) since every act is either
> a first act or a second act; but the first act is the form without its actual
> operation, whereas the second act is the form with its actual operation,
> and thus every act is a form; (ii) but motion is not a form; therefore
> etc.[66]

In (i) "form" stands for any form. In (ii), however, the commentators
implicitly narrow the meaning of this term to the final form induced
through motion. Accordingly, the problem addressed by (C1) is the
following: does Aristotle's characterization of motion as an act imply
that motion is essentially the same as the form to which it is directed?
Of course, the answer of our commentators is negative.

In replying to (C1), they generally appeal to the distinction
between complete and incomplete acts. A form and the operation
resulting from it are both complete acts. There is, however, also an
incomplete kind of act, and motion is an act of this latter kind.[67]

Motion is said to be an incomplete act by Aristotle himself in a
passage of *Physics* III.2.[68] In his commentary, Averroes specifies that

---

totle's definition in two parts is also employed by Adam of Bocfeld in his literal commentary. See Adam of Bocfeld, *In Physicam*, f. 15ra, lin. 8-21.

[65] Cfr. M¹, III, q. 8, f. 109vb, lin. 23-31; G¹, III, q. 8, f. 140ra, lin. 50-rb, lin. 5; M³,
III, q. 6, f. 153rb, lin. 20-28.

[66] M¹, III, q. 8, f. 109vb, lin. 23-26: "Et videtur quod non, quia omnis actus aut est
actus primus aut secundus; actus primus est forma sine actuali operatione, actus
secundus est forma cum actuali operatione (consideratione *ms.*), et ita <omnis> actus
est forma; sed motus non est forma; quare etc.". See also S, III, q. 7, f. 41ra, lin. 27-
31; P, III, q. 12, f. 66vb, lin. 30-34; G¹, III, q. 8, f. 140ra, lin. 50-53; M³, III, q. 6, f.
153rb, lin. 20-23; N, III, q. 9, f. 134ra, lin. 45-rb, lin. 1; M², III, q. 5, f. 126va, lin.
26-33; W, III, q. 5, f. 56va, lin. 6-19. The distinction between *actus primus* and *actus
secundus* derives from Aristotle, *De Anima*, II.1, 412a10-11.

[67] See S, III, q. 7, f. 41ra, lin. 38-46; P, III, q. 12, f. 66vb, lin. 49-52; M¹, III, q. 8, f.
109vb, lin. 31-35; G¹, III, q. 8, f. 140rb, lin. 5-8; M³, III, q. 6, f. 153rb, lin. 28-30; N,
III, q. 9, f. 134rb, lin. 2-4. M² and W also maintain that motion is an incomplete act,
but they reply to argument (1) by distinguishing different meanings of "first act". See
M², III, q. 5, f. 126va, lin. 62-vb, lin. 16; W, III, q. 5, ff. 56vb, lin. 31-57ra, lin. 17.

[68] Aristotle claims that motion is an incomplete act at the end of his review of the
opinions of his predecessors on the nature of motion. According to Aristotle, the diffi-

an incomplete act is an *actus medius inter potentiam et actum*.[69] And this formula (or the equivalent one *actus permixtus potentiae*) is often employed in the Aristotelian tradition to describe the mode of being of successive things,[70] but in itself suggests no definite commitment regarding the ontological status of successive things and in particular of motion. Our commentators, however, seem to perceive that the incomplete form of the *forma*-theory of motion can also be described as an incomplete act, since it is a form not yet fully actualized. Some of them explicitly point out this ambiguity in the notion of incomplete act and try to define the distinction between the incompleteness of motion and the incompleteness of an incomplete form. This is, for instance, the case of S. He introduces his answer to the question "Utrum motus sit actus" with a careful distinction of the senses of *actus*:

> In this regard, it must be said that motion is an act, but there are two kinds of act, viz., a perfect and complete act and an imperfect and incomplete one, that is, an act that is always joined with a potency. And this latter kind of act is twofold. One kind of incomplete act is an incomplete form, which terminates the potency and appetite of matter in an incomplete way, and another one is a perfection and a disposition of the incomplete composite itself or of the thing that has the incomplete form insofar as this thing goes to completion.[71]

Motion, S concludes, is an incomplete act in this latter sense, i.e., not as an incomplete form but as a disposition of the mobile substance that has an incomplete form, this disposition being the *via in actum perfectum*.[72]

---

culties they encountered in determining the exact nature of motion are due to the fact that motion is neither totally a potency nor totally an act, but an incomplete act. See Aristotle, *Physics*, III.2, 201b16-202a3. For some interpretations of Aristotle's doctrine of the incompleteness of motion offered by Aristotelian scholars, see, for instance, Kosman, "Aristotle's definition of motion", p. 56-58; Hussey, *Aristotle's Physics*, Introduction, p. xiv-xv.

[69] Averroes, *In Physicam*, III, t. c. 14, f. 91raC; also t. c. 15, f. 91vaH.

[70] This formula expresses the idea that as long as a motion or more generally a process goes on, some of its phases have still to take place, that is, are still in potency.

[71] S, III, q. 7, f. 41ra, lin. 38-46: "Ad istud dicendum quod motus est actus, sed duplex est actus, scilicet perfectus et completus et imperfectus et incompletus, qui scilicet semper habet secum potentiam annexam. Et hic actus duplex est. Quidam enim est forma incompleta quae incomplete terminat potentiam materiae et appetitum, et quidam est perfectio et dispositio ipsius compositi incompleti vel habentis formam incompletam secundum quod vadit ad completionem".

[72] Ibid., f. 41ra, lin. 47-rb, lin. 1.

Note that the account of S is somewhat ambiguous. For, on one hand, he claims that an incomplete act is always joined with a potency. On the other hand, in the subsequent description of the incomplete act unique to motion as a disposition of the mobile substance he does not further specify in which sense this disposition is joined with a potency and hence incomplete. Rather, it seems that motion is said to be an incomplete act not because the disposition it confers on the mobile substance is in some sense incomplete, but because it is a disposition of an incomplete thing, namely, of the mobile substance characterized by an incomplete form.[73]

This ambiguity does not appear in the solution proposed by P and N. This solution appeals to the distinction between permanent things and successive things, which we have already encountered in the arguments used by our commentators against Averroes' *forma*-theory.[74] The idea is that the incompleteness of form and the incompleteness of motion are two quite distinct types. An incomplete form becomes complete at the end of the motion during which it is acquired, whereas motion never becomes complete. At the end of a motion that motion no longer exists, and during that motion, there are some of its phases which have still to take place. P explains this distinction as follows:

> ...motion is an incomplete act and is of something incomplete, and similarly for the incomplete form. Nevertheless they differ, because the incomplete form is an incomplete act such that it can be totally completed and will become a complete act, which gives complete being to that same thing of which previously it was an incomplete act. But although motion is an incomplete act, it can never be completed in such a way that it persists. For when the entire motion is completed, then it is already corrupted. Motion neither is nor can be the complete act of that thing of which previously it was an incomplete act.[75]

---

[73] According to S, when motion is considered as a disposition of the mobile substance it is said to be a quality. On this point, see § 5, p. 80-81.

[74] See § 3, p. 55.

[75] P, III, q. 12, f. 66vb, lin. 54-59: "motus actus est incompletus et incompleti et similiter forma incompleta. Differunt tamen quoniam forma incompleta est actus incompletus ita quod totaliter compleri potest et fiet actus completus, dans esse completum eidem cuius prius fuit actus incompletus; sed motus, cum sit actus incompletus, numquam poterit compleri ita quod maneat. Completo enim toto motu, iam corrumpitur motus. Nec est motus nec esse potest actus completus eius cuius prius fuit actus incompletus". N, III, q. 9, f. 134rb, lin. 21-28: "... dico quod haec consequentia non tenet: motus est actus incompletus; ergo motus est forma incompleta,

M² proposes a more interesting solution. As in the case of N and P, the general idea of the solution of M² is that motion is incomplete in a more radical way than the incomplete form of Averroes' *forma*-theory. Unlike N and P, however, he does not make explicit use of the *permanentia-successiva* distinction in describing this difference. Rather, he attempts to derive it through an "exegetical" argument, that is, by showing that Aristotle's definition of motion is sufficient to distinguish the incompleteness peculiar to motion from the incompleteness that characterizes its final form when it is still in the process of being acquired. As with the other commentators, M² formulates his solution by distinguishing between different kinds of act:

> I say that there are two kinds of act. For one kind of act is a perfect and complete act; but motion is not an act of this kind. Another kind of act is an incomplete and imperfect act, and this is the act of what is incomplete and imperfect. But this latter kind of act is also twofold, since either it is the act of what is imperfect and incomplete insofar as it is imperfect and incomplete, and in this sense motion is an act of what is incomplete and imperfect, because it makes that to which it belongs incomplete and imperfect, or it can be the act of what is imperfect insofar as it is to some extent perfect, and in this sense the form while it is in process of being acquired is the act of what is incomplete and imperfect.[76]

Thus, the two kinds of incomplete act distinguished by M² are (i) the act of what is incomplete insofar as it is incomplete, and (ii) the act of what is incomplete insofar as it is to some extent complete. If in (i) "incomplete" is replaced by "potentially" we get exactly Aristotle's

---

quia diversimode accipitur actus, cum dicitur 'forma incompleta est actus incompletus' et 'motus est actus incompletus', quia, cum dicitur forma incompleta est actus incompletus, ibi dicitur actus incompletus ratione alicuius <in>completi cuius postea erit actus completus. Cum autem dicitur 'motus est actus incompletus', ibi actus <incompletus> non est gratia alicuius <in>completi cuius postea erit actus completus".

[76] M², III, q. 5, f. 126va, lin. 46-54: "Dico quod duplex est actus. Quidam enim est actus perfectus et completus, cuiusmodi non est motus. Quidam autem est actus incompletus et imperfectus. Et iste actus est incompleti et imperfecti. Et hoc est dupliciter, quia aut erit actus imperfecti et incompleti secundum quod imperfectum et incompletum, et sic est motus actus incompleti et imperfecti, quia facit illud cuius est [est] incompletum et imperfectum; vel potest esse actus imperfecti secundum quod aliquo modo perfectum est, et sic est forma prout est in acquirendo actus incompleti et imperfecti". The characterization of *actus incompletus* as *actus incompleti* is found also in Aristotle's text. See Aristotle, *Physics*, III.2, 201b31-33. A very similar distinction of the senses of *actus* is given by W in III, q. 5, f. 56va, lin. 43-50.

formula for the definition of motion. Let us assume that (i) is equivalent to Aristotle's definition, since the difference between the two is
not very relevant to the following considerations. Then the crucial
question becomes whether it is true that the final form of motion does
not satisfy (i) when it is still incomplete and in the process of being
acquired (*in acquirendo*). This must be true if (i) is to distinguish
between motion and the final form *in acquirendo*, as the solution of M²
pretends. Nevertheless, such a final form does seem to satisfy (i). For
instance, as long as whiteness is in the process of being acquired, it is
(a) an act of what is white in an incomplete way, since during the
process of being acquired whiteness is still in an incomplete state, and
(b) an act of what is white in an incomplete way insofar as its subject
is white in an incomplete way, since, as long as whiteness is in the
process of being acquired, its subject is white in an incomplete way.
In conclusion, (i) does not seem sufficient to differentiate the two
ontologies of motion discussed by our commentaries, since it leaves
undetermined whether, in speaking about the acquisition of whiteness, one means that this process is a *res* distinct from whiteness itself
or is simply a mode of being of whiteness. In particular, the attempt
of M² at an "exegetical" refutation of Averroes' *forma*-theory is not
very successful. On the other hand, once it is assumed that motion is
a *res* distinct from any form involved in motion, it can at least be
explained why M² thinks that (ii) is satisfied by the form in the process
of being acquired and not by motion. In this regard, it is necessary to
anticipate a principle concerning the nature of motion that M²
emphasizes in his discussion of the categorical classification of
motion.[77] According to this principle, motion considered as a *res* in
itself (independently of its relation to its final form, its subject, and the
agent that causes it) is something completely indeterminate, devoid of
formal content. Thus, because of its indeterminacy, motion does not
satisfy (ii), since it cannot confer any sort of perfection on its subject.
The incomplete form, however, has a formal nature, which, despite
its incompleteness, can confer some determination on its subject.

(2) As we have just seen, the commentators try to isolate the
incomplete act unique to motion from the incomplete act as incomplete form by distinguishing different meanings of incomplete act, but
without explicitly identifying the incomplete act of motion with the

---

[77] See below, p. 83.

via ad formam. There is, however, one occasion in which such an identification is explicitly made by most of our commentators. It occurs in another argument against Aristotle's claim that motion is an act. This is formulated by M³ as follows:

> (C2) ... Only that which terminates a potency is said to be an act; but that which terminates a potency is a form or the nature of a form; therefore it seems that, if motion is an act, it is not only the intermediate way, but also the form.[78]

From a doctrinal point of view, the answer to this argument given by most commentators is based once again on the *permanentia-successiva* distinction. A form like whiteness completely actualizes the corresponding potency. Once a substance is white, it is no longer in potency to being white. But motion, as a successive thing, does not completely actualize the corresponding potency, since, during any phase of a motion, the mobile substance is still in potency to those phases which have still to take place.[79] In this context, however, the specific formulation of the answer of our commentators rather than its doctrinal content is relevant, for they all introduce a distinction between two potencies in the mobile thing and describe these potencies in terms of the *forma-via* distinction, as in the following passage from the solution of (C2) given by M³:

> ... being in potency is in two ways: either to the form to be acquired or to the intermediate way through which the form is acquired. For instance, the buildable is in potency to the form of a house and also to the intermediate way through which the form of a house is acquired, i.e., to the act of building, and it is more immediately in potency to the act of building, i.e., to the intermediate way. Similarly, the mobile thing is immediately in potency to the intermediate way, and is mediately in potency to the form. And two different acts correspond to

---

[78] M³, III, q. 6, f. 153rb, lin. 23-25:"... illud solum dicitur actus quod est terminans potentiam; sed illud quod terminat potentiam est forma vel natura formae; quare videtur quod motus, si sit actus, non solum est via media, sed etiam forma". See also M¹, III, q. 8, f. 109vb, lin. 26-28; G¹, III, q. 8, f. 140rb, lin. 1-3. This argument is not proposed by S and P. In N, M² and W a different version of this argument is given: motion is not an act, because it does not terminate the potency to motion, whereas any act terminates the corresponding potency. See N, III, q. 9, f. 134rb, lin. 10-15; M², III, q. 5, f. 126va, lin. 21-24; W, III, q. 5, f. 56rb, lin. 50-va, lin. 3.

[79] G¹, III, q. 8, f. 140rb, lin. 8-15; q. 10, f. 140rb, lin. 57-va, lin. 7; M³, III, q. 7, f. 153va, lin. 30-46; N, III, q. 9, f. 134rb, lin. 32-43; q. 11, f. 134vb, lin. 5-19; M², III, q. 5, f. 126va, lin. 54-60; W, III, q. 5, f. 56va, lin. 50-vb, lin. 21.

these two potencies: one to the first potency, and this is motion; the other to the second potency, and this act is the form. Therefore, when it is said that form is that which terminates potency, this ought to be understood in the first sense <i.e., as to the potency to the form>.[80]

The example of the buildable is employed by Aristotle himself in order to illustrate the definition of motion.[81] In Aristotle's text, however, there is no hint of the above distinction between the two potencies of the buildable, namely, to the act of building and to the form of the house. Nonetheless, the distinction between the potency to motion and that to its final form represents one of those modifications that medieval authors occasionally introduced in Aristotle's original account to make it more intelligible, which, in this particular case, is to explain in what sense is motion an act.[82] This distinction is found, for instance, in Avicenna[83] and later in Thomas Aquinas.[84] Its specific formulation, however, in terms of *forma* and *via ad formam* seems to be unique to our commentators. It is also found in the early questions on the *Physics* by Richard Rufus of Cornwall.[85] It can therefore be con-

---

[80] M³, III, q. 6, f. 153rb, lin. 30-38: "... esse in potentia est duobus modis: aut ad formam acquirendam aut ad viam mediam per quam acquiritur forma. Verbi gratia, aedificabile est in potentia ad formam domus et ad viam mediam per quam acquiritur forma domus, scilicet ad aedificationem, et immediatius est in potentia ad aedificationem sive ad viam mediam. Similiter est mobile in potentia immediate ad viam mediam et est in potentia ad formam mediate. Et huic duplici potentiae respondet duplex actus: unus primae potentiae, et iste est motus; alius secundae potentiae, et iste actus est forma. Quando igitur dicitur quod forma est illud quod terminat potentiam, hoc est intelligendum primo modo". See also M¹, III, q. 8, f. 109vb, lin. 35-39; G¹, III, q. 8, f. 140rb, lin. 8-15; N, III, q. 9, f. 134rb, lin. 32-43; M², III, q. 5, f. 126va, lin. 54-60; W, III, q. 5, f. 56va, lin. 51-vb, lin. 21. The distinction appears also in S and P, although they do not discuss argument (C2). See S, III, q. 9, f. 41va, lin. 18-25; va, lin. 40-vb, lin. 10; P, III, q. 2, f. 65vb, lin. 30-38.

[81] Aristotle, *Physics*, III.1, 201a15-18.

[82] The most important medieval interpretations of Aristotle's definition are quoted and discussed by A. Maier, in *Zwischen Philosophie und Mechanik*, p. 3-57.

[83] Avicenna, *De sufficientia*, II, cap. 1, f. 23rb: "... quia in hora quietis ante motum est illud (*sc.* mobile) in potentia absoluta. Immo, habet duas potentias: unam iam in illo (*sc.* in termino motus), alteram perveniendi ad illud. Ergo habet tunc duas perfectiones". Avicenna specifies that during motion the mobile thing is still in potency not only to the terminus of motion but also to some extent to motion itself, that is to the part of motion that still has to take place. An extensive quotation of Avicenna's exposition of Aristotle's definition is found in Maier, *Zwischen Philosophie und Mechanik*, p. 12-20.

[84] Thomas Aquinas, *In Physicam*, III, lectio 2, p. 145b.

[85] Like most of our commentators, Rufus introduces this distinction in response to argument (C2) quoted above. Argument (C2) is presented by Rufus as a counterargument to the solution of argument (C1) based on the distinction between complete and incomplete act. Rufus, *In Physicam*, III, f. 5rb, lin. 29-35: "Dubitatur de defini-

sidered a representative feature of the English exegetical tradition before Thomas Aquinas' commentary. Furthermore, this indicates that, although our commentators reject Averroes' *forma*-theory of motion, they use his *forma/via* distinction to develop their own exegesis of Aristotle's definition of motion.

5. *The Classification of Motion in the Aristotelian Categories*

As we have seen in Section 3, by adopting the *via*-theory the early English commentators commit themselves to a realist position on the ontological status of motion according to which motion is a *res* over and above both the mobile substance and the form acquired by this substance through motion. Nevertheless, it remains to be seen what kind of *res* motion is. The formulation of this problem as considered by our commentators is more specifically Aristotelian, namely, if motion is a *res*, to which of the ten Aristotelian categories does it belong?

From the perspective of Averroes' *forma*-theory, the answer to this question lies in the classification of the *per se* species of motion established by Aristotle in *Physics* V.[86] For instance, according to Averroes, qualitative motion is not only with respect to a quality, but it is also essentially the same as the quality acquired through it. This is, in fact, the crucial point of the *forma*-theory of motion. It is also clear, however, that this Averroistic answer cannot be given by our commentators. Thus, on the one hand, they accept Aristotle's doctrine of the

---

tione motus sic: (C1) actus est duplex, primus et secundus. Primus ut substantia est actus formae secundum quod dicimus quod scientia in habitu est actus scientis. Secundus autem est ipsa forma cum operatione sua, cuiusmodi est considerare. Sed motus non est actus primus nec secundus; ergo non est actus. Dicendum quod haec divisio actus est divisio actus perfecti et non actus imperfecti. Motus autem est actus imperfectus. (C2) Contra: quod terminat potentiam existentis in potentia hoc est actus; sed forma terminat potentiam acquisitam per motum; ergo forma est actus eius... lin. 37-42: Dicendum ad primum quod ens in potentia est in potentia ad duplicem actum, scilicet ad formam et ad viam in formam, scilicet ad motum, sicut aedificabile ad formam domus et ad aedificationem, quae est via in formam domus. Sed primo et immediate est ens (via *ms.*) in potentia ad motum, qui est via in formam, et ex consequenti est in potentia ad actum, scilicet ad formam. Et primo modo intelligenda est definitio". From this passage it is clear that Rufus knows Averroes' *forma-via* distinction and that he follows the *via*-theory; yet, an explicit discussion of Averroes' position is not found in Rufus' commentary.

[86] See above p. 48-49.

classification of the species of motion, and they often refer to this doctrine by the formula that motion is in the four *genera* of its *per se* termini.[87] On the other hand, some of them also specify that this does not
imply, for instance, that qualitative motion is a quality in an incomplete state, and hence a *res* belonging to the category of quality, but
only that qualitative motion is a *via* through which a quality is
acquired.

The contrast between this interpretation of Aristotle's doctrine of
the species of motion and that of Averroes is most clearly explained
by M[3]. He comments on Averroes' interpretation of the sentence
"motion to a substantial form is in the category of substance"[88] as follows:

> But you should understand that this is false, because the Commentator
> means that motion differs from the form to which it is directed only as
> what is diminished from the complete. Yet, this is false, nor does Aristo-
> tle mean this. Instead, Aristotle does mean, and it is true, that motion to
> a substantial form is in the category of substance as something incom-
> plete, nevertheless, not in the sense in which the Commentator says
> that motion is in the category of substance as something incomplete.
>
> Therefore, I say that something is said to be in a category as something
> incomplete in two ways: (i) either as that which afterwards becomes
> complete and which is a part of that thing to which motion is directed
> while such a thing acquires completion. And in this way the dimin-
> ished form, that is, the potency from which the form comes to be, is in
> the category of substance. And Averroes posited that that incomplete
> thing is motion. But this is false... (ii) In another way something is said
> to be in a category as incomplete not because is a part of a complete
> thing, but as a way through which completion is acquired... And in this
> way motion is in a category as incomplete. For motion does not
> become a form nor complete, but it is the way or the passage through
> which an incomplete nature becomes complete.[89]

---

[87] Cfr. *passim* S, III, qq. 5-6, ff. 40va, lin. 3 ab imo-41ra, lin. 21; P, III, qq. 7-10, ff.
66rb, lin. 9-vb, lin. 7; M[1], III, q. 4, f. 109ra, lin. 13 ab imo-rb, lin. 23; q. 6, f. 109va,
lin. 2-35; G[1], III, q. 4, ff. 139vb, lin. 21 ab imo-140ra, lin. 6; M[3], III, q. 4, f. 152vb,
lin. 18-12 ab imo; N, III, q. 6, f. 133ra, lin. 24-rb, lin. 19; q. 7, f. 133vb, lin. 4-40;
M[2], III, q. 4, ff. 125va, lin. 26-126va, lin. 18; W, q. 3, ff. 53ra, lin. 18-55vb, lin. 13 ab
imo.

[88] M[3], III, q. 5, f. 153rb, lin. 1-3: "Et dicet aliquis, sicut dicit Commentator, quod
motus ad formam substantialem est in praedicamento substantiae. Similiter vult Aristoteles".

[89] Ibid., lin. 3-17: "Sed intellige quod illud falsum est, quia Commentator intendit
quod motus non differt a forma ad quam est nisi sicut diminutum a completo. Sed

This passage indicates that, in the view of our commentators, Aristotle's doctrine of the classification of motion, when "correctly" understood as explained in (ii), does not answer the question of what kind of *res* motion is. We shall refer to this latter question as the problem of the intrinsic, as opposed to the extrinsic, classification of motion. The one classification is based on the nature of motion itself, while the other is based on other elements to which motion is related. Put in these terms, our commentators see Aristotle's classification of motion as extrinsic and not, as Averroes suggests, intrinsic, since it is based on the relation of a motion to its final state, which differs from motion itself. Hence, we must look at their treatment of the intrinsic classification of motion in order to determine where they locate motion as an Aristotelian entity. However, their treatment of this topic is rather brief and often confused. Different commentators tend to propose different solutions, generally inspired by suggestions of Aristotle himself or other authors, and none of them is very convincing.

S and P, for instance, deal with the intrinsic and extrinsic classifications of motion as follows:

> (1) ... motion can be considered in two ways: either in itself and absolutely or in comparison. (i) If in the first way, since motion is nothing other than a continuous succession, if it is considered insofar as a succession, then it is in the category of passion. For every succession is caused by a resistance, and every resistance is primarily and essentially in the category of passion. If it is considered insofar as there is continu-

---

istud falsum est, nec istud vult Aristoteles. Vult tamen Aristoteles, et verum est, quod motus ad formam substantialem est in praedicamento substantiae ut incompletum, non tamen eo modo quo dicit Commentator motum esse in genere substantiae ut incompletum. Dico igitur quod dupliciter dicitur aliquid esse in genere ut incompletum: (i) aut ut illud quod postea fit completum et pars eius ad quod fit motus in acquirendo completionem. Et sic est forma diminuta sive potentia ex qua fit forma in praedicamento substantiae, et illud posuit Commentator esse motum. Sed hoc est falsum; immo illud est natura diminuta sive forma incompleta vel potentia ipsa ex qua. (ii) Alio modo dicitur aliquid esse in genere ut incompletum, non quod sit pars completi, sed ut via per quam acquiritur completio, hoc est illa via per quam incompleta forma sive natura vel potentia fit completa et cedit incompletionem. Et sic est motus in praedicamento ut incompletum. Non enim fit motus forma nec completum, sed est via sive exitus per quem aliqua natura incompleta fit completa". A similar remark is made by M². M², III, q. 4, f. 126ra, lin. 52-58: "... cum terminus ad quem est motus sit in aliquo genere, in eodem genere erit motus ad illum terminum, non tamen est ibi sicut forma incompleta quae vadit ad actum, sed incompletum est dupliciter: (i) vel sicut forma aliqua quae vadit ad complementum (ii) vel sicut via ad complementum. Motus autem est incompletum in genere, sed non sicut forma incompleta, sed sicut via ad formam". See also W, III, q. 3, f. 54vb, lin. 25-45.

ity in that succession, in this way it belongs to the category of quantity, but this is accidental, since the continuity of motion derives from that of the magnitude. (ii) But if we speak of motion in comparison, it is therefore either in comparison to that thing from which it derives, and in this way it will be in the category of action, or it is in comparison to that thing to which it is directed, and this is twofold: either essentially or accidentally. In the first way motion is only in four genera, in the second way it is in all ten. If, moreover, motion is considered in comparison to that thing in which it is, that is, to the mobile thing, this is also twofold: either essentially, and thus it is again only in four genera, or accidentally, and thus it is in ten.[90]

In this passage, part (i) contains the solution of S-P to the intrinsic classification problem, whereas part (ii) contains the solution to the extrinsic classification problem.

In (i) S-P identify the nature of motion with a continuous succession. Then they appeal to the principle that the succession of motion, in this case, its temporal extension, presupposes a resistance offered by the mobile substance to the agent of motion. This resistance is due to the presence in the mobile substance of a form different from that induced through motion. As to the continuity, they seem to refer to a controversial passage from *Physics* IV.11, in which Aristotle claims that the continuity of motion derives from that of the magnitude in the sense of the spatial extension along which motion takes place.[91]

The extrinsic classification given in part (ii) is relatively unproblematic. It seems, however, quite unusual that motion compared to its subject is classified again in the category of its final form. For, although during a motion the mobile thing is characterized by formal

---

[90] S, III, q. 5, f. 40vb, lin. 20-36: "... motus potest considerari dupliciter: aut in se et absolute aut in comparatione. (i) Si primo modo, cum motus non sit nisi successio continua, si consideretur in ratione successionis, tunc est in genere passionis. Successio enim ratione resistentiae causatur: omnis autem resistentia primo et per se est in genere passionis; si ratione continuitatis in successione, sic est de genere quantitatis, sed hoc est per accidens, quia eius continuitas est a continuitate magnitudinis. (ii) Si autem loquamur de motu in comparatione, aut ergo ad illud a quo est, et sic erit in genere actionis, aut ad illud ad quod est, et hoc dupliciter: aut per se aut per accidens. Primo modo est tantum in quattuor generibus, secundo modo in omnibus decem. Si vero consideretur <in comparatione> ad illud in quo est sive ad mobile, hoc est dupliciter: aut per se, et sic adhuc tantum in quattuor generibus erit; si per accidens, sic in decem.". See also P, III, q. 8, f. 66rb, lin. 46-62. The treatment of the classification problem given by P repeats almost *verbatim* that given by S.

[91] Aristotle, *Physics*, IV.11, 219a10-14. We shall discuss the interpretation of this passage given by the commentators in chapter 4.

determinations belonging to the same category as the final form, that mobile thing *qua* subject of motion is more essentially described as a patient in the Aristotelian tradition. Therefore, motion compared to its subject should be more properly classified in the category of passion.[92] Perhaps S-P have decided the category to which motion as compared to its subject belongs on the *ad hoc* grounds that otherwise motion would be both intrinsically and extrinsically classified in the category of passion.[93]

There is a more serious problem concerning the solution given in part (i) to the intrinsic classification problem. Since S-P claim that motion *in se* is a succession, the intrinsic classification of motion as a succession is supposed to specify what kind of *res* succession is. Yet, the account of S-P specifies at most what kind of *res* the resistance causing motion is rather than succession itself. Succession evidently is something other than resistance. In other words, S-P's classification of motion taken as a succession in the category of passion seems to be extrinsic and not intrinsic.

Another problem is that if motion is a *res*, it should be a *res* of just one category. This requirement is acknowledged by S-P. One of the arguments against Aristotle's classification of motion into four categories claims exactly that motion should belong to just one category, since it is just one accident.[94] In their reply to this argument, S-P appeal to the distinction between motion regarded *in se* or *secundum suam essentiam* and motion regarded *per comparationem*, that is, they

---

[92] Aristotle deals with the relation of motion to action and passion in *Physics*, III.3. Aristotle's doctrine is usually formulated by our commentators and more generally in the Aristotelian tradition through the formulas that motion, action and passion are *idem secundum rem*, but not also *secundum rationem* or *secundum essentiam*. For motion regarded insofar as it is caused by an agent (*ab agente*) is said to be an action, and regarded insofar as it is in the patient (*in patiente*) is said to be a passion. So the notion of motion is more extensive than that of action and that of passion, since every motion denotes both an action and a passion. On Aristotle's doctrine of action and passion in *Physics* III.3 see, for instance, Hussey, *Aristotle's Physics*, Introduction, p. xvi-xviii; Gill, "Aristotle's Theory of Causal Action", p. 129-147; Waterlow, *Nature, Change*, p. 159-203. For the treatment of this topic given by our commentators, see S, III, qq. 10-11, ff. 41vb, lin. 18-42ra, lin. 33; rb, lin. 18-34; P, III, qq. 15-16, f. 67va, lin. 22-vb, lin. 36; M¹, III, q. 11, f. 110ra, lin. 23 ab imo-rb, lin. 26; G¹, III, qq. 12-14, f. 140va, lin. 5 ab imo-141ra, lin. 20; M³, III, q. 9, ff. 153vb, lin. 12 ab imo-154ra, lin. 4; N, III, qq. 13-14, f. 135rb, lin. 22-vb, lin. 10 ab imo; M², III, qq. 11-12, ff. 127va, lin. 20 ab imo-128ra, lin. 34; W, III, q. 11, f. 59rb, lin. 18-va, lin. 1 ab imo.

[93] However, it appears also in M³ and N. Cfr. M³, III, q. 5, f. 153ra, lin. 55-57; N, III, q. 6, f. 133va, lin. 37-40.

[94] Cfr. S, III, q. 5, f. 40va, lin. 49-50; P, III, q. 7, f. 66rb, lin. 9-19.

appeal to the distinction between the intrinsic and the extrinsic classification of motion they have set out in passage (1). They correctly
assume that the requirement of univocal classification can be satisfied
only by intrinsic classification: motion has just one essence, although
it is related to essentially distinct things.[95] One can further conclude
that the "intrinsic" classification proposed by S-P in (1) satisfies this
requirement, since motion is said to be a quantity only in an accidental sense, so that essentially it is only a passion. But then in their reply
these commentators add:

> (2) And it should be noted that (i) sometimes motion is in a genus as a
> thing of that genus, as it is in action and passion and also accidentally
> in quantity, as has been said, and also in quality, in the sense of motion
> as compared to the mobile, inasmuch as it confers a quality on the
> mobile, and not inasmuch as it derives from action; (ii) sometimes,
> however, motion is in a genus not as a thing of that genus, but as a
> way; in this latter sense motion is in the genus of substance, which nev-
> ertheless seems to be against Averroes....[96]

It seems quite natural to take the expression "thing of a genus" (*res
generis*) in (2) as referring to the intrinsic classification of motion. But,
in addition to the genera of passion and quantity that we have
already encountered in (1), S-P list also two other genera of which
motion is said to be a *res*: action and quality. The suggestion that
motion is a kind of quality is never offered by Aristotle himself, but
probably derives from the *Liber Sex Principiorum*[97] and is also found in
other commentaries of our group.[98] Thus, passage (2) seems to contradict the requirement of a univocal classification. To avoid this con-

---

[95] S, III, q. 5, f. 40vb, lin. 36-39: "Ad primam tunc dicendum quod motus secundum suam essentiam est unum accidens et sic est in uno genere; per comparationem
autem consideratus non est unum, sicut iam patuit". See also P, III, q. 7, f. 66rb, lin.
22-26.

[96] S, III, q. 5, f. 40vb, lin. 39-46: "Et notandum quod motus quandoque est in
genere sicut res generis, sicut in actione et passione et etiam quantitatis per accidens,
ut dictum est, et etiam qualitatis, secundum quod comparatur ad mobile, in quantum ipsum qualificat, non in quantum infertur ex actione. Aliquando autem est in
genere non sicut res generis, sed sicut via, sicut in genere substantiae, quod tamen
videtur contra Commentatorem...". See also P, III, q. 8, f. 66va, lin. 1-5. N's solution
of the intrinsic classification problem is substantially the same as that given by S and
P. See N, III, q. 6, f. 133va, lin. 23-33; va, lin. 50-vb, lin. 4.

[97] *Liber Sex Principiorum, De actione*, p. 39, lin. 18. This view is explicitly ascribed to
the author of the *Liber Sex Principiorum* by M[1] in III, q. 4, f. 109ra, lin. 5 ab imo.

[98] Cfr. M[1], III, q. 4, f. 109rb, lin. 9-11; G[1], III, q. 5, f. 140ra, lin. 21-22; N, III, q.
6, f. 133vb, lin. 1-3.

tradiction, one might reply that the consideration of motion as a *res generis* does not necessarily reflect its intrinsic classification. In favour of this reply, it can be observed that in passage (1) the classification of motion in the category of action is regarded as extrinsic, but in passage (2) motion in the category of action is regarded as a *res generis*. On the other hand, this reply does not solve the problem completely, since in passage (2) motion is said to be a *res generis* also insofar as it confers a quality on its subject. This implies that the classification of motion in the category of quality should be regarded as intrinsic, since it reflects the ontological status of motion as an accident of the mobile substance. But then from passages (1) and (2) it follows that, according to S-P, motion would be intrinsically classified in at least two categories, namely, passion and quality.

The point that the consideration of motion as an accident of the mobile substance leads to an intrinsic classification of motion is made explicit by Geoffrey of Aspall. In explaining why motion, although it is essentially related both to its subject and to its terminus, is a species of a genus only when it is related to its subject, Aspall claims:

> (3) ... it must be said that anything that is posited in a category <is so posited> either insofar as it has the ratio of a substance or insofar as it has the ratio of an accident. Therefore, if motion must be posited in a category, this will be insofar as it has the *ratio* of an accident; but motion has the *ratio* of an accident in comparison to its subject; therefore, it is placed in a genus in comparison to its subject, whereas in comparison to its final terminus it does not receive the *ratio* of an accident, but that of a way; therefore in comparison to its final terminus it is not posited in a category.[99]

Furthermore, like S-P, Aspall maintains that motion is a sort of quality of the mobile substance. But, again, like S-P, Aspall seems to violate the requirement of univocal classification. For in his solution to the classification problem, he claims:

---

[99] M¹, III, q. 5, f. 109rb, lin. 62-va, lin. 1: "... dicendum quod illud quod ponitur in praedicamento aut ponitur secundum quod habet rationem substantiae aut secundum quod habet rationem accidentis. Si ergo motus debeat poni in praedicamento hoc erit secundum quod habet rationem accidentis; sed in comparatione ad subiectum (substantiam *ms.*) habet rationem accidentis et ita in comparatione ad illud (illum *ms.*) ponitur in genere. In comparatione autem ad terminum in quem non capit rationem accidentis, sed tantum rationem viae; ergo in comparatione ad ipsum non ponitur in praedicamento".

(4) We can also consider motion either as it is a way to a thing of a category or as it is a species in a genus. (i) If it is considered as a way to a
thing of a category, then, since <for instance> the way is directed to
being in a place, it is classified in the category of being in a place. (ii) If
it is considered as a species of a genus, then it can be compared to the
mobile thing to which it gives denomination and a quality, and in this
way it is in the category of quality; but if it is compared to the distance
from which it receives its quantity, in this way it is in the category of
quantity.[100]

The distance in question is the formal "distance" between the *terminus
a quo* and the *terminus ad quem* of motion, which consists of the intermediate forms separating these two termini.[101] Here Aspall uses the
same classifications of motion used by S-P in passage (2). He maintains, however, that motion is a species of the categories of both quality and quantity.

The two main problems contained in the solutions offered by S-P
and Aspall can be summarized as follows: (a) motion is said to be
something determined in itself (a continuous succession), but then its
classification in the Aristotelian system of categories does not properly
reflect this nature (this is the case of S-P); (b) the intrinsic classification
of motion does not succeed in preserving a univocal nature of
motion, since motion is intrinsically posited as a *res* of more than one
category (this is the case both of S-P and Aspall). Similar problems
can be detected in the solutions offered by other commentators.[102]

---

[100] M¹, III, q. 4, f. 109rb, lin. 6-12: "Possumus etiam considerare motum aut ut est
via in rem praedicamenti aut ut est species in genere. (i) Si ut est via in rem praedicamenti, tunc quia est via <in> ubi ibi ponitur. (ii) Si ut est species in genere, tunc
potest comparari ad mobile cuius est denominativum et qualificativum, et sic est in
praedicamento qualitatis; si autem comparetur ad distantiam a qua recipit quantitatem, sic est in praedicamento quantitatis".

[101] In a short question devoted to Aristotle's remark that motion is continuous
(*Physics*, III.1, 200b16-17), Aspall maintains that the general cause of the continuity
of motion is that of the intermediate degrees (*gradus*) between its initial terminus and
its final terminus. See, M¹, III, q. 3, f. 109ra, lin. 38-53.

[102] For instance, M³ declares that the *intentio communis* of motion, i.e., motion
regarded *formaliter*, is the *exitus de potentia ad actum*. He concludes without any explanation that motion considered in this way is in the category of action. This solution evidently runs into problem (a), since it is not clear why a passage from potency to act
should be an action instead of a passion. See M³, III, q. 5, f. 153ra, lin. 48-55. G¹ follows Averroes' solution to the classification problem (see above, p. 52-55), but he
modifies the part of this solution relative to the *via ad formam*. For Averroes, motion as
via ad formam is only in the category of passion. The position of G¹ on this point is
more confused: "... secundo modo (*sc.* ut via ad formam) est in uno genere tantum,

The problems involved in the intrinsic classification of motion are radically avoided by M² and W. The position of these two commentators differs from that of the other commentators of our group, since it explicitly acknowledges that no intrinsic classification of motion is possible. In brief, according to M²-W, motion is a *res* in itself, being a *defluxus*, not however a *res* of some Aristotelian category, since it lacks any formal determination. M² introduces his answer to the classification problem with the following remark:

> I say that motion, once the comparison to the agent, the patient, and the terminus are removed from it, is only a flow and has an indeterminate being. For if it were an act of some determinate being, it would posit that thing to which it belongs in act in some way.[103]

On the basis of this same remark, M² concludes in a later passage that:

> ... For motion in its essence, once any respect is removed from it, that is, the respect to the agent, the patient, and the terminus, is not in any genus.[104]

However, motion can be classified in different categories extrinsically, that is, in virtue of those elements that confer some determination on its being, as explained in the following passage:

> But if motion is to acquire determinate being, this will be in virtue of something that essentially determines its being. And that thing will be either the agent, which effectively gives being to motion, or the patient in which motion is received, or the terminus to which motion is directed.[105]

---

scilicet in genere actionis vel passionis. Prout enim comparatur ad agentem, est in praedicamento actionis; prout ad patientem, est in genere passionis. Et isto modo potest adhuc dupliciter considerari, vel scilicet secundum quod disponit patientem, et sic est qualitas; vel prout infertur ab agente, et sic est passio" (III, q. 5, f. 140ra, lin. 19-23). Thus, the solution of G¹ runs into problem (b). On the position of N see note 96.

[103] M², III, q. 4, f. 126ra, lin. 43-46: "Dico quod motus, circumscripta ab illo comparatione ad agens et patiens et ad terminum, est solus defluxus et esse indeterminati. Si enim esset actus determinati esse, poneret illud cuius est aliquo modo in actu". See also W, III, q. 3, f. 54va, lin. 15-20.

[104] M², III, q. 4, f. 126rb, lin. 50-51: "Motus enim id quod est, circumcripto ab ipso omni respectu, scilicet ad agens, ad patiens et ad terminum, in nullo genere est". See also W, III, q. 3, f. 55rb, lin. 1-5.

[105] M², III, q. 4, f. 126ra, lin. 46-50: "Si autem debeat fieri esse determinati, hoc erit per aliquid suum esse essentialiter determinans. Illud autem aut erit agens quod dat esse motui effective aut patiens in quo motus recipitur aut terminus ad quem vadit".

These three elements conferring determination on motion provide three different categorical classifications of motion:

> If the being of motion is essentially determined by the agent, then motion is in the genus of action and is the action itself of the agent. If its being is determined by the terminus to which it is directed, thus, since the terminus to which motion is directed is in a certain genus, the motion which is directed to that terminus will be in the same genus. Nevertheless, motion is in that genus not as an incomplete form which goes towards its act,... but as a way to the form... Thus, motion is not properly in a genus, since it has no formal being which posits it in any species, but since the formal being of motion derives from the patient itself in which it is received, therefore in the most proper sense motion is in the genus of passion. For what is received is in the recipient according to the mode of the recipient.[106]

Like S-P, M^2-W would probably concede that motion is a species of the categories of action and passion, although they do not usually employ these terms. However, while S-P assert merely that these classifications arise from the comparisons of motion to the agent and patient, M^2-W add that only through these comparisons does motion acquire any formal determination. Furthermore, whereas according to the other commentators motion also confers a sort of quality on its subject, albeit of an unspecified nature, according to M^2-W the relation of motion to its subject is quite the opposite. Indeed, as they make clear at the end of the last passage quoted, the mobile thing is the element that most contributes to the determination of the being of motion, and for this reason motion is most properly in the category of passion. Conversely, they strongly deny that motion confers any sort of formal determination on its subject.[107] In conclusion, for M^2 and W, motion in itself is something real but completely devoid of formal content.

The negative conclusion of M^2 and W on the intrinsic classification

---

[106] Ibid., f. 126ra, lin. 50-55: "Si vero suum esse essentialiter determinetur per agens, sic est motus in genere actionis et est ipsa actio agentis. Si vero per terminum ad quem vadit, sic, cum terminus ad quem est motus sit in aliquo genere, in eodem genere erit motus ad illum terminum, non tamen est ibi sicut forma incompleta quae vadit ad actum... lin. 57-58: sed sicut via ad formam... lin. 63-rb, lin.1: Sic igitur motus proprie in genere non est, quia non habet esse formale ponens ipsum in aliqua specie, sed quia esse formale motus est ab ipso passo in quo recipitur, ideo proprissime est motus in genere passionis. Receptum enim est in recipiente per modum recipientis". See also W, III, q. 3, ff. 54va, lin. 21-55ra, lin. 7.

[107] See, for instance, the passage quoted in note 103.

of motion will be proposed again by Thomas Wylton at the beginning of the fourteenth century. Wylton also rejects Averroes' *forma*-
theory and follows the *via*-theory of motion. But when he is confront-
ed with the question:

> I ask therefore what motion includes in its concept. Since it is some-
> thing in itself outside the soul, it must formally include a thing of some
> one category, because being is exhaustively divided in ten categories,[108]

he replies:

> ... I say that, when motion is considered as to its quidditative notion,
> since its quidditative notion is being a way to a terminus or an act
> which is ordered to a terminus, and since it receives its determination
> only from this terminus, it is therefore in a category only with respect
> to its terminus. As to the form of the argument, when it is said that
> motion is in itself a being, I concede this, if being is distinguished from
> nothing. But when it is further assumed that formally it includes a
> thing of some category, I deny this and I claim that this is not neces-
> sary.[109]

The negative conclusion reached by M[2]-W and Wylton on the possibility of an intrinsic classification of motion in Aristotle's categories
points out a major problem involved in the radically realist positions
on the ontological status of motion like those supported by the early
English commentators. The problem is that, once motion is postulat-
ed as a third *res*, in addition to the mobile substance and the forms
acquired and lost by this substance during motion, this third *res* cannot adequately be accommodated by one of Aristotle's categories,
since the mobile substance and its forms already exhaust the variety
of entities allowed by Aristotle's system. This problem is avoided by
Averroes' reductionist position on the ontological status of motion. It
is also avoided by the moderate realism opposed to Averroes' position
by Thomas Aquinas, Giles of Rome, and William of Bonkes.[110]
Indeed, for these commentators, motion is not simply an incomplete
form, as Averroes holds, but an incomplete form "plus" an *ordo* to
completion. This *ordo*, however, is not regarded as a *res* added to the

---

[108] Thomas Wylton, *In Physicam*, III, q. 7, ed. in C. Trifogli, "Due questioni sul
movimento nel Commento alla *Physica* di Thomas Wylton", *Medioevo*, 21 (1995), p.
59, lin. 278-280.

[109] Ibid., lin. 284-291.

[109] See above, pp. 61-65.

incomplete form, but simply as a *modus essendi* or a modification of this form. On the other hand, the problem does arise for the early English commentators. For, as we have seen throughout this chapter, they assume that motion is a *res* in itself, and this *res* ultimately results from a "reification" of the successive character that appears in every motion. Yet, as M² and W remark, succession taken in itself is devoid of any formal determination. Thus, if motion so reified must be given some formal "content", this can be found only if motion is related to something different from itself, as to the entities of Aristotle's categories. This accounts for most of the difficulties in the attempts by the other commentators of our group to specify the "intrinsic" categorical classification of motion.

CHAPTER TWO

THE INFINITE

Introduction

In general, Aristotle's attitude towards the infinite is negative. From a metaphysical point of view, he assumes that something infinite lacks any formal determination and hence is unknowable. Specifically, he regards infinity as analogous to matter and finiteness as analogous to form.[1] This negative view of the infinite extends from the metaphysical to the physical level. Indeed, Aristotle's physical universe is characterized by formal determinations and differences. As a consequence, the matter-like nature of the infinite implies that it is to be regarded as a deviant element in Aristotle's physical system. Yet, Aristotle concedes that the existence of the infinite in the physical world cannot be absolutely denied, for there are basic physical structures that show some form of infinity: time has no beginning nor end, continuous quantities are divisible into parts *ad infinitum,* and number is infinite.[2] Accordingly, Aristotle's main concern in treating the infinite in *Physics* III.4-8 is to establish precisely which forms of infinity are admissible and which kinds of quantity are in some sense infinite.

As to the problem of the legitimate form of infinity, Aristotle's position is traditionally formulated by means of the distinction between the actual infinite and the potential infinite. Only the potential infinite can be admitted, whereas the existence in any way of the actual infinite must be ruled out. As we have seen in the *Introduction,* Aristotle's general discussion of this distinction is extremely obscure, nor is it easy to integrate all its aspects into a unified interpretation.[3] Here, we shall concentrate instead on Aristotle's application of his general theory of the infinite to the two main types of quantities: (1) magnitudes (continuous, permanent quantities) and (2) numbers (the series of positive integers).

(1) Aristotle maintains that magnitudes can be divided *ad infinitum.*

---

[1] Aristotle, *Physics,* III.6, 206b33-207a32; 7, 207b34-208a4.
[2] Ibid., III.6, 206a9-14.
[3] See above, p. 10-14.

This means that any given part of a magnitude can always be further divided. Therefore, given any magnitude, it is always possible to find a smaller one: the one obtained by dividing the magnitude. Formulated in the technical terms introduced in *Physics* III.6, Aristotle's claim is that (i) magnitudes are potential infinites by division.[4] In Aristotle's view, this is the only form of infinity admissible for magnitudes. Indeed, his position on the extension or extendibility of magnitudes is strictly finitist. He holds not only that (ii) there cannot be an infinitely extended physical body (i.e., a magnitude greater than any finite magnitude),[5] but also that (iii) magnitude cannot be increased *ad infinitum*, since the universe has a finite and fixed size which cannot be exceeded.[6] In Aristotelian terms, (ii) says that magnitude cannot be an actual infinite and (iii) that it cannot even be a potential infinite by addition.

(2) Aristotle claims that numbers represent no exception to the general principle that there is no actual infinite, for he claims that the series of natural numbers constitutes only a potential infinite by addition and not an actual one.[7] This means that there are not infinitely many numbers, although any given number can be further increased. In a general way, Aristotle's restriction of the type of infinity admissible in numbers derives from two different assumptions. The first concerns the ontological status of numbers. For a number *n* to exist, a collection of numerically *n* actually existing things must exist. The second is that there are only finitely many things that actually exist. There are, however, collections of actually existing things the number of which can increase indefinitely in time, and this is why number is potentially infinite by addition. In *Physics* III.7, Aristotle specifically holds that the increase *ad infinitum* of numbers is admitted and accounted for by the divisibility *ad infinitum* of continuous magnitudes, in the sense that the parts divided from a continuum form a collection of things whose number can always be increased.[8]

In summary, the main theses of Aristotle's doctrine of the infinite in magnitude and number are the following:

---

[4] Ibid., 206a14-18.
[5] Ibid., III.5, 204b1-206a8.
[6] Ibid., III.7, 207b15-21.
[7] Ibid., 207b1-15.
[8] On Aristotle's treatment of infinity in number see especially Hussey, *Aristotle's Physics*, Notes, p. 88-90.

(i) Magnitude is potentially infinite by division.
(ii) Magnitude cannot have an actually infinite extension.
(iii) Magnitude cannot be potentially infinite by addition.
(iv) Number is only potentially infinite by addition.

These four theses are generally accepted in the Aristotelian tradition.[9] The early English commentators, in particular, follow Aristotle's view on the infinite in magnitude formulated in theses (i)-(iii). In sections 1 and 2, we shall describe the most significant elements of the exegesis of Aristotle's theory given by this group of commentators. Such elements appear mainly in connection with the negative side of this theory, namely, with the denial of any form of infinity by extension in magnitude stated in theses (ii)-(iii). Section 1 is devoted to the treatment of the actual infinite in magnitude, while section 2 discusses the logical and quantitative aspects of the relation between the notions of actual and potential infinite by addition in magnitudes. Aristotle's treatment of this topic contains some difficulties, which were clearly perceived by Simplicius and Averroes and usually discussed in the thirteenth- and fourteenth-century exegetical tradition. As we shall see, however, such difficulties are passed over by most of our commentators.

While contribution of the early English commentators to Aristotle's theory of the infinite in magnitudes is essentially exegetical, this is not the case for thesis (iv) about the infinite in number. Indeed, Aristotle's finitism about number gives rise to an original debate among our commentators. Some of them hold that, in fact, number is actually infinite. This debate will be analysed in section 3.

1. *Metaphysical Grounds for the Rejection of an Actual Infinite in Magnitude*

In *Physics* III.5, Aristotle claims that a task specific to physical inquiry is to establish whether there is an infinitely extended body.[10] Most of the

---

[9] For a comprehensive survey of the most important medieval interpretations and modifications of Aristotle's theory of the continuum and of the infinite, see A. Maier, *Die Vorläufer Galileis im 14. Jahrhundert* (*Studien zur Naturphilosophie der Spätscholastik*, Bd. 1), Edizioni di storia e letteratura, Roma 1949, p. 155-215 and, for the fourteenth century, J. E. Murdoch, "Infinity and Continuity", in N. Kretzmann, A. Kenny, J. Pinborg (eds.), *The Cambridge History of Later Medieval Philosophy*, Cambridge University Press, Cambridge 1982, p. 564-591.

[10] Aristotle, *Physics*, III.5, 204a34-b4.

arguments he uses to rule out the existence of such a body are said to be physical arguments.[11] Indeed, these kinds of arguments aim at showing that the existence of an infinitely extended body is incompatible with some of the basic structures of the physical world. For instance, Aristotle argues that it is incompatible with the fact the universe is ultimately composed of a finite plurality of elements endowed with different qualities[12] and with the existence of natural places and natural motions.[13]

Aristotle is quite confident in the efficacy of these physical arguments. Yet, it is clear that they are all essentially different formulations of the obvious point that an infinitely extended body, being formless and undifferentiated, cannot be accomodated in Aristotle's formally differentiated physical universe.[14] Accordingly, it is not surprising that in the Greek commentaries, Averroes' commentary, and the thirteenth-century commentaries, Aristotle's physical arguments do not become a matter of debate or of significant philosophical remarks. Indeed, once the basic finiteness of Aristotle's "formal" natural world is accepted, his physical arguments against the existence of an infinite body must be regarded as conclusive. The early English commentators, in particular, occasionally devote questions to clarifying some of Aristotle's assumptions, but their contribution to this part of Aristotle's theory is not very significant. Most of them, however, do try to integrate Aristotle's physical refutation with some considerations pertaining to the "metaphysics" of infinity in continuous magnitudes. More accurately, they propose a set of remarks and arguments that try to show that an infinitely extended body and, in general, infinitely extended magnitudes are already incompatible with the metaphysical structure of Aristotle's universe and not only with some specifically physical presuppositions, such as those explicitly used by Aristotle in his physical arguments. In this section we shall present and comment upon the most characteristic elements of the metaphys-

---

[11] Ibid., 204b10-11. In connection with topics of natural philosophy, Aristotle often uses a distinction between physical arguments and logical arguments. Roughly, by physical argument he means one proceeding from principles that hold for natural things as such, whereas by a logical argument one proceeding from considerations that are not proper to natural things as such. On Aristotle's distinction, see *Aristotle's Physics*, Books I and II, Translated with Introduction, Commentary, Notes by W. Charlton, Clarendon Press, Oxford 1970, Introduction, p. x-xii. See also Hussey, *Aristotle's Physics*, Introduction, p. xxxiii-xxxiv.

[12] Aristotle, *Physics*, III.5, 204b10-205a7.

[13] Ibid., 205a7-b1, b24-206a7.

[14] See above, *Introduction*, p. 10.

ical approach of our commentators.

Although Aristotle does not even try to discuss the problem of the existence of an infinite body in some alternative physical universe which is not immediately incompatible with it, a more general approach to this problem is not totally absent from his treatment of the infinite. In addition to the physical arguments, he also presents a 'logical' argument against the existence of an infinitely extended body,[15] which is formulated by Averroes as follows:

(A) (i) Every body is contained by one or more surfaces; (ii) but everything that is contained by one or more surfaces is finite; (iii) therefore every body is finite.[16]

Clearly, the idea of this argument is that the surfaces are the limits of the three-dimensional extension of the body. The argument is "logical" because it is based on a general definition of body, common to both natural and mathematical bodies, and not on some specifically physical assumption. Because of their "non physical" character, logical arguments are not really appropriate to a physical topic and are not regarded as definitive by Aristotle. Averroes and before him the Greek commentator Philoponus, however, do not find argument (A) in any way conclusive. As these two commentators point out, Aristotle assumes that the major premise (i) expresses a universally accepted definition of body.[17] But, in fact, those who posit an infinite body would not concede that such a body has limiting surfaces, i.e., a figure.[18] Thus Aristotle's argument is in fact only dialectical and not demonstrative.[19] Moreover, one might object against the minor premise (ii) that a body could be "limited" by infinitely extended surfaces. Therefore, Aristotle's argument does not seem to be sound if 'body' is taken in a purely quantitative sense.

---

[15] Aristotle, *Physics*, III.5, 204b4-7.

[16] Averroes, *In Physicam*, III, t. c. 40, f. 103raB: "Omne corpus continetur ab una superficie aut a pluribus; et omne quod continetur ab una superficie aut pluribus est finitum; ergo omne corpus est finitum". Averroes also specifies that a round body is that contained by only one surface.

[17] Hussey remarks, however, that Aristotle more usually defines 'body' as 'three-dimensional magnitude'. Nevertheless, he maintains that argument (A) expresses one of the motives of Aristotle's finitism, namely, that any magnitude has a measurable size and therefore cannot be infinite. See Hussey, *Aristotle's Physics*, Notes, p. 79.

[18] See Philoponus, *In Physicam*, III, p. 417, lin. 14-19; Averroes, *In Physicam*, III, t. c. 40, f. 103raC-rbD.

[19] Ibid., f. 103raB.

Argument (A), however, naturally gives rise to the following question: (a) is it possible to show that a body (or more generally magnitude) is finite, if "body" is taken in its purely quantitative sense as three-dimensional extension, and, if not, (b) what is a non-quantitative notion of body that is incompatible with the notion of infinite extension?

In the rest of this section, we shall try to reconstruct the answer of the early English commentators to this question.

An implicit answer to part (b) of this question given by some of our commentators claims that, if a body is regarded as composed of matter and form, then it cannot be infinitely extended. Indeed, an argument already proposed by Rufus and also found in M^1 and M^3 tries to show that a body is necessarily finite by appealing to the matter-form relation. Geoffrey of Aspall (M^1) formulates this argument as follows:

> (1) ...the form of whatever body is together with the totality of its matter; but if a body is posited as infinite, then its form is not together with the totality of its matter; therefore etc. Proof of the minor premise: what is only in the depth of something is not together with the totality of its matter; but if a body is posited to be infinite, then its form will be only in the depth, since, if it were also in the exterior part, it would terminate this body and make it finite and thus that body would be finite, which is against our hypothesis. Therefore, if an infinite body were posited, its form would not be with the totality of its matter; but this is absurd in a natural thing; therefore, etc.[20]

---

[20] M^1, III, q. 15, f. 110vb, lin. 59-65: "... forma cuiuslibet corporis est cum tota materia eiusdem; sed si ponatur infinitum, forma non est cum tota materia; quare etc. Probatio minoris: quod solum est in profundo alicuius non est cum tota materia eius; sed si ponatur infinitum, forma erit solum in profundo, quia, si esset in exteriori parte terminaret et finitaret et ita esset finitum, quod est contra ypothesim. Si ergo ponatur infinitum, non erit forma cum tota materia; sed hoc est inconveniens in re naturali; quare etc.". (Throughout this chapter, we use the numbering of the questions on the infinite in the early English commentaries published in Trifogli, "Le questioni sul libro III", second part, *Documenti e studi sulla tradizione filosofica medievale*, 4 (1993), p. 166-178). See also, Rufus, *In Physicam*, III, f. 5vb, lin. 37-43; M^3, III, q. 5, f. 155va, lin. 24-32. G^1 and also M^3 propose another version of this argument, in which there is no explicit reference to the form of the body. The external surface is assumed to be the principle which confers actual existence to the body, in the sense that it makes a body physically separated from the surrounding bodies. Thus a body having only 'depth' and not an external surface would be like an undivided part of a larger body and not a body in its own right; therefore, it would not exist in act. G^1, III, q. 2, f. 141va, lin. 2 ab imo-vb, lin. 2: "Quod autem aliquod corpus non sit actu infinitum patet, quia omne corpus habet terminum, quia, si non, vere esset dicere ipsum esse

Argument (1) basically relies on the Aristotelian idea that, from a metaphysical point of view, infinity is always associated with matter and finiteness with form. From this idea it follows that a body composed of matter and form is finite. In argument (1), however, this "traditional" idea is expressed in a very original way. Indeed, this argument tries to reformulate the quantitative description of a body proposed by argument (A) from Aristotle in terms of the metaphysical notions of matter and form. Argument (A) implies that if a body is posited to be infinite, then it should be a three-dimensional extension unbounded by an external surface. In the "metaphysical" version of argument (A) proposed in (1) the three-dimensional extension of a body is replaced by its matter and its surface, as the limit of this extension, is replaced by its form. Accordingly, the idea that an infinite body could not be bounded by an external surface of argument (A) is translated in (1) into the idea that the form of an infinite body could be only in the "interior part" (*in profundo*) of this body, for its form should leave some of the three-dimensional extension, viz. matter, unbounded, that is, there would exist some portion of the matter of an infinite body deprived of form. Thus, while the idea of a three-dimensional extension not bounded by a surface in argument (A) is not contradictory, its "metaphysical translation" in argument (1) is contradictory according to Aristotelian metaphysics, since it implies the existence of matter without form.

A further question is whether the most general notion of body that is incompatible with the notion of infinity is that of a body as three-dimensional material extension endowed with form — in other words, whether form is the sole cause of the finiteness of continuous quantities inhering in natural bodies. A positive answer is explicitly given by N and W.

In his solution to the question "What in a continuous quantity is that which is incompatible with the nature of the infinite", N distinguishes two meanings of 'continuous quantity':

---

ens in profundo et non in ultimo; sed quod est solum existens in profundo non est corpus actu existens, quia est ens in alio, ut eius pars; sed omne corpus carens termino est solum existens in profundo; ergo etc.". See also M^3, III, q. 3, f. 155ra, lin. 30-38. Note that in this second version the term 'actu' refers to the type of existence of the infinite body and not to the type of infinity it has. We shall meet again this kind of association in the treatment of infinity in number given by G^1-M^3. See below p. 121-123.

(2) Therefore, I say that in a continuous quantity there are two things or equivalently two things are denoted by this name 'quantity', namely (i) this extension in matter. And this is the primary and formal meaning of this name 'quantity'. And in virtue of this meaning infinity belongs to quantity. Accordingly, in virtue of its formal meaning quantity is not incompatible with infinity. And in this way Aristotle's saying "the finite and the infinite are proper to quantity"[21] must be understood. Furthermore, something else is given to be understood in a derivative way by this name 'quantity', namely (ii) the form that causes this extension in matter. And in virtue of this meaning quantity is incompatible with the nature of infinity, because it is proper of the form to make finite and to terminate, whereas in virtue of its first and formal meaning quantity is the subject of infinity.[22]

Thus, according to N, continuous quantity in itself, i.e., taken in its primary and formal meaning of extension in matter, can be infinite. Its infinity, however, is ruled out by the fact that it is always caused by a form. In this position, the extension of fire, for instance, is not necessarily finite *qua* extension but only *qua* extension of fire. This principle is emphasized by W. He claims that matter in itself admits of a magnitude of however great extension. Since magnitude, however, is always joined with a natural form, it is, in fact, always finite in the natural world, because any natural form determines a finite quantity of matter in which it inheres.[23]

The position of N and W, which identifies form with the cause of

---

[21] Aristotle, *Physics*, III.4, 202b30-32.

[22] N, III, q. 10, f. 138ra, lin. 24-32: "Dico igitur quod in quanto continuo duo sunt sive duo signantur per hoc nomen 'quantum', scilicet ista extensio in materia. Et hoc est quod primo signatur per hoc nomen 'quantum', et est eius signatum formale. Et gratia huius signati debetur quanto infinitas. Unde ratione formalis signati ipsius non repugnat naturae infiniti. Et hoc modo intelligendum est quod dicit Aristoteles 'finitum et infinitum quantitati congruunt'. Item, aliud datur intelligi ex consequenti per hoc nomen 'quantum', scilicet forma causans istam extensionem in materia. Et gratia huius signati quantum naturae infinitatis repugnat, quia formae est finire et terminare, et quantum ratione primi formalis signati est subiectum infinitatis".

[23] For instance, W answers the question whether a line necessarily has initial and final points, as argument (A) above from Aristotle implies, as follows: "... punctus et linea possunt dupliciter considerari: aut ut sunt ultima materiae naturalis, et sic non est possibile lineam extendi in infinitum. Alio modo possunt considerari non prout sunt ultima materiae naturalis, sed materiae vel magnitudinis absolutae, et sic sunt de consideratione mathematici, sicut dicit Averroes hic, et sic potest linea esse infinita. Primo modo non, quia materia non extenditur nisi sub forma naturali, quam impossibile est operari in magnitudine infinita; ideo etc." (W, III, q. 5, f. 67vb, lin. 22-27). See Averroes, *In Physicam*, III, t. c. 71, f. 119rbD.

the finiteness of the extension of physical body, can be considered the traditional one, since it is already suggested by Aristotle and Averroes,[24] and is repeated in different formulations throughout the medieval tradition. Some of our commentators, however, seem to hold a different position, according to which magnitude in itself, that is, considered purely as magnitude, cannot be infinite. An earlier proponent of this view is Richard Rufus of Cornwall, and in their discussion of this topic M^1-G^1-M^3 seem to be heavily influenced by Rufus.

Like Rufus,[25] the three commentators M^1, G^1, M^3 discuss a short question (henceforth (Q)) on whether an actual infinite is incompatible with magnitude *qua* magnitude or *qua* physical magnitude (*magnitudo naturalis*).[26] The structure and content of (Q) in all three commentaries are very similar. The structure largely consists of a series of *pro* and *contra* arguments with the solution of the question reduced to a sentence claiming that infinity is incompatible with magnitude both *qua* magnitude and *qua* physical magnitude.[27] Overall the arguments adduced by this set of commentators against the possibility of an infinite continuous magnitude *qua* magnitude are not very clear or convincing. For instance, they use argument (1), which, as we have seen, assumes that a body is not purely a three-dimensional extension, but is composed of matter and form. Yet, there is another main argument, which makes no explicit reference to any form. This latter argument assumes that a continuous magnitude is characterized by the property of being a whole and tries to show that this property is incompatible with infinity. G^1 formulates this argument as follows:

> (3) ... (i) in every continuum the notions of whole and part are preserved; (ii) but each of these notions is incompatible with infinity. For (a) a whole is that outside which nothing is and (b) everything of this

---

[24] For Aristotle see note 1. For Averroes in addition to the reference given in the preceding note see also ibid., t. c. 60, f. 114raB; t. c. 72, f. 119vaG.

[25] The title of Rufus' question is "Cum non possumus ponere infinitum esse actu, quaeritur aut hoc est quia continuum aut quia continuum naturale, scilicet continuum in materia naturali" (*In Physicam*, III, f. 5vb, lin. 29-31). This question ends at f. 6ra, lin. 9. It is followed by another very short question (f. 6ra, lin. 10-24) which asks whether the continuum *qua* continuum is infinite by addition, as number is. Rufus' answer to this latter question is negative, and his main concern is to defend it against the objection arising from the fact that the continuum *qua* continuum is divisible *ad infinitum*. Rufus' discussion seems to have influenced our commentators as well. See below note 36.

[26] M^1, III, q. 3, ff. 110vb, lin. 41-111ra, lin. 23; G^1, III, q. 4, f. 142ra, lin. 12-46; M^3, III, q. 5, f. 155rb, lin. 8 ab imo-vb, lin. 30 ab imo.

[27] Even this very minimal form of solution is missing in G^1.

kind is complete, and therefore finite. Furthermore, a part is always said with respect to some whole, and therefore infinity is incompatible with the notions of both part and whole.[28]

This argument shows an original combination of different suggestions made by Aristotle. Premise (i) seems to point to Aristotle's analysis of the continuum in *Physics* V.3, where it is implied that a continuum is not a mere aggregate of parts, but has an intrinsic unity, because its parts join at one common limit. In this respect, a continuum is said to be essentially one and a whole.[29] (a) mentions Aristotle's definition of 'whole' in *Physics* III.6 as that of which no part is outside itself,[30] that is, something complete. It is intuitive that, if a continuum is a whole in the sense of being essentially one, then it is a whole in the sense of something complete. If it were incomplete, then it would be capable of undergoing addition, which would contradict its essential unity. Furthermore, the inference from (a) to (b), that is, from 'whole-complete' to 'finite-perfect' is made by Aristotle in *Physics* III.6.[31] The specific application of this inference, however, in argument (3) seems problematic, for this argument intends to show that a continuum cannot be actually infinite. But it is not clear in what sense an infinitely extended line, for instance, has some of its parts "outside" itself and therefore is not a whole and complete. It is true that, given any part A of an infinite line, there is always another part B outside it, but it does not seem to follow that B is "outside" this line. In fact, B "already" belongs to this line. On the other hand, if we imagine that a finite line is undergoing a process of addition *ad infinitum* in which A has already been added to it, but part B is still to be added, then the inference becomes more plausible.

The problem is that in moving from 'whole-complete' to 'finite' Aristotle takes 'finite' as opposed to 'potentially infinite' and not to 'actually infinite'. Indeed, in a metaphysical sense, a potential infinite is something finite which can nonetheless be expanded *ad infinitum* through addition. Thus, the infinity of a potential infinite consists

---

[28] G¹, III, q. 4, f. 142ra, lin. 23-26: "... in omni continuo salvatur ratio totius et partis; sed ratio utriusque istorum repugnat infinitati. Totum enim est extra quod nihil <est>, et omne tale est perfectum et ita finitum. Pars etiam non dicitur nisi respectu alicuius totius, et ita rationi (ratione *ms.*) utriusque repugnat infinitas". See also Rufus, *In Physicam*, III, f. 5vb, lin. 43-48; M¹, III, q. 3, f. 110vb, lin. 52-57; M³, III, q. 5, f. 155va, lin. 48-57.

[29] Aristotle, *Physics*, V.3, 227a10-17.

[30] Ibid., III.6, 207a8-10.

[31] Ibid., 207a10-15.

exactly in its "extendibility" and, therefore, in the fact that a potential infinite is something essentially incomplete, i.e., not a whole.[32] An actually infinite magnitude, however, is infinitely extended and not extendible.[33]

Thus, argument (3) does not seem adequate to show that continuous magnitudes *qua* wholes cannot be actually infinite.[34] Yet, the connection between continuity, oneness and wholeness or completeness does seem more effective in proving that a potential infinite by addition is incompatible with the nature of magnitude. In fact, M[1], G[1], M[3] make implicit use of this connection in reply to an argument in question (Q) against the thesis that infinity is incompatible with magnitude *qua* magnitude. The argument claims that, if magnitude as such is divisible *ad infinitum*, it can also be increased *ad infinitum* by addition.[35] M[1], G[1], and M[3] reply that only divisibility *ad infinitum* reflects the nature of magnitude, whereas a process of addition *ad infinitum* would be extraneous to its nature. M[1] formulates this reply as follows:

(4) ... it must be said that magnitude has the property that it can be divided *ad infinitum* in virtue of something which is inside itself, namely, in virtue of the infinite parts of its matter, and therefore in magnitude itself there is the essential cause of its division *ad infinitum*. If, however, we imagine that a magnitude is increased *ad infinitum* by addition, this is not in virtue of an intrinsic nature of the magnitude itself or of the body, but in virtue of the nature of something added and hence of an extraneous nature. Therefore, there cannot be a cause in any way

---

[32] Aristotle's definition of the potential infinite reads: "So, that is infinite, of which it is always possible to take some part outside, when we take according to quantity" (III.6, 207a7-8). On Aristotle's metaphysical description of the potential infinity, see especially Hussey, *Aristotle's Physics*, Notes, p. 85-88. Among our commentators, S, P, and N devote short exegetical questions to Aristotle's definition of the infinite. They realize that this definition applies to the potential infinite and not to the actual infinite. See S, III, qq. 7-8, ff. 44rb, lin. 6-47; P, III, qq. 30-31, ff. 74vb, lin. 7 ab imo-75ra, lin. 44; N, III, qq. 21-22, f. 142rb, lin. 19 ab imo-1 ab imo.

[33] Argument (3) is found also in N. In the version given by this commentator the confusion between potential infinite and actual infinite most clearly appears. In order to deny that the infinite is a whole he appeals to Aristotle's analysis of *Physics* III.6. But in order to show that the infinite is not even a part he appeals to the principle "infinitum non derelinquit aliquid extra se", which in fact seems to apply only to an actual infinite. See N, III, q. 10, f. 138ra, lin. 6-11.

[34] Similar problems can be detected in the versions of argument (3) given by Rufus, M[1] and M[3]. References to these versions have been given in note 28.

[35] See M[1], III, q. 3, f. 110vb, lin. 44-46; G[1], III, q. 4, f. 142ra, lin. 36-38; M[3], III, q. 5, f. 155vb, lin. 15-18.

essential of the addition of magnitude *ad infinitum*, but only an accidental one. And consequently we do not say that magnitude can be
increased *ad infinitum* by addition, since this does not follow from its
intrinsic nature.[36]

Thus, infinite divisibility is essential to magnitude because it derives
from something *inside* magnitude, whereas addition *ad infinitum* is only
accidental, because it presupposes something *outside* it. It seems clear
that, taken in purely spatial terms, the relation inside-outside cannot
be the basis of an essential-accidental distinction. It can, however, be
such a basis if magnitude is considered as whole, complete and something essentially unified. For, when magnitude is considered in this
way, what is outside it is accidental. This point is made more explicitly by M[1] when he compares the addition of numbers *ad infinitum* with
that of magnitude. Any number (i.e., any positive integer) is essentially ordered to the next, and therefore it is an essential and intrinsic
property of numbers that any number can be increased by adding a
unity. A magnitude, however, being a whole and one, is not essentially ordered to another magnitude.[37]

In conclusion, the early English tradition supported two different
positions on the "metaphysics" of actual infinity in magnitudes. The
first position is that magnitude in itself can be actually infinite; its
finitess derives precisely from the form of the physical body in which

---

[36] M[1], III, q. 3, f. 111ra, lin. 3-10: "... dicendum quod magnitudo habet quod possit dividi in infinitum gratia alicuius quod est intra magnitudinem, ut gratia partium
infinitarum materiae, et ita in magnitudine est causa essentialis suae divisionis in
infinitum. Si autem imaginetur aliquam magnitudinem crescere in infinitum per
additionem, hoc non est per aliquam intraneam naturam ipsius magnitudinis sive
corporis, sed per naturam additamenti et ita per naturam extraneam. Unde non
potest esse causa aliquo modo essentialis in appositione magnitudinis in infinitum,
sed solum accidentalis, et ita non dicimus quod magnitudo possit crescere in infinitum per additionem, quia hoc non est ex natura sua intranea". Similar answers are
given by the other commentators. See Rufus, *In Physicam*, III, f. 6ra, lin. 15-22; G[1],
III, q. 4, f. 142ra, lin. 40-46; M[3], III, q. 5, f. 155vb, lin. 18-37.

[37] M[1], III, q. 3, f. 111ra, lin. 12-21: "Dicendum quod quilibet numerus est in
potentia de se respectu additionis super ipsum et quaelibet pars numeri ordinatur ad
aliam in infinitum, et ideo dicimus quod numerus per additionem crescit in infinitum, scilicet quia quilibet numerus de se est in potentia ad alium numerum. Et
praeter hoc cuilibet parti numeri debetur forma propria et ita numerus habet diver-
sas potentias quarum quaelibet ordinatur ad aliam, et ideo crescit sive est in potentia
ut crescat etc.. Sed in magnitudine non est ita, quia una magnitudo non ordinatur ad
aliam, et etiam quando una magnitudo additur alteri magnitudini totum fit sub una
forma sive sub uno actu existendi. Unde totum est terminatum sicut fuit prius, et
ideo non crescit in infinitum per additionem". On the different *potentiae* corresponding to the unities added in the addition *ad infinitum* of numbers see below, p. 106-110.

magnitude inheres. This position, which can be regarded as the traditional one, is endorsed by N and W. The second position is that magnitude in itself cannot be actually infinite. This position is found in
the early commentary by Richard Rufus of Cornwall and is adopted
by M[1], G[1], and M[3]. We have pointed out, however, that the most significant arguments for this thesis do not characterize magnitude in
purely quantitative terms. For instance, magnitude is said to be a
whole, something essentially unitary and complete, and these are all
formal characteristics.

As an introduction to the topic of next section, it should be noted
that in both positions supported by our commentators, the "metaphysics" of the actual infinite in magnitudes tends to be closely related to that of the potential infinite by addition. As to the first position,
it is clear that the form of a natural body rules out not only that its
size is actually infinite, but also that it can be increased indefinitely.
As to the second position, we have seen that argument (3) is meant to
be directed against the actual infinite, but, in fact, uses Aristotle's
metaphysical description of the potential infinite. Furthermore, in this
position, a wholeness or completeness prevents magnitudes from
being not only actually infinite, but also potentially infinite by addition, as is shown by argument (4). Although the metaphysical reasons
for rejecting actual infinites and potential infinites by addition in
magnitudes are very similar, nevertheless, from a logical point of
view, actual infinite and potential infinite by addition are generally
taken by Aristotle to be distinct notions. In the next section, we shall
see that most of the early English commentators fail to distinguish
clearly between the logic of the actual infinite in magnitude and that
of the potential infinite by addition.

2. *The Actual Infinite and the Potential Infinite by Addition in Magnitude*

In *Physics* III.6, Aristotle explains that in magnitude a potential infinite by addition is in a sense the same thing as a potential infinite by
division.[38] Aristotle's idea can be illustrated as follows. Take a finite,
continuous magnitude m and divide it in two halves m^1 and m^2. Since
m^2 is also a continuous magnitude, it can be divided in halves *ad infini-*

---

[38] Aristotle, *Physics*, III.6, 206b3-13.

tum. But then m^1 can undergo a process of addition *ad infinitum*. For at each step of the division of m^2, one of two halves obtained at this step can be added to m^1. Regardless of the number of steps, the size of m^1 will be less than the original magnitude m. Indeed, this is the crucial property of the addition *ad infinitum* that is inverse to the division *ad infinitum*.[39] There is, however, another way of defining a process of addition *ad infinitum*, which does not have this property of "finiteness". For instance, if magnitudes of the same fixed size, however small, are repeatedly added to m^1, the size reached by m^1 after a sufficiently large number of steps will be greater than that of m. Aristotle rejects the idea that magnitudes could have a potential infinite by addition of this sort,[40] and he obviously has a strong motivation for doing so. After a sufficiently large number of steps the size reached by m^1 would not only exceed the size of m, but of the whole universe. Yet, the universe – Aristotle assumes – is not only finite, but it has also a fixed size which cannot be expanded. By "potential infinite by addition" (in magnitudes) we shall henceforth mean that whereby any finite magnitude can eventually be exceeded, which is to say, the potential infinite rejected by Aristotle.

In addition to the cosmological argument based on the fixed dimension of the universe, Aristotle adduces another argument to reject the potential infinite by addition, and it is this argument that gives rise to the exegetical problem to be analysed in this section. The argument in question claims that the admission of a potential infinite by addition in magnitudes would also imply the admission of an actually infinite magnitude. The inference on which Aristotle's argument is explicitly based is the following: if, given any magnitude, it is possible to find a greater one, then there is also (or there can be) a magnitude greater than any finite magnitude, i.e., an actually infinite magnitude.[41] This inference seems to be faulty. A sign of this is that, if it

---

[39] It is not necessary, however, to divide a continuous magnitude in halves, but it suffices to divide it in parts having a fixed ratio less than unity; in scholastic terms, the division must be *secundum eandem proportionem*, for in this way it can go on *ad infinitum*, without exhausting the initial magnitude.

[40] Aristotle, *Physics*, III.6, 206b16-20.

[41] The argument in question is the following: "*To be [infinite] so as to exceed every [definite quantity] by addition is not possible even potentially unless there is something which is actually infinite*, accidentally, as the natural philosophers say that the body outside the world-system, of which the substance is air or some other such thing, is infinite. But *if it is not possible for there to be a perceptible body which is actually infinite in this sense, it is manifest that there cannot be one even potentially infinite by addition*, except in the way that has been

were valid, then Aristotle's theory of the potential infinite would be inconsistent. Aristotle holds that the series of numbers is a potential infinite by addition, but denies that it is also an actual infinite, i.e., that there are infinitely many numbers.[42]

Aristotelian commentators are usually aware of the problems arising from Aristotle's inference from a potential infinite by addition to an actual infinite in magnitudes. In the Greek tradition, Simplicius points out some of these problems. At the end of his literal exposition of Aristotle's argument, he raises the following objection to Aristotle's inference:

> But in what sense does Aristotle say: *For a magnitude may exist in act of any size, of which it may exist in potency?* For, from the fact that it is possible to make an addition to any number, it does not follow for this reason that there exists an actually infinite number, nor from the fact that an actually infinite number does not exist does it follow that an infinite addition of number is prevented. Indeed, it is possible to make an addition to any given number. Therefore, one might say: even if an actually infinite magnitude does not exist, what prevents it from existing in potency in the sense that it can be increased to infinity?... But if this is the case, it is not necessary to deny the addition to infinity on the basis of the fact that an actually infinite sensible magnitude does not exist.[43]

---

stated, in inverse correspondence to the division-process" (*Physics*, III.6, 206b20-28; italics is mine). As Hussey remarks: "The reasoning here is faulty. If it is granted that there cannot be an actual infinitely extended body, as Aristotle claims to prove in ch. 5, it still does not follow that there cannot be a corresponding *potential* infinite. That would involve the continual, unbounded, expansion of an always finite universe. So Aristotle needs the extra premiss that the size of the universe is not only finite but fixed, or at least of bounded variation" (Hussey, *Aristotle's Physics*, Notes, p. 85). This extra premiss is explicitly supplied by Aristotle in a later passage in which he takes up again the rejection of a potential infinite by addition in magnitude. But even in this passage the inference from a potential infinite by addition to an actual infinite still appears: "... the continuous is divided into infinitely many parts, but there is no infinite in the direction of 'greater'. *For a magnitude in actual operation may exist of any size, of which a magnitude may potentially exist. Since therefore no perceptible magnitude is infinite, there may not be an exceeding of every definite magnitude* – for then there would be something greater than the world" (*Physics*, III.7, 207b16-21; italics is mine). In view of this latter passage in particular, the question arising from Aristotle's inference is sometimes proposed by medieval commentators under the formulation "Utrum contingat esse magnitudinem tantam in actu quanta est in potentia". This is in fact the title of the question on this inference discussed by Wylton. See Wylton, *In Physicam*, III, ff. 43va, lin. 19 ab imo-44va, lin. 9.

[42] Aristotle, *Physics*, III.7, 207b1-15.

[43] Simplicius, *In Physicam*, III, p. 508, lin. 3-9, 13-14: "Ἀλλὰ πῶς φησιν ὅσον γὰρ ἐνδέχεται δυνάμει εἶναι, καὶ ἐνεργείᾳ ἐνδέχεται τοσοῦτον εἶναι; οὐδὲ γὰρ ἐπειδὴ παντὶ ἀριθμῷ δυνατὸν προσθεῖναι, ἤδη καὶ ἐνεργείᾳ ἐστὶν ἄπειρος ἀριθμός, οὐδὲ ἐπειδὴ μὴ ἔστιν

The quotation at the beginning of this passage contains one of the formulations of the inference from a potentially infinite magnitude to an actually infinite magnitude given by Aristotle in his controversial argument.[44] In the rest of the passage, Simplicius explains in detail the asymmetry between the infinite in magnitude and the infinite in number that results from Aristotle's inference. While in number the actual infinite and the potential infinite are two irreducible types of infinity, and neither of the two implies the other, Aristotle claims that in magnitudes a potential infinite implies an actual infinite. On the other hand, as Simplicius objects, there seems to be no reason for this asymmetry. After raising this objection, Simplicius tries in a variety of ways to defend Aristotle's position either by arguing that Aristotle's resoning implies no asymmetry between the infinite in number and that in magnitude, or by finding some explanation for this asymmetry. He acknowledges, however, that none of his attempts is satisfactory, and he ends his discussion leaving as an open problem Aristotle's argument against the potential infinite in magnitudes.[45]

This controversial argument continued to be discussed throughout the medieval tradition. Unlike Simplicius, however, medieval commentators tend to find some positive solution for the difficulties involved in it. In particular, Averroes' treatment of this exegetical problem deserves to be examined in detail because of its influence on some of the early English commentators. Specifically, most of our commentators do not notice any problem at all in Aristotle's argument, and, as we shall see at the end of this section, they assume and use Aristotle's inference from the potential infinite to the actual infinite in magnitudes. On the other hand, those commentators, namely, S, P, and W, who deal explicitly with the problems arising from Aristotle's argument simply repeat the solution proposed by Averroes.

Averroes discusses the problems arising from Aristotle's argument more than once in his commentary on *Physics* III.4-8. He proposes

---

ἐνεργείᾳ ἄπειρος ἀριθμός, ἤδη διὰ τοῦτο κωλύεται ἡ ἐπ' ἄπειρον τοῦ ἀριθμοῦ πρόσθεσις. παντὶ γὰρ τῷ λαμβανομένῳ προσθεῖναι δυνατόν. ὥστε φαίη ἄν τις, κἂν ἄπειρον ἐνεργείᾳ μέγεθος μὴ ᾖ, τί κωλύει δυνάμει εἶναι τῷ δύνασθαι ἐπ' ἄπειρον αὔξεσθαι; ... εἰ δὲ τοῦτο οὕτως ἔχει, οὐ χρὴ ἐκ τοῦ μὴ εἶναι ἄπειρον ἐνεργείᾳ μέγεθος αἰσθητὸν ἀναιρεῖν τὴν ἐπ' ἄπειρον πρόσθεσιν". Simplicius' discussion is analysed in D. J. Furley, "The Greek Commentators' Treatment of Aristotle's Theory of the Continuous", in N. Kretzmann (ed.), *Infinity and Continuity in Ancient and Medieval Thought*, Cornell University Press, Ithaca and London 1982, p. 34-36.

[44] For this formulation, see above note 41.

[45] See Simplicius, *In Physicam*, III, p. 508, lin. 14-509, lin. 20.

two different types of explanation for the asymmetries arising from Aristotle's proof, one of which can be roughly classified as a meta-physical explanation and the other as a logical one.

A "metaphysical" explanation of the asymmetry between the potential infinite by division and the potential infinite by addition in magnitudes is presented by Averroes in t.c. 60. The problem is to explain why a magnitude can be divided to infinity without this process of division leading to an infinitely small magnitude (i.e., to an actual infinite), whereas if a magnitude were infinitely increased, then, it would lead to an infinitely extended magnitude. Averroes' answer goes as follows:

> ... (a) if we were to posit that magnitude can increase to infinity, then the infinite would become actual and then "potency" would be under-stood as it is understood when we say that this thing is a man in poten-cy. Yet, when we posit that a decrease goes on to infinity, no impossi-bility occurs. (b) The cause of this is that decrease is a process towards nothing, the cause of which is matter, whereas increase is a process towards being, the cause of which is form, and infinity is due to matter, just as finiteness is due to form.[46]

Part (a) of this passage indicates the general strategy of Averroes' explanation, which is to distinguish between two kinds of potency involved in the infinite by division and the infinite by addition. The point of the distinction is that only the first kind of potency is legiti-mate within Aristotle's theory of the potential infinite, since it is never completely actualized. Instead, the potency of the potential infinite by addition in magnitude is analogous to a potency to a form, namely, one that can be completely actualized. On the other hand, as Aristo-tle specifies in introducing the potential infinite in *Physics* III.6, this latter kind of potency is not appropriate to the infinite.[47] In part (b), Averroes explains why the potency of infinite division differs so radi-cally from that of infinite addition. This is because – Averroes claims – the process of division is governed by matter, whereas the process of addition is governed by form. In t. c. 68 Averroes extends this

---

[46] Averroes, *In Physicam*, III, t. c. 60, f. 114ra A-B: "... si posuerimus quod magnitu-do potest crescere in infinitum, tunc infinitum exibit in actum, et tunc potentia intel-ligitur sicut intelligitur cum dicimus quod hoc est homo in potentia. Et cum posuer-imus quod diminutio est in infinitum, non accidit impossibile. Et causa in hoc est quoniam diminutio est ire ad nihil, cuius causa est materia, et additio est ire ad esse, cuius causa est forma. Et infinitas invenitur per materiam sicut finitas per formam".

[47] See above, p. 10-11.

explanation to the case of the potential infinite by addition in number. On this point, he relies on Aristotle's doctrine that the process of addition *ad infinitum* in number is granted by the process of division *ad infinitum* in magnitudes.[48] It follows that also the potential infinite by addition in number is ultimately governed by matter and hence is a "legitimate" form of potential infinite.[49]

In the early English tradition, W reformulates, abridges, and simplifies Averroes' metaphysical explanation of Aristotle's inference from the potential infinite by addition in magnitude to the actual infinite and of the resulting asymmetries in Aristotle's theory of the infinite. In connection with the problem of the asymmetry between magnitude and number, this commentator remarks:

> If you argue that, since it is not possible for any given magnitude to give a greater magnitude unless it is possible to give an infinite in act, as it is said in Aristotle's text, therefore, in the same way, it is not possible for any given number to give a greater number unless it is possible to give a number that is infinite in act, and, yet, it is true that for any given number it is possible to give a greater number, it must be said that the two cases are not similar and this inference does not hold, just as the following inference does not hold "for any given magnitude it is possible to take a smaller one; therefore, it is possible that an actual infinite exists", because the process towards division is a process due to the nature of matter, and a process towards matter is not a process towards act, but towards potency. Therefore, it does not follow, if given any number, it is possible to take a greater one, that for this reason there is an infinite number, because addition in number is on the part of matter, and the process towards matter is a process towards potency and not towards act.[50]

---

[48] See Aristotle, *Physics*, III.7, 207b10-11.

[49] Averroes, *In Physicam*, III, t.c. 68, f. 117vb M: "Quemadmodum enim causa in divisione mensurae in infinitum est materia, similiter est causa in additione unitatum in infinitum. Et additio numeri in infinitum est in potentia, non quod additio infinita exeat in actum, ita quod inveniatur numerus in actu infinitus, sed quod additio numquam cesset". See also ibid., at f. 118ra A.

[50] W, III, q. 7, f. 68va, lin. 32-42: "Si arguas quod non contingit quacumque magnitudine accepta finita dare maiorem nisi contingat actu dare infinitum in actu, in littera, ergo a simili non contingit quocumque numero accepto dare maiorem nisi actu numerum infinitum contingit dare, et in veritate omni numero accepto contingit maiorem accipere, dicendum quod non <est> simile nec sequitur, sicut non sequitur "quacumque magnitudine accepta contingit minorem accipere; ergo contingit infinitum actu esse", quia ire ad divisionem est ire per naturam materiae et ire ad materiam non fuit ire ad actum, sed ad potentiam; ideo non sequitur quod, si quocumque numero accepto contingit accipere maiorem, ut (et *ms.*) propter hoc sit numerus

In this argument, W clearly relies on Averroes' idea that both the process of addition in number and the process of division in magnitude are governed by matter, so that the infinity associated with these processes can only be potential because matter is essentially a potency. The process of addition in magnitude, however, is a process towards an act and thus the infinity associated with this process is actual.

Averroes' metaphysical solution in t.c. 60 and in t.c. 68 to the exegetical problem arising from Aristotle's argument against a potential infinite by addition in magnitude was very influential in the thirteenth century. Some echo of it can be found, for instance, in Thomas Aquinas[51] and Giles of Rome.[52] Indeed, it is an original combination of different ingredients of Aristotle's metaphysics of the infinite. Yet Averroes' explanation seems to be inadequate precisely because of its metaphysical character, for it purports to solve in a "metaphysical" way a problem that belongs specifically to the logical and quantitative part of Aristotle's theory of the infinite. The discrepancy between the logical and quantitative nature of the problem and the metaphysical nature of Averroes' solution can be perceived very

---

infinitus, quia haec acceptio numeri in apponendo fuit a parte materiae et vaditio ad materiam est vaditio ad potentiam, non ad actum". Averroes' explanation in t. c. 60 of the asymmetry between the infinites by division and by addition in magnitudes is also found in B, III, q. 8, f. 19vb, lin. 25-31.

[51] Aquinas argues: "Patet etiam ex praemissis ratio quare non oportet numerum tantum esse in actu quantum est in potentia, sicuti hic dicitur de magnitudine, quia additio numeri sequitur divisionem continui, per quam a toto itur ad id quod est in potentia ad numerum. Unde non oportet devenire ad aliquem actum finientem potentiam. Sed additio magnitudinis ducit in actum, ut dictum est" (*In Physicam*, III, lectio 12, p. 194a). The "Averroistic" elements of Aquinas' metaphysical explanation are the connection between the process of addition in number and that of division in magnitudes, the connection between both these processes and potency, and the connection between the process of addition in magnitude and act.

[52] Giles, for instance, explains the asymmetry between the division *ad infinitum* and the addition *ad infinitum* in magnitude as follows: "... quia ergo dividi et accedere ad partialitatem est accedere ad modum materiae, augeri vero et accedere ad totalitatem est accedere ad modum formae, ideo potentia illa qua continuum dividitur est secundum materiam (numerum *ed.*) et respicit actum in fieri, propter quod non oportet, si continuum potest dividi in infinitum, quod aliquando sit actu divisum in infinitum, quia huiusmodi potentialitas, cum sit secundum materiam, non respicit actum in facto esse; sed si magnitudo poterit augeri in infinitum, quia huiusmodi potentialitas esset secundum formam et respiceret actum completum, quia frustra esset potentia nisi posset poni in actu respectu cuius dicitur, si esset in natura potentia ad augmentum in infinitum, quia, ut dictum est, talis potentialitas respicit actum completum et in facto esse, oportet quod esset dare magnitudinem aliquam actu infinitam" (Giles of Rome, *In Physicam*, III, lectio 13, ff. 66vb-67ra).

neatly in the simplified version contained in the passage above from
W. It juxtaposes a precise formulation of Aristotle's controversial
argument in logical terms with remarks on matter, act, and potency,
which seem to be extraneous to the logical setting of the problem.
The general gesture towards matter and form does not lend any
explanatory weight. For instance, it is not at all clear why in magnitude the process of division is governed by matter, while the process
of addition is governed by form. From a quantitative point of view,
both these processes essentially involve the quantitative parts of a
physical magnitude, and the existence of such parts is ultimately due
to matter endowed with quantity. Accordingly, if the process of division is "governed" by matter because it involves parts, for the same
reason also the process of addition should be "governed" by matter.
Furthermore, it is not clear in which sense the potency of the infinite
by division is analogous to that of matter, whereas the potency of the
infinite by addition is analogous to that to a form. From a logical
point of view, the "potencies" involved in these two types of infinity
are exactly the same. Indeed, according to the process-view of Aristotle's potential infinity, these "potencies" must be understood in the
sense that both the process of division and the process of addition are
endless. According to the modal-view, they must be understood in
the sense that the following propositions are true "given any part of a
magnitude, there could exist a smaller/greater part".[53]

It is likely that Averroes himself was aware of the inadequacy of his
metaphysical solution set out in t.c. 60 and 68. At any rate, in t.c. 69
he takes up again the asymmetry between the potential infinite by
addition in magnitude and number[54] and provides a more logical
type of explanation. It is contained in a particularly difficult and
obscure passage. We shall first quote this passage and then provide
expository comment to clarify its meaning:

> (1) But if someone considers this problem, he will see (a) that the addi-
> tion that can be carried out *ad infinitum* and that, if it is posited, it does

---

[53] For the process-view and the modal-view of Aristotle's potential infinite, see p.
11-14.

[54] Averroes, *In Physicam*, III, t. c. 69, f. 118rbE-F: "Sed quaeret aliquis in hac
propositione dicente quod in quacumque quantitate ponatur magnitudo in potentia
in illa quantitate potest poni in actu, in quo differt ab hac propositione, scilicet quod
in quacumque quantitate ponatur aliquis numerus demonstratus in potentia in illa
quantitate potest poni in actu. Unde existimatur quod non est differentia in hoc quod
sit possibile infinitum esse in potentia in numero et in magnitudine, ut dictum est".

not follow that it would lead to an actual infinite, which is impossible, is the addition of any generated part whatsoever whose possibility is different from the possibility of the other parts and all these possibilities are not all parts of a single demonstrated possibility. And this kind of addition is found in motion and time. (b) But in the addition of any part whose possibility is part of a single demonstrated possibility, that possibility, in whatsoever way it is posited in potency, it follows from that that it is found in act in that disposition. For if it were not so, that potency would be in vain. (2) The addition in a given magnitude is of this latter kind. But the addition in number is an addition of the first kind. And the cause of this is that the potencies in the addition of any part of a magnitude are all parts of a single potency. But this is not so in number, because magnitude is one and continuous, whereas number does not have these properties. And in this way the passage in question must be understood.[55]

In the early English tradition, Averroes' explanation in this passage is followed by S and P and is found also in B, the set of questions on the *Physics* very close to Adam of Bocfeld's literal commentary.[56] This explanation, however, was not highly regarded in the second half of the thirteenth century. For instance, it is quickly dismissed by Aquinas[57] and not even mentioned by Giles of Rome. Yet, in our view, in some respects it is more interesting than Averroes' answer in t.c. 60 and 68.

Part (1) of the passage quoted above contains the "logical" side of Averroes' new explanation. There, he distinguishes two kinds of addition and claims that one of them leads to an actual infinite, while the other is admissible, i.e., represents only a potential infinite. Part (2)

---

[55] Ibid., f. 118rbF-vaH: "Sed, cum aliquis consideraverit hoc, videbit quod additio in qua non cessat infinitum esse et non sequitur, si ponatur, ipsam exire in actum, quod est impossibile, est additio cuiuslibet partis generatae cuius possibilitas est alia a possibilitate alterius partis et non sunt omnes partes unius possibilitatis demonstratae. Et hoc est sicut est dispositio in motu et tempore. In additione autem cuiuslibet partis cuius possibilitas est pars unius possibilitatis demonstratae, ista possibilitas, quomodocumque ponatur in potentia, sequitur ex ea ut inveniatur in actu in illa dispositione, et, si non, contingeret ut potentia esset frustra. Et additio quae est in magnitudine demonstrata est de genere istius additionis et additio quae est in numero est de genere primae additionis. Et causa in hoc quod potentiae quae sunt in additione uniuscuiusque partis partium mensurae omnes sunt partes unius potentiae et non est ita in numero, quoniam, sicut mensura est una et continua et numerus non, secundum hoc igitur intelligendus est iste locus".

[56] S, III, q. 16, f. 46ra, lin. 4-24; P, III, q. 34, f. 75rb, lin. 35-44; B, III, q. 6, f. 19ra, lin. 30-51.

[57] See Thomas Aquinas, *In Physicam*, III, lectio 12, p. 194a.

shows how this general distinction must be applied to the case of magnitude and number.

The two kinds of addition distinguished by Averroes are:

(a) An addition in which the possibility of each added element (i.e., the possibility of adding a given element) is different from the possibility of any other element, and these many different possibilities are not parts of a single possibility.

(b) An addition in which the possibilities corresponding to different elements are numerically distinct, but there is also a single possibility of which these individual possibilities are parts.

Then Averroes claims that an addition of type (a) does not lead to an actual infinity, whereas an addition of type (b) does lead to it. On this point, Averroes seems to be definitively right. To see why this is so, however, it is helpful to introduce some elements of the "propositional analysis"[58] of the potential infinite and of the actual infinite (i.e., the logical analysis of the propositions which express these kinds of infinite) and to try to apply such a propositional analysis to Averroes' distinction between addition of type (a) and type (b).

We denote by S a series that is potentially infinite by addition, for instance, the series of the parts added to a given magnitude. The claim that S is potentially infinite by addition can be translated in the following sentence: (i) 'given any part x in S added to a magnitude, another part y in S *can* still be added'.[59] Notice that in proposition (i) the modal verb 'can' is within the scope of the universal quantifier. Translated in Averroes' terms, this means that there are just as many possibilities as there are items in the series, and not some additional possibility of which these many possibilities are parts. Thus, proposi-

---

[58] This term is introduced by Murdoch to indicate, more generally, the logical analysis of physical problems, typical of the fourteenth century. See especially J. E. Murdoch, "Propositional Analysis in the Fourteenth-Century Natural Philosophy", *Synthese*, 40 (1979), p. 117-146.

[59] I am following the propositional formulation of Aristotle's potential infinite and actual infinite given by Charlton in "Aristotle's Potential Infinites", p. 140-142. Charlton formulates (i) in more general terms, namely 'For all x, if x is a member of S, there could be a y such that y is a member of S, and y is R to x', where S is any series which is a potential infinite and R is a relation which is transitive and irreflexive. In particular, if R is the relation 'being greater than', then this proposition expresses the potential infinite by addition; if R is the relation 'being smaller than', it expresses the potential infinite by division.

tion (i) seems to express in logical terms Averroes' idea of the addition of type (a). As to the addition of type (b), its crucial difference from type (a), according to Averroes, is that there is a single possibility which encompasses all the items in the series. Thus, one may suggest that addition of type (b) is expressed in logical terms by transposing in proposition (i) the modal 'can' and the universal quantifier. Such a transposition yields the sentence: (ii) 'It is possible that, for every part x in S, there *is* another part y in S'.[60] In sentence (ii) there is only "one possibility", since the modal verb or modal determination is not within the scope of a universal quantifier. If addition of type (b) is expressed by sentence (ii), then Averroes is certainly right to claim that it leads to an actual infinite or makes possible an actual infinite. Take the assertoric sentence (*propositio de inesse* in medieval terms) corresponding to (ii), namely (iii) 'For every x in S there is another item y in S'. In the case of the series of numbers, (iii) already expresses the actual infinity of this series, for it means that for every integer n *there is* an integer n+1.[61] In the case of magnitudes, it means that, given any finite magnitude A, *there is* a finite magnitude B greater than A. This also implies that there is a magnitude greater than every finite magnitude, i.e., an actually infinite magnitude. For instance, if the magnitudes in this infinite addition are of a fixed size, (iii) implies that there are infinitely many magnitudes of the same size. Then the magnitude formed by these infinitely many magnitudes is actually infinite. So, in fact, (ii) means (or at least implies) 'It is possible for an actual infinite to exist'.

In part (2) of the passage from t.c. 69, Averroes makes the further claim that addition in numbers is of type (a) and addition in magnitudes is of type (b). In proving this claim, however, he abandons the logical approach to the problem of part (1) and appeals to non-logical and non strictly quantitative properties of magnitude and number.

---

[60] It can be remarked, however, that in other passages Averroes seems to take (ii) and not (i) as expressing potential infinites by addition and division in magnitudes. For instance, this appears in the formulation of a question he raises in t. c. 60 at the end of his exposition of Aristotle's passage from *Physics* III.6 quoted in note 41: "Sed est hic quaestio non modica. Quemadmodum enim unum principiorum quae ponit Geometer est quoniam possibile est accipere ad omnem lineam lineam minorem illa, similiter etiam ponit, quoniam possibile est accipere ad omnem lineam lineam maiorem illa. Additio igitur mensurae procedet in infinitum, sicut eius diminutio" (f. 114raC).

[61] See Hussey, *Aristotle's Physics*, Notes, p. 88.

Indeed, he resorts to a "formal" difference between these two kinds of quantity. Magnitude insofar as it is continuous is homogeneous and essentially one, whereas number insofar as it is discrete is a mere aggregate which lacks intrinsic unity. These different properties of continuous and discrete quantities seem to be transferred by Averroes to the possibilities involved in the processes of addition in these two kinds of quantities. The possibilities corresponding to the parts of magnitude to be added are as homogeneous as these parts are, and therefore can all be parts of a single possibility, in the same way in which these parts can form a single continuous magnitude. The possibilities corresponding to the unities added to a number are heterogeneous, and hence cannot be part of a single possibility.

Part (2) of Averroes' explanation in t.c. 69 is very weak, since it is based on a loose analogy between the logical properties of the modal determinations involved in additions of type (a) and of type (b) and the "formal" properties of continuous and discrete quantities. Thus, even Averroes' "logical" explanation of Aristotle's controversial argument is not very convincing.

In fact, as Simplicius had suspected, Aristotle's argument seems faulty. For this argument is based on the inference:

> (PA) If, for every given magnitude, it is possible that a greater magnitude exists, then it is possible that an infinitely extended magnitude exists.

However, inference (PA) (that is, from potential infinite to actual infinite) is not logically sound, as the propositional analysis that we have applied to the "logical" part of Averroes' explanation of t.c. 69 shows. The antecedent of this inference is, formally, a sentence of type (i) "For every x in S, there can be another item y in S", in which the universal quantifier occurs before the modal verb "can", whereas the consequent can be expanded in a sentence of type (ii) "It is possible that, for every x in S, there is another item y in S", in which the modal determination occurs before the universal quantifier. The inference from (i) to (ii), however, is formally invalid, because of the transposition between the universal quantifier and the modal determination on which it is based.[62] Furthermore, even apart from these

---

[62] See for instance Charlton, "Aristotle's Potential Infinites", p. 141. As Charlton explains, the difference between (i) and (ii) is fundamentally that between (i') p is pos-

logical aspects, it is quite clear that the antecedent of (PA) simply implies that every magnitude can be increased *ad infinitum*. From this follows the unwanted consequence for Aristotle that the extension of the universe can eventually be exceeded, but not that there exists an actually infinite magnitude, as Aristotle contends in his controversial argument.[63]

Yet, in the early phase of the reception of Aristotle's theory of the infinite, inference (PA) enjoyed some success. The case of the early English commentators G^1, M^3, and W is very instructive in this regard. They all treat the issue extensively and include a question on the problem of the *existence* of an actual infinite in magnitudes and one on the *possibility* of this kind of infinite. And among the *pro* arguments of the latter question there are some that are based precisely on the inference (PA).[64] It is interesting to see how our commentators deal with the most significant examples of these kinds of arguments.

The general logical structure of the arguments in question is illus-

---

sible and q is possible and (ii') it is possible (p and q). A typical counterexample to the validity of the inference from (i') to (ii') is when p and q stands for contingent facts which cannot hold simultaneously. For instance, it is possible that Socrates sits and it is possible that Socrates stands, but it is not possible that Socrates sits and stands.

[63] This point is shown very clearly by William of Ockham: "... circa probationem Philosophi qua probat quod non potest omni magnitudine esse maior quia tunc esset infinitum in actu, est sciendum quod ista consequentia non est formalis et evidens 'omni magnitudine potest esse maior magnitudo, ergo est aliqua magnitudo infinita', nec̄ etiam sequitur quod possit esse magnitudo infinita, nec Philosophus intendit talem consequentiam facere. Quod enim talis consequentia non valet, patet. Quia quantumcumque posset fieri maior magnitudo et magis maior, ex quo tamen ille processus non poterit terminari, semper acceptum poterit esse finitum, immo nisi una additione addatur infinitum, semper acceptum de necessitate erit finitum. Quia quaero: aut processus ille finietur aut non finietur; si finietur, ergo non vadit in infinitum, sed aliquando erit una additio unius infiniti vel totum erit finitum; si non stabit sed ibit in infinitum, ergo quocumque addito semper totum acceptum erit finitum et per consequens si numquam processus finietur, numquam pervenietur ad infinitum, et ita quamvis sine fine fieret additio, numquam tamen esset infinitum in actu sicut numquam ille processus finiretur." (*In Pysicam*, III, cap. 13, p. 559, lin. 138-154). At the beginning of this passage, Ockham claims that inference (PA) is not that intended by Aristotle. He adds that: "Sed Philosophus intendit istam consequentiam 'omni magnitudine est maior magnitudo, ergo est aliqua magnitudo infinita'" (ibid., lin. 155-156). He maintains that this latter consequence is necessary. On this point Ockham is certainly right, as the propositional analysis of the actual and of the potential infinite shows (see above p. 109). More questionable, however, is Ockham's attempt to save Aristotle's position by maintaining that Aristotle's argument is based on the latter consequence.

[64] G^1, III, q. 2, f. 141va, lin. 11 ab imo-vb, lin. 5; q. 3, ff. 141vb, lin. 5-142ra, lin. 12. M^3, III, q. 3, f. 155ra, lin. 5-46; q. 4, f. 155ra, lin. 20 ab imo-rb, lin. 9 ab imo. W, III, q. 4, f. 67ra, lin. 8-rb, lin. 23; q. 5, ff. 67rb, lin. 24-68ra, lin. 19.

trated by the following argument taken from W's question "Whether it is possible that magnitude is infinite":

> (1) ... given whatsoever magnitude, it is possible to take a greater one; but this would not happen unless it were possible for a magnitude to be infinite; therefore etc..[65]

The major premise claims that magnitude is potentially infinite by addition, i.e., that sentence (i) above is true for magnitudes. The minor premise expresses precisely inference (PA). For the validity of the minor premise, W invokes Aristotle's authority.[66] He then rejects argument (1) by claiming that the major premise is false.[67] We have already seen that the major premise is certainly false in Aristotle's view, for whom it is impossible to increase the size of the universe.[68] But what happens in a more flexible universe in which the major premise holds?

W considers the case of mathematical magnitudes, for which he admits that this premise does hold. He admits, however, that in this case also argument (1) holds.[69] This shows that he takes for granted the validity of inference (PA).

Another relevant case considered in our commentaries is what happens when argument (1) is formulated in a theological context. The theological version of (1) is based on the principle, stated by Aristotle in *Physics* VIII.10, that an infinite power (*virtus*) can exist only in an infinite body.[70] The principle holds for those powers whose quantity is proportional to the extension of the body in which they inhere.

---

[65] W, III, q. 5, f. 67rb, lin. 27-29: "... accepta quacumque magnitudine, possibile est maiorem accipere; sed hoc non esset nisi contingeret magnitudinem esse infinitam; ergo etc.".

[66] Ibid., lin. 29-31: "Minor patet in littera: non contingit extollere omnem magnitudinem finitam accipiendo maiorem nisi actu contingit (contingit *rep. ms.*) ponere infinitum". W seems to refer to the first passage from *Physics* III.6 quoted in note 41.

[67] More precisely, in order to reject the major premise he uses Aristotle's principle according to which an infinite by addition can take place in the natural world only as the inverse of a process of division. But then, as we have explained at the beginning of this section, it is not true that the size of any magnitude can be exceeded through such an addition. See W, III, q. 5, f. 67rb, lin. 29-41; vb, lin. 28-32.

[68] Although, as Hussey remarks, nowhere does Aristotle actually prove this impossibility. See Hussey, *Aristotle's Physics*, Introduction, p. xxiii.

[69] Indeed, he concedes that mathematical magnitude, i.e., magnitude considered in abstraction from the form of the natural body with which it is necessarily joined, can be infinite. See W, III, q. 5, ff. 67rb, lin. 39-va, lin. 3; 67vb, lin. 32-68ra, lin. 9.

[70] Aristotle, *Physics*, VIII.10, 266a24-b6.

The power considered by Aristotle is the capacity of producing motion, while the power considered by our commentators is the "metaphysical power" of being good which inheres in the heavenly body.

Unlike God, the heavens certainly have a finite goodness, but, as P argues, one may ask:

> (2) ... whether the Creator can give it a greater goodness than that it actually has or not. If not, then the Creator is not omnipotent. If he can, since he can give it a greater goodness *ad infinitum*, then the heavens could have an infinite goodness and thus an infinite power.[71]

But then from Aristotle's principle it follows that the heavenly body can have infinite extension. As argument (2) makes clear, it seems that this theological version of argument (1) cannot be rejected by denying that the goodness of the heavenly body constitutes a potential infinite by addition, i.e., by denying that it can be increased *ad infinitum*. For this would apparently contradict the omnipotency of God. Consequently, the only alternative left seems to be the rejection of inference (PA). According to P, however, this is not really the case. His answer is:

> (3) ...that God from his own part can make the world better *ad infinitum*. But from the part of the world itself he cannot make the world better *ad infinitum*, since the world cannot receive an infinite goodness, and therefore it does not have an infinite power.[72]

We can reformulate the distinction introduced in (3) by means of the sentences (a) 'God can make the world better *ad infinitum*' and (b) 'The world can be made better *ad infinitum*'. According to P, (a) is true, and so the omnipotency of God is saved. But (b) is false. There is, however, a problem with the argument adduced by P against (b). For this argument is exactly based on inference (PA): if (b) were true, the world could receive an infinite goodness. This clearly shows that

---

[71] P, III, q. 16, f. 71va, lin. 1-4: "... aut ergo potest dare maiorem quam habet aut non. Si non, ergo non est omnipotens. Si sic, ergo, cum in infinitum posset ei dare maiorem bonitatem et maiorem, caelum potuit habere bonitatem infinitam et sic virtutem infinitam".

[72] Ibid., lin. 28-31: "... quod Deus potest in infinitum meliorare mundum quantum est a parte sui. Quantum est tamen a parte ipsius mundi, non potest ipsum in infinitum meliorare, quia non est receptivum bonitatis infinitae, et ideo non est virtutis infinitae".

P accepts inference (PA). But then the solution of P to argument (2) begs the question.

Argument (2) is also proposed by G[1], M[3], N, and W. Their discussion shows that all of them seem to accept inference (PA) and accordingly experience very similar difficulties to that encountered in P. In the end, they leave argument (2) without a satisfactory answer.[73]

As has been suggested, the problems related to the acceptance of inference (PA) come out most explicitly in a theological context, because there the possibility of a potential infinite by addition is always granted. So one might expect these problems to be emphasized even more in the case of numbers, for the growth *ad infinitum* of numbers is granted in a very natural way within Aristotle's universe. Indeed, the infinite divisibility of a continuum does not grant the possibility of growth *ad infinitum* of magnitudes, as we have seen at the beginning of this section, but it does grant that of numbers. However large the number of parts already divided from a continuum might be, it can still be enlarged, since the continuum can always be further divided. Yet, our commentators do not mention the problems we have encountered with argument (2) in the case of numbers. In particular, they do not try to show that numbers can be actually infinite owing to the fact that they are potentially infinite by addition and, more generally, they do not use inference (PA) in their treatment of infinity in numbers.[74] This suggests that the early English commentators do not have a firm grasp of the logic of the potential and actual infinite. Furthermore, it confirms that, like Averroes himself, they tend to assume that inference (PA) is valid only for magnitudes and not for numbers. Unlike Averroes, however, they do not make any original attempt to explain this controversial asymmetry in Aristotle's theory of the infinite.

3. *The Infinite in Number*

The problem of the infinite in number is much debated by the early English commentators. They all agree that number as considered by Aristotle is only potentially infinite. Some of them, however, maintain that there is also a more general kind of number which is, in fact,

---

[73] Cfr. G[1], III, q. 3, f. 141vb, lin. 18-35; M[3], III, q. 4, f. 155ra, lin. 50-61; rb, lin. 12-23; N, III, q. 9, f. 137va, lin. 2-26, 41-47; W, III, q. 5, f. 67va, lin. 3-vb, lin. 14.

[74] The only exception is the passage from W quoted in note 69.

actually infinite. The sparse command of the logical aspects of Aristotle's theory of the infinite exhibited by our commentators and the fragmentary character of their discussion make it difficult to reconstruct the details of their arguments and to reach an exhaustive and coherent view of the different assumptions at work in them. Despite these obstacles to a full understanding, the debate about the infinite in number in the early English tradition is of great interest and originality. And it is so for two main reasons:

(1) The type of arguments from which the debate arises.
(2) The ontological commitments about number from which the infinitist position supported by some of our commentators seems ultimately to derive.

As to point (1), it can be remarked that the traditional source of objections to Aristotle's claim that every kind of number is only potentially infinite is represented by Aristotle's doctrine of the eternity of the world. Indeed, the most relevant discussion about the infinity of number before the time of our commentators goes back to the Greek commentator Philoponus. The context of Philoponus' discussion is exactly the cosmological problem of the eternity of the world. Philoponus follows Aristotle in maintaining that number is only potentially infinite, but he argues that the Aristotelian finitism about number could not be saved if the world were eternal, for then the number of men who lived in this beginningless world would be actually infinite. The same would be true for the number of revolutions of the sun and other planets, and so on.[75] These "cosmological" examples of an actually infinite number are essentially the only ones considered by Philoponus. And they hardly appear in the early English debate on the infinity of number. Instead, in this debate the dominant source of arguments in favour of an actually infinite number is Aristotle's theory of the infinite divisibility of a continuum. This "innovative" aspect of the early English debate will be presented in detail in section 3.1.

Point (2) hints at another very original, though latent, aspect of the debate, which we shall try to make explicit in section 3.2.

---

[75] Philoponus' "infinity" arguments against the eternity of the world and Simplicius' reply to them are discussed by R. Sorabji in *Time, Creation and the Continuum*, p. 210-224, and Id., "Infinity and the Creation", in R. Sorabji (ed.), *Philoponus and the Rejection of Aristotelian Science*, Duckworth, London 1987, p. 164-178.

3.1 *The Finitist Position and the Infinitist Position About Number*

In the debate under discussion, there is a main argument that gives rise
to the dispute and on which the commentators are sharply divided.
The argument in question is usually presented as a counterexample to
Aristotle's general principle that any kind of infinite exists only in
potency, which is equivalent to existing *in fieri*.[76] This standard formula
used in the medieval tradition to indicate Aristotle's theory of infinity is
in itself quite vague and ambiguous. In the case of numbers, however,
Aristotle makes it sufficiently clear what this formula means. He claims
that the infinity of numbers is to be accounted for by the divisibility *ad
infinitum* of a continuum. The number of parts actually divided from a
continuum is always finite, but it can always be increased, since a continuum can be further divided.[77] Our commentators feel that Aristotle's
analysis of the relation between infinity in numbers and the infinite
divisibility of a continuum is, as it stands, somewhat incomplete, for it
takes into account only the parts actually divided from a continuum. A
continuum, however, also has parts of a different kind, namely, its
potential parts which do not yet actually exist, but can be brought into
existence by further division. So one might still ask whether the potential parts of a continuum are finitely many and whether they actually
have a number. These questions are occasioned by the argument
debated by our commentators. M[3] formulates it as follows:

> (1) ... (i) the continuum has infinitely many parts in potency; (ii) there-
> fore, its parts have infinitely many potencies; (iii) therefore, the number
> of potencies is infinite.[78]

---

[76] When applied to the infinite, the expression 'in potentia' is considered as equivalent to 'in fieri' and the expression 'in actu' as equivalent to 'in factum esse'. This
derives from Aristotle's description of the way in which the infinite exists in potency.
As we said in the *Introduction* (see above, p. 11), Aristotle specifies that this is not the
way in which a statue exists in potency: the statue can also exist in act, whereas the
infinite can only exist in potency. Rather, the infinite has the mode of being proper
to days and athletic contests, i.e., in medieval terms of things which are *in fieri* and
not *in factum esse*. In fact, Aristotle's potential infinite is always related to a process of
addition or division. For an analysis of the difficult passage of *Physics* III.6 (206a14-
206b2) where the potentiality of the infinite is explained see especially Hussey, *Aristotle's Physics*, Notes, p. 82-83; Charlton, "Aristotle's Potential Infinites", p. 140-141.
[77] Aristotle, *Physics*, III.7, 207b10-15.
[78] M[3], III, q. 8, f. 156rb, lin. 12-13: "... infinitae sunt partes continui in potentia;
ergo infinitae potentiae sunt partium; igitur numerus potentiarum est infinitus". See
also P, III, q. 19, f. 72rb, lin. 5-7; M[1], III, q. 7, f. 111rb, lin. 12-19; G[1], III, q. 6, f.
142rb, lin. 37-40; N, III, q. 14, f. 139va, lin. 31-34; W, III, q. 6, f. 68ra, lin. 29-32.

Premise (i) claims that the undivided parts of a continuum are infinitely many, but these parts exist only in potency, i.e., they are mere possibilities.[79] Indeed, they are actualized only when the continuum is actually divided. But then at any time only finitely many of them are actualized. Thus, they are infinitely many only as possibilities, that is, as premise (ii) claims, there are infinitely many possibilities or potencies in a continuum. In short, the point of M[3]'s argument is the following: Aristotle stresses that because the continuum has infinitely many parts *in potency* there can be *no actual* infinity; M[3] remarks that, although there is *no actual infinity of parts*, there is an *actually infinite number of potencies*.

All our commentators seem substantially to agree on premises (i) and (ii). The matter of contention is rather the inference from premises (i)-(ii) to conclusion (iii), about the infinity of the number of the potencies. More precisely, the question is whether the potencies corresponding to the undivided parts of the continuum have a number, or, as our commentators often put it, whether they have a number in act, despite the fact that they are potencies. If they actually have a number, since this is the number of a 'collection' of infinitely many possibilities, then it is also an actually infinite number. If they do not have a number, then argument (1) is not conclusive and hence is not a counterexample to Aristotle's claim that number is only potentially infinite. G[1] and M[3] are in favour of the first alternative, S, P, M[1], W in favour of the second,[80] whereas N reports both alternatives but

---

[79] An interesting analysis of the problem of the potential or undivided parts of the continuum in Aristotle is given by Charlton, in "Aristotle's Potential Infinites", p. 131-140. In particular Charlton (p. 134-135) is reluctant to ascribe to Aristotle the view that the infinite divisibility of a continuum implies that infinitely many parts exist in it as possibilities. This view, however, seems to be accepted by our commentators. In the fourteenth-century English tradition, Ockham even maintains that an undivided continuum contains infinitely many parts which are to some extent in act. Ockham holds that all parts of actually existent things, like continua, actually exist, although these parts are not separately existing wholes. On Ockham's treatment of the infinite divisibility of the continuum, see J. E. Murdoch, "William of Ockham and the Logic of Infinity and Continuity", in *Infinity and Continuity*, p. 183-201.

[80] S in fact does not discuss argument (1). Nevertheless he sides with P, M[1], and W on the problem of the number of potentially existing things. For instance, he raises the following objection to Aristotle's doctrine that the infinite does not exist in act: "... numerus potest actu esse indifferenter in his quae sunt potentia et quae sunt sub actu; sed in potentia sunt actu infinita; ergo erunt infinita in actu in his quae sunt actu et, si hoc, possunt accipi; quare etc. Probatio antecedentis: a Deo numerantur aliqua in potentia sicut in actu, sicut duo in potentia, tria, quattuor, quinque etc.; iste autem numerus actu est, licet numerentur ea quae sunt in potentia, et ita numerus

takes no definite position.[81] We shall refer to the first alternative as to the infinitist position and to the second one as to the finitist position.

A variation of argument (1) occurs in the earlier questions on the *Physics* by Richard Rufus of Cornwall.[82] Rufus seems to accept this argument and hence can be regarded as an exponent of the infinitist position. Historically, Rufus is certainly a source of the debate we are examining and apparently had a direct influence on M^3.[83] Yet, his short discussion of the actual infinite in number does not entirely match the central topic of this debate. Indeed, the problem of whether a collection of potentially existing things has an actual number is not clearly addressed by Rufus.[84] In what follows, by 'expo-

---

infinitus erit" (III, q. 9, f. 44va, lin. 14-21). He replies that the potencies are not numbered insofar as potencies; having a number or being numbered presupposes a discretion and therefore some form of actuality: "... dico quod bene possunt numerari ea quae sunt in potentia, sed secundum quod subiacet signatio reducitur illud quod est in potentia aliquo modo ad actum, cum ibi sit quodammodo discretio, distinctio, signatio et ita statim est ibi actualitas, quia ubi est discretio et signatio ibi erit secundum hoc [erit] actualitas; et ita considerantur secundum quod in actu sunt et non secundum quod in potentia sunt, et ita non concludit ratio" (ibid., f. 44vb, lin. 6-14).

[81] See N, III, qq. 14-15, ff. 139va, lin. 19-140ra, lin. 49.

[82] Rufus, *In Physicam*, III, f. 6ra, lin. 24-28: "De infinito in numero sive in discretis dubitatur sic: in hoc plano sive in hac superficie sunt infinitae figurae, quia qua ratione una et alia, et sic omnis superficies est a natura; natura ergo facit in hac superficie infinitas figuras; ergo numerus harum figurarum est infinitus, et ille numerus est sicut in factum esse; ergo infinitum est actu". A version of Rufus' argument is also found in Roger Bacon. See *In Physicam*, IV, p. 148, lin. 5-12: "Item, in unoquoque corpore, ut in lapide, sunt infinite figure in potentia, ut figura triangularis et quadrangularis et sic in infinitum, unde ibi sunt propositiones infinite actu per quas infinitum actu cum figuris; set propositiones nichil sunt; ergo oportet quod fundentur in aliqua natura reali; quare erit infinitum in actu quod erit aliqua natura realis, et ita videtur quod sit ponere infinitum actu, quod est quantitas discreta". This passage is probably corrupt but the argument seems to infer the existence of an actually infinite number from the existence of infinitely many propositions, those that signify the existence of infinitely many figures in a continuous body. Bacon rejects this argument by denying that the human intellect can form infinitely many propositions. See Roger Bacon, *In Physicam*, IV, p. 148, lin. 27-32. Like Rufus, Bacon does not seem to focus the problem addressed by our commentators and, despite his rejection of the argument quoted, he cannot be regarded strictly speaking as an exponent of the finitist position.

[83] See below, note 89.

[84] After formulating the argument quoted above in note 82, Rufus is mainly concerned with the problem of the *pertransibilitas* of an actual infinite arising from it. One of the senses of the term 'the infinite' distinguished by Aristotle in the dialectical phase of his inquiry is 'something which cannot be traversed'. See Aristotle, *Physics*, III.4, 204a4-6. Yet, the argument in question seems to show that the actual infinity of the figures potentially existing in the surface has been 'traversed', i.e., in this case, has been produced by nature. Rufus' reply to this objection is, in short, that it is not absurd that this infinite collection of figures has been traversed, because it is con-

nents of the infinitist position' we shall mean only G^1 and M^3.

The exponents of the infinitist position appeal to the principle that the actuality of a number does not depend on the actuality of the things that form the collection in which this number inheres. This is asserted by M^3 in the following argument:

> (2) (i) ... what is common to potentially and actually existing things and to beings and non-beings does not receive its actuality from any of them; but number is of this kind; therefore etc. (ii) Furthermore, the actuality of a number is the discreteness of its units, and there is a discreteness of units in the number of potencies just as in the number of acts.[85]

In the major premise of (i) M^3 lays down a very general criterion, which may perhaps be accepted. The crucial question is how this criterion applies to number and, in particular, in what sense do potentially existing things have a number. M^3 leaves this question without an answer. In part (ii) a more specific criterion for the actuality of number is stated: it must be a collection of distinct units. But again in this case it is not explained in which sense this criterion is satisfied when the units in question are potencies or possibilities. In fact, from an Aristotelian perspective, this criterion does not seem to be satisfied by potencies as such, because these can apparently be distinguished only when they are referred to the corresponding acts. For instance, the potency to being black is distinct from the potency to being white only in so far as black is distinct from white. This Aristotelian principle is used in the reply to argument (1) given by P, an exponent of the finitist position:

> (3) ... it must be said that number is a discrete quantity, whose parts are mutually distinct and separate. And since only act divides and distinguishes, as Aristotle says in the seventh Book of the *Metaphysics*, therefore, the things which are numbered insofar as they are numbered must have some actuality. But potency does not have an act in itself, unless it is compared to its form. Similarly it is not distinct from another potency unless it is compared to its act. Therefore, when it is said that the potencies or the parts in a continuum are infinite in

---

tained in something finite, namely a surface. See Rufus, *In Physicam*, III, f. 6ra, lin. 28-rb, lin. 2.

[85] M^3, III, q. 8, f. 156rb, lin. 26-30: "... quod indifferenter est rerum existentium in potentia et in actu et entium et non entium non contrahit actualitatem ab aliquo eorum; sed talis est numerus; quare etc. Et praeter hoc actualitas numeri est discretio suarum unitatum, et est discretio unitatum in numero potentiarum sicut actuum". See also G^1, III, q. 6, f. 142rb, lin. 46-49.

potency, it does not follow from this that the number of the potencies
is actually infinite, since the potencies are only numbered by the comparison to the act, as to the actual division of this or that part. And
since these acts cannot be infinitely many in act, therefore nor can the
number of potencies be infinite, unless only in potency.[86]

In this passage, P offers an interesting integration of Aristotle's analysis of the relation between infinity in numbers and the divisibility *ad
infinitum* of the continuum. He takes from Aristotle that the parts
actually divided from a continuum are always finite or equivalently
that the divisions of the continuum actually made are finite. To deal
with the case of the undivided parts or of the potencies corresponding
to the undivided parts, he appeals to the principle that a number is
ascribed not to a mere multiplicity, but to a multiplicity in which
each of its members is actually or formally distinct from each of the
other members. According to this principle, potencies in general form
a multiplicity having a number only if they can be related to some
acts and described in terms of these acts. But the only acts to which
the potencies of the parts of the continuum are related are the acts of
division and, according to Aristotle, these are finite.

There is clearly another way of assigning a number to the undivided parts of a continuum, that is, through a conceptual division, namely, by counting. Then, of course, one can only count finitely many
potential parts.[87] This is, in short, the reply to argument (1) given by
Geoffrey of Aspall in the following passage, in which he systematically
distinguishes the senses in which a number is said to exist in act:

(4) ... it must be said that a number can exist in act in two ways: (i)
either in such a way that it actually inheres in things which are divided

---

[86] P, III, q. 19, f. 72va, lin. 2-9: "... dicendum quod numerus est quantitas discreta,
cuius partes sunt distinctae et separatae ad invicem. Et quia solus actus, ut dicitur in
septimo, dividit et distinguit, ideo quae numerantur secundum quod huiusmodi
quandam debent habere actualitatem. Potentia autem non habet actum de se nisi
prout ad formam suam comparatur; similiter nec habet distinctionem ab alia potentia nisi prout comparatur ad suos actus. Cum igitur dicitur quod potentiae vel partes
in continuo sunt infinitae in potentia, non sequitur propter hoc quod numerus potentiarum sit actu infinitus, quia non numerantur potentiae nisi per comparationem ad
actum, ut ad actualem divisionem huius partis vel illius. Et quia isti actus non possunt
esse infiniti numero actualiter, ideo nec est numerus potentiarum infinitus nisi solum
in potentia".
[87] Aristotle's 'logical' argument against an actually infinite number is based on the
principle that number or what has a number can be counted. See Aristotle, *Physics*,
III.5, 204b7-10.

(*signata*) and distinct one from the other. Aristotle wants number to be in act in this way, since he claims that number increases according to the actual division of the continuum, and in this sense number is not infinite. (ii) In another way number exists in act, because it is in the act of our marking off or counting. And this can be in two ways: (a) either by counting the multiplicity taken as a whole. And in this way number can be infinite. For <in this sense> it is well said that in this continuum infinitely many points exist. (b) Or by counting the single discrete elements one by one in such a way that each of these elements in itself is made distinct through our act. And in this latter way it is impossible that something is infinite <in number>.[88]

The main distinction introduced by Aspall is that between (i) number as an accident that inheres in a collection of extramental things and (ii) number as a mental process of counting. When number is taken in sense (i), then – Aspall implicitly assumes – the extramental things in which it inheres must be physically separated and distinct from each other as the divided parts of the continuum. The potential parts of the continuum, however, are not things of this kind, and so they can have a number only in sense (ii), i.e., in the sense that we can count them. It is clear that we can count the totality of these parts only in a very improper sense, without singling out each of its members. The mental process of counting is necessarily finite, as is the physical process of dividing the continuum.

These objections are not explicitly answered by the infinitists G^1 and M^3. Their position, however, becomes clearer if one examines other arguments adduced by M^3 to reinforce the claim that even potentially existing things have a number. In the following proof, in

---

[88] M^1, III, q. 7, f. 111va, lin. 26-34: "... dicendum quod numerum esse in actu contingit dupliciter: vel ita quod sit actualiter in rebus signatis et distinctis invicem. Et sic vult Aristoteles quod numerus sit in actu, quia dicit numerum crescere secundum actualem divisionem continui, et isto modo non est numerus infinitus; alio modo est numerus in actu, quia est in actu nostrae signationis sive numerationis. Et hoc contingit dupliciter: vel sub una summa numerando, et sic potest esse infinitum. Bene enim dicitur 'infinita puncta sunt in hoc continuo'. Vel sub singulis discretionibus numerando ita quod quodlibet (quaelibet *ms.*) sub proprio numerabili signetur ab actu nostro. Et sic est impossibile aliquid esse infinitum". In connection with this kind of argument, Prof. Marilyn McCord Adams remarks that God is aware of infinitely many *possibilia* as distinct, even though he has no need to count them by any temporally successive process, and she wonders why for Aristotelian commentators divine consciousness of the distinction of *possibilia* is not enough for infinite number. She suggests that this reflects an oddity in Aristotle's notion of number, as if Aristotle makes number an *operational* concept.

particular, he seems to give more precise indications concerning the 'actuality' of number:

> (5) ... the dimension of the number of potentially existing things is the same as that of the <corresponding> actually existing things; but the dimension of a number is in some sense the actuality of number itself; therefore, the number of potentially existing things is a number in act, just as the number of actually existing things.[89]

The dimension of a number is not explicitly defined, but one can infer that it is the number of units of which it is composed. So the dimension of number 10 is ten. The point of argument (5) is probably the following: if one admits that number 10 actually inheres in a collection of ten actually existing things, one also has to admit that it inheres in a collection of ten potentially existing things. Such inherence requires only that the things in question be ten, whatever these things are and, in particular, whether they are potencies or acts.

This same point is emphasized in the following argument:

> (6) ... the number of ten potencies and that of the ten acts corresponding to them are the same; therefore, if either of them is a number in act, so is the other; therefore, potentially existing things have an actual number. I concede this because, since number has its actuality from the discreteness of the potencies as well as from that of the acts, it follows that the number of potentially existing things is an actual number.[90]

---

[89] M³, III, q. 8, f. 156rb, lin. 22-26: "... eadem est dimensio numeri rerum existentium in potentia quanta est rerum existentium in actu; sed dimensio numeri est quodammodo actualitas ipsius numeri; quare numerus rerum existentium in potentia est actu numerus, sicut numerus rerum existentium in actu". This argument is found also in Rufus' commentary. In connection with the problem of the *pertransibilitas* of the infinite (see above, note 84), Rufus examines a solution according to which it is not absurd that the infinite collection of the figures contained in a surface is traversed, because this is a collection of potentially existing things. He replies that this solution is not satisfactory adducing the following argument: "Ostendi potest quod est inconveniens, quia quod natura non potest pertransire infinita hoc est propter magnitudinem dimensionis infiniti; sed figurarum potentialiter existentium dimensio tanta est quanta esset si actu in infinitum esset figurarum actus; ergo sicut non pertransibit infinita actu existentia, sic nec infinita potentialiter existentia" (Rufus, *In Physicam*, III, f. 6ra, lin. 13 ab imo-9 ab imo). It is likely that the argument from M³ is adapted from that used by Rufus. A similar argument, where 'dimensio' is replaced by 'actualitas', is formulated also by G¹: "... tanta est actualitas numeri rerum existentium in potentia quanta est rerum existentium in actu; sed si omnes partes quae sunt potentia in continuo esse<n>t actu, esset numerus earum actu infinitus actu, ipsis existentibus tantum in potentia" (III, q. 6, f. 142rb, lin. 44-46).

[90] M³, III, q. 8, f. 156rb, lin. 35-39: "... idem est numerus decem potentiarum et

As with argument (2) above, this argument does not specify in what sense potencies have discreteness. Thus, the finitist might still raise the following objection that even if one allows that a 'collection' of potencies has a number, this number depends on the fact that the collection of the corresponding acts has a number, since the potencies can be distinguished one from the other only by reference to the corresponding acts. Therefore, since acts are necessarily finite, in Aristotle's view, the 'number' of potencies is also finite. It is not clear how the exponents of the infinitist position might have replied to this objection. Perhaps they would observe that the reference to the corresponding acts is only required to give a formal description of the potencies, and not to make them 'many', i.e., simply numerically distinct.[91] On the other hand, it seems that each potency associated with a point of a continuous line is numerically distinct from any other, for, given any two points a and b, when the potency of dividing the line at a is actualized, that of dividing it at b can still remain unactualized.

This interpretation might suggest that the debate on the actual infinity of number arising from the potential parts of the continuum ultimately reduces to deciding between loose and strict criteria for a multiplicity to have a number. For the exponents of the infinitist position, any multiplicity has a number. For those of the finitist position, this is not true; only a multiplicity of actual things, or at least of things which are actualized by a process of counting, has a number. Reduced to these terms, the problem debated by our commentators

---

actuum decem eis respondentium; quare, si unus est numerus actu, et reliquus; quare rerum existentium in potentia est numerus actualis, quod concedo, quia, cum numerus habeat suam actualitatem a discretione potentiarum sicut actuum, sequitur quod numerus rerum existentium in potentia sit actu numerus". This argument seems to be suggested by a similar one proposed by G^1: "... idem est numerus decem hominum et decem equorum; ergo idem <est> numerus partium infinitarum in potentia et in actu, et sic <in>finitarum potentiarum est infinitus numerus in actu" (III, q. 6, f. 142rb, lin. 49-51). In the chapter on time, we shall see that the principle of the identity of number belonging to collections of different things, used here by G^1, plays an important role in the discussion of the unity of time.

[91] Probably M^3 wants to suggest the idea that the potencies are simply numerically distinct in the following argument: "... actualitas numeratorum est indivisio eorum secundum quod numerata sunt; sed tam rerum existentium actu quam rerum existentium potentia est indivisio actualis. Possum enim dicere quod potentia est in se indivisa et ab aliis divisa. Quare actualitas numeratorum secundum quod numerata sunt est ideo rerum existentium in potentia sicut et in actu; quare actualis numerus eis respondet sicut illis" (III, q. 8, f. 156rb, lin. 30-35).

will be given an apparently very natural solution in the fourteenth
century by William of Ockham and Walter Burley, who distinguish
between loose and strict senses of the term 'number'. If number is
taken in a broad sense (*large loquendo*), then the infinitist position can
be maintained, whereas if it is taken in a strict sense (*stricte loquendo*),
only the finitist position, i.e., that of Aristotle, can be accepted. Burley, in particular, introduces this distinction in response to an objection to Aristotle's 'logical' argument against the possibility of an actually infinite number. Aristotle's argument is that every number is necessarily finite, because only finitely many things can be counted.[92]
Burley agrees that in order to be counted a number must be finite,
but then objects that there are numbers which are infinite, such as
the number of the parts of a continuum.[93] In reply to this objection,
Burley argues:

> It must be said that number is taken in two senses, namely, in a broad
> sense and in a strict sense. Broadly speaking, every multiplicity of dis-
> tinct things of whatsoever sort is said to be a number. If number is tak-
> en in this sense, it is true that there is an infinite number, because the
> number of the parts of a continuum and also the number of points in a
> line is infinite. When we speak of number in this sense, it is not true
> that every number can be counted in act, and the Philosopher does not
> speak here of number taken in this sense. In another way number is
> taken strictly, namely, for every multiplicity of beings that exist per se
> and on their own or that can exist per se and separately. In this sense it
> is true that every number can be counted in act, because every num-
> ber of this kind is finite, and in this way the Philosopher speaks here
> about number.[94]

---

[92] See above, note 87.

[93] Burley, *In Physicam*, III, f. 73rb: "Sed dubitatur hic quia non videtur quod omnis
numerus possit esse actu numeratus, quia numerus partium continui est infinitus,
cum continuum sit divisibile in infinitum, et etiam numerus punctorum existentium
in linea est infinitus, et nullum infinitum potest esse actu numeratum; ergo falsum est
dicere quod omnis numerus potest esse actu numeratus".

[94] Ibid.: "Dicendum quod numerus accipitur dupliciter, scilicet large et stricte.
Large loquendo, sic omnis multitudo quorumcumque distinctorum dicitur numerus.
Et sic accipiendo numerum verum est quod aliquis numerus est infinitus, quia
numerus partium continui et etiam numerus punctorum in linea est infinitus. Et sic
loquendo de numero non est verum quod omnis numerus possit esse actu numeratus,
et sic non loquitur Philosophus hic de numero. Alio modo accipitur numerus stricte,
scilicet pro multitudine entium per se et seorsum existentium vel possibilium per se et
separatim existere. Et sic est verum quod omnis numerus potest esse actu numeratus,
quia omnis talis numerus est finitus; et isto modo loquitur hic Philosophus de

Certainly, there are similarities between Burley's argumentation and certain aspects of the debate in the early English tradition examined in this section. The most remarkable similarity is that both Burley (and Ockham) and the early English commentators take the relevant counterexample to Aristotle's finitism about number from the parts of a continuum. Furthermore, Burley's idea that, strictly speaking, only collections of actually distinct things have a number reflects some of the objections of the finitist position presented above. Yet, Burley's view that the instances of infinite collections can be said to be a number only in a broad sense does at all not reflect the intention of the infinitist position supported by G^1 and M^3. In fact, as we shall see in section 3.2, although G^1 and M^3 eventually resort to a distinction between two kinds of number to save Aristotle's doctrine, it is totally different from that between loose and strict senses of 'number' used by Burley in the passage quoted. Rather, it seems that by relaxing the conditions under which a multiplicity may have a number, G^1 and M^3 intend in some sense to emphasize the ontological independence of number from the collection in which it inheres.

3.2 *Ontological Aspects of the Infinitist Position*

The ontological assumptions about number underlying the discussion of G^1 and M^3 about the infinity of the potential parts of a continuum can be detected in their critique of Aristotle's approach to the problem of infinity in number. More precisely, these two commentators claim that infinity is not a derivative property of number, as Aristotle claims when he asserts that infinity in number stems from the infinite divisibility of a continuum, but that it is an intrinsic property, since it derives from the 'nature' of number itself. This point is presented by G^1 as follows:

---

numero". A similar distinction is used by Ockham. See Ockham, *In Physicam*, III, cap. 15, p. 575, lin. 58-576, lin. 100. It must be remarked, however, that for Ockham the parts of an undivided continuum exist to some extent in act (see note 79). Among our commentators, W admits that these parts have some weak form of actuality but he denies that this is sufficient for the actuality of their number: "... aliquid esse actu in toto suo est dupliciter: aut in actu completo et integro aut in actu imperfecto; partes magnitudinis sunt in magnitudine sub actu secundo modo. Sunt enim sub magnitudine actu per formam quae est actus totius et per consequens partium. Sed quando separantur partes a magnitudine, habent actu formam illam in actu completo quam prius habuerunt sub actu incompleto. Sed non sequitur quod, licet sint in actu aliquo modo in toto, quod propter hoc habeant numerum infinitum sibi correspondentem nisi essent in actu completo" (III, q. 7, f. 68va, lin. 16-23).

(1) Therefore, it can be said that infinity is in number neither in virtue of the division of the parts of magnitude nor in virtue of the intellect carrying on an addition, but in virtue of the fact that the parts of number are ordered according to before and after, in such a way that what is before in number is in potency to what comes after in number; hence, infinity in number derives from that thing from which the endless addition of the next part to the preceding one derives; but this endless addition derives from number itself and not from something else. Hence, according to Aristotle, infinity is in discrete quantities in the same way as in successive things, namely, in virtue of the fact that it is always possible to take something further.[95]

In this passage, 'number' stands for the series of positive integers and 'parts of number' for the individual integers (2, 3 and so on). The infinity of this series, – according to the passage –, consists in the fact that each integer has a successor, in the ordering of the integers, according to which, for any given integer n, there is an integer n+1. G^1 claims that this ordering is not grounded on the fact that, once n parts have been divided from a continuum, an n+1-th part can be divided or on the mental process of counting. Rather, it is a primary and underived property of the series of positive integers, for each number in this series is in potency, i.e., is essentially ordered, to the next.[96]

---

[95] G^1, III, q. 6, f. 142va, lin. 36-42: "Potest igitur dici quod non est infinitas in numero propter decisionem partium magnitudinis nec etiam propter intellectum apponentem, sed propter hoc quod partes numeri ordinantur secundum prius et posterius, ita quod prius in numero est in potentia ad illud quod posterius est in eodem. Unde ab eodem est infinitas in numero a quo est continua appositio partis (partis *ante* appositio *ms.*) posterioris ad partem priorem in infinitum; sed haec continua appositio est ex parte numeri et non aliunde. Unde, secundum Aristotelem, infinitas est in discretis sicut in successivis, in eo quod semper est aliquid accipiendum extra". See also M^3, III, q. 10, f. 157ra, lin. 21-27.

[96] The references at the end of passage (1) to the potency of each number to the next and to Aristotle's definition of the potential infinite (*Physics*, III.6, 207a7-8) might suggest that, according to G^1-M^3, the series of positive integers is potentially infinite in a propositional-analytical sense, namely, that it is expressed not by proposition (a) 'For each integer n there is an integer n+1', but by proposition (b) 'For each integer there can be an integer n+1'. Indeed, propositions (a) and (b) are never explicitly distinguished by G^1 and M^3. Nevertheless, passage (1) makes clear that the increase *ad infinitum* in numbers is not at all based on a temporal process, i.e., on collection of things whose number can increase in time, as for Aristotle, but on a logical one; accordingly, proposition (a) seems more appropriate to express the position of G^1 and M^3 on the type of infinity of number. On the 'atemporal' character of infinite number see also passage (4) quoted below.

In order to make more explicit the contrast between the attitudes of Aristotle and G¹, it is helpful to quote a parenthetical remark made by Aristotle in the passage of *Physics* III.7 in which he proposes the reduction of the infinity of number to the infinite divisibility of the continuum. Aristotle's remark is that

> 'three' and 'two' are derivative names, and similarly each of the other numbers.[97]

But one might ask in what sense 'three' and 'two' are derivative. The reply is that they are derivative with respect to the use of the words 'three' and 'two' as applied to actual collections composed of three and two things respectively, as Hussey explains. This derivation between terms rests on a corresponding relation of ontological dependence between the things denoted by the terms.[98] Hussey illustrates this point:

> (2) The existence of, and our understanding of, the number 3, is derived from the existence of, and our understanding of, actual trios.[99]

Accordingly, since there are no actual collections of infinitely many things, an actually infinite number neither exists nor can be understood. What can be understood and can exist is a finite but continuously increasing number, and this is made possible by the infinite divisibility of the continuum. This suggests that Aristotle's approach to the problem of the infinity of number is a consequence of a reductionist ontology of number.[100] Passage (1) quoted above makes clear that the approach of G¹ differs radically from that of Aristotle, at least as far as the problem of 'our understanding' of an infinite number is concerned. According to G¹, the infinity of number can be understood

---

[97] Aristotle, *Physics*, III.7, 207b8-10.

[98] Hussey, *Aristotle's Physics*, Notes, p. 90. In their interpretation of Aristotle's remark, G¹ and M³ take 'derivate names' even more strictly to indicate that numbers are those associated with collections of parts divided from a continuum. This appears in the following argument that G¹ presents in favour of Aristotle's position: "Quod autem numerus non sit actu infinitus videtur, quia in toto isto capitulo vult Aristoteles quod infinitas sit in discretis per divisionem continui. Dicit enim quod haec nomina 'unum', 'duo' etc. denominativa sunt, quia non separantur a divisione magnitudinis. Ex quo igitur divisio continui non est actu infinita nec erit infinitas in discretis in actu" (III, q. 6, f. 142va, lin. 22-25). See also M³, III, q. 10, f. 157ra, lin. 1-4).

[99] Hussey, *Aristotle's Physics*, Notes, p. 90.

[100] See ibid., p. 89 and Additional Notes, p. 182-184.

from the internal, ordered structure of the series of integers, without any reference to actual collections of things continuously increasing in number. However, the problem of the existence of an infinite number is more delicate and is not dealt with very clearly by G[1]. The preceding discussion about the potential parts of a continuum at least establishes that G[1] is less reductive in his attitude towards the existence of numbers than Aristotle. In the view of G[1], the actual existence of numbers does not depend on the existence of collections of actually existing things.[101] Furthermore, G[1] seems to imply the stronger claim that the existence of an infinite number, in particular, does not require the existence of any sort of collection of infinitely many things:

> (3) (i) ... number is something mathematical which has no position and therefore cannot become something natural; mathematical magnitude, however, can become something natural, since it has a position or a 'situs'. This is why an infinity of numbered things is not required for the infinity of number, whereas magnitude cannot be infinite in act, unless its parts are infinite in act.
>
> (ii) It is evident from this that it does not follow 'number is the measure of numbered things; and measure does not exceed what is measured; therefore, since measured things are not infinite in act, neither is number infinite in act', because in discrete quantities it is not necessary that measured things be infinite in act, if the measure is infinite in act, but this is true only for continuous quantities.[102]

The passage is rather obscure, and we shall attempt only a partial reconstruction of its meaning. In part (i) of this passage, the term 'position' probably refers to the distinction between unit and point, the principles of discrete quantity and continuous quantity respectively: a unit is an indivisible without position, whereas a point is an indivisible with a position. Thus, number considered as a mathematical

---

[101] Yet, it must be conceded that some, for instance Charlton, ascribe to Aristotle the view that for a number to exist is for a set with that number of members to be *possible*. See Charlton, "Aristotle's Potential Infinites", p. 143. This view seems to be similar to that supported by G[1]-M[3] in the discussion on the potential parts of the continuum.

[102] G[1], III, q. 6, f. 142va, lin. 42-48:"... numerus est quoddam mathematicum non habens positionem, ideo non potest fieri naturale; magnitudo tamen mathematica potest, quia habet positionem sive situm. Hinc est quod ad infinitatem numeri non exigitur infinitas numeratorum, magnitudo autem actu infinita non potest esse nisi suae partes sint actu infinitae. Ex hoc patet quod non sequitur 'numerus est mensura numeratorum, et mensura non excedit mensuratum; ergo, cum mensura<ta> non sunt actu infinita, nec numerus', quia in discretis non necesse est mensurata esse infinita actu, licet mensura sit actu infinita, sed solum habet veritatem in continuis".

entity, that is, as a collection of units, cannot be instantiated as such in the physical world, since this world is characterized by entities having a position (physical bodies).[103] What about numbered things, i.e., the collection of things having a number? In (3) G[1] seems to adhere firmly to Aristotle's finitism on this point. On the other hand, he also maintains that this does not rule out the existence of an actually infinite number. In this regard, he appeals to the principle that in the case of discrete quantities the measure, i.e., number, can be infinite in act, although the things measured by it are not infinite in act. This principle (henceforth (P)) is, however, ambiguous. It can be interpreted in two very different ways, depending on whether the expression 'in act' refers to 'infinite' or to the mode of existence of number and the numbered things.

In the first interpretation, (P) means that an infinite number can exist, despite the fact that the numbered things are finite. This interpretation seems to be confirmed by the fact that (P) is adduced against the minor premise of the argument mentioned in (ii), namely 'measure does not exceed what is measured'. This interpretation, however, is problematic, for our commentators generally tend to regard numbers as accidental forms inhering in collections of things. For instance, the number 2 is a form inhering in a collection of two stones, just as whiteness inheres in a white substance.[104] Hence, for an infinite number to exist, a collection of infinitely many things must exist.

In the second interpretation, (P) means that an infinite number can exist actually, despite the fact that the infinite numbered things exist only potentially. So construed, (P) is the principle already familiar to us from the discussion about the potential parts of a continuum, and is most probably the correct one.[105] This interpretation seems confirmed

---

[103] Probably, however, the point of this remark is that, since number can belong to things having no position, even if an infinite number does exist, i.e., it actually inheres in a collection of things, from this it does not follow that there are infinitely many actually existing things and in particular infinitely many things having a position. This is not the same for magnitude, since magnitude can inhere only in physical bodies.

[104] We shall come back to this point in the chapter devoted to time. See below, p. 224-226.

[105] It explicitly appears in the passage of M[3] parallel to passage (3): "Et quia actualitas numeri non requirit actualem existentiam in actu numeratorum, ideo nec oportet quod ad hoc quod numerus sit in actu quod [in] ipsa numerata sint (sicut *ms.*) in actu. Est enim numerus actualis potentiarum actu numeratarum sicut rerum actu existentium. Dico quod simpliciter est numerus <aliquid> mathematicum, ita quod

by the reply of G¹ to the objection against the existence of an infinite number based on Aristotle's discussion in *Physics* III.7. In his reply, G¹ introduces a distinction between two kinds of number: the one considered by Aristotle, which is not an actual infinite, and another one, which is. In connection with this latter kind of number, he explicitly refers to the principle, used in the discussion of the potential parts of the continuum, that number is found in both beings and non-beings:

> (4) To the objection based on Aristotle's text in this chapter it can be said that he only refers to a number joined with a natural thing. This kind of number proceeds and increases *ad infinitum* only through the division of a magnitude. And it is clear that he means this kind of number, since he refers exclusively to a number that is associated with motion and succession. But what has been said about number, i.e., that it is infinite in act, must be understood about the number of forms and taken in an absolute sense, which is common to beings and non-beings.[106]

For the sake of brevity we call 'natural number' the number inhering in natural things. According to G¹, Aristotle maintains that number is only a potential infinite by addition, but he denies the existence of an infinite number, because he considers only natural numbers, whose finiteness derives from the finiteness of natural things. Numbers that can be infinite are first characterized by G¹ as the numbers of forms. Here, as it seems, 'forms' must be taken in a broad sense including immaterial and unextended things, and even non-beings or possibilities. G¹ remarks that this latter type of number is that taken in an absolute sense (*simpliciter*) and is found in the same way (*indifferenter*) in beings and non-beings. This introduces a new kind of number, which also includes natural numbers, since they belong to a kind of being. In connection with the problem of infinity, the point of the remark by

---

non habet positionem aliquam, et ideo non potest fieri aliquid naturale; ideo non oportet quod ad eius actualem existentiam requiratur existentia actualis rerum numeratarum. De magnitudine autem non est ita, quia concernit positionem et situm, et ita fieri potest naturalis, et ideo non potest esse infinitas in magnitudine nisi res ipsa sit actu infinita. Respondeo igitur uni rationi per illud, quia numerus excedit actualem existentiam rerum numeratarum, ut iam patet, magnitudo autem non sic facit" (III, q. 10, f. 157ra, lin. 34-44).

[106] G1, III, q. 6, f. 142va, lin. 48-54: "Ad hoc autem quod obicitur per litteram Aristotelis in hoc capitulo, potest dici quod solum intendit de numero coniuncto rei naturali. Huiusmodi non procedit in infinitum nec crescit nisi per divisionem magnitudinis. Et quod sic intendat patet, quia non intendit de numero nisi secundum quod est cum motu et successione. Quod autem dictum est de numero, scilicet quod <est> actu infinitus, intelligendum est de numero formarum et simpliciter sumpto, qui indifferenter est entium et non entium".

G¹ is the following: although, as in the case of a continuum, an infinite number exists only as the number of a collection of non-beings or possibilities, this does not imply that it is a number in a somewhat loose or improper sense, for a number in its nature can belong to both beings and non-beings. In other words, the formal nature of a number is unaffected by the fact that it is a number of beings or of non-beings.

In the simplified report of passage (4) made by M³ 'number of forms' is replaced by 'formal number'. Although this commentator does not clarify in which sense the number of forms is formal, he emphasizes the idea that this number reflects the full and unrestricted nature of number:

> (5) ... this number is formal and is not subject to restrictive conditions, but it belongs indifferently to whatsoever kind of things, i.e., to those that exist in potency as well as to those that exist in act.[107]

---

[107] M³, III, q. 10, f. 157ra, lin. 47-49: "... iste numerus est formalis et non respiciens aliquam condicionem contrahentem, sed est indifferenter quarumcumque rerum, scilicet tam existentium potentia quam existentium actu". In his report of the infinist position, N claims that the number that can be actually infinite is the *numerus mathematicus* or *numerus simpliciter*, that is, the one which can belong indifferently to beings and non-beings, and not the *numerus naturalis*. But he also interprets the distinction between natural number and mathematical number as a distinction between number as discrete quantity and number as measure: "Dicitur quod numerus potest esse actu infinitus. Et hoc intelligendum est de numero mathematico. Unde in numero duo possunt considerari, scilicet substantia numeri, quae est aggregatio unitatum, et aliud, scilicet ut mensura, quae est unitas totiens replicata. Considerando numerum quo ad substantiam numeri est numerus quantitas discreta. Et hoc modo non potest numerus esse actu infinitus, quia hoc modo habet numerus esse in rebus numeratis et est quiddam naturale. Et hoc modo, existentibus numeratis finitis, non potest numerus esse actu infinitus. Considerando numerum quo ad secundum, scilicet quo ad mensuram, quae est unitas totiens replicata, est numerus quiddam mathematicum nec habens situm nec positionem, et est indifferenter entium et non entium, actuum et potentiarum. Et sic non sequitur: numerus est infinitus in actu; ergo et numerata. Et hoc quia numerus sic consideratus non habet esse in rebus discretis secundum quod numerata sunt" (III, q. 15, f. 140ra, lin. 34-47). But the distinction between discrete quantity and measure is not used at all by G¹-M³ in their discussion of the problem of infinity. It is used, however, by most of our commentators in relation to the problem of the identity of numbers inhering in different collections of things, which we shall analyze in the chapter devoted to time. Hence N probably introduces this distinction on the basis of the assumption of the infinitist position that number can belong in the same way to potencies and acts, beings and not beings. See also the argument of G¹ quoted in note 90, where he refers to the same number ten belonging to a collection of ten men and to that of ten horses. Another motivation for introducing this distinction might be the discussion of the relation between number and numbered things contained in passage (3) quoted above.

This passage makes clear that the distinction between 'formal number' and 'natural number' used by G^1 and M^3 to save Aristotle's finitism is not at all a distinction between a loose sense and a strict sense of 'number', along the lines of that used by Burley and Ockham for the same purpose. It is, in fact, rather the opposite. Indeed, it turns out that according to G^1 and M^3 the proper sense of number is given by formal number, i.e., by the number that can be infinite, since this kind of number expresses the full nature of number. Natural number, which is necessarily finite, is instead a 'contracted' type of number.

In conclusion, the debate among the early English commentators about the actual infinite in number arises from an argument based on the potential parts of a continuum. They all agree that there are infinitely many potential parts in a continuum. The matter of dispute is whether this collection of parts has a number. Thus, the debate is not really focused on a topic pertaining to the infinite itself, but on one pertaining to number. Indeed, the basic assumption of the exponents of the infinitist position is that number by its own nature can inhere in the same way in collections of beings and non-beings, of acts and potencies. For the infinitists, Aristotle's finitism ultimately derives from a restrictive view of number, according to which only collections of actually existing things have a number. We have suggested that behind this contrast there are diverging views on the ontological status of number. Aristotle tends to reduce number to the collection of numbered things, while the exponents of the infinitist position tend to stress the autonomy of number from this collection. In chapter four, devoted to time, we shall meet another case in which all our commentators depart from Aristotle's position on the status of number.

CHAPTER THREE

PLACE

Introduction

In *Physics* IV.4, Aristotle argues that the place of a body A is the limit of the body B that contains A and is in contact with A.[1] For instance, the place of the water contained in a vessel is the innermost surface of the vessel, namely, the surface in contact with the water. This makes it clear that in Aristotle's view the location of a body must be defined in terms of its surroundings rather than in terms of something that receives the located body and is occupied by it. A 'receptive' notion of place would intuitively lead to the positing of an incorporeal, three-dimensional extension or space occupied by bodies. It is well-known, however, that the existence of any form of incorporeal extension is not admissible in Aristotle's ontology, according to which the only kind of extension is that inhering in corporeal substances.[2] On the other hand, the 'surrounding' notion of place defined in *Physics* IV.4 is ontologically admissible, for although place is a two-dimensional extension (i.e., a surface) which does not belong to the located body, it does belong to the containing and surrounding body.

Medieval commentators usually agreed with Aristotle's view that the location of a body can be defined without positing any form of incorporeal space and even accepted Aristotle's definition of place as the limit of the surrounding body.[3] They realized, however, that Aristotle's

---

[1] Aristotle, *Physics*, IV.4, 212a5-6a.

[2] See especially Aristotle's refutation of a void in *Physics* IV.6-9. Most of his arguments against the possibility of a void are in fact directed against incorporeal space. On this point, see Hussey, *Aristotle's Physics*, Introduction, p. xxxv-xxxvi.

[3] Yet, as prof. Richard Sorabji remarks, no Neoplatonist commentators agreed with Aristotle's view of place, although they tend to separate their disagreement from their exegesis. See R. Sorabji, *Matter, Space and Motion, Theories in Antiquity and Their Sequel*, Duckworth, London 1988, p. 186-201. In particular, Philoponus rejected Aristotle's notion of place and advocated the existence of an incorporeal space. On Philoponus' position see especially D. Sedley, "Philoponus' Conception of Space", in R. Sorabji (ed.), *Philoponus and the Rejection of Aristotelian Science*, Duckworth, London 1987, p. 140-153. For a comprehensive survey of the medieval discussions on place, space, and void space see especially E. Grant, "Place and Space in Medieval Physical

account of place in *Physics* IV.1-5 is not fully consistent. They pointed out two main problems, one arising from Aristotle's claim that place is immobile, and the other from the place of the heavens, i.e., of the universe as a whole and of the outermost celestial sphere in particular.

The treatment of these two traditional problems of Aristotle's doctrine in *Physics* IV.1-5 given by the early English commentators will be analysed in sections 4 and 5 respectively. First, however, we shall reconstruct their position on the problem of the relationship between Aristotle's doctrine of place in *Physics* IV.1-5 and his short account of place given in the *Categories*. This is certainly the most original and interesting aspect of the discussion of place in our commentaries. In section 3 we shall see that their exegesis of the definition of place of *Physics* IV.4 is heavily influenced by Aristotle's view in the *Categories* and point out the ontological problems involved in their interpretations of Aristotle's theory. But first, in order to clarify the background of the discussion of the early English commentators, we shall give an outline of the problem of the relationship between Aristotle's treatments of place in the *Physics* and the *Categories*.

1. *Place in the* Categories *and Place in the* Physics

At the beginning of his discussion of the category of quantity (*Categories* 6), Aristotle distinguishes between discrete and continuous quantities. The latter are those whose parts join at a common boundary. Among continuous quantities he lists not only line, surface, and body, but also time and place.[4] This suggests that place and surface are different kinds of quantity, contrary to what is implied in *Physics* IV. Aristotle's subsequent account of the continuity of place confirms this suggestion beyond doubt, as it tries to establish that the continuity of place is supplied by that of the located body:

> (C) Place, again, is one of the continuous quantities. For the parts of a body occupy some place, and they join together at a common boundary. So the parts of the place occupied by the various parts of the

---

Thought", in P. K. Machamer and R. G. Turnbull (eds.), *Motion and Time, Space and Matter*, Ohio State University Press, Columbus (Ohio) 1976, p. 137-167; Id., *Much Ado about Nothing, Theories of space and vacuum from the Middle Ages to the Scientific Revolution*, Cambridge University Press, Cambridge 1981, p. 3-147.

[4] Aristotle, *Categories*, 6, 4b20-25.

body, themselves join together at the same boundary at which the parts of the body do. Thus place also is a continuous quantity, since its parts join together at one common boundary.[5]

This passage almost exhausts Aristotle's treatment of place in the *Categories*, but it is enough to show that the notion of place at work there is radically different from that defined in *Physics* IV as the innermost limit of the containing body.[6] First, note that in the *Categories* a body and its parts are said to *occupy* a place. This suggests a 'receptive' concept of place rather than the 'surrounding' view in *Physics* IV. Furthermore, the parts of a body are said to have a place, whereas in *Physics* IV Aristotle explicitly denies that such parts have a place in their own right distinct from that of the whole body.[7] Indeed, in the 'surrounding' view of place of the *Physics* only those things that are physically separated from their surroundings can be in a place, but the parts of a continuous body are not things of this kind. More generally, passage (C) seems to imply that place is a three-dimensional extension coextensive with that of the located body, but in *Physics* IV Aristotle strongly denies the existence of such an extension.[8]

Aristotelian commentators are aware of the conflict between the systematic treatment of place given in the *Physics* and the brief account found in the *Categories*.[9] In the medieval tradition, in particular, arguments taken from the account of the *Categories* usually appear among the *contra*-arguments of the question "Whether place is a surface" discussed in the commentaries on *Physics* IV.1-5. As E. Grant has pointed out, there is also a 'standard' solution to this kind of *contra*-arguments offered by medieval commentators.[10] This is clearly formulated by Walter Burley:

---

[5] Ibid., 5a8-14. The English translation is that of J. Ackrill in *Aristotle's Categories and De Interpretatione*, Translated with Notes by J. L. Ackrill, Clarendon Press, Oxford 1963, p. 13.

[6] Aristotle's view in the *Categories* and its contrast with his doctrine in the *Physics* have been recently discussed in H. Mendell, "Topoi on Topos: The Development of Aristotle's Concept of Place", *Phronesis*, 32 (1987), p. 206-231, and in K. Algra, *Concepts of Space in Greek Thought*, Brill, Leiden-New York-Köln 1995, p. 123-136.

[7] At *Physics*, IV.4, 211a29-b5 Aristotle explicitly contrasts the sense of 'in' in which a part is said to be *in* the whole and that in which something is said to be *in* a place. The first relation holds between two things that are not separated one from the other, the second one holds only between separated things. At IV.5, 212b3-6 he also specifies that the undivided parts of a continuum are only potentially in a place, and they are actually in a place, once they have been actually divided from the continuous whole.

[8] See especially Aristotle, *Physics*, IV.4, 211b5-29; 8, 216a26-b21.

[9] On Greek commentators, see below note 21.

[10] See Grant, "Place and Space", p. 138.

And when it is said that place and surface are distinct species, as is evident in the *Categories*, I say that this is not true. For there the Philosopher speaks according to the famous opinion of the ancients, who posited that place is a separate space. And if place were such a space, it would specifically differ from a surface. Thus, the reason why the Philosopher speaks according to a famous opinion could be that he had not yet declared what place is, and therefore he spoke according to a common opinion until he declared what place is.[11]

Thus, according to the standard medieval solution, the true Aristotelian doctrine of place is that of *Physics* IV. The concept of place found in the *Categories* is merely famous, that is, it reflects a common point of view about place, which Aristotle provisionally adopts until he comes to treat this notion systematically in the *Physics*.[12]

We have already encountered this kind of solution to Aristotle's conflicting views on a given topic. Averroes uses the same strategy to reconcile Aristotle's different categorical classifications of motion in the *Categories* and in the *Physics*. Averroes regards as merely famous the way of classifying motion in the category of passion as proposed in the *Categories*, while he considers Aristotle's true position to be the way of classifying it in the category of its final state, as established in the *Physics*.[13] Although in his commentary on *Physics* IV.1-5 Averroes does not even mention Aristotle's account of place in the *Categories*, the standard medieval solution to the problem of Aristotle's conflicting notions of place is undoubtedly inspired by Averroes' tendency to disregard Aristotle's views in the *Categories* when these are in con-

---

[11] Burley, *In Physicam*, IV, ff. 99vb-100ra: "Et quando dicitur quod locus et superficies sunt species distinctae, ut patet in *Praedicamentis*, dico quod non est verum, sed Philosophus ibi loquitur secundum opinionem famosam antiquorum ponentium locum esse spatium separatum. Et si locus esset tale spatium, differret specifice a superficie. Unde ratio quare Philosophus loquitur secundum opinionem famosam potest esse quia nondum declaraverat quid est locus et ideo locutus est ut plures quousque declarabit quid est locus".

[12] A similar interpretation of Aristotle's conflicting views on place has been recently supported by K. Algra. He maintains that there is a 'development' in Aristotle's concept of place from the *Categories* to the *Physics*, where 'development' is here to be understood in the sense that "... a thinker's thought on a specific subject was at first inchoate and inarticulate (e.g. because the subject did not interest him, or because he was unaware of the inherent problems), whereas he later developed a conscious and articulate theory" (*Concepts of Space*, p. 143). Algra also acknowledges the similarity of his view with that expressed by the standard medieval interpretation. See ibid., p. 152-153.

[13] See above, p. 48.

flict with other parts of the *Corpus aristotelicum*.[14] Accordingly, the standard medieval solution can be simply labelled 'the Averroistic solution'.

Contrary to what one might expect, however, our early English commentators do not even mention the Averroistic solution. Instead, as we have seen in the case of motion, our commentators are rather reluctant to disregard Aristotle's account of place in the *Categories*, as will be clear from section 3. Hence, on this topic they tend to follow what K. Algra calls in his recent comprehensive study on Aristotle's conceptions of place the 'synthetizing approach'.[15] As the expression itself suggests, the synthetizing approach consists in the attempt to reconcile Aristotle's view on place in the *Physics* with that in the *Categories*. In order to determine the particular form of the synthetizing approach that appears in our commentaries, we shall set out in next section the relevant exegetical context.

2. *The Synthetizing Approach in the Early English Tradition*

Attempts to reconcile Aristotle's conflicting views in the *Physics* and in the *Categories* are found in two surviving works belonging to the English tradition. They immediately precede our period and were probably known to our commentators. These are B, the exposition with some questions on Aristotle's *Physics* very close to Adam of Bocfeld's commentary, and the questions on the *Physics* by Roger Bacon. Historically, the positions of these two commentators are important, since they represent exactly the two possible ways in which a synthesis of Aristotle's conflicting views could be achieved: B tries to show that Aristotle's account of place in the *Categories* can be interpreted along the lines of his doctrine in the *Physics*, while, conversely, Roger Bacon modifies the doctrine of the *Physics* in order to make it compatible with that of the *Categories*.

---

[14] In addition to the case of the categorical classification of motion, Averroes' tendency appears also in the case of Aristotle's conflicting views in the *Categories* and in the *Metaphysics* on motion as a species in the category of quantity. In the first work Aristotle does not list motion among the species of quantity, as he does instead in the *Metaphysics*. Averroes remarks that in the *Categories* Aristotle lists only the 'famous' species of quantity. See Averroes, *In Metaphysicam*, V, t. c. 18, f. 125vaI-vbK.

[15] See Algra, *Concepts of Space*, p. 136-137.

In B the sequence of the *contra*-arguments of the question 'Whether place is a surface' starts as follows:

> (1) That place is not a surface appears from this: (i) the parts of the body join at the parts of place and conversely; (ii) but the parts of the body are three-dimensional; (iii) therefore, it seems that in the same way the parts of place are three-dimensional. For, if this were not so, how could the parts of place join at the parts of the body? (iv) Therefore the parts of place would be bodies, since they are three-dimensional. Thus, place is a body.[16]

Evidently, the major premise (i) of this argument derives from passage (C) of the *Categories*, where Aristotle accounts for the continuity of place in terms of that of the located body.[17] In (ii) and (iii) B makes explicit that the correspondence between the parts of place and those of the located body assumed by Aristotle in (C) can hold only if body and place are extended in the same way, namely, if they are both three-dimensional extensions. Finally, the further conclusion inferred in (iv), i.e., that place and its parts are bodies, reflects Aristotle's ontology in the *Physics*, according to which there is no three-dimensional extension apart from that of corporeal substances.[18] We shall see in next section that some of the early English commentators try to show that the three-dimensionality of place can, in fact, be maintained without identifying place with a body or violating Aristotle's ontology. On the contrary, B more traditionally assumes that the inference from the three-dimensionality of place to the identity between place and a body is valid. Accordingly, his answer to argument (1) consists in denying the three-dimensionality of place and showing that premise (i) from the *Categories* can be interpreted in such a way that it does not imply that place has three dimensions:

> (2) To the first argument it must be said that the parts of the body join at the parts of place only by means of the surface of the body, so that the parts of the surface of the body immediately join at the parts of

---

[16] B, IV, q. 12, f. 24rb, lin. 40-43: "Quod autem non sit superficies sic videtur: (i) partes corporis copulantur ad partes loci et econverso; (ii) sed partes corporis habent trinam dimensionem; (iii) quare videtur similiter quod partes loci habeant trinam dimensionem. Qualiter enim aliter copularentur haec ad istas? (iv) Quare partes loci corpora essent, cum trinam habeant dimensionem; quare locus corpus".

[17] However, B gives an unfaithful report of that argument. For Aristotle does not say that the parts of the body *join* at the parts of place, but that they *occupy* the parts of place.

[18] See above note 2.

place. And therefore it does not follow that the parts of place are bodies or that place is a body.[19]

As in (1), so in (2) B tacitly assumes that the spatial correspondence stated in premise (i) can exist only between extensions having the same type
of dimensions. Thus, the crucial point of his answer in (2) is that the correspondence in question is to be understood between the parts of place
and those, not of the located body, but of its surface. Indeed, these latter
parts are clearly bidimensional; therefore, the parts of place, at which
the parts of the surface of the located body join, are also bidimensional.
In short, according to B, in passage (C) from the *Categories*, 'parts of the
body' means in fact 'parts of the surface of the body'. On this interpretation, the correspondence between the parts of place and the parts of the
located body of the *Categories* turns out to be a correspondence between
bidimensional extensions, and the conclusion that place is a surface, as
Aristotle maintains in the *Physics*, can legitimately be inferred.

The exegesis of passage (C) proposed by B can be regarded as a
traditional one, since it is substantially the same as that found in the
Greek commentators Ammonius, Philoponus, and Simplicius.[20]
Although this exegesis does not succeed in completely reconciling the
account of place in the *Categories* with Aristotle's doctrine of the
Physics,[21] it reflects very neatly the ontological commitments of this
latter doctrine. As we shall see in next section, however, this line of
interpretation is not pursued by the early English commentators, who
instead tend to follow the alternative approach found in Bacon's
Questions on the *Physics*.[22]

---

[19] B, IV, q. 12, f. 24va, lin. 9-11: "Ad primum sic quod partes corporis non copulantur ad partes loci nisi mediante superficie corporis, cuius quidem superficiei partes
immediate copulantur ad partes loci, et propter hoc non sequitur quod partes loci
corpora sint aut locus corpus".

[20] See Algra, *Concepts of Space*, p. 137-139.

[21] For instance, it leaves unexplained why Aristotle in the *Categories* says that the
parts of the located body occupy a place, whereas in the *Physics* he says that they are
not in a place. Simplicius tries to solve this problem as well by maintaining that in
the *Categories* too, as in the *Physics*, Aristotle means that the parts of a body do not
occupy a place in their own right nor are in a place in their own right. Simplicius'
attempt to explain this point is rather weak. For Simplicius' attempt, see D. J. Furley,
"The Greek Commentators'", p. 19-20.

[22] Our references to Bacon's questions on the *Physics* are all to the second set of
questions on this work by Bacon (*Questiones altere*). Bacon's attempted interpretation of
Aristotle's theory of place in the *Physics* along the lines of Aristotle's account in the
Categories is found only in this set of questions. In his first set of question on the *Physics*,
instead, Bacon follows closely Aristotle's doctrine in the *Physics*, without combining it

If, roughly speaking, B's synthesis of Aristotle's conflicting views is achieved by subtracting a dimension from the three-dimensional notion of place in the *Categories*, then Bacon's opposite synthesis is achieved by adding a dimension, namely, depth, to the two-dimensional notion of place in the *Physics*.

To the question 'Is place a surface?' Bacon answers that place and surface are two distinct species of quantity. His argument for this claim is, in short, the following. Bacon focusses on the class of things that have two dimensions, namely, longitude and latitude (*dimensio in longum et latum*), and then proceeds to split this class into two mutually distinct subclasses. The first is that formed by those two-dimensional things that satisfy three further requirements: containment (*continentia*), immobility (*immobilitas*), and depth (*profunditas*). Thus, the second subclass is that formed by those two-dimensional things that lack any of these three requirements. Every surface clearly belongs to the second subclass, since, by definition, it has no depth. The first subclass, – Bacon claims –, consists exactly of those two dimensional things which are places.[23]

The three additional elements that, in Bacon's view, are required for place and make it something other than a surface deserve closer inspection. Immobility and containment are both properties of place given by Aristotle in the *Physics*. Indeed, they are both included in the final formulation of the definition of place as the immobile limit of the containing body.[24] Depth, however, is not at all a property of Aristotle's notion of place in the *Physics* but rather in the *Categories*. Indeed,

---

with that of the *Categories*. For Bacon's different interpretations of Aristotle's doctrine of place, see C. Trifogli, "Roger Bacon and Aristotle's Doctrine of Place", *Vivarium*, 35 (1997), 2, p. 155-176.

[23] Bacon, *In Physicam*, IV, p. 184, lin. 35-185, lin. 5: "... et natura duarum dimensionum potest dividi in duo, in unum supra quod adduntur ille tres conditiones, scilicet continentia, immobilitas et profunditas, et hec facit unam speciem quantitatis que est locus; opposita istarum trium conditionum faciunt aliam speciem que est superficies, sicut si dividatur animal in rationale et irrationale... (lin.19-22): Unde iste due dimensiones in quantum sunt hujusmodi sunt communes superficiei et loco et per differentias specificas contrahuntur in naturam loci vel superficiei". Bacon's account is clearly problematic. There are two main difficulties: (1) bidimensionality is usually the defining property of a surface, not just its genus; (2) when the third dimension, i.e., depth, is added to place, place can no longer be considered a species of bidimensional quantity. Similar difficulties in the exegesis of Aristotle's definition of place are involved in our commentators' account. See below, p. 152-159.

[24] Aristotle, *Physics*, IV.4, 212a20-21: "So that is what place is: the first unchangeable limit of that which surrounds".

other sections of Bacon's questions on place make it clear that, in fact, depth is introduced mainly on the basis of passage (C) from the *Categories*. For instance, in his answer to the question "Is place a body?", he denies that place is a body but argues that it has depth, because:

> ... it does not alone suffice that the located body be contained within the sides of the container, but it is required that <place> immerse itself in the middle of the located body. Therefore, according to that saying, *the single parts of place are joined to the single parts of the located body and* <these latter parts> *occupy* <the parts of place>, and therefore place immerses itself in some way...[25]

This passage clearly echoes argument (C) from the *Categories*, which requires that the internal parts of the located body also occupy a place. It thus implies that place does not simply surround the body located in it, but must also be to some extent internal to the located body. Accordingly, depth is needed to make place a three-dimensional extension that coexists spatially with the located body. In Bacon's words, depth is the dimension in virtue of which place immerses itself (*profundat se*) in the located body.

Like Bacon, the early English commentators appeal to passage (C) from the *Categories* to ascribe place a depth in some sense and to maintain that, because of its depth, place not only surrounds, but also 'immerses itself' in the located body.[26]

3. *The 'Immersive' Notion of Place*

There is no universal agreement among our commentators on precisely how the immersion of place in the located body should be con-

---

[25] Bacon, *In Physicam*, IV, p. 186, lin. 25-30: "... dico quod locus non est corpus, tamen habet aliquo modo profunditatem, quia non solum sufficit quod locatum contineatur inter latera continentis, immo oportet quod profundet se per medium; unde secundum illud *singule partes loci copulantur ad singulas partes corporis et occupant* et ideo profundat se locus aliquo modo...". (emphasis is mine). On Bacon's attempt to distinguish place from a body, despite the fact that they are both three-dimensional extensions, see below, note 59.

[26] Among Aristotelian scholars, H. King and A. E. Taylor also defend the view that Aristotle in the *Physics* holds a three-dimensional notion of place as that found in the *Categories*. See H. King, "Aristotle's Theory of TOPOS", *Classical Quarterly*, 44 (1950), p. 76-96; A. E. Taylor, *A Commentary on Plato's Timaeus*, Clarendon Press, Oxford 1928, p. 664-677. Their interpretations have been discussed and criticized by Algra in *Concepts of Space*, p. 139-142.

strued. The context of the *Categories* seems to leave no doubt that this immersion has a specifically quantitative meaning, i.e., that it is associated with a notion of place as three-dimensional extension. Indeed, this is the view that we have found in Roger Bacon's questions on the *Physics* and that appears in most of our commentaries, namely, S, P, G[1], and M[3]. T, however, holds a different position, according to which the immersion of place must be explained by appealing to Aristotle's theory of natural places, without modifying the quantitative structure of the notion of place of *Physics* IV.1-5. N and G[3] do not show a fully consistent position on this topic, but they tend largely to juxtapose the position of S, P, G[1], and M[3] with that of T. In section 3.1 the position of T will be first examined. In sections 3.2 and 3.3 the quantitative theory of three-dimensional place supported by the other early English commentators and the ontological problems it involves will be analysed. Finally, in section 3.4 we shall present Roger Bacon's refutation of this theory in his later work *Communia naturalium*.

3.1 *Immersive Place as Natural Place (T, N, G³)*

T devotes a short question to the problem of whether place immerses itself in the located body.[27] He proposes a counter-argument based on the quantitative notion of immersion, according to which the extension of place penetrates the extension of the located body. This would imply that place is a three-dimensional extension. From this, in turn, it would follow that place is a body. But then two bodies, namely, place and the located body, would interpenetrate, which is clearly impossible.[28] The crucial assumption of this argument is that every three-dimensional extension inheres in a corporeal substance. As with B, T accepts this assumption and concludes that:

---

[27] T, IV, q. 11, *Utrum locus profundat se in locatum*, f. 42ra, lin. 6-32. Throughout this chapter, the numbering of the questions on place in the early English commentaries is that published in Trifogli, "Le questioni sul libro IV", Appendice, A: Questioni sul luogo, p. 78-90.

[28] Ibid., f. 42ra, lin. 9-16: "... si profundaret se, aut (i) per intersectionem corporis usque ad centrum corporis aut (ii) per circulationes quasdam primo maiores et postea minores per appropinquationem (appropriationem *ms.*) ad centrum. Si primo modo, tunc esset locus [n]aeque dimensionatus et esset corpus et essent duo corpora simul, et item sic partes essent in toto actu. Si secundo modo, cum illae circulationes non possunt intelligi nisi cum continuitate, essent tamen corpora et ita adhuc corpora duo simul". Not all the details of this argument are clear. The distinction between ways (i) and (ii) in which place can be thought of as something that immerses itself in

(1) ... nothing belonging to place is in the located body in such a way that it is in the depth of this body. For place is outside this body, as Aristotle intends.[29]

Against this conclusion, however, T raises an objection based on passage (C) from the *Categories* that posits a correspondence between the parts of place and the parts of the located body, thus apparently implying that place does immerse itself in the located body.[30] He also mentions an interpretation of this passage very similar to that found in B,[31] which avoids the immersive view of place by taking 'parts of the body' to mean the parts of the surface of the located body. But he finds this solution unsatisfactory.[32] On the contrary, he seems to admit that passage (C) implies that place is in some sense present in the internal parts of the located body, but nevertheless, is not necessarily present in a spatial sense. The alternative sense of immersion that T has in mind is suggested by Aristotle's theory of natural place.[33]

In our commentators' interpretation of this theory, natural place preserves the nature of the body naturally located in it. In medieval terms, natural place has a preserving power (*virtus salvativa*) with

---

the located body is probably based on a distinction between two ways of defining the parts of a body, which is used by our commentators in the case of the celestial region (see below p. 189-190). T seems to imagine that the contained body is spherical; its parts can be defined as either (i) the sectors included between two planes passing through its center or (ii) the concentric spherical parts.

[29] Ibid., lin. 16-17: "... nihil loci est in corpore locato ita quod in profundo eius. Extra enim est, ut vult Aristoteles".

[30] Ibid., lin. 17-20: "Sed tunc quaeritur (i) qualiter partes corporis correspondent partibus loci vel econverso vel qualiter partes corporis et loci copulantur ad unum terminum et (ii) qualiter locus salvat et quis". (i) is the objection taken from passage (C), whereas (ii) is an objection against the conclusion that place is external to the located body and is taken from the theory of natural place. According to T, both these objections can be solved in the same way. See below p. 144-145.

[31] See above, p. 138-139.

[32] T, IV, q. 6, f. 41ra, lin. 44-50: "... et dicunt partes loci copulari ad terminum communem ut ad superficiem, quia pars interior corporis locati est in loco per respectum ad superficiem corporis, quia potest imaginari per sectores corporis transeuntes per centrum corporis ab una superficie ad aliam vel a centro undique ad superficiem, si debent copulari. Hoc difficile est".

[33] For instance, in replying to the argument quoted in note 30, T claims that both passage (C) from the *Categories* and the 'preserving' power of place refer primarily to the heavens. T, IV, q. 11, f. 42ra, lin. 20-23: "Dicendum [quod] ad hoc quod utrumque hoc habet intelligi de caelo primo quod primo influit in sibi proximum et illud proximum, ut ignis, manifestum (?) et sic conservat". The 'influence' of the heavens on the body immediately contained by it reflects a feature of the heavens regarded as natural place.

respect to the located body.[34] The effect of this power must be sensible in the body as a whole: not only in its outermost surface but also
in its internal parts. Because of its preserving power, – T claims –,
place can also be said to be inside the located body and to immerse
itself in it, although spatially it only touches the outermost surface of
this body. Thus, relying on an interpretation of passage (C) based on
the theory of natural place, T holds that all that is needed to resolve
the conflict between this passage and the negative conclusion on the
immersion of place stated in passage (1), is to qualify this conclusion
in the following sense: nothing of place is inside the located body
except the influence of its preserving power.[35]

Clearly, in the interpretation of T, 'immersion' is not a property of
every kind of place, but only of natural place. This point is brought
out explicitly in the answer of T to the question "Whether place is a
surface". He maintains that place is essentially distinct from surface,
since a surface is the limit of any body whatsoever, whereas place,
according to Aristotle's definition in *Physics* IV.4, is the limit of the
containing body. As T puts it:

> (2) Therefore, the limit of the containing body, insofar as it is limit, is a
> surface, whereas insofar as it is containing is place.[36]

However, he adds a further distinction between two kinds of containment:

> (3) But 'insofar as containing' can be taken in two ways, as has been
> said: either only insofar as it surrounds, and thus it is mathematical
> place, or insofar as it has some influence in the depth of the located
> body, and thus it is natural place.[37]

---

[34] On the explanation on natural place in our commentaries, see below p. 171-175.

[35] This qualification is made by T at the end of his report of an interpretation of
passage (C) according to which the common limit at which the parts of the located
body and of place join is the centre of the located body. T, IV, q. 6, f. 41ra, lin. 30-
38: "... ad hoc quod dicit quod partes loci etc., ad hoc dicitur diversimode. Uno
modo quod partes loci copulantur ad terminum communem. Hoc est intelligendum
ad centrum corporis: quia locus non solum est superficies absolute, sed superficies
continentis unde locus est cum profundatione ad centrum corporis, ideo dicitur quod
partes loci copulantur ad illum eundem terminum, ut ad centrum. *Nec tamen intelligatur hoc quod locus sit aliquid intra corpus nisi quo ad illam virtutem influxam*".

[36] Ibid., f. 41ra, lin. 26-27: "Unde ultimum continentis in quantum ultimum est
superficies, in quantum continens est locus".

[37] Ibid., lin. 27-30: "Sed 'unde continens' potest sumi dupliciter, ut dictum est: aut
solum in quantum circumscribit, et sic locus mathematicus est, aut in quantum influit
aliquid in profundum locati, et sic naturalis est". T's position, however, does not

In this passage, the distinction between mathematical place and natural place is associated with the distinction between purely quantitative and formal senses of containment. In the former sense, a container is something that spatially surrounds what is contained by it; in the latter sense, it exercises some kind of formal causality over it. For our purpose, the relevant point is that the 'presence' of place inside the located body is associated exclusively with the formal sense of containment, i.e., with natural place. Accordingly, mathematical and natural place have the same quantitative structure, that is, they are both two-dimensional extensions, since the 'depth' of natural place is not of a quantitative kind.

The same identification of immersive place with natural place is found in N and G³. In their solution to the question 'Is place a surface?', these commentators distinguish between the material and formal aspects of place. Roughly, the material aspect of place corresponds to its genus, whereas the formal aspects correspond to its specific differences. The material aspect of place is its being the limit of a body, i.e., a surface. As to the formal aspects, N and G³ further distinguish the cases of mathematical and natural place. In the case of mathematical place,

> (4) ... the formal aspects of mathematical place are only two, namely, containment and immobility. And that place is the surface which only surrounds but does not immerse itself.[38]

For natural place,

> (5) ... the formal aspects of natural place are three, namely, containment, immobility, and the power through which every body rests in its proper place and every body moves towards its proper place when it is

---

seem to be fully consistent. In a subsequent passage he repeats that a surface can be called place only insofar as limit of the containing body . Then he adds the following distinction of the senses of 'insofar as limit of the containing body': "Hoc tamen dupliciter potest esse, quia (i) circumscribens solum et sub ratione continentiae, et sic est locus mathematicus, aut (i') secundum profundationem per respectum ad illos sectores sine virtutis influxione, et sic adhuc non absolvitur a loco mathematico, aut (ii) cum virtutis influxione ita quod faciat ad locati salvationem, et sic est naturalis" (Ibid., f. 41rb, lin. 5-11). Sense (i') is problematic. It does not appear in the preceding passage and it states that mathematical place also has an 'immersion' in the located body.

[38] N, IV, q. 16, f. 146rb, lin. 33-35: "... formalia autem loci mathematici sunt tantum duo, scilicet continentia et immobilitas. Et ille locus est sola superficies circumdans et non profundans se". See also, G³, IV, q. 15, f. 160ra, lin. 16-22.

outside of it. But this potency of place is diffused through every part of the located, viz. contained, body. And because this potency is diffused through the depths of the located body, for that reason it is said that place has accidentally three dimensions, in the sense that they derive from those of the located body.[39]

As to passage (4), we recall that 'limit', 'containment' and 'immobility' are all notions that appear in Aristotle's definition of place in *Physics* IV.4.[40] Accordingly, what N and G[3] call 'mathematical place' is in fact nothing else than Aristotle's notion of place taken in its most general sense. In passage (5) this general notion is contracted to natural place by adding the requirement of formal causality exerted by natural place on the located body. This requirement also reflects Aristotle's 'axiom' on place that holds specifically for natural place.[41] Aristotle, however, does not in any way associate the formal character of natural place with the spatial notion of 'depth', as do N and G[3] in the conclusive sentence of passage (5). We have already found this association in T and shown that it originates from passage (C) from the *Categories*.

In conclusion, T, N, and G[3] acknowledge that Aristotle's account in the *Categories* implies an immersive notion of place, according to which place does not simply surround the located body, but is also inside it. They deny, however, that the immersion of place is to be taken in a spatial sense. On the contrary, they hold that place is spa-

---

[39] N, IV, q. 16, f. 146ra, lin. 41-48: "... formalia autem loci naturalis sunt tria, scilicet continentia et immobilitas et potentia per quam unumquodque quiescit in suo loco proprio et per quam potentiam movetur unumquodque ad suum locum proprium, cum fuerit extra ipsum. Haec autem potentia loci diffunditur in omnem partem corporis locati sive contenti. Et propter hoc quia ita est quod ista potentia loci diffunditur in profundum corporis locati, ideo dicitur quod locus habet tres dimensiones per accidens, ut a corpore locato". See also G[3], IV, q. 15, f. 159vb, lin. 16-23.

[40] See above, note 24.

[41] Aristotle lists six 'axioms' on place, i. e., general principles about place, which are immediately evident and from which its definition must be deduced. Aristotle, *Physics*, IV.4, 21Ob34-211a6: "We require, then, (1) that place should be the first thing surrounding that of which it is the place; and (2) not anything pertaining to the object; (3) that the primary [place] should be neither less nor greater (than the object); (4) that it should be left behind by each object [when the object moves] and be separable [from it]; further, (5) that every place should have 'above' and 'below'; and (6) that each body should naturally move and remain in its proper places, and this it must do either above or below". Axiom (6) is that quoted by N and G[3]. On the methodological meaning of the axioms on place in Aristotle's dialectical discussion see Hussey, *Aristotle's Physics*, Notes, p. 111. More generally, for Aristotle's method in the treatment of place in *Physics* IV, see Algra, *Concepts of Space*, p. 153-181.

tially external to the located body. What is 'internal' to the body is the effect of natural place considered as a formal cause.

It is evident that the interpretation of Aristotle's account of place in the *Categories* based on the theory of natural place to which our commentators resort is totally implausible. For in passage (C), in particular, Aristotle uses the 'immersion' of place to explain continuity, which is a quantitative property of place. This requires, however, a corresponding quantitative notion of immersion, namely, the three-dimensionality of place. Nevertheless, if this interpretation is more generally viewed as an attempt to use the theory of natural place to reply to arguments or intuitions which immediately suggest a three-dimensional view of place, then it cannot be regarded as an isolated case in the medieval, exegetical tradition. Other important examples are found in Albert the Great's paraphrase of *Physics* IV.1-5.[42] Furthermore, since in the interpretation of T, N, and G³ immersive place still retains the quantitative structure of Aristotle's place in the *Physics*, the synthetizing approach that it reflects is, properly speaking, of the same type as that found in the Greek commentators and in B.[43] That is, it is an attempt to interpret Aristotle's view in the *Categories* along the lines of his doctrine in the *Physics*. The other commentators in our group employ the same approach, but reconcile the texts in the opposite sense, as will be made clear in section 3.2.

3.2 *Immersive Place as Three-Dimensional Extension (S, P, G¹, M³)*

The quantitative interpretation of immersive place given by S, P, G¹, and M³ is clearly seen when we compare their answer to the question

---

[42] In his solution to some arguments in favour of the identification of place with space (which he ascribes to the Epicureans) Albert resorts to the theory of natural place. See *In Physicam*, IV, tract. 1, cap. 10, p. 219a, lin. 32-221a, lin. 32. For instance, the first argument he presents is based on the intuitive view that place must contain the body as a whole and not only surround it: "Prima fuit, quod corpori non debetur locus ratione suae superficiei, sed ratione corporis, inquantum habet tres dimensiones. Sed si superficies esset locus, non contineretur corpus in loco nisi secundum superficiem; ergo superficies includens non est locus, sed potius spatium separatum, quod tres dimensiones habet" (ibid., f. 219a, lin. 33-39). He replies: "Dicemus enim ad primum, quod corpus locatum gratia sui totius est in loco, sed tamen virtus loci coniungitur ei primo per superficiem et per superficiem diffunditur in toto locato" (ibid., p. 220b, lin. 58-62). This reply suggests that Albert takes the claim 'corpus locatum gratia sui totius est in loco' to mean that place must have some power on the whole located body; accordingly he explains how this is possible, despite the fact that place only touches the surface of this body.

[43] See above, p. 139.

'Whether place is a surface' with that of T, N, G^3, examined in 3.1.
P, following S, replies as follows:

> (6) On this topic it perhaps should be maintained that place is not
> merely a surface. For the surface of the containing body has only two
> dimensions, but place has three dimensions in some way. For other-
> wise (i) it would neither be equal to the located body in each of its parts
> (ii) nor would the parts of place join at the same boundary at which the
> parts of the body join. (iii) Nevertheless, place does not have these
> three dimensions essentially, but it acquires the third dimension,
> namely depth, from the located body which enters and separates the
> sides of the containing body. (iv) Therefore, place immerses itself in the
> depth of the located body, and this is not suited to a surface, and hence
> place is not absolutely the same thing as a surface.[44]

In this passage, no reference is made to the theory of natural place
in connection with the immersion of place in the located body.
Rather, it is implied that the immersion of place derives from the
fact that it has a third dimension, i.e., depth. Furthermore, the two
arguments given in (i) and (ii) for ascribing three dimensions to
place both appeal to quantitative properties of place. Indeed, in (ii),
as in the argument used by Roger Bacon to explain why place
should have a depth,[45] the famous passage (C) from the *Categories* is
clearly echoed. The argument in (i) more probably derives from
Aristotle's 'axiom' in *Physics* IV.4 that place must be equal to the
located body.[46] Equality apparently is a relation between extensions
of the same type. Therefore, the equality between body and place
seems to imply that place too is a three-dimensional extension.
Although this objection based on the axiom of equality was usually
raised in medieval commentaries against Aristotle's denial of a
three-dimensional place, it is quite clear from the context of *Physics*
IV.4 that Aristotle, in fact, means that place, understood as the sur-

---

[44] P, IV, q. 21, f. 79ra, lin. 11-18: "Ad istud forte putandum quod locus non est
sola superficies. Superficies enim corporis continentis tantum habet duas dimensiones, locus vero habet tres aliqualiter. Alioquin enim (i) non adaequaretur corpori
locato secundum omnem sui partem, (ii) neque partes eius ad eundem terminum
copularentur ad quem particulae corporis copulantur. (iii) Istas tamen tres dimensiones non habet locus de se, sed tertiam dimensionem, scilicet profunditatem,
acquirit sibi per corpus locatum ingrediens et separans latera corporis continentis. (iv)
Unde locus profundat se secundum profundationem corporis, et hoc non convenit
superficiei, et ideo non est locus idem simpliciter quod superficies". See also S, IV, q.
8, f. 48va, lin. 37-44.
[45] See above, p. 141.
[46] This is axiom (3) in the passage quoted in note 41.

face of the containing body, is equal to the surface of the located body.[47] It was along these Aristotelian lines that medieval commentators usually solved the objection in question.[48] P, however, uses it in support of the thesis that place has three dimensions.

We shall reserve comment on statement (iii), concerning the dependence of the three-dimensionality of place on the located body, until section 3.3, where the ontological problems arising from three-dimensional place will be discussed more extensively. We wish to concentrate presently on the exegetical problem posed by this notion of place, that is, its apparent conflict with Aristotle's definition of place as the limit, i.e., surface, of the containing body.

The commentators of this group are aware of this problem. For instance, in P one of the *pro*-arguments of the question 'Whether place is a surface' is based on Aristotle's definition:

> (7) ... one body has only one boundary or limit; therefore, since place is the limit or boundary of the containing body, as Aristotle shows below, and similarly a surface is the limit or boundary of this same body, then place will be entirely the same thing as surface.[49]

We recall that T, N, and G³ solved this kind of objection against the immersive view of place by introducing the distinction between mathematical place and natural place, to the effect that mathematical place is that which reflects Aristotle's general notion of place as limit of the container and is not immersive, while natural place is immer-

---

[47] In fact axiom (3) aims at distinguishing first or proper place from common place. The former is that which contains exactly one body, whereas the latter contains more than one body. See Aristotle, *Physics*, IV.4, 211a23-29.

[48] On the property of place of being equal to the located body, Albert the Great, for instance, remarks: "... et in hoc, licet videatur convenire cum inani sive vacuo, non tamen convenit, quia vacuum non est et ideo neque aequale neque inaequale est locato. Est autem hic accipienda aequalitas secundum extensionem, quia locus proprius non extenditur extra quantitatem locati, licet non sit aequalis secundum omnem dimensionem, quia locus non habet tres dimensiones, sed duas" (*In Physicam*, IV, tract. 1, cap. 7, p. 214a, lin. 30-b, lin. 37). Here 'void' means incorporeal three-dimensional extension. Following Averroes, medieval commentators also often qualify the equality between place and located body as an equality *secundum continentiam*; this means that the extension contained or surrounded by place is equal to that contained by the outermost surface of the located body. On the equality *secundum continentiam*, see Averroes, *In Physicam*, IV, t. c. 43, f. 142rbD-E.

[49] P, IV, q. 21, f. 78vb, lin. 38-40: "... unius corporis est tantum unum ultimum vel unus terminus; quare, cum locus sit terminus vel ultimum ipsius corporis continentis, ut ostendit Auctor infra, et similiter superficies sit terminus vel ultimum ipsius, erit locus penitur idem cum superficie". See also S, IV, q. 8, f. 48rb, lin. 32-35.

sive. This solution is no longer available for the exponents of the three-dimensional view of place, so it is difficult to see how they could possibly solve the objection. P attempts the following solution:

> (8) ... although the boundary of the containing body is both place and a surface, nevertheless it is not both in the same way. For the limit of the containing body is said to be a surface insofar as it does not immerse itself in the depth of the contained body, whereas it is said to be place insofar as it immerses itself and as its parts join at the same boundary at which the parts of the located body join.[50]

The solution of P is evidently unsound. The limit of the containing body, being a bidimensional extension, can in no way be also immersed in the located body, if immersion is taken in a spatial sense.

A similar difficulty can be detected in the answer of G^1 and M^3 to the question 'Whether place is a surface', which the first of these two commentators formulates as follows:

> (9) (i) It can be said that neither is place merely a surface nor does the containing body contain the contained body merely along its surface. For, according to Aristotle, the parts of the body are joined at a common boundary, i.e., at a point in the centre of the body, and the parts of place join at the same boundary at which the parts of the body join. (ii) If, however, a surface is thought of as actually extended in virtue of the distance of the intervening body and that this surface, being extended in this way, does not only surround, but also immerses itself up to the centre of the body, in this way a surface can be said to be place. (iii) But if this surface were to be considered qua surrounding, then it is the limit of the body, whereas if it were to be considered qua immersing itself, then it has the role of a container. Therefore, since the term 'surface' in itself means a surface qua surrounding, therefore this proposition 'place is a surface' is false, if taken *per se*. For it is accidental for a surface to be containing and to be immersing itself in the contained body. Therefore, it is accidental for it to be a place, because the property of containing, which is essential to place, is accidental to a surface.[51]

---

[50] P, IV, q. 21, f. 79ra, lin. 25-28: "... licet ultimum corporis continentis sit locus et superficies, non tamen eodem modo, quoniam ultimum corporis continentis dicitur superficies secundum quod non profundat se secundum profundationem corporis contenti. Locus vero dicitur inquantum profundat se et habet copulationem suarum partium ad eundem terminum ad quem partes corpori copulantur". See also S, IV, q. 8, f. 48vb, lin. 17-20.

[51] G^1, IV, q. 13, f. 146rb, lin. 27-38: "(i) Potest dici quod locus non est sola superficies, nec [est] corpus continens continet solum contentum secundum superficiem,

In (i), as in passage (6) from P, the claim that place is not only a surface is argued once more by an appeal to passage (C) from the *Categories*. This confirms that G¹ also identifies immersive place with
three-dimensional place. (ii) and (iii) pertain to the attempt of G¹ to
reconcile a three-dimensional immersive place with Aristotle's definition. In (ii) he explains in which way a surface can be said to be a
place. This requires, in particular, that a surface immerses itself in the
located body. Such a requirement, however, cannot be satisfied by a
surface, not even in an accidental sense, as G¹ pretends in (iii). Furthermore, a distinction between surrounding and containing is
assumed and immersion is associated with containing. But even this
distinction does not seem to be plausible. 'Containing', in fact, is conceptually associated with the notion of surrounding and not with that
of immersion. Thus, neither do (ii) and (iii) succeed in squaring Aristotle's definition of place with the three-dimensional, immersive
notion of place.[52] More generally, the difficulties in the treatment of
this exegetical problem given by our commentators stem from the

---

quia, secundum Aristotelem, partes corporis copulantur ad aliquem terminum communem, scilicet ad punctum in medio, et partes loci copulantur ad eundem terminum ad quem et particulae corporis. (ii) Si tamen intelligatur superficies distensa
actualiter per distantiam corporis intercepti, et quod haec superficies sic distensa non
sit solum circumdans, sed profundans se usque ad medium corporis, sic[ut] potest
superficies dici locus. (iii) Si autem consideretur haec superficies in ratione qua circumdans est, sic est terminus corporis; si in quantum profundans, sic est in ratione
continentis. Quia igitur superficies suo nomine solam dicit superficiem in ratione qua
circumdat, ideo falsa est haec "locus est superficies" per se loquendo. Accidit enim
superficiei quod fuerit continens et profundans se in corpus contentum; ideo accidit
ei quod fuerit locus, quia haec condicio, quae est essentialis loco, scilicet continere,
accidentalis est superficiei". See also M³, IV, q. 11, f. 162ra, lin. 13-22. This passage,
quoted from G¹, appears in N and, in an abridged version, in G³ as an answer to the
question 'whether place is a surface', in addition to the response contained in passages (4) and (5) quoted above. See G³, IV, q. 15, f. 159vb, lin. 40-47; N, IV, q. 16, f.
146rb, lin. 9-17.

[52] This seems to be acknowledged to some extent by G¹ himself. In his answer to
the argument in favour of the identity between place and a surface based on Aristotle's definition, he explains how the definitory formula 'limit of the container' must
be analyzed from a logical point of view. In the standard interpretation, 'limit' and
'of the container' are taken to represent the genus and the specific difference of place
respectively, so that 'limit of the container' represents the species of place. But he
holds that this standard interpretation is not correct: "Dicendum ergo ad rationem
quae fuit per definitionem, scilicet quod locus est ultimum sive ultima superficies corporis continentis, quod haec definitio non datur per formalem causam, quia definitio
physica. Unde in ea non ponitur genus vel differentia, sed fit quasi per principium ex
quo definitum naturaliter oritur, et huiusmodi est superficies. Unde antiqui dicebant
quod locus non est superficies, sed aliquid ab ea innascitur. Unde 'ultimum continentis' in definitione loci non dicit speciem vel rationem loci, sed principium ex quo"

fact that a three-dimensional immersive place can only lead to a 'receptive' view of place, that is, to a concept of place as a three-dimensional extension which receives and is occupied by the located body. This, however, contrasts sharply with the "container" view of place reflected by Aristotle's definition of *Physics* IV.4.

3.3 *Ontological Problems in the Three-Dimensional Notion of Immersive Place*

The ontological problems involved in the three-dimensional notion of place are very serious. They can be introduced by the following dilemma: if place has three dimensions, then it is either (A) a body or (B) a three-dimensional incorporeal extension commonly called 'space'. Evidently, (A) can be ruled out, at least if place is not simply identified with a body external to the located body. In particular, it cannot be admitted in the immersive and receptive view of place supported by our commentators, for then the immersion of place into the located body would violate the principle of impenetrability of bodies.[53] (B) must also be ruled out, since, in Aristotle's ontology, there is no extension over and above that inhering in corporeal substances, which is to say that space does not exist.[54]

Our commentators do not explicitly address the ontological dilemma just outlined, but their implicit answer can be in part reconstructed. They accept both the principle of the impenetrability of bodies and Aristotle's denial of space. Nevertheless, they seem to assume that the ontological dilemma is only apparent. Indeed, for them, once the way in which place has three dimensions is properly qualified, the

---

(IV, q. 13, f. 146rb, lin. 38-43). Even in this unusual interpretation of Aristotle's definition of place, however, it is not at all clear in which sense the surface of the container can be thought of as the principle from which the third dimension of place and its immersive nature originate. As a very similar passage in N and M^3 suggests, in this interpretation Aristotle's definition expresses the material cause of place (M^3, IV, q. 11, f. 162ra, lin. 39-42; N, IV, q. 16, f. 146rb, lin. 17-22). This perhaps refers to Aristotle's view that the subject of place and hence its material cause is the containing body. On the problem of the subject of place, see below p. 157-159.

[53] (A) is ruled out explicitly by Aristotle himself in a dialectical argument against the existence of place based on the common-sense view that place has three dimensions: "For all that, it is a problem, if place is, *what* it is: whether it is some kind of bulk of body or some other kind of thing – for we must first inquire what its genus is. (1) It has three dimensions, length, breadth, and depth, by which every body is bounded. But it is impossible that place should be a body, for then there would be two bodies in the same thing" (*Physics*, IV.1, 209a2-7).

[54] See above, note 2.

dilemma disappears. In the rest of this section, we shall examine how our commentators qualify the dimensions of place.

S and P deal directly with (A), reproducing an argument based on the inference 'if place has three dimensions, then it is a body'.[55] In their reply, S and P appeal to the distinction between essential (*per se*) and accidental properties. Since place, unlike body, has three dimensions only accidentally, they maintain that this inference is invalid. To specify in what sense place has three dimensions accidentally, they use a further distinction, which P introduces as follows:

> (10) ... But if we speak of that which has three dimensions accidentally, this is of two kinds, namely either (i) because it is applied to that which has three dimensions essentially or (ii) because it is impressed on a thing of this kind <i.e., having three dimensions essentially>. Place has three dimensions accidentally in the first way, whereas every material form, viz. every form impressed on a body, – be it substantial or accidental – has three dimensions in the second way. And it does not follow that something that has three dimensions in either of these two ways is a body.[56]

For the sake of brevity, we shall refer to senses (i) and (ii) with 'accidentally by application' and 'accidentally by impression', respectively. Since G[1] and M[3] also use the distinction between (i) and (ii) in another context,[57] we can safely ascribe the answer to (A) contained in

---

[55] P, IV, q. 20, f. 78va, lin. 46-49: "In principio *Caeli et Mundi* dicitur quod omnis magnitudo habens tantum unam dimensionem est linea, et habens duas est superficies et habens tres est corpus. Quare, cum locus habeat tres dimensiones, eo quod continet corpus habens dimensiones tres secundum omnem sui partem, erit locus corpus". See also, S, IV, q. 7, f. 48rb, lin. 6-10.

[56] P, IV, q. 20, f. 78vb, lin. 15-20: "... Si autem loquamur de eo quod habet dimensiones tres per accidens, hoc est dupliciter: aut scilicet (i) quia applicatur ei quod habet tres dimensiones per se, aut (ii) quia imprimitur eidem. Primo modo habet locus tres dimensiones per accidens, secundo modo habet omnis forma materialis sive impressa corpori – et hoc sive fuerit substantialis sive accidentalis – tres dimensiones, et neutro istorum modorum ultimorum sequitur quod illud quod habet tres dimensiones sit corpus". See also S, IV, q. 7, f. 48va, lin. 7-20.

[57] It is used in the answer to an objection against Aristotle's doctrine that the subject of place is the containing body and not the located body. The objection claims that, since the extension of place derives from the located body, then its subject is the located body (G[1], IV, q. 15, f. 146vb, lin. 34-35; M[3], IV, q. 13, f. 162va, lin. 4-6). G[1] replies: "Aut potest dimensionatum esse dupliciter, scilicet per se, et hoc est solum corpus, aut per accidens. Et hoc dupliciter. Aut enim per hoc quod est alii impressum, et sic omnes passibiles qualitates habent distensionem, et huiusmodi tantum a suis subiectis distenduntur. Aut per hoc quod est alicui alii applicatum; et sic se habet locus respectu locati, et quod sic distenditur non est necesse quod distendatur per subiectum proprium" (IV, q. 15, f. 146vb, lin. 38-42). See also M[3], IV, q. 13, f. 162vb, lin. 37-44. On the problem of the subject of place see below.

passage (10) to all the commentators of our group.

'Accidentally by application' corresponds to the traditional Aristotelian sense in which quantitative determinations of qualities and more generally of non-quantitative forms derive from the extended subjects of these forms. 'Accidentally by application', however, seems to be used *ad hoc* by our commentators to deal with the case of the three-dimensionality of place. The essentially three-dimensional thing to which place 'applies', in our commentators' view, in order to acquire its three-dimensional extension is the located body.

Although they do not specify how the 'application' of place to the located body is to be thought of, their idea on this point is expressed by the explanation of the derivative character of the depth of place given in (iii) of passage (6) above. There, P maintains that place acquires a depth in virtue of the located body which separates the sides of the containing body. Intuitively, the physical situation that our commentators have in mind arises when a solid body is placed in a fluid container, for instance, a wooden sphere in water. The surface of water is at first flat, but once the wooden sphere is immersed in water, it becomes concave. It would seem that, according to our commentators, the concavity between the inner surface of water formed by the wooden sphere is the place of the sphere. This concavity is a three-dimensional extension, but its existence depends on the body located in it.[58] Thus, unlike a body, place has three dimensions in a derivative and hence accidental way, and therefore (A) of the ontological dilemma stated above is avoided. Roger Bacon employs a very similar strategy to avoid (A). Although he does not use the distinction between 'accidentally by impression' and 'accidentally by application', he maintains, like our commentators, that the *profundatio* of place derives from the located body, which separates the sides of the container.[59]

We turn now to (B), namely, that place is incorporeal space. In order to evaluate whether our commentators avoid (B), it is necessary to distinguish between two versions of the principle of the depen-

---

[58] It should be remarked, however, that the application of place to the located body seems immediately to explain only that the surface of the container is concave, and not also that place has depth, as our commentators believe. Indeed, the fact that place 'applies' to the located body does not suggest any immersive view of place. But in the "surrounding" view of place, the "application" does suggest that place cannot be a flat surface, since it must surround the three-dimensional extension of the located body.

[59] See for instance, Bacon, *In Physicam*, IV, p. 188, lin. 27-34.

dence of the extension of place on the extension of the located body:

(S) A strong version, according to which the extension of place and that of the located body are really the same, although they differ with respect to a mode of being or merely in the sense that they are the same extension regarded in different ways.[60]

(W) A weak version, according to which the extension of place is ontologically dependent on that of the located body, but is not really the same as it, so that the extension of place does not inhere in the located body.

Only the strong version (S) of the 'dependence principle' can avoid (B); the weak version (W) is not sufficient. Aristotle himself rules out this latter version in the case relevant to the discussion of our commentators. He explicitly makes the claim that inside the inner surface of the containing body there is no other three-dimensional extension apart from that of the located body, and not merely that there is no three-dimensional extension ontologically independent from that of the located body, as (W) states.[61]

Our commentators do not seem to follow consistently either of the two versions (S) and (W).

We can illustrate the ambiguity of the position of our commentators with the case of P, the only commentator who devotes a short question to whether place is the space between the sides of the container. Following Aristotle, who explicitly rejects such a candidate for place, P gives a negative answer, which is formulated as follows:

> (11) Therefore, it must be said that place is not such a void space between the sides of the container, because the sides of the container are distant only in virtue of the intervening body ... and therefore there cannot be any void between the sides of the container.[62]

---

[60] It should be remarked that the strong version (S), by identifying a body's place with the extension of this body, violates Aristotle's requirement of immobility of place. For it is clear that, since the located body is subject to motion, also its extension, i.e., its place, is subject to motion. I owe this remark to Prof. Richard Sorabji. On the immobility of place, see below, p. 164-167.

[61] In fact, in the dialectical discussion which leads to the definition of place, Aristotle considers the space between the sides of the container as a possible candidate for place, but he eventually denies the existence of such a space. See Aristotle, *Physics*, IV.4, 211b5-29. On Aristotle's arguments against this candidate for place, see especially Mendell, "Topoi on Topos", p. 219-226.

[62] P, IV, q. 29, f. 80rb, lin. 25-28: "Dicendum igitur quod locus non est tale spatium vacuum contentum inter latera continentis, quoniam non distant latera

The ambiguity of the answer of P derives from the addition of the adjective 'void'. Indeed, this introduces a distinction between occupied space (i.e., occupied by a body) and unoccupied space (i.e., void). The answer of P apparently implies that only unoccupied space cannot exist, so that it seems to support only to the weak version (W) of the 'dependence' principle. In fact, the strong version (S), by assuming all extension to be corporeal extension, rules out both unoccupied and occupied space.

A similar ambiguity is found in M³. He raises the question "whether place has its own distance and extension different from the dimension of the contained body",[63] and he answers:

> (12) I say that place has its own extension only in virtue of the distance of the located body.[64]

When the formulation of the question is considered, it seems that, in giving a negative answer, M³ commits to the strong version (S) of the principle of dependence. The actual answer of M³, however, is also compatible with the weak version (W), since it only makes reference to the dependence of the extension of place on that of the located body, and not to the identity of the two extensions. In fact, both (S) and (W) appear in different passages of M³. For instance, M³ claims:

> (13) To speak of the distension of place insofar as the located body produces such or such a distance in the parts of place is to say that this distance or dimension belongs essentially to the located body and accidentally to place.[65]

Here (S) seems to be assumed, since only one distance is mentioned with respect to both the body and place. Yet, in a subsequent passage, when M³ comes to specify in what sense place is accidentally a

---

continentis nisi per corpus interpositum et quanto plus intrat ipsum corpus, tanto plus dividuntur latera, et ideo non potest aliquid vacuum esse inter latera continentis".

[63] M³, IV, q. 10, f. 160vb, lin. 64-65: "... an locus habeat distantiam et extensionem propriam aliam a dimensione corporis contenti...".

[64] Ibid., ff. 160vb, lin. 65-161ra, lin. 1: "Dico quod non habet distantiam propriam nisi per distantiam locati".

[65] Ibid., f. 161ra, lin. 59-62: "Dico quod, loquendo de distensione loci prout corpus locatum facit partes loci distare sic vel sic, est dicere quod ista distantia sive dimensio est corporis locati per se et loci per accidens".

quantity, that is in what sense it has its quantity from the located body, he maintains:

> (14) ... I say that place is not a quantity in virtue of something else in the same way as whiteness. Whence I say that something can be a quantity in virtue of something else in two ways: (i) either in virtue of its own subject in which it inheres; and in this way whiteness has a quantity in virtue of the quantity of the body. (ii) In another way not in virtue of its own subject in which it inheres, but in virtue of something else from which it is divided; and in this way place has a quantity in virtue of the quantity of the located body.[66]

In (ii) it is emphasized that the located body is not the subject of place. But this is clearly incompatible with (S). Indeed, this passage points out one of the major obstacles to the acceptance of (S). For if (S) saves Aristotle's ontology of extension, on one hand, it is in contrast with the ontological status of Aristotle's place of *Physics* IV, on the other, since this place is an accident of the containing body and not of the located body. This obstacle is at least partially removed by the "two-subjects" theory of place, according to which the subjects of place are both the containing body and the located one. This theory is already discussed in Bacon's questions on the *Physics*.[67] Among the early English commentators, an exponent of this theory is Geoffrey of Aspall. In his answer to the question devoted to the subject of place, he writes:

> (15) It must be said that place can be considered in two ways — and we are speaking of the place of sublunar bodies — (i) either insofar as it is something that contains and surrounds the located body from outside, that is, insofar as it is the limit of the containing body and originates from its principles, and in this sense place is in the locating body as in its subject and, according to the author of the book on *Six Principles*, in the containing body, (ii) or place is considered not only as an external container, but as a certain habit acquired by the located body that immerses itself up to the centre of this body as an internal mea-

---

[66] Ibid., f. 161rb, lin. 10-14: "... dico quod non similiter est locus quantum ab alio sicut albedo. Unde dico quod esse quantum per aliud est dupliciter: (i) aut per aliud ut per proprium subiectum cui inheret; et sic est albedo quanta a quantitate corporis. (ii) Alio modo per aliud non per subiectum proprium cui inheret, sed per aliud a quo est divisum; et sic est locus quantum a quantitate locati".

[67] See Bacon, *In Physicam*, IV, p. 188, lin. 5-10. On Bacon's treatment of the two-subjects theory of place, see Trifogli, "Roger Bacon and Aristotle's Doctrine of Place", p. 166-167.

sure in some way, since the parts of place correspond to the parts of
the body, not in virtue of their own dimension, but of the dimension of
the located body. And in this way place is in the located body as in its
subject.[68]

In (ii) Aspall refers to immersive place. He assumes the strong version
(S) of the principle of dependence and, accordingly, identifies the subject of immersive place with the located body. When (i) is taken into
account, it is clear that, in the end, the two-subject theory splits place
into two quite distinct things. (a) One is Aristotle's place of the *Physics*,
namely, the limit of the containing body. (b) The other, however,
does not exactly correspond to Aristotle's description of place in the
Categories, for while it retains the idea of place having three dimensions, those dimensions belong to a body, as required by Aristotle's
ontology in the *Physics*.

Our commentators also discuss the two-subject theory of place.
Indeed, it is probable that G^1 and M^3 have Aspall in mind when they
present this theory as an *opinio magnorum*.[69] However, like Bacon,[70]
they reject it and support Aristotle's view in the *Physics* that place has
only one subject, namely, the containing body.[71] But this makes the
ontological status of immersive place even more complicated and
confused. If this place is a three-dimensional extension inhering in
the containing body, then in Aristotle's ontology it is difficult to avoid
the conclusion that place is the extension of the locating body itself.

---

[68] M^1, IV, q. 2, f. 112rb, lin. 62-va, lin. 4: "Dicendum quod est considerare locum
dupliciter. Et loquamur de loco inferiorum. (i) Aut secundum quod est quiddam
extra continens et ambiens ipsum extra, ut secundum quod est terminus corporis
continentis egrediens ex principiis eius. Et sic est in locante ut in subiecto, et sic vult
auctor *Sex principiorum* quod sit in continente. (ii) Aut non solum ut est extra continens, sed ut est habitus quidam acquisitus locato, profundans se usque in centrum
corporis ut quodammodo mensura intra, quia partes loci correspondent partibus corporis non sub dimensione propria, sed sub dimensione corporis locati. Et sic est in
locato ut in subiecto". The numbering of the questions on place that form the fragment of Aspall's commentary on Book IV is that published in Trifogli, "Le questioni
sul libro IV", p. 68.

[69] See G^1, IV, q. 15, f. 146va, lin. 24-32; M^3, IV, q. 13, f. 162va, lin. 13-15.

[70] See reference in note 67 above.

[71] See S, IV, q. 3, f. 47rb, lin. 42-va, lin. 9; q. 5, ff. 47va, lin. 36-49; vb, lin. 29-
48ra, lin. 20; P, IV, q. 16, f. 78ra, lin. 4-23; q. 18, f. 78ra, lin. 59-rb, lin. 16; G^1, IV,
q. 15, f. 146va, lin. 24-vb, lin. 42; M^3, IV, q. 13, f. 162rb, lin. 42-vb, lin. 58; G^3, IV,
q. 13, f. 158va, lin. 39-vb, lin. 3; vb, lin. 11-19; q. 14, ff. 158vb, lin. 20-159rb, lin. 7;
N, IV, q. 13, f. 145ra, lin. 44-rb, lin. 6; rb, lin. 13-20; q. 15, f. 145va, lin. 29-vb, lin.
10. T, however, follows Aspall in maintaining that place has two subjects. See T, IV,
q. 7, f. 41va, lin. 17-20.

But then it cannot be immersive, since this violates the principle of the impenetrability of bodies.

In conclusion, relying on Aristotle's view in the *Categories*, S, P, G¹, and M³ maintain that immersive place is a three-dimensional extension coextensive with that of the located body. This reflects a 'receptive' conception of place, according to which place is something in which the located body is received and which is occupied by it. Therefore, this conception is also committed to admitting incorporeal space. Accordingly, immersive place is inconsistent with Aristotle's views in the *Physics*, where he advocates a 'surrounding' notion of place and rejects incorporeal space. This inconsistency is apparent from the insurmountable difficulties in our commentators' attempts to reconcile immersive place with Aristotle's view in the *Physics*.

3.4 *Roger Bacon's Rejection of Immersive Place in the* Communia Naturalium[72]

In his questions on the *Physics*, as we have seen, Roger Bacon defends the view that place has a depth in virtue of which it immerses itself in the located body.[73] His theory of immersive place faces the same ontological problems as those just examined in the early English commentators. Some time after his Questions on the *Physics*, however, Bacon himself became aware of these problems. In fact, in the first book of his later work *Communia naturalium* (ca. 1260-1267), Bacon devotes a significant part of his treatment of place to the refutation of the view that place has depth. It is probable that the extensive discussion of immersive place in the early English commentaries contributed to Bacon's awareness of the difficulties involved in this theory. Indeed, Bacon is very likely referring to some early English exponent of the theory of three-dimensional, immersive place when, in the first book of his *Communia naturalium* , he raises the following question:

> (1) ... it is asked what is required by place properly speaking in addition to a surface. And first it is asked whether some depth, namely, a third dimension, is required, as some think, for they say that (i) place is a surface, not merely insofar as this surface surrounds, but insofar as it actually has a distance intervening between its opposite sides; (ii) nevertheless, place does not have this distance in its own right, but in

---

[72] In this section I follow closely the section on this topic in my paper "Roger Bacon and Aristotle's Doctrine of Place", p. 168-175.

[73] See above, p. 139-141.

virtue of the located body; and that (iii) the depth of place is none other than the depth of the body....[74]

Bacon adds some short arguments presented by the exponent of this
position. His report, however, is not enough to establish whether he is
making reference to the specific position of one of our early English
commentators. In fact, as we have seen in section 3.3, points (i)-(iii) of
passage (1) above can be found in a number of early English commentaries. Moreover, points (i) and (ii) reflect Bacon's own view in his
earlier Questions on the *Physics*. Point (iii) corresponds to the strong
version of the principle of the dependence of the depth of place on
the depth of the located body, according to which the dependence in
question implies that the depth of place is really the same as the
depth of the located body. This strong version of the principle of
dependence cannot be found in Bacon's questions on the *Physics*. We
do, however, occasionally find it in some early English commentators, although they are not able to hold it consistently.[75]

The ontological problems arising from this principle and, more
generally, from the three-dimensionality of immersive place that we
have pointed out in section 3.3 are clearly addressed by Bacon in his
refutation of the theory. In dismissing the arguments presented by the
exponents of this theory, he writes:

> (2) Therefore, these arguments are not valid and the position itself is
> not true, namely, that place has a third dimension, i.e., depth between
> the sides of the containing body. (i) For it is evident that (a) there is no
> distance of a void space, as has been proved, (b) nor is there a distance
> of the locating body, which is a dimension of this body, because noth-
> ing belonging to this body exists between its sides, (c) nor is there any-
> thing else apart from the located body. Therefore, this distance is the
> dimension of the located body. (ii) Yet, place is an accident not of the
> located body, but of the locating body and is nothing of the located
> body. Therefore, the dimension of the located body is not place or
> anything belonging to place.[76]

---

[74] Bacon, *Communia Naturalium*, I, pars 3, p. 194, lin. 35-195, lin. 7: "... queritur,
quid ultra superficiem requiritur ad locum, proprie dictum. Et primo queritur; an
aliqua profunditas, ut tercia dimensio, requiratur, secundum quod aliqui volunt;
dicunt enim quod locus est non tantum superficies circumdans, set in quantum hec
superficies habet actualem distanciam per medium inter partes oppositas; hanc
tamen distanciam non habet a se; set a locato, et quod profundum loci non est aliud
a profundo corporis...".

[75] See above, p. 155-159.

[76] Bacon, *Communia naturalium*, I, pars 3, p. 195, lin. 24-33: "Raciones igitur non

In part (i) of this passage, Bacon considers three possible candidates for the depth of place: (a) an incorporeal dimension; (b) a dimension of the containing body; (c) a dimension of the located body. Following Aristotle's ontology of extension in the *Physics*, he rules out (a). Bacon can also immediately rule out (b), since the containing body cannot be extended also in the region inside its concave surface. Therefore, only (c) is left. However, as Bacon points out in part (ii), alternative (c) cannot be reconciled with the assumption that place is something other than the located body and, in particular, that it does not inhere in the located body as in its subject.

Once alternative (c) is accepted, the only possible way to render the ontological status of three-dimensional place consistent is to adopt the two-subject theory of place. As we have seen in section 3.3, this theory is discussed in the early English commentaries, but is generally rejected. Bacon too in his earlier questions on the *Physics* rejects the two-subject theory,[77] but in that work he also implicitly assumes that it is not entailed by a three-dimensional view of place. Apparently, like the early English commentators, Bacon had in mind at that time a longer list of candidates for the depth of place, which also included depth inhering in the containing body, but spatially external to it. There is little doubt that the absence of such a candidate from the list in the above passage of the *Communia naturalium* shows that Bacon had developed a much more lucid view of the ontological aspects of the theory of three-dimensional place. This led him to reject radically this theory by denying its basic assumption, namely, the existence of a third dimension of place.

Yet, in the *Communia naturalium*, one can still find an echo of this theory. For instance, in dealing with the problem of the difference between place and a surface, Bacon writes:

> (3) I say, therefore, that if the limit of the locating body is considered in itself, insofar as it limits the locating body, then it is a surface, properly speaking. But if that limit is regarded as something capable of containing, then it is concave. If it is regarded as something which actually contains, then it is on its way to becoming a place, but must still be

---

valent, nec ipsa posicio in se est vera, quod locus habet tertiam dimensionem, scilicet, profunditatem inter latera continentis, quia constat quod distancia nulla est vacui spacii, ut probatum est, nec corporis locantis, que sit ejus dimensio, quia nichil ejus est inter latera sua nec aliquid nisi corpus locatum; ergo, hec distancia est dimensio corporis locati; set locus non accidit corpori locato set locanti, et nichil est ipsius locati, ergo dimensio locati non est locus nec aliquid loci".

[77] See above, p. 157.

completed by two conditions, namely, by a relation to the space or
depth between the sides of the containing body and by a respect to the
limits of the universe.[78]

This passage is parallel to that of the *Questions on the Physics,* where
Bacon argues that the surface that represents the limit of the containing body must satisfy three further requirements in order to be the
place of a body: containment, immobility and depth.[79] Bacon also
gives the first two of these requirements in the present passage (3)
from the *Communia naturalium.* The capacity of containing is here
expressed geometrically by concavity. Immobility corresponds to the
respect (i.e., distance) that the limit of the containing body has to the
limits of the universe. Such a correspondence is based on a particular
solution to the problem of the immobility of place, which Bacon
adopts in both the questions on the *Physics* and the *Communia naturalium.* This theory will be examined in detail in section 4.[80] The third
requirement, namely depth, is also present to some extent in passage
(3), but with a very important modification, for "having depth" has
been replaced by "having a relation to depth". Bacon further specifies that the depth in question is simply the depth of the body located
between the sides of the container, in agreement with Aristotle's
ontology in the *Physics.* He also insists that place has only a relation to
such a depth, but in itself has no depth.

The question naturally arises why Bacon maintains, in the *Communia naturalium,* that place has a relation to the depth of the located
body, the nature of which relation remains obscure. One implicit reason is that, by insisting that place is somehow related to a third dimension, Bacon is attempting to minimize the difference with his earlier
view on place in the questions on the *Physics.* Yet, Bacon also gives an
explicit reason for positing this relation, which is the same one he gave
in the questions on the *Physics* in connection with the requirement of
the depth of place:[81] a relation of place to the depth of the located

---

[78] Bacon, *Communia naturalium,* I, pars 3, p. 183, lin. 4-10: "Dico, ergo, quod si ultimum locantis consideretur in se, ut terminat corpus locans, sic est superficies, et
nominatur vere et proprie. Si vero consideretur illud ultimum, ut natum est continere, sic est concavum: si vero ut actu continet, sic incipit fieri locus, set completur
per duo, scilicet, per respectum ad spacium sive profundum inter latera continentis,
et per respectum ad terminos mundi".
[79] See above, p. 140.
[80] See below, p. 175-186.
[81] See above, p.140-141.

body is required by Aristotle's account of the continuity of place in the *Categories*.[82] This is not at all surprising, since we have seen in sections 2 and 3 that Aristotle's short treatment of place in the *Categories* is the major source of the theory of three-dimensional place in both Bacon and the early English commentators. Yet, even without mentioning the details of Bacon's explanation in the *Communia naturalium*, it should be clear that he could hardly be successful in his attempt to save Aristotle's account of the continuity of place in the *Categories* by means of a notion of place as two dimensional extension having simply a relation to the depth of the located body. In Aristotle's account each part of the located body occupies a corresponding part of place, which accordingly must also have a third dimension, and not simply a relation to a third dimension. Bacon himself seems to be aware that his "weakened" notion of "three-dimensional" place in the *Communia naturalium* cannot be reconciled with Aristotle's view of place in the *Categories*. In fact, the failure of a similar attempt at reconciliation is acknowledged by Bacon in his questions on the *Physics*.[83] But in the *Communia naturalium*, instead of adding a third dimension to place, he eventually decides to dismiss Aristotle's view in the *Categories*:

> However, when in the *Categories* Aristotle posits that place is a species of quantity, he does not posit a new species essentially distinct from surface, but one distinct only in relation. And since place is a quantity extrinsic to the located body, and not intrinsic, as are a line, a surface, and a body, and since he had to take into account this difference in the *Logical works*, where he speaks superficially, therefore there he also lists place <among the species of quantity> and distinguishes it from a surface. But he does not do this in the *Metaphysics*,[84] where he speaks according to a deeper truth, or in the *Natural works*, where he says that place is the limit of the containing body and that this is a surface.[85]

---

[82] Bacon, *Communia naturalium*, I, pars 3, p. 183, lin. 10-19: "Quod vero habeat respectum necessario ad spatium et profundum inter latera continentis, patet per hoc, quod Aristoteles dicit in *Predicamentis*, quod partes loci copulantur ad eundem terminum ad quem copulantur partes corporis locati, set partes sue profunditatis copulantur ad superficiem, que est ymaginanda inter partes ejus; ergo partes ejus copulantur ad eandem superficiem. Ergo locus necessario habet profundum corporis contenti, vel respicit de necessitate profundum illius, seu quod habet respectum essencialiter et necessario ad illud profundum".

[83] On this point, see Trifogli, "Roger Bacon and Aristotle's Doctrine of Place", p.158-160.

[84] See above, note 14.

[85] Bacon, *Communia naturalium*, I, pars 3, p. 184, lin. 23-32: "Quod autem

This passage shows that Bacon is aware that the respect of place to depth is not enough to make place a species of quantity distinct from a surface, as Aristotle implies in the *Categories*. In short, Bacon admits that Aristotle's conflicting views of place in the *Categories* and in the *Physics* cannot strictly speaking be reconciled. Consequently, he has to decide which of the two views is the "true" one. On this point he appeals to the "Averroistic" solution of this conflict, according to which the true view of place is that of the *Physics*, where Aristotle focuses on the true nature of things, whereas in the *Categories* he proceeds superficially, introducing distinctions that deeper investigation shows to be devoid of a firm basis.[86] This "Averroistic" solution is the one commonly given in the later medieval tradition. Thus, although the *Communia naturalium* still bears the traces of Bacon's earlier theory of three-dimensional place, it also contains the exegetical tool that will forestall the use of this theory in the later tradition. Indeed, we have not found traces of this theory after Bacon's *Communia naturalium*. This suggests that, although the theory of three-dimensional place finds its most authoritative exponent in Roger Bacon and his questions on the *Physics*, it seems to have come to an end with the *Communia naturalium* by the same author.

4. *The Immobility of Place*

While in sections 1-3 we have analysed the conflict between Aristotle's definition of place in the *Physics* and his account of place in the *Categories*, here we shall focus on an internal problem that arises from the requirement of immobility introduced by Aristotle in his final definition of place in *Physics* IV.4.[87] In fact, in chapter 4 Aristotle first defines the place of a body A as the limit of the body B containing A that is in contact with A.[88]

Aristoteles ponit locum esse speciem quantitatis in *Predicamentis*, non ponit novam speciem distinctam per essenciam a superficie, sed distinctam in respectu. Et quia extrinseca quantitas est rei locate, non intrinsica, sicut linea superficies et corpus (et hanc distinccionem debuit notare in *Logicalibus*, nisi (*pro* ubi) superficialiter loquitur), et ideo connumerat locum, et distinguit a superficie; set non fecit hoc, ubi loquitur in *Metaphysica*, magis in profundo veritatis, nec in *Naturalibus*, ubi dicit quod locus est ultimum continentis, et hoc est superficies".

[86] See above, p. 135-137.

[87] The problem of the immobility of place in Aristotle's theory has been extensively discussed by Algra, who also takes into account the solutions proposed by some Greek commentators. See Algra, *Concepts of Space*, p. 222-230. See also R. Sorabji, *Matter, Space and Motion, Theories in Antiquity and Their Sequel*, Duckworth, London 1988, p. 186-201.

[88] Aristotle, *Physics*, IV.4, 212a5-6a.

Thus, according to this first definition, the place of a ship in a river is the surface of water in contact with the ship. Later in the chapter, however, Aristotle makes clear that, since this first definition is to some extent incomplete, it remains provisional. Needed is a further requirement to distinguish place from any container whatsoever. In the following passage, which leads to the final definition of place, Aristotle argues that the requirement in question is immobility:

> And, just as a vessel is a mobile place, so place is an immobile vessel. Therefore, when an enclosed thing moves and changes within something that moves, like a ship in a river, it has the surrounding thing serving as a vessel rather than as a place. But place should be immobile. Therefore, the whole river is rather the place, because the whole is immobile. So the first immobile surface of the surrounding thing, that is place.[89]

This passage, which is nearly the whole of Aristotle's treatment of the immobility of place, is puzzling in several respects. First, although the difference between an immobile place and a mobile vessel formulated at the beginning of the passage is clear in its abstract formulation, its subsequent illustration with the case of a ship in a river is problematic. Since the water surrounding the ship continuously flows, then – Aristotle claims – the place of this ship should rather be identified with the "whole river", which is immobile. The meaning of the expression "the whole river" is not specified by Aristotle, but it can be probably taken to mean either the banks and the bed of the river or the totality of water enclosed by them as opposed to the portion of water immediately in contact with the ship. In both cases, "the whole river" stands for something that is certainly more fixed than the flowing surfaces of the water in contact with the ship. Yet, even when the meaning of "the whole river" is thus specified, Aristotle's example cannot be taken as a positive account of the immobility of place. On the contrary, from other aspects of his theory of place, it follows that the whole river cannot be regarded, strictly speaking, as the place of the ship. For, in *Physics* IV.2, Aristotle distinguishes between common place and proper place. The common place of a body A is that which also contains other bodies besides A, whereas the proper place of A contains only A, being a containing surface that encompasses exclusively A.[90] Only proper place is regarded as "true" place by Aristotle.

---

[89] Ibid., 212a14-21. The English translation of this passage is taken from Algra, *Concepts of Space*, p. 223.

It is clear, however, that the whole river, as opposed to the surface of water in contact with the ship, is not at all the proper place of the ship, since it contains many other bodies besides the ship.

One might suggest that in claiming that the place of a body is immobile, Aristotle means that a body must have some immobile place, but that such an immobile place needs not be its proper place. This suggestion, however, cannot be accepted. In fact, Aristotle refers to proper place, as is proven by the occurrence of the adjective "first" in the final definition stated at the end of the passage quoted above ("the first immobile surface of the surrounding thing"). According to the standard interpretation, here "first" serves to specify the surrounding surface with which place must be identified, namely, with that in contact with the located body (the first surface in spatial order after that of the located body itself).[91] Thus, "first" is used here precisely to distinguish proper place from common place. As a consequence, a first difficulty in the passage is that Aristotle's account of the immobility of place, as illustrated with the case of the ship in a river, seems incompatible with the requirement that proper place must also be in contact with the located body. This first difficulty was already detected by Simplicius[92] and was commonly raised in the medieval tradition.[93]

A second and even more radical difficulty in Aristotle's passage derives from the ontological status of place. In Aristotle's view of the *Physics*, although place is separated from the located body, it does not exist over and above physical bodies. In fact, it is the limit, that is, an accident, of the containing body. But the containing body, being a natural body, can be subject to motion. Therefore, its limit, namely place, can also be subject to motion, although in a derivative sense: when the containing body moves, it carries along its limiting surface.

---

[90] On the distinction between proper place and common place, see above, note 47.

[91] For this interpretation, see, for instance, Simplicius, *In Physicam*, IV, p. 584, lin. 15-20; Averroes, *In Physicam*, IV, t.c. 41, f. 140ra B; Thomas Aquinas, *In Physicam*, IV, lectio 6, p. 227b; Giles of Rome, *In Physicam*, IV, lectio 7, f. 80vb.

[92] See Simplicius, *In Physicam*, IV, p. 584, lin. 20-27.

[93] This has been pointed out especially by E. Grant in his survey of the main medieval solutions to the problem of the immobility of place. See E. Grant, "The Medieval Doctrine of Place: Some Fundamental Problems and Solutions", in A. Maierù and A. Paravicini-Bagliani (eds.), *Studi sul XIV secolo in memoria di Anneliese Maier*, Edizioni di storia e letteratura, Roma 1981, p. 59-60. For a traditional study on the medieval theory of place, see also P. Duhem, *Le Système du Monde. Histoire des doctrines cosmologiques de Platon a Copernic*, vol. VII, Hermann, Paris 1956, p. 158-302.

Thus, as it seems, the requirement of immobility cannot be reconciled with the ontological status of place as an accident of a mobile body. This ontological difficulty represents the most common and crucial objection raised by medieval commentators against Aristotle's account of the immobility of place.[94] Nevertheless, most medieval commentators tried to reconcile the requirement of immobility of place with its ontological status of limit of the containing body and therefore proposed different solutions, all of which involved significant modifications to Aristotle's doctrine.[95]

The treatment of the problem of the immobility of place given by the early English commentators is largely a review of preexisting opinions on this topic. Three opinions are invariably discussed by all our commentators, and we shall concentrate on them in this section. Following the order in which they are presented in our commentaries, we shall begin with Averroes' opinion. This is the only opinion whose exponent is explicitly mentioned by our commentators.

4.1 *Averroes' Opinion*

Averroes himself is not very sensitive to the problems arising from Aristotle's requirement of the immobility of place. In particular, he devotes no specific doctrinal or doxographical digression to this topic, as he does in the other traditional problem case – viz., the place of the heavens. The opinion that medieval latin commentators usually ascribe to Averroes is largely an extrapolation from some expository remarks in his comment 41 of Book IV. In the opening sentence, Averroes gives the following interpretation of Aristotle's distinction between place and a vessel:

> (1) In the definition of place Aristotle posits another difference between place and a vessel. And this difference is that a vessel is a container and is essentially mobile, whereas place is a container that is immobile, if not accidentally.[96]

---

[94] Among Greek commentators, the ontological difficulty was pointed out most notably by Philoponus. See Philoponus, *In Physicam*, IV, p. 587, lin. 30-588, lin. 6.

[95] A review of the most important solutions proposed by medieval commentators is given in Grant, "The Medieval Doctrine of Place", p. 57-72.

[96] Averroes, *In Physicam*, IV, t. c. 41, f. 139vbL: "In definitione loci aliam differentiam ponit inter ipsum et vas. Et est quoniam vas est continens et mobile essentialiter, locus vero est continens immobile, nisi per accidens".

While Aristotle simply contrasts the mobility of a vessel with the immobility of place, Averroes qualifies Aristotle's claim. In particular, in the concluding words of the above passage Averroes implies that place is not absolutely immobile, since it can be mobile accidentally.[97] This is the crucial point of passage (1). It leads to the formula with which the early English commentators summarize Averroes' opinion: place is essentially (*per se*) immobile, but accidentally mobile. Our commentators also agree on the meaning of this formula. In Aristotle's view the only things that are essentially subject to motion are bodies (e.g., a vessel). Place, however, is not a body, but the limit of a body. Therefore, place can be subject to motion only in the accidental and derivative sense that the containing body of which it is the limit is essentially subject to this motion.

Among the early English commentators, T alone accepts Averroes' solution.[98] The others reject the interpretation of the immobility of place given by Averroes on the grounds that it does not at all reflect Aristotle's intention. For instance, they point out that any other property of a body (e.g., whiteness) can be said to be immobile in the weak sense of being mobile only accidentally. Accordingly, if place is regarded as immobile in this weak sense, then it is left unexplained why in fact Aristotle thinks that it is necessary to add 'immobility' to

---

[97] Among Greek commentators, this interpretation of Aristotle's requirement of the immobility of place is suggested by Themistius and Simplicius. See Themistius, *In Physicam*, IV, p. 118, lin. 29-30; Simplicius, *In Physicam*, IV, p. 583, lin. 1-3.

[98] See T, IV, q. 13, f. 43va, lin. 11-12. T, however, ascribes to Averroes a more articulated opinion. Referring to the problem of the immobility, he says: "Et dicendum quod multipliciter dicitur ad hoc. Uno modo sic, secundum Averroem dicentem quod (i) locus se habet ad sua subiecta sicut alia accidentia ad sua et quod movetur aliquo modo per motionem sui subiecti. (ii) Distinguit tamen ut salvat rationes sic dupliciter esse loqui de loco: aut de loco ubi (non *ms.*) primo et per se reperitur natura loci, ut de concavitate (continuitate *ms.*) orbis lunae, et huiusmodi locus, licet sit [im]mobilis motu circulari, est tamen immobilis de loco ad locum. Et sic, ut dicit ipse, sumitur immobilitas in definitione loci, et sic intendit Aristoteles. Alio modo est loqui de loco non primo et per se, cuius<modi> locus est hic inferius; et huiusmodi aliquo modo movetur, ut patet de loco liquoris contenti in vase, quod movetur, cum vas moveatur, sicut dicit Commentator" (T, IV, q. 13, f. 42vb, lin. 8-20). In this passage, (i) reports the standard interpretation of Averroes' position. (ii) implies a different solution to the problem of immobility, according to which 'immobility' stands for the absence of rectilinear local motion (i.e., the passage from one place to another). In this sense the concavity of the lunar orb is immobile, since it moves only with circular motion. More generally, the locations associated with celestial bodies are immobile in this sense. The solution in (ii) is not found in Averroes' commentary, although it probably originates from some suggestions by Averroes in t. c. 41, f. 140raB and t. c. 42, f. 140rbF.

the definition of place, but not to that of any other property of a body. Similarly, in Aristotle's view, since immobility is a defining property of place, then the contrary property of mobility cannot belong to place, even in an accidental sense.[99]

In general, the treatment of Averroes' opinion given by the early English commentators makes no significant contribution to the medieval discussion on the immobility of place. In fact, in their refutation of his opinion, they simply restate in more accurate terms the ontological question involved in Aristotle's position. If the reality of place consists of being the limit of a natural and hence movable body, then Averroes seems right in maintaining that only a weak kind of immobility can be ascribed to place. But, as our commentators remark, Aristotle's emphasis on the immobility of place appears unjustified. Yet, a more remarkable aspect of the discussion of Averroes' opinion can be found in S and P. In defending the view that place is not even accidentally mobile, S and P maintain that Averroes' contrary position on this topic derives from his 'erroneous' assumption that place is the same thing as the limit of the containing body. Referring to Averroes' opinion, S writes:

(2) To that it is said that place considered in its proper being is essentially and also accidentally immobile. For place has the nature

---

[99] For instance, P argues against Averroes as follows: "(i) Nulla species definita per aliquam differentiam potest recipere praedicationem oppositae differentiae, nec per se nec per accidens; sed locus definitur per immobile; quare locus non erit mobilis nec per se nec per accidens. Maior videtur per hoc quod homo non recipit praedicationem irrationalis, nec per se nec per accidens, nec linea recipit praedicationem latitudinis per se vel per accidens, et sic in omnibus aliis. Minor patet per Auctorem in littera. (ii) Item, secundum Aristotelem in VII *Metaphysicae*, ultima differentia definitionis convertitur cum definito; quare, cum 'immobile' sit ultima differentia definitionis loci, erit immobile convertibile cum loco. Si igitur immobile, quod est differentia loci ultima, sit immobile per se, mobile tamen per accidens, cum omne accidens sit tale, scilicet quod est mobile per accidens, ut motu subiecti, immobile tamen per se, esset omne accidens locus, quod patet impossibile. Impossibile ergo videtur quod locus sit mobilis per accidens et per se immobilis" (P, IV, q. 30, f. 80vb, lin. 28-38). Argument (ii) is evidently *ad hominem*. For even if 'absolutely immobile' is the ultimate difference of the definition of place, then reasoning in the same way one would infer that everything that is absolutely immobile is place; but this conclusion does not seem to be true. For the refutation of Averroes' opinion see also S, IV, q. 13, f. 49va, lin. 4-18; G¹, IV, q. 16, f. 146vb, lin. 55-57; G³, IV, q. 16, f. 160ra, lin. 51-rb, lin. 8; N, IV, q. 17, f. 146va, lin. 11-21. Bacon also discusses in a short question the view that place is only essentially immobile, but accidentally mobile, although he does not ascribe it to Averroes. He rejects this view with arguments very similar to those found in our commentaries. See Bacon, *In Physicam*, IV, p. 189, lin. 34-190, lin. 20.

of a surface, and not only this, but in addition to the nature of a surface, it is also immersive in every part of the located body. Therefore, although place accidentally moves according to the being of a surface, viz., insofar as it is the limit of the containing body, it does not nevertheless move either essentially nor accidentally according to its proper being. But in positing that place and surface are entirely the same, Averroes was deceived and accordingly it was necessary for him to posit that this kind of place is accidentally mobile. And this makes clear the solution to the counter-arguments, because place moves accidentally only insofar as it is the limit of the containing body, and not insofar as it is place, i.e., insofar as it is immersive.[100]

Evidently, this passage shows that S-P's attempted strategy in supporting the absolute immobility of place consists in resorting to the 'immersive' nature of place that we have analysed in section 3. Abstractly, this strategy is rather appealing. The quoted passage, however, gives no positive indications on how it could be carried out. If, as the passage seems to imply, place has a composite quantitative structure, being the limit of the containing body plus a depth, and if the limit of the containing body can in fact move accidentally, then place can be absolutely immobile at most according to its depth. But we have seen that in S-P's view the depth of place is ontologically dependent on the located body. Consequently, the recourse to immersive place seems to duplicate the problem of the immobility rather than to solve it, since this kind of place turns out to be ontologically dependent on two movable substances, i.e., the located body and the containing body.

S and P are probably aware of these difficulties, since they drop any further mention of immersive place in their subsequent discussion. They eventually accept the third opinion on the immobility of

---

[100] S, IV, q. 13, f. 49va, lin. 18-27: "Ad illud dicitur quod locus sub (*forte pro* secundum) esse loci immobilis est per se et etiam per accidens. Locus enim habet naturam superficiei, et non solum hanc, immo super naturam superficiei addit profundationem secundum omnem partem locati. Unde licet secundum esse superficiei, in quantum scilicet est terminus continentis corporis, movetur per accidens, non tamen secundum esse loci movetur, scilicet nec per se nec <per> accidens. Commentator vero in hoc quod ponit locum et superficiem penitus idem deceptus fuit et ideo necesse est ponere hunc locum esse mobilem per accidens. Per istud satis patet ad rationes in contrarium, quoniam secundum quod terminus continentis est tantum, movetur per accidens, non secundum quod locus est, id est secundum quod profundationem dicit". See also P, IV, q. 30, f. 80vb, lin. 38-52.

place, which, as we shall see, makes no reference to a three-dimensional place.[101]

It should be noted that, if immersive place is more generally viewed as a three-dimensional extension that is coextensive with the located body, it can indeed represent an absolutely immobile place, provided that it is regarded as incorporeal space ontologically independent from any body. Among Aristotelian commentators this conception is supported by Philoponus.[102] On the other hand, it clearly subverts Aristotle's ontology of extension. But in section 2 we have seen that our commentators do not go so far as to posit an incorporeal space independent from bodies. Thus, although our commentators constantly employ Aristotle's requirement of immobility in their counter-arguments to the question 'Whether place is a surface',[103] when they turn to the discussion specifically devoted to this requirement, they make little use of immersive place.

Finally, Averroes' position on the immobility of place reflects a "negative" solution to this problem. Indeed, Averroes makes no attempt to find a positive solution which would show that place is absolutely immobile. Such a positive solution is instead attempted in the other two opinions on the immobility of place discussed by the early English commentators.

4.2 *The Second Opinion on the Immobility of Place: The Immobility of the Celestial Nature*

The second opinion predates our commentators, since it is reported by Richard Rufus of Cornwall, Roger Bacon and B. The treatment of this opinion given by our commentators is very similar to that found in Rufus' Questions on the *Physics*, which are a direct source at least for some of our commentaries.

In Rufus' report the opinion in question is presented as follows:

> (3) For some say that a celestial nature, such as light, is propagated throughout the whole sphere of the elements, and this nature persists,

---

[101] See below p. 177-178.

[102] On Philoponus' rejection of Aristotle's doctrine of place, see above, note 3.

[103] See S, IV, q. 8, f. 48rb, lin. 42-47; P, IV, q. 21, f. 78vb, lin. 40-49, 60-61; T, IV, q. 6, f. 41ra, lin. 5-8, 15-20; G¹, IV, q. 13, f. 146ra, lin. 45-51, 53-60; M³, IV, q. 11, f. 161va, lin. 64-vb, lin. 7; vb, lin. 15-26; G³, IV, q. 15, f. 159rb, lin. 35-va, lin. 2; va, lin. 36-47; N, IV, q. 16, ff. 145vb, lin. 34-42; 146ra, lin. 22-31.

when air, water, and the other bodies are in motion; and place persists in this nature as in its subject, when the containing body moves. And they say that the place of my hand is not the limit of air insofar as it is air, but rather insofar as air is joined with this nature. And therefore because this nature persists, place persists.[104]

As our commentators concisely put it, according to this opinion, the immobility of place derives from the nature or power (*virtus*) that is propagated from the last celestial sphere to the sublunar world. Rufus' report identifies this nature with light. This might suggest that the opinion in question originates from the circle of Robert Grosseteste. In his commentary on the *Physics*, however, Grosseteste himself makes no reference to light or to any celestial nature in order to explain the immobility of place.[105]

The exponents of the second opinion seem to acknowledge tacitly that, since place is ontologically an accident, it can only be absolutely immobile, if its subject is absolutely immobile. Elemental bodies and more generally natural bodies do not have this property. Nevertheless – they maintain – there is something in the universe that is absolutely immobile and permeates every body, namely, the celestial nature. This is, in fact, to be regarded as the subject of place, for place is not the limit (i.e., in general, an accident) of the containing body *qua* natural body (e.g., air or water) but *qua* endowed with the immobile celestial virtue. In other words, in the second opinion, two formal elements must be distinguished in a natural body: its specific nature in Aristotle's sense, which is a principle of motion, and a more universal and 'cosmological' nature, the celestial nature, which is a principle of persistency that guarantees the immobility of place.

---

[104] Rufus, *In Physicam*, IV, f. 7ra, lin. 4-9: "Aliqui enim dicunt quod per totam sphaeram elementorum diffunditur natura caelestis aliqua, sicut lux, et haec manet, moto aere et aqua et aliis corporibus motis; et in hoc manet locus tanquam in subiecto, moto continente. Et dicunt quod locus manus meae non est terminus aeris in quantum aer, sed magis in quantum habet secum hanc naturam coniunctam; et propterea, manente hac natura, manet locus". See also Bacon, *In Physicam*, IV, p. 191, lin. 11-14; B, IV, f. 24rb, lin. 7-9; S, IV, q. 14, f. 49rb, lin. 44-46; va, lin. 35-36; P, q. 31, f. 80vb, lin. 9-14; T, IV, q. 13, f. 43ra, lin. 33-39; G^1, IV, q. 16, f. 146vb, lin. 57-62; M^3, IV, q. 14, f. 163ra, lin. 14-17; G^3, IV, q. 16, f. 160rb, lin. 51-va, lin. 5; N, IV, q. 17, f. 146vb, lin. 15-19.

[105] R. Wood remarks that it reflects a view somewhat similar to that of Philip the Chancellor. See Wood, "Richard Rufus: Physics at Paris before 1240", p. 107-109. Prof. Richard Sorabji suggests that the most likely origin of this view is Proclus' theory of place as light. This suggestion is very interesting and deserves further investigation. On Proclus' theory, see Sorabji, *Matter, Space and Motion*, p. 106-119.

The general attitude towards this opinion of our commentators is that it (i) does not save the immobility of place, but (ii) correctly assumes that the celestial nature is a formal element inhering in each natural body in addition to its specific nature.

As to point (i), the main objection raised by Rufus and our commentators against this opinion's explanation of immobility concentrates on the claim that the celestial virtue can function as a subject for place. This objection is very clearly formulated by G¹ in the following argument:

> (4) This nature is either a body or not. If not, then place is not in this nature as in its subject. For place is an accident of a body, since it is its limit. On the other hand, if this nature were a body, then it would be either a mathematical or a natural body. If it were a mathematical body, then this is not pertinent to our problem. (a) If it were a natural body, then it would be endowed with motion, since every natural body is endowed with some motion, as Aristotle intends in the book *On the heavens and the universe*. Therefore, because of the persistency of this nature, the immobility of place cannot be saved. (b) Furthermore, it follows 'it is a natural body and it is together with air; therefore, two bodies are in the same place'.[106]

Following Aristotle, G¹ claims that place is an accident of a natural body, so that the celestial nature could be a subject for place only if it were a natural body. But then evidently, as implied in (a), the ontological difficulty concerning Aristotle's requirement of immobility surfaces once again. (b) points out that, in virtue of the principle of the impenetrability of bodies, the identification of the celestial nature with a natural body is also incompatible with its property of being propagated throughout the whole corporeal extension of the sublunar world.

Turning to point (ii), while the appeal to the celestial nature is not

---

[106] G¹, IV, q. 16, ff. 146vb, lin. 62-147ra, lin. 5: "Haec natura aut est corpus aut non. Si non, tunc locus non est in ea ut in subiecto. Est enim locus accidens corporis, cum sit eius terminus. Si autem haec natura fuerit corpus, aut ergo mathematicum aut naturale. Si mathematicum, tunc nihil ad propositum. (a) Si naturale, ergo ei debetur motus, <quia> cuilibet corpori naturali debetur aliquis motus, ut vult Aristoteles in libro *Caeli et mundi*. Propter igitur permanentiam huius corporis non potest salvari immobilitas loci. (b) Item, est naturale et cum corpore aeris; quare duo corpora in eodem loco". See also Rufus, *In Physicam*, IV, f. 7ra, lin. 9-24; S, IV, q. 14, f. 49vb, lin. 2-10; P, IV, q. 31, f. 81ra, lin. 1-12; T, q. 13, f. 43ra, lin. 45-rb, lin. 6; M³, IV, q. 14, f. 163ra, lin. 17-25; G³, IV, q. 16, f. 160va, lin. 5-16; N, q. 17, f. 146vb, lin. 19-26.

adequate to save the immobility of place, it does account, in our commentators' view, for another aspect of Aristotle's doctrine of place, namely, the theory of natural place. As Aristotle implies at the very end of *Physics* IV.1-5, the natural place of an elemental body is the limit not of any containing body whatsoever, but of a body which is of the same kind of the located body.[107] In our commentators' terms, a homogeneity (*unigeneitas*) must be assumed between a body and its natural container. On the other hand, the substantial forms of the containing and contained elements are not homogeneous. Air, for instance, is the natural place of water. Aristotle himself seems to perceive this difficulty. He thinks, however, that the homogeneity in question must be understood as a peculiar relationship between the substantial forms of the located and naturally locating bodies.[108] Rufus and our commentators apparently ignore Aristotle's explanation.[109] On the contrary, they maintain that the homogeneity at issue cannot be explained by the substantial forms of the elements alone. Instead another formal principle must be added to their substantial forms, which is the celestial nature that appears in the second opinion on the immobility of place.[110]

---

[107] Aristotle, *Physics*, IV.5, 212b29-213a1.

[108] He claims that water is analogous to the matter of air and conversely air is in some sense the form and the actuality of water. Thus water and air are in some sense the same thing, but water is this thing in potency, whereas air in actuality. See ibid., 213a1-10. On Aristotle's theory of natural place, see especially Algra, *Concepts of Space*, p. 195-221.

[109] Our commentators usually assume that the homogeneity between natural place and the body naturally located in it derives from the fact that they have a common nature; then they argue that this nature can be neither matter nor a form common to them as intrinsic constituent of each of them. For instance, G[1] writes: "Ultimo quaeritur de unigeneitate quae est inter locum et locatum. Dicit enim Aristoteles quod quaedam sunt unigenea, separata et divisa, cuiusmodi sunt locus et locatum. Haec autem unigeneitas, cum sit natura, quaeritur an sit materia vel forma. Quod non materia videtur, (i) quia sic quodlibet elementum esset locus alterius. Conveniunt enim elementa in materia. (ii) Item, proprium est materiae contineri et loci continere; ergo etc. Quod autem haec natura non sit forma substantialis patet, (i') quia corruptibile et incorruptibile, ut habetur in fine decimi, plus differunt quam secundum genus, et sic non sunt in eodem genere; ergo nullam naturam generis communicant; a forma autem substantiali sumitur genus; ergo etc. (ii') Item, si haec natura esset forma substantialis, tunc elementa non differrent specie, cum ipsorum sit eadem materia. (iii') Item, sic ultimum caeli et ignis contentus non differrent specie, quod falsum est" (IV, q. 18, f. 147va, lin. 40-50). See also Rufus, *In Physicam*, IV, f. 7va, lin. 1-7; S, IV, q. 20, ff. 50vb, lin. 45-51ra, lin. 20; P, IV, q. 48, f. 83rb, lin. 23-35; T, IV, q. 14, f. 43va, lin. 13-42; M[3], IV, q. 17, f. 164rb, lin. 16-27; G[3], IV, q. 18, f. 161va, lin. 36-vb, lin. 2; N, IV, q. 19, ff. 147vb, lin. 48-148ra, lin. 9.

[110] G[1] replies to the question mentioned in the preceding note as follows: "Potest

In conclusion, the early English commentators accept the existence of a celestial nature conceived of as a somewhat universal and cosmological formal principle, distinct from the substantial forms of natural bodies, and which alone accounts for the preserving power of natural place. They deny, however, that this nature can account for the immobility of place. From a historical point of view, it is likely that both the second opinion on the immobility of place and the interpretation of the theory of natural place transmitted by Rufus and our commentators were originally parts of a single exegesis of Aristotle's doctrine of place.[111] In next section, we shall see why they make no significant attempt to save the part of this exegesis concerning the immobility.

4.3 *The Third Opinion on the Immobility of Place: The Identity of the Distance from the Fixed Points of the Universe*

It is not yet clear why our commentators insist that place must be absolutely immobile. Although Aristotle himself is not very explicit on this point, it is apparent that in his view place cannot be essentially subject to motion, for this would lead to an infinite regress: since things that essentially move essentially have a place, then there would be a place of a place, and so *ad infinitum*. On the other hand, this infinite regress is also avoided if place is given only a weak kind of immobility, such as found in Averroes' interpretation discussed in section 4.1. Explicit arguments in favour of a stronger kind of immobility are

---

dici quod haec natura est forma substantialis, non tamen forma quae sit pars rei. In omnibus enim corporibus, elementis et elementatis, est aliqua natura corporis caelestis (contenti *ms.*), continens et salvans formam quae est pars rei in sua propria materia. Et haec natura sic diffusa diversificatur secundum propinquius et remotius. Primo enim diffunditur in loca et secundario in locata, ita quod in concavo orbis lunae competit corpori ignis, et in concavo ipsius ignis recipit talem diversitatem quod competit corpori aeris, et sic deinceps" (IV, q. 18, f. 147va, lin. 50-56). See also, Rufus, *In Physicam*, IV, f. 7va, lin. 7-18; S, IV, q. 20, f. 51ra, lin. 20-33; P, IV, q. 48, f. 83rb, lin. 35-41; T, IV, q. 14, f. 43va, lin. 42-vb, lin. 11; M³, IV, q. 17, f. 164rb, lin. 27-34; G³, IV, q. 18, f. 161vb, lin. 2-14; N, q. 19, f. 148ra, lin. 9-24.

[111] For instance, Albert the Great emphasizes the role of the *virtus caelestis* in the theory of place that he ascribes to Aristotle and more generally to the Peripatetics. Furthermore, he appeals to this *virtus* also in solving some objections against the immobility of Aristotle's place. See Albert the Great, *In Physicam*, IV, tract. 1, cap. 10-11, p. 219a-224a. Nevertheless, the second opinion on the immobility of place as reported by the early English commentators does not appear in Albert the Great's commentary.

not found in Aristotle's text but are supplied by Aristotelian commentators. The most common arguments point to the difficulties posed by describing locomotion and rest in terms of a place that is mobile even in an accidental sense. Such difficulties are well illustrated by two arguments taken from G[1]. These arguments are actually directed against the identity of place and the surface of the containing body, a position which would imply at least the accidental mobility of place:

> (5) ... (i) if place and a surface were the same thing, then something that changes place can remain in the same surface. This is evident as follows: let us imagine that a body is carried about in flowing water in such a way that during all that motion a single part of water is in contact with that body. Then this body always remains in the same surface, and nevertheless it continuously changes place. (ii) Again, if place and surface are substantially the same, then a thing at rest would change place. The proof is that, if they were the same, then that thing which continuously changes its containing surface would also continuously change place; but something can continuously change its surrounding surface and nevertheless be at rest. For example, if a body were fixed in some continuously flowing water, then it would change the surface of its container and therefore a thing at rest would change place.[112]

We recall that immersive place plays no meaningful role in the discussion of our commentators about the immobility of place.[113] So in this context we can assume that place is merely the surface of the containing body. Then replacing 'surface' with 'place', these arguments point out two "paradoxes" arising from locomotion and rest: (i) something which changes place is at rest (i.e., does not change place) and (ii) something which is at rest changes place.

---

[112] G[1], IV, q. 13, f. 146ra, lin. 53-60: "... (i) si locus et superficies essent idem, tunc aliquid transmutans locum potest manere in eadem superficie. Quod patet sic: imaginemur corpus delatum in aqua fluente et in toto motu coniuncta si<n>t una pars aquae et illud corpus. Et sic semper manet in eadem superficie, et tamen continue transmutat locum. (ii) Item, si locus et superficies sint idem in substantia, tunc quiescens locum transmutaret. Probatio, quia, si essent idem, tunc quod continue mutat superficiem et locum; sed aliquid potest continue mutare superficiem circundantem et tamen quiescere. Verbi gratia, si corpus fuerit fixum in aqua fluente, continue transmutaret superficiem continentis et sic quiescens locum transmutaret". See also S, IV, q. 8, f. 48rb, lin. 42-47; P, IV, q. 21, f. 78vb, lin. 40-49; T, IV, q. 6, f. 41ra, lin. 15-20; M[3], IV, q. 11, f. 161vb, lin. 15-26; G[3], IV, q. 15, f. 159rb, lin. 46-va, lin. 2; va, lin. 36-47; N, IV, q. 16, f. 146ra, lin. 22-31.

[113] See above, p. 170-171.

For a modern reader, these paradoxes are only apparent and their solution is easily seen. Locomotion and rest can be defined only with respect to a frame of reference. This means that it is necessary to specify with respect to which things a body is relatively in motion or at rest. Thus it is absurd that a body be both at rest and in motion with respect to the same frame of reference, but not with respect to different ones. Indeed, this latter case is that presented by both examples given by G^1. In both these examples two frames of reference are, in fact, assumed. Let us take, for instance, the second example. A body immersed in flowing water changes place with respect to its immediate surroundings; nevertheless, it is also said by G^1 to be fixed or at rest. Clearly, another frame of reference is implicitly assumed. This is, as it will soon be clear, the cosmological frame of reference formed by the centre of the universe and its poles (north, south, east, and west), which are the fixed points of the universe. So in fact the body fixed in flowing water is in motion with respect to its immediate surroundings, but at rest with respect to the cosmos.

This anachronistic account of the examples quoted from G^1 does not adequately reflect the view of our commentators. Firstly, the choice of frame of reference seems largely arbitrary. On the contrary, our commentators assume that there is only one possible choice, so that there is a privileged frame of reference with respect to which we can alone speak of a body being at rest or in motion. This is the cosmological frame of reference, which determines the 'cosmological' coordinates of bodies. Secondly, in their view, the place of a body must be defined in such a way that, when a body is in motion (with respect to the cosmological system), it also changes place, that is, it is also in motion with respect to the frame corresponding to its place, and similarly for rest. The third opinion on the immobility of place reported by our commentators aims at showing how Aristotle's notion of place can be intrinsically related to the cosmological frame of reference in this way.

G^1 describes this opinion as follows:

(6) There is another subtler opinion which saves the immobility of place, claiming that the place of my hand is not the air surrounding my hand or the limit of this air, insofar as it is air, but by means of another nature, namely by the respect to the centre and to the circumference. And this seems to be Aristotle's intention, since he saves the immobility of place by means of the respect to the extremes of the universe. Therefore, a concave surface, whose centre is at a certain dis-

tance from the east pole, a certain distance from the west pole, a certain distance from the north pole and a certain distance from the south
pole, can in this way be called place. Therefore, although where now
there is air, water may submerge my hand – my hand remaining
immobile – nevertheless its place remains the same, because the distance from the extremes of the world always remains one and the
same. For the limit of air or water is not called place in an absolute
sense, but in comparison to the extremes of the world. And thus, when
air recedes and water comes in, the limit of both is said to be numerically the same place by means of the aforesaid respect.[114]

The solution proposed by this opinion is found also in Richard
Rufus' Questions on the *Physics*,[115] and it is reported and accepted by

---

[114] G[1], IV, q. 16, f. 147ra, lin. 7-16: "Alia opinio subtilior est salvans immobilitatem loci, dicens quod aer circumdans manum meam vel eius terminus non est
locus manus meae secundum quod aer, sed per aliam naturam, scilicet per respectum ad centrum vel circumferentiam. Et hoc videtur Aristoteles velle, <quia> salvat
immobilitatem loci per respectum ad mundi terminos. Potest igitur superficies conca-
va, cuius centrum tantum distat ab oriente, tantum ab occidente, tantum ab austro,
tantum ab aquilone, secundum hoc dici locus. Licet igitur aqua inundet manum
meam ubi nunc est aer, manu mea manente non mota, nihilominus manet idem
locus, quia semper manet una et eadem distantia ad mundi terminos. Terminus
enim aeris vel aquae non dicitur locus absolute, sed in comparatione ad terminos
mundi. Et sic, recedente aere et adveniente aqua, terminus utriusque dicitur idem
locus numero mediante praedicto respectu". See also S, IV, q. 15, f. 49vb, lin. 17; P,
IV, q. 32, f. 80vb, lin. 14-20; T, IV, q. 13, ff. 42vb, lin. 44-43ra, lin. 1; M[3], IV, q. 14,
f. 163ra, lin. 61-rb, lin. 9; G[3], IV, q. 16, f. 160va, lin. 38-45; N, IV, q. 17, f. 146vb,
lin. 44-51. In maintaining that the opinion in question also reflects Aristotle's intention, G[1] probably refers to the following remark that concludes Aristotle's discussion
of the immobility of place: "And it is for this reason that the centre of the world and
the extreme limit (with respect to us) of the circular motion [of the heavens] are
thought by everyone to be 'above' and 'below' in the primay way more than anything else, because one of them is always at rest, and the limit of the circular motion
remains in the same state" (Aristotle, *Physics*, IV.4, 212a21-24). However, with this
remark Aristotle simply seems to point out that there are immobile or fixed places,
i.e., 'above' and 'below', the two primary kinds of natural places.

[115] Rufus, *In Physicam*, IV, f. 7rb, lin. 35-45: "Qualiter ergo debemus dicere de
immobilitate loci? Debemus dicere sicut prius dictum est quod terminus huius aeris
non in quantum huius aeris, sed in quantum talem habet respectum ad universum
locus est. Quia iste respectus manet idem, recedente aere et adveniente aqua circa
manum, propterea terminus aeris et terminus aquae consequenter advenientis sunt
idem locus manus meae, quia per eandem naturam sunt locus. Et hoc sustinendum
est, cum dicit terminus continentis immobilis, quia hoc est dictu: terminus ipsius aeris
continentis infra ut talem habet respectum ad universum, qui respectus manet immobilis et manet idem, quia aer per suam propriam naturam non est locus aquae... sed
secundum respectum quem habet ad universum". Rufus' discussion on the immobility of place and on the place of the heavens has been analyzed in detail by R. Wood
in "Richard Rufus: Physics at Paris", p. 110-115.

Roger Bacon[116] and B.[117] The main idea on which it relies already appears in Robert Grosseteste's commentary on the *Physics*.[118] Different versions of it will be proposed repeatedly in the thirteenth century. From the late thirteenth century on, this opinion is associated with Thomas Aquinas and Giles of Rome. In particular, Giles formulates his solution in terms of a distinction between 'material place' and 'formal place', where material place is the surface of the containing body and formal place the distance of this surface from the fixed points of the universe. Giles' distinction forms the basis of the standard version of this solution reported by late medieval commentators.[119] Thus, unlike the second opinion that we have examined in 4.2, the third opinion reflects one of the traditional solutions to the problem of the immobility of place.[120]

This opinion can be broadly interpreted as a sort of 'geographical' version of the second one. According to the second opinion, the place of a body is the limit of the containing body, not insofar as it is a natural body, but insofar as it is endowed with the celestial nature. Similarly, according to this third view, place is not the limit of the containing body insofar as it is natural, but insofar as it has a certain distance or respect to the fixed points of the universe, namely, its centre and poles. So, in passing from the second opinion to the third opinion, the metaphysical and formal notion of celestial nature is replaced by the

---

[116] Bacon, *In Physicam*, IV, p. 192, lin. 13-20; 193, lin. 10-29.

[117] B, IV, q. 10, f. 24rb, lin. 10-14: "Quidam autem alii dicunt quod locus per se est terminus immobilis, et ista immobilitas est eadem distantia et idem respectus semper ad universum. Et quamdiu manet idem ille respectus, tamdiu manet idem locus. Si maneat terminus in eodem respectu ad universum, dicunt quod manet idem locus. Nec refert si <non> sit terminus aeris aut terminus aquae aut aliorum, et sic dicunt quod locus semper est immobilis".

[118] Grosseteste, *In Physicam*, IV, p. 80-81. Grosseteste's discussion of the immobility of place is, however, extremely impenetrable.

[119] For instance, Burley writes: "Ad hanc dubitationem dicunt aliqui quod locus accipitur dupliciter, scilicet vel pro materiali in loco vel pro formali. Si accipiatur pro materiali, sic est mobilis, quia materiale in loco est superficies, et certum est quod superficies est mobilis. Si vero accipiatur pro formali, sic est distantia communicata ab orbe sive a polo mundi et <est> a centro terrae, et sic totus locus est immobilis, quia semper manet eadem distantia ad orbem lunae sive ad polos mundi" (Burley, *In Physicam*, IV, f. 100va). On Giles' and Aquinas' solution see C. Trifogli, "La dottrina del luogo in Egidio Romano", *Medioevo*, 14 (1988), p. 254-290. On the reception of the notion of formal place and its role in the explanation of the immobility of place see also Grant, "The medieval doctrine of place", p. 63-72.

[120] Among Greek commentators, the idea of defining the immobility of place in terms of the cosmological frame of reference appears in Eudemus. See Algra, *Concepts of Space*, p. 252-254.

geographical notion of distance from the fixed points of the universe. Certainly, this replacement marks an important step in the reception of Aristotle's theory of place, since it constitutes a deeper and more mature insight into the physical question of the immobility of place. Only the notion of distance from "cosmological" points addresses directly and explicitly the problems involved in the description of local motion and rest in terms of mobile place raised by passage (5) from G^1.

The summary of the third opinion given by G^1 indicates how a situation analogous to (ii) of passage (5) can be dealt with without leading to the paradox of the body being at rest and at the same time changing place. When my hand is at rest, its place also remains the same, despite the fact that its immediately surrounding body is initially air and then water, because its place is the limit of the containing body, not qua air or water, but qua having a certain distance from the fixed points of the universe. Moreover, this distance does not vary as long as my hand is at rest. Therefore, as long as my hand is a rest, it has numerically the same place.

In this account, there is clearly an ontological difficulty. The distance from the fixed points of the universe is ontologically an accident and hence has a subject. This subject, as our commentators assume, is the containing body or its limit. Therefore, the distance cannot remain numerically the same when the subject changes. For example, according to the usual medieval interpretation of the numerical identity of accidents, the distances inhering in water and air are numerically distinct.[121] Thus, the third opinion does not seem to solve the ontological problem from which the debate on the immobility of place originates, but simply shifts it from the limit of the containing body to its distance from the fixed points of the universe. In fact, this is the main objection raised in the fourteenth century against Giles of Rome's theory of the identity of formal place.[122]

---

[121] Not all Aristotelian scholars, however, accept this interpretation. In a fundamental and much debated paper, G. E. L. Owen defends the opposite view that individual accidental properties can inhere in more than one subject, i.e., they are repeatable. See G. E. L. Owen, "Inherence", *Phronesis*, 10 (1965), p. 97-105.

[122] This difficulty is pointed out most clearly by Walter Burley. Referring to formal place (see above note 119) he argues: "Tertio arguo principaliter contra illud formale. Et hoc sic: si esset tale formale in loco, cum illud non sit substantia, oportet quod sit in aliquo subiecto. Aut igitur illud formale est subiective in illo ultimo corporis locantis aut est in corpore locante aut in caelo subiective. Si detur quod est subiective in ultimo corporis continentis locatum vel in ipso locante, cum tam corpus

Some of our commentators are aware of this difficulty. For instance, in order to prevent the ontological objection we have just outlined, G¹ introduces his question on the immobility of place by laying down a general principle on the numerical identity of accidents. In short, the principle states that an accidental property can inhere in numerically distinct subjects and nevertheless itself be numerically the same.[123] The specific application of this principle that G¹ has in mind is clear: the accidental property of having a certain distance from the fixed points of the universe is numerically the same in the distinct containing bodies in which it actually inheres. In next chapter, we shall find this same principle applied to the case of the unity of time.[124] Nevertheless, the principle assumed by G¹ is at variance with the usual medieval interpretation of the numerical identity of accidents[125] and, so it seems, is introduced *ad hoc* by this commentator to deal with the cases of the immobility of place and the unity of time.

S attempts to solve the ontological problem involved with the third

---

locans quam ultimum corporis locantis sit mobile, sequitur quod illud formale est mobile vel saltem sequitur quod, remoto corpore locante, non remanet idem respectus vel ordo ad caelum quod prius erat, et sic non manebit idem formale. Et quod idem respectus vel ordo non possit remanere, recedente corpore locante et succedente alio corpore locante, patet quia ille respectus vel formale illud aut remanet sine subiecto aut in subiecto. Non sine subiecto, ut certum est, quia illud esset contra rationem accidentis, scilicet esse per se sine subiecto. Si vero sit in subiecto, aut igitur in eodem subiecto in quo prius erat vel in alio. Non in eodem, quia, cum illud subiectum moveatur et non remaneat ubi (ut *ed.*) prius, sequitur quod illud formale moveatur et non remaneat ubi prius fuit, quod est propositum. Si vero detur quod illud formale remanet ubi prius et in alio subiecto quam prius, illud est impossibile, quia sic accidens migraret de suo subiecto in subiectum, quod est impossibile" (*In Physicam*, IV, ff. 100vb-101ra). For similar reactions against Giles' solution, see Grant, "The Medieval Doctrine of Place", p. 65-72; Trifogli, "La dottrina del luogo", p. 275-290.

[123] G¹, IV, q. 16, f. 146vb, lin. 42-45: "Sequitur quaerere de immobilitate loci. Et ad evidentiam suae immobilitatis supponatur in principio haec propositio, scilicet quando aliquibus diversis inest aliquod unum numero, gratia cuius unius est aliquid in ipsis diversis, non est dicere illud quod sic inest esse multa propter ista diversa, sed potest manere unum numero, ipsis existentibus diversis". At the end of his exposition of the third opinion (see passage (5) above), he suggests that the account of the immobility of place given by it is in accordance with the principle formulated in this passage: "... Et sic recedente aere et adveniente aqua, terminus utriusque dicitur idem locus numero mediante praedicto respectu. Et huic consonat illa propositio 'quando aliquid inest duobus diversis etc.'" (ibid., f. 147ra, lin. 15-16). The same principle is introduced by M³. See M³, IV, q. 14, f. 163rb, lin. 3-9.

[124] See below p. 253.

[125] The usual interpretation is well represented by Burley's remark in the passage quoted in note 122 above that an accidental property does not "migrate" from one subject to another.

opinion without apparently modifying the standard view on the numerical identity of accidental properties. Referring to the distance from the fixed points of the universe, he remarks:

> (7) (a) ... it can be considered in two ways: either (i) insofar as it is a quantity and insofar as inhering in a body or (ii) insofar as it has a certain measure, i.e., a certain longitude. If distance is considered in the first way, then it varies and in this way does not contribute to place or to the subject of place. If it is considered in the second way, then it contributes to place and to the subject of place. For measure always persists, but neither quantity nor accident persist. Accordingly, this solves all the counter-arguments. (b) For all bodies that follow one another taken together are the subject of place, not, however, insofar as they are many, but insofar as they are one. Therefore, in a way the distance varies, i.e., according to its quantity, but in another way it does not. And it is not absurd that divided and distinct things, insofar as they are joined together, are a subject of something. Therefore, it does not follow that an accident passes from one subject to another, because all bodies that follow one another are one subject in virtue of the unity and respect from the centre to the circumference....[126]

This passage is rather obscure. Parts (a) and (b) seem to present two different solutions, which are not very well integrated. In (a) it is said that, although the body varies in which distance inheres, the distance itself persists insofar as it is a certain measure, i.e., a determinate distance x (for instance, being x^1 miles away from the centre of the universe, x^2 miles away from the north pole and so on). Distance varies, however, when considered as a quantity and an accident. Thus, in short, the strategy of the solution proposed by S in (a) is the following. Since an accident numerically varies when its subject varies, then the

---

[126] S, IV, q. 5, f. 48ra, lin. 3-19: "... (a) potest tunc considerari dupliciter: aut (i) secundum quod quantitas est et secundum quod inhaerens corpori aut (ii) secundum quod in ea est aliqua certa mensura, scilicet talis longitudo. Si primo modo, tunc variatur distantia et tunc non facit ad locum nec ad subiectum loci. Si secundo modo consideratur, tunc facit ad locum et ad subiectum loci. Mensura enim semper manet, [distantia] quantitas autem non nec accidens. Unde per hoc patet ad omnes rationes. (b) Omnia enim corpora succedentia simul sumpta erunt subiectum loci, non tamen secundum quod multa sunt, sed secundum quod unum sunt. Unde uno modo variatur, quia secundum quantitatem, alio modo non. Et hoc non est inconveniens quod ali<qu>a divisa et distincta secundum quod coniuncta sunt sint subiectum alicuius. Unde non sequitur quod accidens transferat se ad diversa subiecta, quia omnia succedentia sunt unum subiectum per unitatem et respectum a centro ad circumferentiam..."

distance of the containing body from the fixed points of the universe, insofar as it persists while its subject changes, is not an accident. In fact – S claims – it must be regarded as a measure and not as an accident. Part (b) repeats this point, but also introduces a subject for the distance regarded as measure which is identified with the totality of all the containing bodies having the same distance or respect to the fixed points of the universe. Hence, the strategy in (b) is to claim that the distance from the fixed points of the universe does not vary because its subject, in fact, does not vary. Indeed, its subject does not consist of the individual containing bodies that are continuously displaced, but of the totality of all these bodies considered as one insofar as they are unified by the property of having the same respect to the fixed points of the universe.

The solutions to the ontological problem of the immobility of place proposed by S are not very successful. As to solution (a), it is not easy to see how the distance from the fixed points of the universe can persist when regarded as a measure but vary when regarded as an accident and a quantity. If 'persisting' and 'varying' are states having some reality, then their existence cannot depend on a way of regarding the thing to which they are ascribed. As to solution (b), the individual containing bodies are said to be a single subject for place. Their unity, however, is apparently motivated by the fact that they all have the same respect to the fixed points of the universe. Yet, this violates the principle of the identity of an accident accepted by S, for if the containing bodies are numerically distinct, they cannot have, strictly speaking, the same respect to the fixed points of the universe.

As we shall see in next chapter, S, along with other early English commentators, formulates a very similar solution for the problem of the unity of time.[127]

In this context, it should be noted that the early English commentators try to find a "positive" solution to the ontological problem related to the immobility of place, in the sense that they try to show that place can be immobile or persist even if it is an accident of a mobile body. Furthermore, the tendency towards a "positive" solution is typical of the thirteenth-century tradition, appearing also in Thomas Aquinas and Giles of Rome. On the contrary, fourteenth-century commentators usually acknowledge that the absolute persis-

---

[127] See below, p. 246-253.

tence of place is incompatible with its ontological status as an accident of a mobile substance and do not attempt a positive solution.

Certainly, the "negative" fourteenth-century approach marks a new phase in the history of the debate on the problem of the immobility of place. In order to appreciate the innovations introduced in the fourteenth century, one should recall the "paradox" of rest and locomotion that forms the main objection raised in the medieval tradition against a non-persisting place.[128] The paradox is the following: take the case of a body at rest; if its surrounding body changes, then its place also changes, since in Aristotle's view place depends ontologically on the surrounding body; but what changes place, by definition, undergoes locomotion; it follows that the same body is simultaneously at rest and in local motion. There are two main ways out of this paradox. The first consists in showing that the place of a body at rest does not change, notwithstanding the change occurring in the bodies surrounding it. The second way is to modify the definition of locomotion and rest in such a way that a body at rest does not move locally, even when its surroundings change. The early English commentators, Thomas Aquinas, Giles of Rome and, in general, the thirteenth-century exponents of the positive solutions to the problem of the immobility of place take the first approach. All the fourteenth-century commentators who acknowledge that place to some extent does not persist take the second approach. Accordingly, the fourteenth-century negative positions on the problem of the immobility of place also contain more accurate formulations of the definitions of locomotion and rest. This complex of definition-problems is another major innovation of the fourteenth-century debate on the immobility of place. Nevertheless, the fourteenth-century debate does not discard the basic intuition of the dominant thirteenth-century, positive solution that the respect of the containing body to the fixed points of the universe plays a fundamental role in the description of locomotion and of rest.

For instance, this is illustrated by Duns Scotus' position, one of the most influential in this debate.[129] Although he maintains that place

---

[128] See above, p. 176.

[129] On Scotus' position, see especially R. Cross, *The Physics of Duns Scotus. The Scientific Context of a Theological Vision*, Clarendon Press, Oxford 1998, p. 208-213. On the fortune of Scotus' position in the fourteenth century, see E. Grant, "The Medieval Doctrine of Place...", p. 65-72.

does not persist while the containing body is subject to locomotion, Scotus also claims that place is incorruptible "by equivalence with respect to locomotion" (*per aequivalentiam quantum ad motum localem*). The meaning of this expression is explained in the following passage taken from the section of his *Ordinatio* devoted to the place of the angels:

> ... (i) although place is corrupted when its subject moves locally, so that, when air moves locally, the *ratio* of place in air does not remain the same as before... nor can the same *ratio* of place remain in the water that succeeds the air, because the same accident in number cannot remain in two subjects, (ii) nevertheless, the posterior *ratio* of place (which is distinct from the preceding one) is in truth the same as the preceding *ratio* by equivalence with respect to local motion. For, it is just as impossible that a local motion takes place from that preceding place to the posterior place as if these two places were absolutely the same place in number. In fact, no local motion can take place from an *ubi* to another *ubi* unless those two *ubi* correspond to two specifically different places, namely, to places which have a different respect, not only numerically, but also specifically, to the whole universe. Hence, those respects that are only numerically different seem to be one in number, because they are just as indistinct with respect to local motion as if they were just one respect.[130]

In part (i), by appealing to the principle of the numerical identity of accidents, Scotus argues that local motion of the containing body implies the corruption of the place associated with this body, so that absolute immobility of place is incompatible with its ontological status

---

[130] Duns Scotus, *Ordinatio*, liber II, dist. 2, pars 2, q. 1, p. 257, lin. 12-258, lin. 9: "... licet locus corrumpatur moto eius subiecto localiter, ita quod, moto aere localiter, non manet in eo eadem ratio loci quae prius (sicut patet ex iam probato), nec eadem ratio loci potest manere in aqua succedente, quia idem accidens numero non potest manere in duobus subiectis, – tamen illa ratio loci succedens (quae est alia a ratione praecedente) secundum veritatem est eadem praecedenti per aequivalentiam quantum ad motum localem, nam ita incompossibile est localem motum esse ab hoc loco in hunc locum sicut si esset omnino idem locus numero. Nullus autem motus localis potest esse ab uno 'ubi' ad aliud 'ubi', nisi quae duo 'ubi' correspondent duobus locis differentibus specie, quia habentibus alium respectum – non tantum numero sed etiam specie – ad totum universum; ex hoc illi respectus qui sunt tantum alii numero, videntur unus numero, quia ita sunt indistincti respectu motus localis sicut si tantum essent unus respectus". (The second parentheses in this passage should be closed after *secundum veritatem*). A very similar position on the immobility of place is that of Thomas Wylton. See C. Trifogli, "Thomas Wylton on the Immobility of Place", *Recherches de Théologie et Philosophie médiévales*, 65 (1998), p. 12-22.

as an accident of a mobile body. In part (ii), Scotus introduces his original doctrine of the immobility of place "by equivalence". Although in (ii) Scotus does not explicitly mention the paradox of local motion and rest arising from a changing place, it is clear that he implicitly provides a solution to this paradox. For in (ii) Scotus' main concern is to establish what condition two distinct places must satisfy in order to be the termini of a local motion, i.e., Scotus seems to formulate a precise definition of local motion. As Scotus formulates this condition, two distinct places can be the termini of a local motion provided that they are not only numerically distinct but also specifically different. The formula "equivalent with respect to local motion" is used by Scotus to describe those places that, though numerically distinct, cannot constitute the termini of local motion. Two places that differ only in number can be considered equivalent, from the viewpoint of local motion, to the same place, because, in fact, local motion cannot occur between these two places, any more than it can occur from one place to the same place. Instead, local motion can occur only between two specifically different places. What is most important in this context is that the specific difference of two places, in Scotus' view, does not derive from the specific difference of the surfaces of the bodies in which they inhere, but from that of the respect of the bodies to the whole universe (or, equivalently, to the fixed points of the universe). Thus, the thirteenth-century notion of respect to the fixed points of the universe still plays a fundamental role in Scotus' doctrine of the immobility of place "by equivalence".[131]

5. *The Place of the Heavens*

At the beginning of *Physics* IV.5, Aristotle lays down a general criterion for being in a place:

---

[131] In emphasizing the importance of the respect to the fixed points of the universe in Scotus' solution, we depart from Lang's interpretation according to which "incorruptible by equivalence" means incorruptible mathematically, i. e., in the sense that places of the same size and shape are equivalent and interchangeable. In the passage from the *Ordinatio* that we have quoted in the preceding note and to which Lang refers there is no mention of the size or shape of place. See H. S. Lang, *Aristotle's Physics and Its Medieval Varieties*, State University of New York Press, Albany 1992, p. 178. Cross rightly maintains that Lang misunderstands Scotus' position. See Cross, *The Physics of Duns Scotus*, p. 209-210, note 64.

Therefore, the body that has an external body containing it is in a place, whereas the body that does not have an external container is not in a place.[132]

This criterion is an immediate consequence of the definition of place reached by Aristotle in *Physics* IV.4: if the place of a body is the limit of the body containing it, then it is clear that having a container is at least a necessary condition for being in a place. On the other hand, when the structure of Aristotle's universe is considered, this criterion also suggests a natural candidate for a body without place, the last celestial sphere or the heavens. Indeed, Aristotle's physical universe is enclosed within the last celestial sphere and outside this sphere there is nothing. Thus, the heavens lack an external body containing them and, therefore, are not in a place. Yet, this negative conclusion on the place of the heavens is in contrast with a guiding principle of Aristotle's theory of place, according to which there is an essential connection between place and local motion. Indeed, in the preliminary discussion which leads to the definition of place, Aristotle claims that the existence of local motion is the primary motivation for the inquiry. He even adds that, because the heavens always move, we think that they are in a place.[133] Thus, the cosmological problem of the place of the heavens points to the following inconsistency in Aristotle's theory: the heavens cannot be in a place, since they do not have an external container, but, on the other hand, they must be in a place, since they move with local motion.

In the Aristotelian tradition, the cosmological problem of the place of the heavens is the most frequently discussed aspect of Aristotle's doctrine of place in the *Physics*. Among the Greek commentators, Simplicius and Philoponus take a very radical position on this problem. They maintain that it shows an unavoidable contradiction in Aristotle's theory of place and are subsequently induced to reject this theory.[134] Apart from Simplicius and Philoponus, Greek, Arabic, and Latin Aristotelian commentators generally show a more constructive attitude towards this

---

[132] Aristotle, *Physics*, IV.5, 212a31-32.

[133] Ibid., 211a12-14.

[134] The objections raised by these two commentators against the consistency of Aristotle's theory of place and their alternative theories of place are mainly formulated in the non exegetic sections of their respective commentaries on *Physics* IV that go under the title *Corollarium de loco*. See Simplicius, *In Physicam*, IV, p. 601, lin. 1-645, lin. 19; Philoponus, *In Physicam*, IV, p. 557, lin. 8-585, lin. 4.

problem. Indeed, they try to remove the contradiction by modifying
some of the principles from which it derives, without giving up the
whole Aristotelian doctrine of place. In *Physics* IV.5, after stating the
criterion for being in a place quoted above, Aristotle himself attempts
to find a solution to the cosmological problem arising from it. His solution, however, contains some obscurities and ambiguities that allow different interpretations. Accordingly, although all Aristotelian commentators start from Aristotle's discussion of the place of the heavens in
Physics IV.5, they follow different routes to save Aristotle's doctrine,
routes which often go far beyond what Aristotle says or means and,
especially in the medieval tradition, give rise to a running debate.[135]

As in the case of the immobility of place, the treatment of the place
of the heavens given by the early English commentators is on the
whole a review of preexisting opinions. We shall, therefore, concentrate on those most commonly and extensively discussed by this
group of commentators, namely, that of Aristotle, Averroes, and one
probably originating in the twelfth century, which holds that the
place of the heavens is their convex surface. These three opinions are
also considered by Richard Rufus of Cornwall and Roger Bacon in
their questions on the *Physics*.[136] Thus, from a historical point of view,
it can be said that they characterize the debate on the place of the
heavens in the early phase of the reception of Aristotle's *Physics*. We
shall see that most early English commentators, like Rufus, accept the
third opinion.

5.1 *Aristotle's Opinion*

The strategy of Aristotle's attempted solution to the cosmological
problem consists in "weakening" the local character of circular
motion. While he does not deny the principle that every body subject

---

[135] A traditional study of the debate on the place of the heavens in the Greek and
Latin tradition is found in Duhem, *Le Système du Monde*, vol. 1, p. 197-205, 297-350;
vol. 7, p. 158-302; vol. 10, p. 50, 79-81, 100, 157-160, 204-210, 396-412. For the
Greek commentators' solutions see also Sorabji, *Matter, Space*, p. 194-196; C. Trifogli,
"Il luogo dell'ultima sfera nei commenti tardo-antichi e medievali a *Physica* IV.5",
Giornale critico della filosofia italiana, 68 (1989), p. 144-152. For the main solutions pro-
posed by Arabic and Latin commentators, see Grant, "The Medieval Doctrine", p.
72-79.

[136] In fact, these are the only opinions discussed by Bacon, whereas Rufus also
refers to Avempace's position reported by Averroes. References to Bacon's and
Rufus' discussions are given below in the notes to this section.

to local motion must be in a place, he also admits that this principle can be interpreted in a weak sense in the case of circular motion. Aristotle claims that in circular motion the rotating body as a whole does not change place and therefore need not be in a place. The parts of the rotating body, however, do change place, and hence must be in one. Accordingly, since the heavens are subject to circular motion, they do not have and do not need a place strictly speaking, i. e., they do not have or require an external container. Nevertheless, they can be said to be in a place in a derivative sense, according to their parts, since, according to Aristotle, each of these parts is contained by another part.[137]

In the Aristotelian tradition, Aristotle's solution is summarized by the formula that the heavens are in a place according to their parts (*per partes*). This formula, however, is ambiguous because Aristotle's discussion is unclear concerning the term "parts". Indeed, in the passage from *Physics* IV.5, Aristotle mentions both the heavens and the universe, so that the term "parts" can stand (a) for the continuous parts of the last sphere, or (b) for the single celestial spheres as parts of the whole celestial region, or even (c) for both the celestial spheres and the sublunar elements as parts of the universe. In the context of the cosmological problem of the place of the heavens, only the ambiguity concerning the meanings (a) and (b) of the term "parts" is relevant. In fact, this ambiguity gives rise in the Aristotelian tradition to different positions on this problem.[138] This ambiguity can also be found in the treatment of Aristotle's position by the early English commentators. Nevertheless, among the arguments which they make against Aristotle's opinion that the heavens are in a place because of their parts, the one that recurs most frequently is unaffected by the ambiguity concerning the term "parts". The argument in question, which is already found in Rufus,[139] is formulated by G¹ as follows:

(1) ... the parts of the heavens can be assigned in two ways: either (i) as the parts next to each other, as when the heavens are divided into sections; or (ii) as those which are one inside the other, as when the heavens are divided into orbs. But in neither of these ways are the heavens in a place in virtue of their parts; therefore etc. The first part of the

---

[137] Aristotle, *Physics*, IV.5, 212a32-b22.
[138] For a classification of the principal solutions that originate from the ambiguity of Aristotle's discussion, see Trifogli, "Il luogo dell'ultima sfera", p. 145-155.
[139] Rufus, *In Physicam*, IV, f. 6va, lin. 23-30.

minor premise is clear, since any part <of type (i)> is not contained in some direction, namely, in that of its convexity. The second part of the minor premise is also evident, because outside the last circle there is no container, and therefore this circle is not essentially in a place. Therefore the whole will not be accidentally in a place in virtue of the fact that its parts are essentially in a place.[140]

In this argument, the term 'the heavens' stands for the whole celestial region. In addition to the physically separated parts represented by the orbs (i.e., those of type (ii)), in (i) a more geometrical type of parts is also considered, namely, the sectors defined by a system of planes passing through the center of the universe and reaching its outermost surface (or by a system of lines, in the two-dimensional representation of the celestial region to which the argument seems to refer). But evidently, since the outermost celestial orb does not have a surrounding and containing body, neither all orbs nor any of the sectors can be completely surrounded and contained. In particular, each sector cannot be completely surrounded, since it has a part which lies exactly on the outermost sphere. Accordingly, the argument also shows that, even if the term 'the heavens' stands for the outermost sphere, it is not true that its parts are essentially in a place in the sense that they are completely surrounded, for the parts of the outermost sphere are just the parts of the sectors lying on this sphere.

As it is clear from this argument, the early English commentators, following Richard Rufus[141] and Roger Bacon,[142] attack a specific ver-

---

[140] G¹, IV, q. 17, f. 147ra, lin. 57-62: "... dupliciter est assignare partes caeli: aut scilicet (i) partes iuxta se positas, ut si dividatur per sectiones; aut (ii) ita quod quaelibet sit infra aliam, ut si dividatur in orbes. Sed neutro istorum modorum est caelum in loco <per> partes; ergo etc. Prima pars minoris patet, quia quaelibet pars a parte una est non contenta, ut a parte convexitatis. Secunda pars minoris patet, quia extra ultimum circulum nihil continens est, et sic non est in loco per se. Quare non erit totum in loco per accidens quia partes per se". See also S, IV, q. 26, f. 52rb, lin. 29-36; M³, IV, q. 15, f. 163rb, lin. 21-28; G³, IV, q. 19, f. 162va, lin. 45-vb, lin. 4; N, q. 20, f. 149ra, lin. 8-18. Another very common objection against Aristotle's opinion is based on Aristotle's principle that the parts of a whole are not strictly in a place, but only in the whole. In this second objection 'parts' stands for the continuous parts of the last celestial sphere. See S, IV, q. 26, f. 52rb, lin. 40-46; G¹, IV, q. 17, f. 147ra, lin. 55-56; M³, IV, q. 15, f. 163rb, lin. 20-21; G³, IV, q. 19, f. 162va, lin. 44-45; N, IV, q. 20, f. 149ra, lin. 4-8.
[141] Rufus, *In Physicam*, IV, f. 6va, lin. 23-24: "Dubitatur qualiter caelum sit in loco per accidens. Et videtur littera protendere quod caelum sit in loco per accidens, quia partes eius sunt in loco per se".
[142] Bacon, *In Physicam*, IV, p. 217, lin. 23-30.

sion of Aristotle's solution, according to which all the parts of the heavens are essentially (*per se*) in a place, i.e., each of them has a surrounding place as defined in *Physics* IV.4. Certainly, if Aristotle's claim that the heavens are in a place in virtue of their parts is interpreted in the strong sense that each of these parts is in a place essentially, then it can be refuted on very simple geometric grounds, as in passage (1). On the other hand, it is doubtful whether Aristotle himself advocates this strong version. As to the last sphere in particular, for which the problem actually arises, he seems rather to maintain that this is in a place because all its parts are in some sense in a place, without implying that the place of each of these parts is the limit of a body containing it according to the definition of *Physics* IV.4.[143] This more faithful interpretation of Aristotle's text will be given a precise and articulate meaning by Thomas Aquinas.[144] As we shall see, some of the early English commentators also make an attempt to integrate Aristotle's position with the opinion that they support, namely, that the place of the last sphere is its convex surface.[145] Nevertheless, most of these commentators feel that there is something basically wrong with any attempt to define the place of the heavens in terms of the place of their parts. The reason is that this would imply that the heavens are ontologically inferior to the lower bodies. On this point the following argument against Aristotle's position proposed by S is illuminating:

> (2) ... the heavens are less dependent on their parts than is a sublunar body, because there is less composition in the heavens than in any sublunar body; but no sublunar body receives its place from its parts; therefore neither do the heavens.[146]

This argument indicates that the heavens (here the last sphere) have an ontological priority over their parts, due to the fact that they are essentially continuous and one, so that their parts exist only potentially. But the ontological priority of the heavens is in contrast with the derivative type of location that Aristotle's position ascribes to them.

---

[143] See Hussey, *Aristotle's Physics*, Notes, p. 120.

[144] See Thomas Aquinas, *In Physicam*, IV, lectio VII, p. 232b-233a. On Aquinas' solution, see Grant, "The Medieval Doctrine of Place", p. 78; Trifogli, "Il luogo dell'ultima sfera", p. 148-150.

[145] See below, p. 201-202.

[146] S, IV, q. 26, f. 52rb, lin. 37-40: "... caelum minus dependet a suis partibus quam aliquod corpus inferius, quia minor est compositio in caelo quam in aliquo inferiori; sed nullum corpus inferius capit locum a suis partibus; ergo nec caelum".

Indeed, a recurrent idea in our commentaries is that the place of the heavens should reflect the superiority of their nature. As we shall see next, the appeal to the ontological priority of the heavens over the sublunar region also has an important role in the refutation of Averroes' position.

5.2 *Averroes' Opinion*

At the beginning of his lengthy doxographical digression devoted to the cosmological problem of the place of the heavens,[147] Averroes makes clear that this problem essentially concerns the last celestial sphere, since this is, in fact, the only body that lacks a container.[148] Thus in this section we can use the terms 'the heavens' and 'last celestial sphere' interchangeably. Averroes' solution of this problem can be summed up as follows: the heavens are in a place accidentally in virtue of the fact that the centre of the universe, i.e., the earth, is essentially in a place. Hence the Latin tradition refers to Averroes' opinion with the formula *caelum est in loco per centrum*.

Although in this short formulation Averroes' solution may appear extravagant, the general idea on which it relies is very appealing and is repeatedly proposed in the thirteenth and fourteenth centuries.[149] Averroes accepts Aristotle's principle that every body subject to locomotion is in a place, but he also wonders whether this place must necessarily be the containing place defined in *Physics* IV.4. In his view, the answer to this question essentially depends on which of the two basic kinds of local motion, namely, rectlinear motion and circular motion or rotation, a body is subject to. If it is subject to rectilinear motion, then it must have a containing place. But if it rotates, as

---

[147] This digression is contained in t. c. 43 and continues also in t. c. 45. The Greek and Arabic commentators whose opinions are reported and discussed by Averroes are Philoponus (t. c. 43, f. 141rbF), Themistius (t. c. 43, f. 141rbF-vbM), Avempace (t. c. 43, f. 141vbM-142raG), Alexander (t. c. 43, f. 143raA-C), and Avicenna (t. c. 45, f. 144rbE-vaI). Among our commentators, only G³ and N report systematically the main points of Averroes' digression. See G³, IV, q. 19, ff. 161vb, lin. 32-162rb, lin. 30; N, IV, q. 20, f. 148ra, lin. 43-va, lin. 51. A detailed report of this digression is found also in B, who accepts Averroes' solution according to which the heavens are in a place in virtue of their centre, i.e., the earth. See B, IV, qq. 4-6, ff. 22va, lin. 5-23va, lin. 47.

[148] Averroes, *In Physicam*, IV, t. c. 43, f. 141rbE.

[149] On the fortune of Averroes' solution see Grant, "The Medieval Doctrine of Place", p. 75-76.

the heavens do, then Aristotle's containing place seems to play no role. Up to this point, Averroes' intuition reflects well the guiding principle of Aristotle's discussion in *Physics* IV.5 mentioned above.[150] Yet, Averroes introduces a crucial innovation when he comes to specify the relevant local element in the rotation of the heavens. In Averroes' view, such an element is not the location of the parts of the heavens, as Aristotle maintains, but, in modern terms, the centre of rotation, i.e., the thing around which the heavens rotate.[151]

This same idea about the significant place involved in rotation also appears in Avempace's solution of the problem of the place of the heavens, as reported by Averroes. Avempace, however, makes an unusual 'choice' for the centre of the rotation of a celestial sphere, namely, the convex surface of the sphere immediately contained by it (the convex surface of Saturn in the case of the sphere of the fixed stars). This choice seems to be dictated mainly by his attempt to show that Aristotle's definition of place in *Physics* IV.4 applies to both rectilinear motion and rotation.[152] While Averroes rejects Avempace's attempt to give an unifying interpretation of Aristotle's definition,[153] he does retain Avempace's idea that circular motion involves a place

---

[150] See above, p. 188-189.

[151] Averroes, *In Physicam*, IV, t. c. 43, especially ff. 142vbM-143raA; t. c. 45, ff. 143vbM-144raB.

[152] Ibid., t. c. 43, ff. 141vbM-142raA: "Avempace vero respondit in hoc loco sic, quoniam sphaera secundum quod est sphaera non est in loco quia aliquid extrinsecum continet illam, et quod hoc proprium est corpori recto, non corpori rotundo. Et locus sphaerae qui fingitur ab isto, secundum quod est sphaera, est convexum centri circa quod revolvitur, quasi igitur locus eius est superficies convexi quod continet sphaera, et est quodammodo continens sphaeram. Et nititur dicere quod definitio quam induxit Aristoteles in loco, quoniam est continens divisum a re, debet intelligi in corporibus rectis ab extrinseco et in rotundis ex intrinseco". Thus, as Averroes remarks, in Avempace's view both the sublunar contained bodies and the celestial spheres have a *per se* place in sense of Aristotle's definition, because in the definitory formula 'limit of the container', 'container' must be taken to mean the external container in the case of sublunar bodies, and the 'internal' container in the case of celestial spheres. From a metaphysical point of view, Avempace finds an explanation for the lack of an external container of the heavens in the geometrical 'perfection' of the sphere, which is in itself bounded: "Et dicit quod causa in hoc est quoniam corpus rotundum finitur per se et corpus rectarum dimensionum finitur per aliud. Et ideo corpora recta, scilicet elementa, indigent in hoc quod finiantur corpore rotundo, rotundum vero non indiget corpore extrinseco. Et causa in hoc est quoniam linea rotunda est perfecta et non potest recipere additionem aut diminutionem, linea vero recta est diminuta" (Ibid., f. 142raA-B). Avempace's idea that the lack of a container for the heavens must be explained by its perfection is accepted and emphasized by Rufus. See Rufus, *In Physicam*, IV, f. 6vb, lin. 24-47.

[153] Averroes, *In Physicam*, IV, t. c. 43, f. 142raC-vaG.

'around which' (*circa quem*) it rotates. Furthermore, Averroes more naturally identifies the centre of the rotation of the heavens with the centre of the universe, which is the earth. Averroes' most explicit reason for this identification occurs in the famous passage where he introduces his own solution at the end of his refutation of Avempace:

> (3) But let us say that, since the heavens as a whole are fixed, it is necessary that in this way they are at rest. And since they are at rest because of the rest of the centre, which is in the earth, and the centre is at rest because it is essentially in a place, therefore it is said that the heavens are in the same place and do not move from this place, not even accidentally, namely, because their centre is essentially in a place. And this is what Aristotle intends when he says that the heavens are accidentally in a place.[154]

With the claim that the heavens as a whole are fixed or at rest Averroes means that they lack any translational motion, i.e., they simply rotate. This is due to the fact – he maintains – that the earth around which they rotate is absolutely immobile and in particular is not subject to translation.[155]

In Averroes' position the earth plays two distinct roles with respect to the heavens: (i) a logical role in the description of their rotation, since the earth represents the geometric centre around which they rotate; (ii) the causal role that is pointed out in passage (3). There it is implied that the heavens or their rotation do in some sense causally depend on the earth and its immobility.

The fortune of Averroes' solution in the later thirteenth- and fourteenth-century tradition is substantially determined by point (i) rather than by (ii). This is to some extent true also for the early English commentators. Among them, only P accepts Averroes' solution, but in his report of this solution the causal role of the earth is almost completely neglected and its conceptual role in the description of the rotation of the heavens is emphasized:

---

[154] Ibid., f. 142va, G-H: "Nos autem dicamus quoniam, cum sit fixum secundum totum, necesse est ut hoc modo sit quiescens. Et quia quies est ei propter quietem centri, quod est in terra, et quies est quia est in loco essentialiter, ideo dicitur caelum esse in eodem loco et non transmutatur ab eo per accidens, i.e., quia centrum eius est in loco essentialiter. Et haec est intentio sermonis Aristotelis dicentis quod caelum est in loco per accidens".

[155] For our commentators' report of Averroes' opinion, see S, IV, q. 27, f. 52ra, lin. 33; T, IV, q. 15, f. 43vb, lin. 43-45; G¹, IV, q. 17, f. 147rb, lin. 15-18; M³, IV, q. 15, f. 163va, lin. 5-12; G³, IV, q. 19, f. 161vb, lin. 32-37; N, IV, q. 20, f. 148ra, lin. 43-48. For P, see next note.

(4) The third opinion is that of the Commentator himself. And it seems to concern specifically the third meaning of the term 'the heavens', namely, as it stands exclusively for the eighth sphere. And his opinion is that the heavens are in a place accidentally, viz. since the centre is essentially in a place. And he means by 'centre' the earth itself, which is fixed in its place, around which, as around a support, the heavens move with circular motion. Therefore, the last circumference is said to be accidentally in a place because of the respect which it has to this centre, which centre is essentially in a place. Therefore, when 'the heavens' is taken in the third meaning, it is safer to follow the Commentator rather than saying that the heavens are neither essentially nor accidentally in a place, for they have something around which they move, although they do not have a place towards which they move.[156]

In this passage, the earth is repeatedly described as that around which the heavens rotate. Furthermore, the fixity of the earth is not

---

[156] P, IV, q. 41, f. 82va, lin. 20-27: "Tertia vero opinio est ipsius Commentatoris. Et videtur esse specialiter de caelo tertio modo dicto, scilicet secundum quod nominat tantum octavam sphaeram. Et est quod caelum est in loco per accidens, scilicet quia centrum est in loco per se. Et intendit per centrum ipsam terram, quae est fixa in suo loco, circa quam, tanquam circa sustentamentum, movetur caelum circulariter. Unde circumferentia ultima propter respectum quem habet ad istud centrum, quod est per se in loco, dicitur per accidens esse in loco. Unde forte, loquendo de caelo tertio modo, securius ponitur imitando Commentatorem quam dicendo quod non est in loco nec per se nec per accidens. Habet enim locum circa quem movetur, licet non habeat locum ad quem movetur". At the end of this passage P refers to the second opinion that he reports, according to which the last sphere does not have a place even in an accidental sense. This is the following: "Alia est opinio de loco caeli, scilicet quod caelum dicitur tripliciter. Uno enim modo nominat caelum universum, alio vero modo nominat totum corpus caeleste, scilicet aggregatum ex octo sphaeris supremis, tertio modo nominat tantum sphaeram octavam sive extremam sphaeram. Si igitur fiat quaestio de caelo primo modo vel secundo, dicitur quod caelum est in loco per accidens secundum se totum, quia partes eius sunt per se in loco. Non tamen est hoc intelligendum de omnibus eius partibus, quoniam sphaera ultima sive extrema, quae est pars caeli primo modo vel secundo dicti, non est in loco per se nec etiam alio modo... Si autem fiat quaestio de tertio modo, dicitur quod non est in loco nec per se nec per accidens, cum nihil sit extra ipsum, nec sufficit quod habeat motum secundum locum nisi simul cum hoc habeat continens extra ad hoc quod ponatur in loco" (ibid., f. 82va, lin. 5-17). This opinion is also reported by G³ and N, who classify it as an *opinio magistralis*. See G³, IV, q. 19, f. 162rb, lin. 30-31; va, lin. 9-24; N, IV, q. 20, f. 148va, lin. 51-vb, lin. 1; vb, lin. 30-41. It appears also in S, who, however, does not report it as an opinion. See S, IV, q. 28, f. 52va, lin. 41-50. Nevertheless, S cannot be considered an exponent of this opinion. For referring to the claim that the last sphere does not have a place even in an accidental sense, he remarks: "Verumtamen illud videtur dissonare Aristoteli, eo quod caelum isto modo tertio dictum corpus est et omne corpus locum habet secundum ipsum" (Ibid., f. 52va, lin. 50-vb, lin. 2).

given a causal role with regard to the rotation of the heavens. Instead, the reference to the 'respect' of the heavens to a central, fixed earth suggests that the earth merely forms part of the cosmological frame of reference, as has been explained in the analysis of the problem of the immobility of place.[157] Although, as we shall see in next subsection, other early English commentators also acknowledge that the centre has this kind of role in the description of the rotation of the heavens, following Rufus,[158] they reject Averroes' solution. Their most basic and general objections to Averroes' solution are directed against precisely the ontological priority of the earth over the heavens that it implies.

For instance, G[1] argues:

> (5) ... the local motion of the heavens is prior by nature to all motions of sublunar bodies; therefore, it is also prior to their rests, since motion is prior by nature to rest as a habit is prior to privation. Therefore, the heavens have their motion prior by nature to any sublunar body having rest; but the heavens have local motion and place simultaneously; therefore, the heavens are not in a place in virtue of the nature of the earth resting in place.[159]

---

[157] This interpretation of Averroes' opinion appears even more explicitly in B. He accepts this opinion, but he denies the causal role of the earth over the heavens. B, IV, q. 6, f. 23va, lin. 6-19: "Ad hoc dicendum quod circumferentia et centrum maxime respiciunt se, et motus circularis circumferentiae et etiam eius fixio maxime respicit fixionem centri. Cum ergo caelum sit circumferentia et terra centrum, caelum et terra maxime respiciunt se, et motus circularis caeli et eius fixio, ut fixum est, maxime respiciunt fixionem terrae. Si ergo caelum debeat poni in loco per accidens per naturam corporis alicuius, maxime oportet poni in loco per accidens per naturam terrae. Et solus Averroes inter omnes expositores aperiebat illud per subtilem et profundam inquisitionem. Et illud vult Aristoteles expresse in libro *De Caelo et mundo*, ubi vult quod motus circularis caeli fixus est super terram fixam et quietam. Non tamen vult Aristoteles quod fixio terrae natura praecedat motum circularem caeli nec eius fixionem nec quod sit causa eius per se. Immo, magis secundum veritatem est econverso: motus circularis caeli et eius fixio natura et causalitate praecedunt fixionem terrae. Et similiter nec vult Averroes quod caelum sit fixum et quietum fixione et quiete terrae, ita quod fixio caeli causetur a fixione terrae". Bacon also follows Averroes' opinion. See Bacon, *In Physicam*, IV, p. 218, lin. 25-220, lin. 2. On the debate between Rufus' and Bacon' on the place of the heavens, see Wood, "Richard Rufus: Physics at Paris", p. 118-124.

[158] Rufus, *In Physicam*, IV, f. 6vb, lin. 1-23.

[159] G[1], IV, q. 17, f. 147rb, lin. 62-va, lin. 3: "... motus localis caeli est praecedens natura omnes (omnis *ms.*) motus corporum inferiorum; quare et quietes illorum, cum motus naturaliter praecedat quietem sicut habitus privationem. Caelum igitur prius natura habet motum localem quam aliquod corpus inferius quietem; sed caelum simul habet motum localem et locum; ergo non erit in loco per naturam terrae quiescentis in loco". See also T, IV, q. 15, ff. 43vb, lin. 45-44ra, lin. 1; M[3], IV, q. 15, f.

Similarly, S argues:

> (6) (i) The heavenly body is prior by nature to the centre; therefore,
> place must first be ascribed to it; therefore, it does not have a place in
> virtue of the centre. (ii) Furthermore, as the heavenly body is prior by
> nature to the centre, similarly motion is prior by nature to rest; there-
> fore, the heavenly body by nature is in motion prior to the central
> body being at rest; therefore, since place follows the motion of the
> heavens, their place is not in virtue of the nature of the centre.[160]

Evidently, our commentators regard these objections as having force
against Averroes' thesis that the heavens and their motion are causally dependent on the resting earth, as asserted in passage (3), but not
against the idea that the earth is the fixed point around which the
heavens rotate. More generally they discourage any attempt to define
the place of the heavens in terms of the place of something that is
ontologically or naturally posterior to them. On the other hand, since
the heavens are by nature prior to any other part of the cosmos, it
seems to follow that one can look for their place only 'inside' the
heavens themselves. This is, in fact, what is done in the last opinion
we are going to present.

5.3 *The Place of the Heavens as Their Convex Surface*

The opinion that the place of the heavens is the convex surface (i.e.,
the outermost surface) of the heavens themselves probably originates
in the twelfth century. Albert the Great, for instance, ascribes it to
Gilbertus Porretanus.[161] The early English commentators do not
name any author of this opinion. S, in particular, regards it as traditional (*opinio communis*), like those of Aristotle and Averroes[162] and presents it as a third explanation, in addition to those offered by Aristotle
and Averroes, of the dictum that the heavens are in a place acciden-

---

163va, lin. 55-59; G³, IV, q. 19, f. 161vb, lin. 43-47; N, IV, q. 20, f. 148rb, lin. 4-8.
See also B, IV, f. 23rb, lin. 47-va, lin. 6.

   [160] S, IV, q. 27, f. 52rb, lin. 48-va, lin. 5: "(i) Corpus caeleste per naturam prius est
quam centrum; ergo prius ei debetur locus; ergo non per naturam centri habebit
locum. (ii) Item, ita est quod, sicut corpus caeleste per naturam prius est quam centrum, similiter motus prius per naturam est quam quies; ergo per naturam corpus
caeleste prius est motum quam corpus centri quiescens; quare, cum locus sequatur
motum in caelo, non erit locus per naturam centri".

   [161] See Albert the Great, *In Physicam*, IV, tract. 1, cap. 13, p. 228b, lin. 54-60. On
the sources of this opinion see also Wood, "Richard Rufus: Physics at Paris", p. 112.

   [162] S, IV, q. 28, f. 52va, lin. 30-35.

tally. This explanation is condensed by S in the title of the short question which asks:

> (7) ... whether the heavens are accidentally in a place, because they do not require an external place that entirely contains and preserves them, but rather their convex surface, because of its finiteness, suffices to locate the heavens, and therefore they are accidentally in a place, and also because their proper place is not outside, but inside.[163]

This passage is a bit condensed, but its meaning can be expanded as follows.[164] While in Aristotle's and Averroes' views the heavens are in a place accidentally in the sense that something other than the heavens, to which they are to some extent related, is essentially in a place, this third opinion holds that the heavens themselves have a place, i.e., their convex surface. Nevertheless, they are in a place accidentally, because their place does not satisfy all the requirements of place defined by Aristotle in *Physics* IV.4 as the limit of the containing body. Passage (7) suggests two axioms on place that the convex surface does not satisfy: (a) place must contain the located body, but be separate from it, and (b) it must exert a preserving influence on the nature of the located body.[165] Evidently, (a) is not satisfied by the convex sur-

---

[163] Ibid., f. 52va, lin. 11-16: "... utrum caelum sit in loco per accidens quia non indiget loco extrinseco penitus continente et salvante, immo sua superficies convexa propter sui terminationem sufficit ad locandum caelum et ideo est in loco per accidens, quia etiam non habet locum deputatum extra, sed intra". See also P, IV, q. 41, f. 82rb, lin. 51-54; T, IV, q. 15, f. 44ra, lin. 21-31; G¹, IV, q. 17, f. 147va, lin. 30-37; M³, IV, q. 16, f. 164ra, lin. 52-rb, lin. 3; G³, IV, q. 19, ff. 162rb, lin. 31-36; 162vb, lin. 51-163ra, lin. 18; N, IV, q. 20, ff. 148vb, lin. 1-6; 149rb, lin.11-28. On Rufus' and Bacon's versions, see Rufus, *In Physicam*, IV, f. 7ra, lin. 41-46; Bacon, *In Physicam*, IV, p. 218, lin. 4-7.

[164] In this regard, we also rely on Rufus' more extensive treatment of this opinion, on which our commentators' discussion seems to depend, and in particular on Rufus' detailed reply to an objection against it. The objection is that this opinion is in contrast with Aristotle's view that place is the limit of the containing body. Referring to Aristotle's view, Rufus replies as follows: "Dicendum quod, cum sic definitur locus, definitur locus proprie dictus. Et deficit locus caeli a proprietate loci in duobus: et ex parte potentiae loci et ex parte continentiae. Locus enim qui est terminus continentis, quia continens nobilius est, et propterea habet potentiam et naturam loci per quam potest salvare locatum. Sed cum caelum sit corpus nobilissimum, non indiget aliquo nobiliore salvante se. Deficit similiter a continentia loci. Continens enim dicit esse receptivum, receptivum in quantum est de se dicit esse divisum et distinctum ab ipso recepto et denudatum ab eo. Hoc proprie invenitur in loco qui est terminus continentis, quia ibi recipiens nihil est ipsius recepti, et hoc non proprie invenitur in loco caeli, cum sit terminus ipsius recepti et contenti et non terminus continentis et recipientis" (Rufus, *In Physicam*, IV, f. 7rb, lin. 15-25).

[165] On the axioms on place, see above note 41. Axiom (a) corresponds approxi-

face of the heavens. More accurately, this surface contains in the sense that it surrounds the heavens, but since it inheres in the heavens themselves, it is not separate from them. Nor is axiom (b) satisfied, since, according to our commentators, the 'preserving' power of place in Aristotle's sense depends on the fact that the nature of the containing body has some kind of superiority over that of the contained and located body. As our commentators put it, the containing body is more noble (*nobilius*) than the contained body. Since, however, the nature of the heavens is superior to that of all other bodies, they do not have and do not need a preserving place and an external container.

Axiom (a) deserves more attention because, when it is read against its Aristotelian background, it indicates the metaphysical character of the position that identifies the place of the heavens with their convex surface. In the dialectical discussion that leads to the definition of place, Aristotle also considers the form of the located body as a candidate for its place.[166] He eventually denies that place is this form and distinguishes between place and form as follows: both contain the located body, but place must be a container separated from it, whereas the form is not.[167] Thus, axiom (a) is posited by Aristotle precisely to distinguish place from the form of the located body. Therefore, the physical meaning of Aristotelian place is essentially determined by its separation from the located body.[168] Moreover, Aristotle points out that a non-separated place is inadequate for describing local motion, for when a body moves, he wants to say that it leaves its former place and acquires a new one. This, however, would not be possible if place

---

mately to axioms (1) and (2) in Aristotle's passage quoted in note 41 and axiom (b) to axiom (6).

[166] Aristotle, *Physics*, IV.2, 209a31-b5; IV.4, 211b10-12.

[167] Ibid., IV.2, 209b30-31; IV.4, 211b10-14.

[168] Indeed, the main objection raised by our commentators against the third opinion points out that it does not respect Aristotle's axiom on the separation of place from the located body. The "standard" solution which appears in our commentaries is that also found in Rufus' commentary. This is based on the principle that simpler quantities are logically prior to more complex ones. Thus a surface, being a bidimensional extension, is logically prior to the body in which it inheres, and therefore can also be thought of as separated from this body. See Rufus, *In Physicam*, IV, f. 7rb, lin. 25-33; S, IV, q. 28, f. 52va, lin. 16-31; vb, lin. 6-18; P, IV, q. 41, f. 82rb, lin. 54-61; G¹, IV, q. 17, f. 147va, lin. 37-40; M³, IV, q. 16, f. 164rb, lin. 3-16; G³, IV, q. 19, ff. 162rb, lin. 36-49; 163ra, lin. 18-29; N, IV, q. 20, ff. 148vb, lin. 6-19; 149rb, lin. 29-36. Of course, this solution does not show that place conceived of as the surface of the located body has any physical meaning.

were the surface of the located body.[169] Accordingly, from an Aristotelian perspective, positing that the place of the heavens is their convex surface is not far from positing that their place is their form. However, this renders place devoid of any specifically physical meaning. Since the cosmological problem of the place of the heavens arises from the physical circumstance of being subject to motion, it is not surprising that the opinion that identifies their place with their convex surface does not enjoy much success in the thirteenth-century Aristotelian tradition.

On the contrary, the early English commentators are attracted by this opinion, because to them it seems to be the only one that respects the ontological priority of the heavens over any other parts of the universe. However, some of them realize that it is not very well suited to providing an adequate physical definition of the place of the heavens. Its inadequacy in this respect is acknowledged and accepted, for instance, by S. At the end of his refutation of Averroes' position he adds the following remark:

> (8) It must be known, however, that the heavens have two properties, namely being mobile and being most perfect. Thus, insofar as they are most perfect, they do not require a place, and thus we could say that they are accidentally in a place. But, since they are mobile, it is necessary that they have something around which they move, since they are circular, and not something in which they move; and this is the centre, not in the sense that the heavens are in the centre as in their place, but the centre is that around which they move.[170]

The claim that the heavens do not require a place must probably be understood in the sense that they do not require a place totally distinct from themselves and outside themselves, which is in accordance with the third opinion.[171] Thus, S agrees with Averroes that the

---

[169] Aristotle, *Physics*, IV.2, 209b22-30.

[170] S, IV, q. 27, f. 52vb, lin. 22-29: "Sciendum autem quod caelum proprietates habet, scilicet ut sit mobile, ut sit perfectissimum. Ratione tunc qua perfectissimum est non indiget loco, et sic possemus dicere quod esset in loco per accidens. Quia tamen mobile est, de necessitate oportet quod habeat aliquid circa quod movetur, cum sit circulare, et non in quo, cuiusmodi est centrum, non quia sit in centro tamquam in loco, sed illud circa quod movetur".

[171] This is in fact the opinion that S seems to accept. Referring to the argument which shows that the heavens do not have a place even accidentally (see above note 156), he claims: "Ad argumentum dico sustinendo quod caelum est in loco per accidens, quia habet superficiem convexam et ambientem" (IV, q. 28, f. 52vb, lin. 3-4). But the position of S does not seem to be fully coherent, because immediately after passage (7) he adds: "Sumendo tunc caelum pro omnibus sphaeris, sic habet locum

motion of the heavens is necessarily related to something distinct from the heavens themselves, i.e., the centre around which they rotate. However, unlike Averroes, he maintains that the place of the heavens must reflect their metaphysical state of perfection rather than their physical state of motion.

The other commentators who support the third opinion (G[1], M[3], N-G[3]) are reluctant to render the place of the heavens devoid of any physical meaning. They eventually give a more complex description of the place of the heavens, which takes into account not only their convex surface, but also the parts of this surface, the centre of the universe and the 'respect' of these parts to the centre. The origin of this 'physical' version of the third opinion seems to be an objection raised by Rufus. He points out that the parts of the convex surface of the heavens in fact move when the heavens rotate; but if the place of the heavens is their convex surface, then these parts are also parts of the place of the heavens. Aristotle, however, – the objection concludes – requires place to be immobile.[172] It should be noticed that, if place is something separate from the located body, as in Aristotle's view, the question of whether place remains immobile while the located body moves makes sense, at least in principle. But if place is not separate from the moving body, then, *a priori*, there can only be a negative answer. By requiring that place must be separate from the located body, Aristotle shows himself well aware of this point. Rufus, however, does not seem to see this. As an exponent of the immobility of place based on the identity of the distance or respect of place to the fixed points of the universe,[173] he applies this theory to solve the objection in question. He states that the parts of the convex surface of the heavens are parts of their place only when they are regarded as having a certain respect to the centre. He further notes that parts of the surface having the same respect to the centre represent the same part of place.[174] On the basis of Rufus' solution, G[1], M[3], N-G[3] specify

---

in sphaera ignis. Si autem sumatur caelum pro octava sphaera, sic movetur circa immediatam sphaeram, ut Saturni, tamquam in loco suo" (Ibid., lin. 29-32). This rather resembles Avempace's position (see above note 152). S takes it as an interpretation of Aristotle's claim that the heavens are in a place because of their parts (ibid., lin. 32-48). Thus the apparent inconsistency in the account of S can probably be explained as an attempt to avoid a complete rejection of Aristotle's opinion.

[172] Rufus, *In Physicam*, IV, f. 7ra, lin. 3 ab imo-2 ab imo.
[173] See above, p. 178.
[174] Rufus, *In Physicam*, IV, f. 7ra, lin. 2 ab imo-rb, lin. 7: "Propterea debemus scire

the place of the heavens as follows: it is the convex surface of the heavens not simply insofar as it is their surface, but insofar as its parts have a certain respect to the earth. These commentators assume that this physical version of the third opinion also represents the views of Aristotle and Averroes, for it includes in the definition of the place of the heavens both their parts and the earth, as, respectively, Aristotle and Averroes maintain.[175]

Evidently, the physical version of the third opinion proposed by Rufus and followed by some of our commentators combines different and not very well integrated suggestions and therefore does not succeed to give a coherent solution to the problem of the place of the heavens. Yet, when this physical version is viewed as an attempt to mitigate the metaphysical character of the third opinion and to confer some physical meaning to it, it is historically very important, since it shows that the approach of the early English commentators corresponds to a shift in the debate over the place of the heavens from a perspective that was not specifically physical to the more mature, physical view that characterizes the late thirteenth-century debate.

---

quod partes huius superficiei non sunt partes loci secundum hoc quod sunt superficiei, sed ut sunt distantes a centro, ut dicatur quod haec pars est ex hac parte centri et haec ex hac. Hoc hinc possumus videre: cum aliqua pars circumferentiae est in tali respectu a centro, ipsa recedit, et cum advenit alia, tunc habet ipsa adveniens eundem respectum quem habuit pars prior a centro. Et propterea, si ex tali respectu fiat pars superficiei pars loci, ergo ex eodem respectu pars eadem. Ergo pars adveniens et pars recedens sunt eadem pars loci, cum tamen sint diversae partes superficiei, tamen eundem respectum habent a centro". On Rufus' position on the place of the heavens, see Wood, "Richard Rufus: Physics at Paris", p. 112-115.

[175] For instance, referring to the parts of the surface of the heavens, G[1] claims: "... Alius autem est respectus prout quaelibet pars ab aliquo alio respicitur, ut a centro. Et quantum ad istum respectum dicitur caelum esse in loco per partes. Determinatur enim locus caeli per respectum istarum partium ad centrum. Et secundum hoc potest intelligi sermo Commentatoris, cum dicit caelum esse in loco propter centrum. Ex respectu enim partium superficiei convexae, quae ponitur locus caeli, ad ipsum centrum est solum accipere immobilitatem loci ipsius. Est igitur locus totius caeli et partium universi ista superficies convexa, non absolute, sed prout est in tali respectu. Et in quantum est profundans se ad convexum ignis <est locus ignis>, et superficies ignis profundans se ad convexum aeris est locus aeris, et ita de aliis" (IV, q. 17, f. 147va, lin. 26-33). See also M[3], IV, q. 16, f. 164ra, lin. 38-58; G[3], IV, q. 19, f. 162vb, lin. 17-33; N, IV, q. 20, f. 149ra, lin. 28-47.

CHAPTER FOUR

TIME

Introduction

In Aristotle's view, time is an attribute of motion. The nature of this attribute is specified by the definition of time in *Physics* IV.11, which claims that it is the number of motion in respect of the before and after.[1] Generally speaking, this definition implies that time is a sort of successive quantity that inheres in motion. Yet, its exact meaning and in particular the description of time as a number are not very clear.[2] In both the Greek and medieval traditions, however, the debate on Aristotle's doctrine of time developed independently of a precise understanding of its definition. Aristotelian commentators treat Aristotle's definition of time in much the same way as his definition of motion. While accepting and providing detailed exegesis of Aristotle's definition of time, they nevertheless hold different positions on time's reality and ontological status. Furthermore, it is often difficult to discern a commentator's own position in his exegesis of Aristotle's definition. In any case, the debate on time in the Aristotelian tradition focusses on three main topics, which are not immediately concerned with its definition. These are (1) the existence of time, (2) the extramental reality of time and the relation of time to motion, and (3) the unity of time.

(1) In *Physics* IV.10, Aristotle opens his account of time by presenting some arguments against the existence of time,[3] the solution to which he never explicitly provides. The objections raised in these arguments derive from the successive character of time, that is, from the fact that the parts of time do not exist simultaneously, but only one after the other. Because of Aristotle's arguments, the existence of successive entities and, in particular, of time becomes matter of debate among Aristotelian commentators. In the end, they admit that such entities exist, but, relying on different suggestions offered by

---

[1] Aristotle, *Physics*, IV.11, 219b1-2.
[2] See Introduction, p. 19-20.
[3] Aristotle, *Physics*, IV.10, 217b32-218a8.

Aristotle himself, propose different criteria for their existence.

(2) The definition of time as a number of motion makes clear that time has the ontological status of an accident and not that of a substance. Indeed, according to Aristotle, number does not exist over and above the collection of numbered things; accordingly, neither does time exist over and above the motion that it numbers. On this point as well there was nearly universal agreement among Aristotelian commentators.[4] The controversy arises, however, over whether time is an extramental accident of motion or rather depends in some essential sense on our mental activities. Aristotle himself seems to imply the latter view in a passage of *Physics* IV.14 where he maintains that there would be no time if there were no soul, since time is a number and only the soul can count.[5] While in the Greek tradition Aristotle's suggestion that time depends on the soul was usually rejected, in the medieval tradition it was accepted by Averroes. Averroes' position was very influential and became, in fact, the standard starting point of the debate on the extra-mental reality of time in the thirteenth and fourteenth centuries.

(3) In *Physics* IV.14, Aristotle claims that there is just one time and tries to argue this point on the basis of the nature of time as a sort of number. Greek and most thirteenth-century commentators follow Aristotle in maintaining that time is unique. Yet, the unity of time is perhaps the most disputed problem in the Aristotelian tradition. Indeed, the claim that time is unique seems to be in contrast with its ontological status of accident of motion, which apparently implies that there are as many times as there are motions. This problem is clearly analogous to that of the immobility of place. As in the case of place, so too in the case of time Aristotelian commentators formulate a variety of solutions that give rise to an articulate debate.

In this chapter, we shall analyze the position of the early English commentators in the debates on these three main problems of Aristotle's doctrine of time. Their treatments of time as successive entity and of time as accident of motion will be examined in sections 1 and 2 respectively. We shall see that, as in the case of motion, our com-

---

[4] An exception is recorded by A. Maier. It is the case of the fourteenth-century Franciscan Gerardus Odonis, who maintained that time is not an accident of motion. See A. Maier, *Metaphysische Hintergründe der Spätscholastischen Naturphilosophie*, Edizioni di storia e letteratura, Roma 1955, p. 134-137.

[5] Aristotle, *Physics*, IV.14, 222b21-29.

mentators hold a realist position according to which the reality of time does not depend on our soul in any significant way. Specifically, they react against Averroes' claim that the actual existence of time derives from our mental 'division' of the successive phases of a motion. In section 3 we shall examine their treatment of the unity of time.[6] Here too most of our commentators reject Averroes' solution, which is certainly the most influential in the thirteenth century.

1. *Time as Successive Entity*

At the beginning of his account of time in *Physics* IV.10 Aristotle asks whether time is among the things that exist or those that do not exist.[7] He presents two main arguments in favour of the latter alternative,[8] which are reported quite faithfully in the following passage from M²:

> (1) The first argument is: everything that is composed of non-beings is a non-being; but time is composed of non-beings; therefore etc. Aristotle proves the minor premise as follows: time is composed of the past and the future; but the past does not exist, because it has passed away, and nor does the future exist, because it is only in potency.
> The second argument is: for every finite continuum, if it exists, it is necessary that either all its parts or at least some of its parts exist; but no part of time exists, because neither the past nor the future exists nor anything of time exists apart from the instant, which is not a part of time.[9]

---

[6] The most comprehensive survey of the Scholastic debate about Aristotle's doctrine of time is given by A. Maier in chap. 2 (*Das Zeitproblem*) of her study *Metaphysische Hintergründe*, p. 47-137. In subdividing the present chapter in three sections, devoted respectively to time as successive entity, to the extramental reality of time and its relation to motion, and to the unity of time, we have followed the structure of A. Maier's study.

[7] Aristotle, *Physics*, IV.10, 217b31-32.

[8] Ibid., 217b32-218a8.

[9] M², IV, q. 1, f. 130rb, lin. 36-41: "Prima est: omne compositum ex non entibus est non ens; sed tempus est compositum ex non entibus; ergo etc. Minorem ostendit sic: tempus componitur ex praeterito et futuro; nunc autem praeteritum non est, eo quod factum est; nec futurum, eo quod solum in potentia est. Secunda ratio est: cuiuslibet continui finiti, si sit, necesse est omnes partes aut saltem aliquas esse; sed temporis nulla pars est, quia nec praeteritum nec futurum nec est aliquid de tempore nisi instans quod non est pars temporis". See also T, IV, q. 1, f. 49rb, lin. 30-36. Throughout this chapter the numbering of the questions on time in the early English commentaries is that published in Trifogli, "Le questioni sul libro IV", Appendice, C: Questioni sul tempo, p. 99-114.

In both these arguments time (or any period of time) is viewed as a continuum composed of two parts: a past part and a future part, which join at the present indivisible instant. Then the non-existence of time is inferred from the non-existence of each of these two parts. These arguments suggest that the past and the future do not exist because they do not exist 'now', that is, unlike the present instant, they are not present. Thus they rely on the following general criterion of existence: for a divisible thing to exist, some of its parts must exist now.[10] As medieval commentators often put it, some parts of an existing thing must exist simultaneously (*simul*). In the medieval tradition, those things that satisfy this criterion of existence are called permanent entities (*permanentia*). A paradigm case of a permanent entity is a natural substance. Its parts are naturally taken to be its physical parts, which can all exist in the present instant. These remarks make clear that, although Aristotle's arguments are directed specifically against the existence of time, they work just as well or badly against the existence of any non-permanent thing.[11] In other words, they raise the question whether permanent entities are the only class of existing things. In the Aristotelian tradition, the common answer to this question is negative. The other relevant class of existing things is that of successive entities (*successiva*), which include not only time, but also motion. Unlike permanent entities, successive entities are characterized by temporally extended parts or phases, which therefore do not exist in the durationless present instant and simultaneously, but follow one another in time.

We have already encountered the *permanentia-successiva* distinction in the chapter devoted to motion, and have seen that it is one of the main conceptual tools used by the early English commentators against Averroes' *forma*-theory, according to which motion is not really distinct from its final form.[12] We also remarked that our commentators assume a

---

[10] For a recent discussion of Aristotle's arguments in *Physics* IV.10 and his implicit solution of them, see Inwood, "Aristotle on the Reality of Time", p. 151-178. For other traditional studies on this topic, see especially G. E. L. Owen, "Aristotle on Time", in J. Barnes, M. Schofield, R. Sorabji (eds.), *Articles on Aristotle*, vol. 3 (*Metaphysics*), Duckworth, London 1979, p. 140-158; Miller, "Aristotle on the Reality of Time", p. 132-155. See also Introduction, p. 22.

[11] In fact, our commentators reformulate Aristotle's arguments to use them against the existence of motion. See S, III, q. 1, f. 39vb, lin. 10 ab imo-5 ab imo; P, III, q. 1, f. 65va, lin. 11 ab imo-6 ab imo; M¹, III, q. 1, f. 108vb, lin. 11-15; G¹, III, q. 1, f. 139rb, lin. 12-11 ab imo; M³, III, q. 1, f. 152rb, lin. 10-11; N, III, q. 1, f. 132ra, lin. 12-19 ab imo; M², III, q. 3, f. 125ra, lin. 1 ab imo-rb, lin. 4; W, III, q. 1, f. 52ra, lin. 26-29.

[12] See, chap. 1, p. 55-57.

very sharp distinction between successive and permanent entities. Indeed, the idea that the successive character of motion can be accounted for by the permanent entities involved in motion (the mobile substance and the form acquired by this substance) is completely extraneous to their view.[13] Here, however, we shall try to reconstruct their position on the problem of defining a criterion for the existence of successive entities and, in particular, of time. Abstractly, the question is: in virtue of what can successive entities be legitimately said to be existing things, despite the fact that none of their parts exists in the present? Since this problem is not dealt with very accurately and systematically by our commentators, it is helpful to introduce first the two main solutions proposed in the thirteenth and fourteenth centuries, which have been brought to light by A. Maier in her comprehensive investigation on the Scholastic debate on the reality of time:

> (S1) The first solution posits the existence of the present instant and from that concludes the existence of time; similarly, the existence of motion is guaranteed by the existence of its instantaneous present element (the *mutatum esse*).
>
> (S2) The second solution envisages a distinct mode of existence for motion and time taken as wholes, different from that of permanent entities. In particular, even the parts of successive things exist, although in a different sense from the parts of permanent things.[14]

As we shall see later in this section, both these solutions originate from different suggestions offered by Aristotle. Even from the abstract formulation that we have just given them, it appears that (S1) and (S2) are two quite distinct solutions. Indeed, according to (S1), only what is present is strictly real, and the reality of successive entities derives from that of their present element. According to (S2), the past and the future are in some sense real in their own right. In the Greek tradition, the difference between (S1) and (S2) is stressed by Simplicius, who adopts (S2) and radically rejects (S1), arguing that the present instant plays no role in the reality of time.[15] In the thirteenth century, howev-

---

[13] Ibid., p. 57.

[14] Cfr. Maier, *Metaphysische Hintergründe*, p. 52. A. Maier also remarks that (S1) was usually proposed by Franciscans and (S2) by Dominicans.

[15] Simplicius' solution of the arguments of *Physics* IV.10 is contained in his *Corollarium de tempore*. There Simplicius reports two solutions formulated by his teacher Damas-

er, (S1) and (S2) are not always regarded as two mutually exclusive
views on the reality of time as successive entity. Albert the Great, for
instance, presents both solutions in different passages.[16] As a general
tendency, this is also the case in the early English tradition. This general tendency can be further specified in two points: (S2) is the dominant solution, whereas (S1) is proposed almost exclusively in the case
of time and in a very specific formulation, which is not absolutely in
contrast with (S2). In what follows, (I) we shall illustrate the first point
with some examples. As to the second point, (II) we shall explain what
our commentators usually mean when they claim that the reality of
time depends on the instant, and in what sense their position differs
from the 'standard' version of (S1) recorded by A. Maier.

(I) In presenting the objections to the existence of time raised in
passage

(1), G[1] explains Aristotle's assumption that the past and the future
do not exist by appealing to their definition:

(2) For the past is defined thus: that which was and is not; the
future: that which will be and is not.[17]

In replying to these objections, he distinguishes two senses of the verb
'to be' and claims that in one of these two senses the past and future
and time itself as composed of the past and future *are*:

(3) ... it can be said that 'to be' must be distinguished into two types,
namely *esse facti*, and as such time has no being, and *esse fientis*, and as
such time has being. Therefore, although the past or the future *is not*
insofar as 'to be' is taken for the *esse facti*, it *is*, however, insofar as 'to
be' is taken for the *esse fientis*, and the being of every successive thing is
of this kind.[18]

---

cius. According to the first, the element of time that exists simultaneously and in the
present is not the indivisible instant, but is an extended part of time, so that there is
in fact a part of time that exists in the present. This solution is very original, but Simplicius rejects it. According to the second solution, time has the mode of existence
peculiar to successive entities, whose being consists in their becoming, i.e., in the fact
that their parts follow one another in time. Furthermore, Simplicius, following Damascius, even denies that the present instant actually exists. See Simplicius, *In Physicam*,
IV, *Corollarium de tempore*, p. 795, lin. 27-799, lin. 30. On Damascius' solution and
Simplicius' criticisms of it, see Sorabji, *Time, Creation*, p. 56-62.

[16] The relevant passages from Albert the Great are quoted by A. Maier in *Metaphysische Hintergründe*, p. 58.

[17] G[1], q. 1, f. 150ra, lin. 1: "Praeteritum enim sic definitur: quod fuit et non est;
futurum: quod erit et non est".

[18] Ibid., lin. 16-19: "... potest dici quod esse distinguitur dupliciter, scilicet in esse

On the basis of this distinction of the senses of 'to be', our commentators often say that motion and time, unlike substances and permanent entities, are *in fieri* (in becoming) and not *in factum esse*. An equivalent (but less usual) distinction uses the pair act-potency: permanent entities exist in act, whereas successive entities exist in potency or in an act always joined with a potency. This latter distinction is used by S in his answer to the arguments in (1) formulated against the existence of motion:

> (4) To the first counterargument it is said that this proposition, namely, 'that of which no part is <is not>', must be understood with regard to permanent entities and not to successive entities. We can distinguish two kinds of being, that is, being in act and being in potency. The parts of motion, although not in act, are, nevertheless, in potency and *in fieri*. Successive entities *are* and are said to exist by virtue of the parts which are *in fieri* .[19]

The formulation of the distinction between the types of being of permanent and successive entities in terms of both the pair *factum esse-fieri* and the pair act-potency used by our commentators derives from a passage of *Physics* III.6, which is in fact the *locus classicus* for (S2). In this passage, Aristotle explicitly distinguishes between the type of being of a substance, like a man or a house, and that of other entities, like a day or an athletic contest and also time, that is, in medieval terms, of successive entities. The latter type of being is described as a being in potency or also in generation and corruption.[20] T and M³, for instance, appeal directly to *Physics* III.6 in their answer to the arguments against the existence of time.[21]

---

facti, et sic non habet tempus esse, et in esse fientis, et sic habet tempus esse. Unde, licet praeteritum vel futurum non sit ut 'esse' copulet esse facti, est tamen ut 'esse' copulat esse fientis, et huiusmodi est esse cuiuslibet successivi". See also G³, IV, q. 1, f. 171rb, lin. 31-35; N, IV, q. 1, f. 155va, lin. 2-6; M², IV, q. 1, f. 130va, lin. 32-34.

[19] S, III, q. 1, f. 40ra, lin. 15-21: "Ad primam rationem in contrarium dicitur quod ista propositio intelligenda est de permanentibus et non de successivis, scilicet illud cuius nulla pars etc. Possumus tamen distinguere sic quod duplex est esse, scilicet actu et potentia. Partes tamen motus, licet non sint in actu, sunt tamen in potentia et fieri. Ratione autem partium fiendarum sunt et existere dicuntur".

[20] Aristotle, *Physics*, III.6, 206a14-b2. The distinction is introduced by Aristotle in order to specify which is the admissible type of existence for the infinite. On Aristotle's application of this distinction to the infinite, see above, chap. 2, p. 116.

[21] T, IV, q. 1, f. 49va, lin. 35-39: "Dicendum tamen, sicut dicit in littera, quod quaedam sunt in permanentia, ut homo <et> aes; quaedam <in> successione, ut dies et ago est. Entitas ergo quae respondet rei permanenti potest [rem] permanere et habere omnes partes simul, entitas respondens successivo non". M³, IV, q. 1, f.

Aristotle's distinction of two types of being on which (S2) is based does not seem, as it stands, to give an explicit answer to the problem of determining the criteria for the existence of successive entities. One may remark, for instance, that the claim that time and motion are in a process of coming to be (*in fieri*) cannot be understood in the sense that they eventually exist in the present, as when one says that a substance is in a process of coming to be, because no time or motion exists in the present. The early English commentators, however, are not very concerned with this kind of problem. They tend to take it as a primitive and unanalyzable fact that motion and time exist in the sense that they become.

Our commentators are more concerned with emphasizing that the becoming of time and motion derives from the becoming of substances and permanent accidental forms of substances. This point can be illustrated with the following example. Suppose that a substance passes from being white to being black, and let m be the motion through which it passes from being white to being black, and t the time associated to this motion. In this situation, they assume that there are three parallel processes of becoming: that of blackness (i. e., the generation of blackness in the white substance), that of m, and that of t. Now, blackness necessarily requires motion m in order to be generated in the substance. Then the question is: does the becoming of m and t imply that it is necessary to postulate motions m^1 and m^2, different from m, through which m and t respectively become? The answer of our commentators is negative. They maintain that only the becoming of blackness requires a motion m different from blackness, and not also the becoming of m and t, since this is ontologically dependent on that of blackness. In other words, it is because the substance becomes black that m becomes, and because m becomes, t becomes. Thus, these three parallel processes are in fact connected by a relation of derivation in which the becoming of blackness occupies the first step. Some modern scholars remark that the fact that the becoming of time derives from that of motion saves Aristotle's theory

---

167ra, lin. 12-18: "Supposito igitur quod tempus sit, ad primum obiectum intelligendum <quod> haec est divisio Aristotelis: eorum quae sunt quaedam habent esse permanens, ut homo et aes; quaedam in fieri, ut dies et ago. Debilius autem esse habent ultima quam prima, et ideo sufficit quod suae partes sint successivae et non simul entes. Ad permanentiam igitur sive existentiam successivi non exigitur quod partes eius sint simul entes, sed simul invicem succedentes, et per hoc quaelibet pars salvatur in suo esse".

from 'hypertemporal regresses', namely, from the necessity of postu-
lating a 'hypertime', different from the ordinary one, in which the
becoming of ordinary time occurs. Indeed, since the becoming of
time ultimately depends on and is ontologically posterior to that of
substances, and since substances come to be within ordinary time,
also the becoming of time occurs within ordinary time, so that no
hypertime is needed.[22] The emphasis of the early English commentators on the derivative character of temporal becoming is, instead,
explicitly motivated by the exegetical problem of reconciling this
becoming (and that of motion) with Aristotle's restriction of the existence of motion or change to the four categories of substance, quality,
quantity and being somewhere (*ubi*).[23] This restriction means that
only substantial forms, qualities, quantities and being in a definite
place come to be through motion. Therefore, there is no motion
through which motion and time come to be. According to our commentators, this implies that time and motion are not primarily the
end-states of motion, but only in the accidental and derivative sense
that has been illustrated in the case of becoming black.[24] Yet, it can
be suggested that behind their insistence on the derivative character
of the becoming of motion and time there is also an ontological concern. Indeed, as has been seen in chapter 1, these commentators
assume that motion is a *res* distinct from the mobile substance and, as

---

[22] See Miller, "Aristotle on the Reality of Time", especially p. 152-154.

[23] On this aspect of Aristotle's doctrine of motion, see above, chap. 1, p. 41.

[24] For instance, S proposes the following argument against the existence of time:
"Item, si sic, aut in permanentia aut in fieri. Non in permanentia, quia eius partes
non sunt simul. Non in fieri, quia, si sic, ergo fieret (ergo fieret *ante* quia *ms.*) aut per
mutationem aut per motum. Non per mutationem. Tunc enim esset fieri in indivisibili, quod est falsum. Nec per motum, quia tunc motus ordinaretur ad tempus et ita
esset in genere quando" (S, IV, q. 1, f. 56va, lin. 17-23). He replies: "Ad aliud quod
est in fieri. Unde ad obiectum dico quod tempus fit, sed non per se, sed per accidens.
Et hoc in tertio gradu, quia primo <fieri> terminatur ad formam, secundo ad
motum, tertio ad tempore, et ita per accidens est fieri in motu et tempore. Et ulterius
respondeo quod fit per motum, hoc est verum per accidens; et ulterius erit in quando, hoc est verum per accidens" (ibid., f. 56va, lin. 49-vb, lin. 5). See also T, IV, q. 2,
f. 49vb, lin. 2-9, 20-24; M², IV, q. 1, f. 130va, lin. 5-12, 17-20; vb, lin. 7-21. For similar objections against the becoming of motion, see S, III, q. 1, ff. 39vb, lin. 4 ab imo-
40ra, lin. 1; 40ra, lin. 1-10, 21-27, 24 ab imo-17 ab imo; P, III, q. 2, f. 65vb, lin. 11-
16, 25 ab imo-17 ab imo; q. 5, f. 66ra, lin. 23-25, lin. 31-35; M¹, III, q. 1, ff. 108vb,
lin. 27-28, 28-35, 7 ab imo-1 ab imo; 108vb, lin. 1 ab imo-109ra, lin. 6; G¹, III, q. 1,
f. 139va, lin. 4-11, 12-18, 25 ab imo-22 ab imo, 38-43; M³, III, q. 1, f. 152rb, lin. 14-
16, 16-18, 30 ab imo-va, lin. 1; M², III, q. 3, f. 125rb, lin. 14-16; va, lin. 4-25; W,
III, q. 1, f. 52ra, lin. 10 ab imo-8 ab imo; rb, lin. 14 ab imo-vb, lin. 15 ab imo.

will be seen later in this chapter, that time is a *res* distinct from both
motion and the mobile substance. Accordingly, the becoming of the
movable substance is something different from the becoming of both
motion and time. In this realist perspective, it is then clear that the
ontological dependence of the becoming of time and motion on the
becoming of substance is the only way out of an infinite regress of
'hypermotions' and 'hypertimes'.

We shall see next that, relying on another Aristotelian doctrine,
our commentators are also able to describe temporal becoming
intrinsically, that is, in temporal terms, despite its derivation from
substances. In this intrinsic description of temporal becoming the present instant plays a fundamental role.

(II) The early English commentators occasionally mention the relation between time as successive entity and the instant in the questions
on the existence of time,[25] but the *locus classicus* for this discussion is
the set of questions on the instant itself. In most cases, this relation is
expressed very neatly in the question devoted specifically to the
obscure saying, ascribed to Aristotle, that the instant is the whole substance of time.[26] For instance, M³ maintains that this statement is true
in some sense, but also admits that the analogous statement for a
point and the line to which it belongs would not be true:

> (5) ... I say that an instant in time and a point in a line are similar in
> one respect, but not in another, for (i) they are similar in the sense that,
> as the point makes continuous and divides the line, in the same way
> the instant of time continues and divides; (ii) in being and subsisting,
> however, a point and an instant are not similar, because the instant, in
> virtue of its flow in time, confers being to time. Indeed, since the
> instant flows, it gives substance to time in virtue of a succession of dif-
> ferent beings, since the being of time is in a flow and in a succession. A
> line, however, is not in a succession, but permanent, and therefore a
> point does not flow in the line in such a way as to give being to the line
> in virtue of a succession of different beings.[27]

---

[25] See below, notes 43 and 45.

[26] They probably refer to *Physics* IV.11, 220a3-4 where Aristotle compares time to
number and the instant to the unit of number.

[27] M³, IV, q. 16, f. 171ra, lin. 34-43: "... dico quod nunc in tempore simile esse
habet puncto in linea quo ad unum et quo ad aliud non, quia (i) quo ad hoc quod,
sicut punctus continuat et dividit, sic et nunc in tempore se habet in continuando et
dividendo; (ii) in essendo tamen et subsistendo non similiter se habent punctus et
nunc, quia nunc per fluxum suum in tempore quod habet dat esse ipsi. Nunc enim,

(i) refers to Aristotle's analogy between time and a line. Both are unidimensional continuous quantities, since they are composed of parts which join at an indivisible common boundary, an instant and a point respectively, at which they can be divided.[28] (ii) asserts that the instant is the 'substance' of time because, unlike the point, the instant flows and its flow constitutes the successive being of time.

The ideas in (ii) also have an Aristotelian background. In fact, they are related to what some Aristotelian scholars call the theory of the 'persisting present'.[29] This theory refers to the analogy between an instant of time and a mobile object used by Aristotle in a passage of *Physics* IV.11, where he sets out to determine whether the instant is always the same or always different in time. He replies that, as to sameness and difference, what is true of the mobile object in motion is true of the instant too. To illustrate this point, Aristotle remarks that Coriscus in the Lyceum and Coriscus in the marketplace are in a sense the same and in another sense not the same, since they are the same thing under different descriptions. As medieval commentators generally put it, they are the same in substance (*secundum substantiam*), but different in being (*secundum esse*). The same holds for the now. In time there is just one now in substance, which varies, however, in being, so that the now in some sense persists in time as the mobile substance persists in motion.[30]

Aristotle's theory of the persisting present is an obscure and controversial part of his doctrine of time. Among Greek commentators, this theory was criticized and rejected by Simplicius. This commentator is very perplexed, in particular, by Aristotle's claim that the instant is the same with respect to its substrate:

---

cum sit fluens, per esse sua nova diversa dat substantiam tempori[s], quia esse temporis in fluxu et successione est; linea vero non est in successione, sed permanens, et ideo non habet punctus fluxum in linea, ita <quod> per esse diversa dat esse ipsi lineae". See also S, IV, q. 21, f. 60rb, lin. 3-5, 45-50; P, IV, q. 21, f. 92ra, lin. 49-54; G³, IV, q. 15, f. 175va, lin. 32-37; N, IV, q. 15, f. 158rb, lin. 9-13.

[28] Aristotle, *Physics*, IV.11, 220a9-21.

[29] See Hussey, *Aristotle's Physics*, Notes, p. 152-157; Inwood, "Aristotle on the Reality of Time", p. 163-168.

[30] Aristotle, *Physics*, IV.11, 219b10-33. For our commentators' exposition of Aristotle's analogy between the instant and the moving substance, see S, IV, q. 21, f. 60ra, lin. 29-30, 48-rb, lin. 10; rb, lin. 42-50; P, IV, q. 22, f. 92rb, lin. 33-38; T, IV, q. 9, f. 51rb, lin. 43-va, lin. 1; M³, IV, q. 17, f. 171rb, lin. 16-21; G³, IV, q. 16, f. 176ra, lin. 14-20; N, IV, q. 16, f. 158va, lin. 25-31; M², IV, q. 6, f. 131va, lin. 51-58.

In this regard, I think that it is worth noticing in what sense Aristotle
says that the before and after are the same thing with respect to their
substrate. Indeed, in what sense is the past the same thing as the present and what no longer exists the same thing as what exists? For it is
true to say that the body that is subject to local motion and that takes
on successively different positions is the same with respect to its substrate, because it persists in its being, but as to motion, time and, in
general, all things that have their being in becoming, in what way
could they be the same with respect to their substrate? Indeed, nothing
prevents assuming this for the point, because magnitude, insofar as it is
generated by the flow of the point, persists as a whole and does not
have its being in becoming, the way time does. In what sense, then, is
the instant like the mobile body and the point, and how did Aristotle
show this starting from the mobile body and the point, when the difference between entities that persist and those that do not is so vast?
Therefore, how could that which does not persist have, similarly to
that which persists, the property of being the same thing with respect
to its substrate?[31]

The point of Simplicius' objections is that, since time is a successive
entity, no intrinsic element of time can persist. In particular, unlike a
natural substance, the instant does not persist in time.[32]

In the Aristotelian tradition before the fourteenth century, Simplicius' rejection of Aristotle's theory of the persisting present is an isolated case. Philoponus, Themistius, Averroes, and most thirteenth-
century commentators accept this theory and often tend to repeat
Aristotle's analogy between the instant and the moving object without really explaining it. This general tendency is also followed by the

---

[31] Simplicius, *In Physicam*, IV, p. 724, lin. 27-725, lin. 4: "ἐν δὴ τούτοις ἐπιστάσεως
ἄξιον εἶναί μοι δοκεῖ, πῶς τὸ πρότερον καὶ ὕστερον τῷ ὑποκειμένῳ τὸ αὐτό φησιν εἶναι. πῶς
γὰρ τὸ παρεληλυθὸς τῷ ἐνεστηκότι καὶ τὸ μηκέτι ὂν τῷ ὄντι; τὸ μὲν γὰρ φερόμενον καὶ
ἄλλοτε ἀλλαχοῦ γινόμενον ἅτε ἐν τῷ εἶναι ἀληθὲς εἰπεῖν ὅτι τῷ ὑποκειμένῳ τὸ αὐτό ἐστιν, ἡ
δὲ κίνησις καὶ ὁ χρόνος καὶ ὅλως ὅσα ἐν τῷ γίνεσθαι τὸ εἶναι ἔχει πῶς ἂν εἴη τὰ αὐτὰ τῷ
ὑποκειμένῳ; τῇ μὲν γὰρ στιγμῇ τοῦτο ἐνορᾶν οὐδὲν κωλύει· κατὰ γὰρ τὴν ταύτης ῥύσιν
ὑφιστάμενον τὸ μέγεθος ὑπομένει ὅλον καὶ οὐκ ἐν τῷ γίνεσθαι τὸ εἶναι ἔχει ὥσπερ ὁ χρόνος.
πῶς δὲ τῷ φερομένῳ καὶ τῇ στιγμῇ τὸ νῦν ἀκολουθεῖ κατ' ἐκεῖνα καὶ ἀπ' ἐκείνων τοῦτο ἔδειξε
τοσαύτης οὔσης αὐτῶν τῆς διαφορᾶς, ὡς τὰ μὲν ὑπομένειν, τὰ δὲ μὴ ὑπομένειν; πῶς οὖν [ἂν]
τὸ μὴ ὑπομένον τῷ ὑπομένοντι ὁμοίως ἂν ἔχοι τὸ τῷ ὑποκειμένῳ τὸ αὐτὸ εἶναι...".

[32] In a later passage, in order to save Aristotle's theory to some extent, Simplicius
maintains that the sameness of the instant must be understood as a sameness in
species and not in substrate. Simplicius there means that in time there is, in fact, only
a succession of always different instants; these instants, however, can be said to be the
same in species, because they differ only in being one before the other. See Simplicius, *In Physicam*, IV, p. 725, lin. 9-19.

early English commentators. Indeed, they assume that the instant is a temporal entity which persists in time and is a sort of substrate of time, a temporal counterpart to the moving object, and that the different beings of the instant are the counterparts of the stages reached by the moving object in motion. Moreover, they specify that, unlike the moving object, the instant is not a substance, but an accident.[33] Further elements of their interpretation of the theory of the persisting present will be seen in section 2.

In this context, it is worth noting that our commentators stress the 'dynamic' aspects of the analogy between the moving object and the instant. They assume that, as the moving object constitutes motion by successively taking on different determinations, so the persisting instant constitutes time by taking on different beings. Accordingly, there are not different instants, but just different beings of the same instant. This is, in short, the background of the idea that the instant in virtue of its flow causes time. Although this point is not formulated so explicitly by Aristotle, it was in fact read into his theory of the persisting present by Philoponus,[34] Averroes,[35] and Roger Bacon.[36] Our commentators refer to this same idea when they claim that the existence of time depends on the existence of the instant. For instance, N gives the following reply to the question 'In virtue of the nature of what does time have being':

> (6) To that problem I say that time has being in virtue of the nature of the instant. For the instant, being one and the same in substance, flows and in virtue of its flow causes time; therefore, time is nothing other than the flowing instant.[37]

---

[33] See S, IV, q. 19, f. 60ra, lin. 11-13; P, IV, q. 19, f. 91vb, lin. 20-64; T, IV, q. 11, f. 52ra, lin. 15-25; G³, IV, q. 13, f. 175ra, lin. 31-rb, lin. 42; N, IV, q. 13, ff. 157vb, lin. 46-158ra, lin. 37; M², IV, q. 26, f. 135Bra, lin. 14-22.

[34] See Philoponus, *In Physicam*, IV, p. 727, lin. 21-728, lin. 2.

[35] In the course of his exposition of Aristotle's analogy between the instant and the moving body, Averroes remarks: "... et secundum hunc modum translatio sequitur translatum et tempus instans, quoniam instans agit tempus, sicut translatum translationem et punctus mensuram, ut geometrae dicunt, quoniam, cum movetur, facit mensuram" (*In Physicam*, IV, t. c. 104, f. 183vaG). 'Mensura' here means a line.

[36] Bacon, *In Physicam*, IV, p. 263, lin. 6-31.

[37] N, IV, q. 2, f. 155va, lin. 26-29: "Ad illud problema dicendum quod tempus habet esse per naturam instantis. Instans enim unum et idem secundum substantiam continue fluit et illud causat tempus per sui fluxum; tempus igitur nihil aliud est quam instans fluens". See also G³, IV, q. 2, f. 171va, lin. 14-18.

This kind of explanation of the reality of time based on that of the instant must be distinguished from another, which relies instead upon the analogy between the present instant and a point of a line. For the sake of brevity, we shall refer to the explanation given by N in passage (6) as the dynamic explanation and to the other as the geometric explanation. A. Maier's study makes it clear that the latter explanation should be regarded as standard in the later medieval tradition.[38] For example, the geometric explanation appears in the English commentator Thomas Wylton. To clarify the difference between the two explanations, we shall briefly present the main points of Wylton's answer to the arguments against the existence of time (and of motion) in *Physics* IV.10.

Wylton first remarks that time and motion are continua. He further assumes that the conditions for the existence of time and motion are the same as the conditions for the existence of a continuous quantity insofar as it is continuous. These assumptions are also implicitly made by Aristotle in *Physics* IV.10. At this point, however, Wylton introduces a crucial difference in the way of regarding a continuum. In Aristotle's arguments, a continuum is characterized as something divisible into parts, and the non-existence of time and motion as continua is inferred from the non-existence of their parts. Wylton relies, instead, on the characterization of the continuum expressed by the definition of *Physics* V.3, according to which a continuum is a quantity whose parts join at a common boundary.[39] Then he infers that for a continuum to exist, it is enough that this common boundary actually exists. On the other hand, in the case of time and motion Aristotle himself recognizes that this boundary exists, being respectively the present instant and the durationless present element of motion. Wylton also specifies that the actual existence of the parts of a continuum is not necessary for the existence of the continuum qua continuum, but only for the existence of a particular kind of a continuum, that is, a permanent continuum, like spatial magnitude, and not also for the existence of a successive continuum, like time and motion.[40]

---

[38] This seems to be in fact the explanation given by the exponents of solution (S1) considered by A. Maier: Henry of Ghent, Johannes Baconthorp, Johannes Canonicus. See Maier, *Metaphysische Hintergründe*, p. 52-57.

[39] Aristotle, *Physics*, V.3, 227a10-17.

[40] Wylton, *In Physicam*, IV, f. 61ra, lin. 4-rb, lin. 5: "Circa quod sciendum quod magnitudo sive continuum in hoc consistit eius entitas vel unitas quod partes eius habeant aliquam unitatem et sint unum in aliquo indivisibili, sicut apparet per defi-

Wylton's position can be summarized as follows. The reality of time is based on the reality of the instant conceived of as the continuative element of time, namely, as the common boundary at which its past and future parts join. The 'geometric' nature of Wylton's explanation derives from the fact that it regards the instant as completely analogous to a point in a line, for it makes no reference to the dynamic character of the instant, which is, according to the early English commentators, the feature of the temporal instant that distinguishes it from the point.[41] The idea that the existence of time is guaranteed by the instant conceived of as the continuative element of time is suggested by Aristotle[42] and is occasionally found in our commentaries, but not in the purely 'geometric' version given by Wylton. On the contrary, it is almost always joined with the dynamic version. For instance, M[2] in his answer to Aristotle's arguments of *Physics* IV.10 explains in what sense the past and the future exist:

---

nitionem continui in *Praedicamentis* et quinto huius... Haec ratio continuitatis est communis omni continuo, et per consequens tempori et motui. Ex quo infero: cum entitati rei correspondet esse conveniens illi entitati, quod esse proprium cuiuslibet continui in quantum tale consistit in hoc quod partes eius actu sunt copulatae ad aliquid indivisibile in actu. In hoc tamen differentia est inter continuitatem magnitudinis ex una parte, motus et temporis ex alia, quod sicut ad existentiam actualem magnitudinis requiritur aliquid actu partes continuans, ita exigitur quod partes copulatae sint in actu, quod non accidit magnitudini ex hoc quod continua, sed ex hoc quod sic continua, puta permanens. Unde partes continui permanentis oportet quod sint actu continuatae et simul entes eadem mensura indivisibili qua terminus continuans copulans. Sed in continuo successivo, cum successio sit differentia opposita permanentiae, et in successivo sic est quod non solum ipsum comprehendens partes copulatas ad indivisibile est successivum, sed utraque pars est successiva vel quid successivum, sicut et totum. Ideo [expresse] existere successivi in actu consistit in hoc quod actu una pars, puta prior, est copulata cum posteriori, et ad hoc sufficit quod copulans sit in actu. Immo, eo ipso quod successivum, repugnat sibi quod plus sit in actu simultatis... Quamvis instans continuans nec sit tempus nec pars temporis nec similiter mutatum esse ipsius motus, tamen tam in tempore quam in motu, eo ipso quod utrumque successivum est, ad existere temporis vel motus sufficit esse in actu alicuius indivisibilis continuantis priorem partem in posteriori absque hoc quod aliqua pars sit in actu, quod accidit ex natura successivi, quod potest declarari in exemplo. Licet enim caput hominis non sit homo, tamen homo totus denominatur crispus ex hoc quod crispitudo denominat caput. Et causa in proposito est quia crispitudo non est nata ut homini secundum plures partes vel aliter sibi insit quam secundum caput".

[41] In fact, Wylton does not accept the intuitive view that the instant flows in time. See, Wylton, *In Physicam*, IV, ff. 69ra, lin. 3 ab imo-70ra, lin. 5. On Wylton's doctrine of the instant, see C. Trifogli, "Thomas Wylton on the Instant of Time", in *Mensch und Natur im Mittelalter (Miscellanea Mediaevalia*, 21/1), ed. by A. Zimmermann, De Gruyter, Berlin-New York 1991, p. 308-318.

[42] See Aristotle, *Physics*, IV.11, 219b33-220a21.

(7) ... For past time exists in some sense and similarly future time. Indeed, since they are times, they do not require permanent and simultaneous being, but have a weaker kind of being. Therefore, they are said to exist because they join at one now, which flows from the past to the future.[43]

Here the present instant is clearly considered both in the role of continuative element of time and in the dynamic role of the persisting substrate which flows through time.

To summarize, part (I) of this section has pointed out that the early English commentators generally reply to Aristotle's arguments of *Physics* IV.10 by claiming that motion and time have a peculiar kind of existence, different from that of substances. Motion and time exist in the sense that they become. With this reply our commentators follow (S2), one of the two solutions recorded by A. Maier. (S2) makes no explicit reference to the role of the temporal instant in the existence of time. Part (II) has shown that in their treatment of the temporal instant our commentators do in fact ascribe a fundamental role to the instant for the reality of time as successive entity, since, relying on Aristotle's doctrine of the persisting present, they maintain that the instant is a sort of persisting substrate that with its flow causes time.

This dynamic view of the instant does not stand in contrast to (S2). With (S2) our commentators assert the reality of temporal becoming, whereas in their treatment of the instant they specify that the instant is the basic structural element that grants this reality. Furthermore, when (S2) is supplemented with the doctrine of the flowing instant, it suggests further grounds for rejecting Aristotle's arguments of *Physics* IV.10. Indeed, these arguments regards the instant simply as an indivisible element of time, analogous to a static point on a line, whereas, in the view of our commentators, the instant is analogous to a flowing point, which by flowing extends itself in some sense and generates the whole line.[44] M^2 in passage (7) quoted above and some other com-

---

[43] M^2, IV, q. 1, f. 130va, lin. 37-40: "Tempus enim praeteritum aliquo modo est, similiter et futurum. Cum enim sunt tempora, non quaerunt esse permanens et totum simul, sed habent esse debilius. Unde dicuntur esse quia copulantur ad unum nunc, quod fluit ab uno in alterum".

[44] The importance of the notion of the persistent present for replying to the arguments of *Physics* IV.10 has recently been emphasized by M. Inwood. See, Inwood, "Aristotle's on the Reality of Time", esp. p. 178. On the contrary, Hussey maintains that this notion complicates Aristotle's theory of time. See Hussey, *Aristotle's Physics*, especially *Introduction*, p. xliv.

mentators[45] do have some intuitions of this kind, but they do not develop them into a systematic answer to Aristotle's arguments. In general, their actual answer to these arguments and their assumptions on the instant, although not in contrast, tend to remain unrelated.

2. *The Extramental Reality of Time and Its Ontological Status*

The two main medieval solutions to Aristotle's arguments against the existence of time presented in the preceding section[46] are realist, in the sense that both assume that the being of time and in general of successive entities, although in some sense weaker than the being of permanent entities, is nevertheless extramental. The realist approach to the arguments of *Physics* IV.10 is dominant among the Scholastics. A strong reason for this is that the same arguments can be equally well formulated against the existence of motion, whose extramental reality is regarded as axiomatic in Aristotle's natural philosophy.[47] There is, however, another medieval debate about whether the existence of time is mind-dependent or extra-mental, and this too has an Aristotelian background. In a passage of *Physics* IV.14, Aristotle asks whether there would be time if there were no soul. He answers that it would not exist. His argument is based on time's property of being a kind of number, the number of motion in respect of the before and after, as the definition of time in *Physics* IV.11 states:

> One could ask whether, if soul would not exist, time would exist or not. Indeed, if it is impossible that the thing that counts exists, it is also impossible that something countable exists. Therefore, it is clear that number too would not exist. For number is what has been counted or

---

[45] After claiming that Aristotle's arguments are solved by the distinction between two kinds of being of *Physics* III.6 (see note 21 above), T presents another solution according to which time (i. e., an extended period of time) can be said to be present because of the flow of the present. See T, IV, q. 1, f. 49va, lin. 39-45.

[46] See above, p. 207.

[47] In connection with the arguments of *Physics* IV.10, however, Averroes remarks that motion and time do not exist completely in extramental reality: "... esse eorum componitur ex actione animae in eo quod est in eis extra animam, et entia completa sunt illa in quorum esse nihil facit anima, ut post declarabitur de tempore, scilicet quoniam est de numero entium quorum actus completur per animam" (Averroes, *In Physicam*, IV, t. c. 88, f. 174raA-B). On the other hand, Averroes' position does not seem to be fully consistent. For, when, in t. c. 131, he explains in what sense the actual existence of time depends on the soul, he also assumes that motion can exist completely in extramental reality. On this point, see below, p. 223.

can be counted. Thus, if nothing but the soul or the intellect of the soul
can count, it is impossible that time exists, if the soul does not exist,
except that the substratum of time can exist, as if, for instance, it is
possible that motion exists without the soul.[48]

This passage exhausts Aristotle's discussion of the relation between
time and the soul. Though some aspects of it are too condensed and
obscure, the main point of Aristotle's argument for the dependence of
time on the soul is clear. Time is a number, but the existence of number depends on something capable of counting, and this can only be
the soul.

As some Aristotelian scholars remark, behind Aristotle's argument
there is an "anti-Platonist" theory of number,[49] which denies that
number is a real property of collections of things. Rather, in extramental reality only collections of things exist, and a number is associated with them only insofar as we count the members of these collections.[50] In the Greek tradition, Simplicius and Philoponus reject this
anti-Platonist theory, and maintain that the existence of number does
not depend on counting. Simplicius, for instance, claims that:

> ... the fingers of my hand are five, even if nobody counts them.[51]

Similarly, Philoponus denies that number is just what can be counted
and therefore:

> ... the "ten" of stones, when the soul is destroyed, is destroyed only as
> countable, not however, as number. For the "ten" of stones exists,
> even if the soul does not exist.[52]

Accordingly, by rejecting the anti-Platonist theory from which Aristotle's argument of *Physics* IV.14 derives, Simplicius and Philoponus deny
the dependence of time on the human soul implied by that argument.[53]

---

[48] Aristotle, *Physics*, IV.14, 223a21-28.
[49] A classical study on this topic is Annas, "Aristotle, Number and Time", p. 97-
113. See also Hussey, *Aristotle's Physics*, Notes, p. 173; Additional Notes, p. 176-184.
See also Introduction, p. 19-20.
[50] On this theory of number, see also above, chap. 2, p. 127-128.
[51] Simplicius, *In Physicam*, IV, p. 765, lin. 30.
[52] Philoponus, *In Physicam*, IV, p. 770, lin. 21-23.
[53] Though these commentators try to save Aristotle's saying that time depends on
the soul, by arguing that both time and motion depend on soul viewed as the efficient
cause of any motion in the sublunar world. See Simplicius, *In Physicam*, IV, p. 766, lin.
27-33; Philoponus, *In Physicam*, IV, p. 770, lin. 27-771, lin. 3. This interpretation is
suggested also by Themistius. See Themistius, *In Physicam*, IV, p. 161, lin. 6-8.

In the medieval tradition, the dependence of time on the soul is defended by Averroes. The *Commentator* does not deal extensively with the theory of number that lies behind Aristotle's argument or with the application of this theory to the case of time. Yet, he does make explicit to what extent the existence of time depends on the soul and how the ontological status of time viewed as the number of motion should be conceived of. Averroes' position becomes the starting point of most medieval discussions on the extramental reality of time and on its ontological status more generally. In the early English commentaries, in particular, the discussion focusses on Averroes' position. These commentators strongly reject it, and maintain that time exists extramentally as a real property of motion.

In this section, we shall present the position of our commentators on the extramental reality of time and its ontological status in two main steps. We shall first examine their reaction to Averroes' position, and then present some significant aspects of their treatment of the relation between time and motion.

2.1 *The Rejection of Averroes' Position*

In t. c. 131 of his commentary on Book IV, Averroes summarizes Aristotle's treatment of the relation between time and the soul with the following argument:

> (A) Since it has been declared that, if that which numbers did not exist, number would not exist either. And since it is impossible that something other than the soul and specifically other than the intellect numbers, it is evident that, if the soul did not exist, number would not exist either, and if number did not exist, neither would time.[54]

Averroes believes that this argument must be accepted. Immediately after, however, he specifies to what extent number depends on the soul:

> (1) ... the being of number in the soul is not being in the soul in every way, because, if it were so, then number would be something fictitious and false, like a chimera and a goatstag. But its being outside the mind

---

[54] Averroes, *In Physicam*, IV, t. c. 131, f. 202rbD-E: "Cum sit declaratum quod, cum numerans non fuerit, non erit numerus, et est impossibile aliquid aliud numerare praeter animam et de anima intellectus, manifestum est quod, si anima non fuerit, non erit numerus; et cum numerus non fuerit, non erit tempus".

is being in potency in virtue of its proper subject, and its being in the soul is being in act, that is, when the soul exerts that action in a subject prepared to receive that action which is called number.[55]

Here Averroes suggests that number has a composite ontological status, since it exists potentially in extramental reality, but actually only in the soul or by means of the soul. His point seems to be that a collection of two stones exists in extramental reality, and this is the subject of the number two, but the number two is not an extramental accident of this collection. Rather, it is the result of our mental process of counting the stones belonging to that collection. Hence, in Averroes' terms, the actual existence of the number two depends on the action of counting exerted by our soul on the extramental collection of two stones. The same composite ontological status must be ascribed to time considered as the number of motion. Motion functions here as the extramental subject of time, which grants its potential extramental existence. Specifically, the extramental 'collection' relevant to time as number is that of the successive phases of motion, i.e., the before and after in motion. Time actually exists when our soul 'counts', that is, discerns, the successive phases of motion:

> (2) ... motion would exist, even if the soul did not exist. And insofar as before and after in motion are numbered in potency, time exists in potency, and insofar as they are numbered in act, time exists in act. Therefore, time does not exist in act, unless the soul exists; but it exists in potency, even if the soul did not exist.[56]

Thus, as in the case of the collection of two stones, the number two is nothing other than the two stones insofar as they are counted, similarly time as the number of motion according to the before and after is nothing other than the before and after in motion insofar as they are "numbered", i. e., perceived as distinct by our soul.[57]

---

[55] Ibid., f. 202rbE: "... esse numeri in anima non est omnibus modis esse in anima, quoniam, si ita esset, esset fictum et falsum, ut chimera et hircocervus; sed esse eius extra mentem est in potentia propter subiectum proprium, et esse eius in anima est in actu, scilicet quando anima egerit illam actionem in subiecto preparato ad recipiendum illam actionem quae dicitur numerus".

[56] Ibid., f. 202rbF: "... motus erit, etsi anima non erit. Et secundum quod prius et posterius sunt in eo numerata in potentia, est tempus in potentia, et secundum quod sunt numerata in actu, est tempus in actu. Tempus igitur in actu non erit nisi anima sit; in potentia vero, licet anima non sit".

[57] Ibid., f. 202vaG: "... non potest aliquis dicere quod tempus est, etsi anima non

In t. c. 109, Averroes formulates his thesis on the composite ontological status of time in terms of the distinction between the material
and formal elements of time, which correspond respectively to the
extramental element and the mental element of time. In this context
Averroes sets out to explain why time is defined in terms of number,
despite the fact that it is a continuous quantity:

> (3) Therefore, to this question let us say that outside the mind only
> motion exists and time comes to be only when the mind divides
> motion into the before and after, and this is the meaning of the expres-
> sion 'number of motion', i.e., that motion is numbered. Therefore, the
> substance of time, which has the role of form in time, is number, and
> that which has in it the role of matter is continuous motion, since time
> is not number in an absolute sense, but the number of motion.[58]

Thus, in Averroes' view, the defining formula 'time is the number of
motion' expresses the composite ontological status of time, since
'motion' stands for the extramental element of time, whereas 'number' for the mental element.

There are certainly obscurities and difficulties in Averroes' treatment of the relation between time, motion, and the soul, but his basic
idea that time exists partially in the soul and partially in extramental
reality enjoyed great success in the thirteenth and fourteenth centuries.[59] Indeed, this idea fits well with the more general view about
the ontological status of time that posits no real distinction between
time and motion. In the first half of the thirteenth century, however,
this idea was rejected by Richard Rufus of Cornwall, Roger Bacon,
and some years later by Albert the Great. These three authors oppose
Averroes with a realist position according to which time exists completely and actually in extramental reality. All early English commentators are also exponents of this thirteenth-century realist tradition.[60]

---

erit, nisi quia motus est, etsi anima non fuerit; et similiter sunt in eo prius et posterius, et tempus nihil aliud est quam prius et posterius in motu, sed secundum quod
numerata, et ideo indiget in hoc quod sit in actu anima, scilicet secundum quod est
prius et posterius numerata".

[58] Ibid., t. c. 109, f. 187raC: "Dicamus igitur ad hoc quod extra mentem non est nisi
motus (motum *ed.*), et tempus non fit nisi quando mens dividit motum in prius et posterius, et haec est intentio numeri motus, i. e., motum esse numeratum; ergo substantia temporis quae est in eo quasi forma est numerus, et quod est in eo quasi materia
est motus continuus, quoniam non est numerus simpliciter, sed numerus motus".

[59] See Maier, *Metaphysische Hintergründe*, p. 65-91.

[60] B instead follows Averroes' view on the ontological status of time. See B, IV, q.
19, f. 29rb, lin. 17 ab imo-9 ab imo; q. 28, ff. 31va, lin. 19 ab imo-32rb, lin. 33.

In particular, unlike Averroes, they find argument (A) inconclusive, and reject the main aspects of Averroes' view that time is ontologically composite. In what follows, (I) we shall first present the reply of our commentators to argument (A) and then (II) the criticism that they specifically address against Averroes.

(I) We recall that behind argument (A) there is a position about the ontological status of number which claims that the number two, for instance, is not an extramental accident of a collection of two stones, but simply the result of our counting the members of this collection. This 'economical' position does not reflect the view of the early English commentators on number. Like Simplicius and Philoponus, they usually assume that number two is, in fact, an extramental accident of the collection of two stones and in general of any collection of two things. This realist view on number is also found in Richard Rufus, Roger Bacon, and Albert the Great. Specifically, in replying to argument (A) all our commentators, with the exception of M², adopt some version of Rufus' answer:

> Therefore, how shall we respond to the argument that if number exists, then that which counts exist? As it seems to me, it should be said that "to count" is equivocal. For in one sense to count means to determine a thing under a definite discreteness. And in this sense it follows that, if number exists, then that which counts exists. But this number (*perhaps read*: in this way what counts) is not the soul, but the form of those things that are counted, as, for instance, the form of the stone replicating itself in some subjects determines for them some definite discreteness and counts them. In another sense to count something means to determine for oneself the discreteness of some things or to declare to oneself some things under a definite discreteness. And in this sense the soul is that which counts, and it does not follow that if number exists, then that which counts exists.[61]

---

[61] Rufus, *In Physicam*, IV, f. 8va, lin. 45-vb, lin. 3: "Qualiter ergo respondebimus argumento: si numerus est, numerans est? Dicendum, ut mihi videtur, quod numerare est aequivocum. Numerare enim aliquid uno modo est determinare rem sub certa discretione. Et sic sequitur: si numerus est, numerans est. Sed hic numerus (*forte pro*: sic numerans) non est anima, sed forma ipsorum numeratorum, sicut forma lapidis sic replicans se in aliqua supposita determinat eis aliquam certam discretionem et numerat ipsa. Alio modo aliquid numerare est determinare sibi discretionem aliquorum vel declarare sibi ali<qu>a sub certa discretione. Et sic anima est numerans, et non sequitur: si numerus est, numerans est". See also Bacon, *In Physicam*, IV, p. 250, lin. 6-15; S, IV, q. 2, f. 57ra, lin. 13-18; P, IV, q. 5, f. 89va, lin. 27-34; T, IV, q. 5, f. 50vb, lin. 3-10; G¹, IV, q. 9, f. 151ra, lin. 61-rb, lin. 4; M³, q. 12, f.

The significant point of Rufus' reply consists exactly in denying that the inference "if number exists, then that which numbers exists" is valid when 'that which numbers' stands for the mental act of counting the members of a collection of things. Indeed, in Rufus' view, the number two exists when it actually inheres in a collection of two stones, for instance, but its actual inherence does not at all require that we count the members of this collection. It only requires that there be two stones. This, of course, does not depend on the soul, but on the extramental condition that the form of the stone replicates itself in the two individual stones, as Rufus puts it. This is the extramental sense of "that which counts" used by Rufus to save Aristotle's inference from the existence of number to the existence of something that counts.

A more direct refutation of the 'economic' position on the ontological status of number is attempted by M[2] in his reply to argument (A):

> (4) I say that, when the soul numbers, it numbers only through something that is in the numbered things themselves by which it numerates. Therefore, not only numerable things, but also that by which the soul numerates them are outside the soul. Accordingly, that by which we numerate is of two kinds, viz., effectively or formally. That by which we numerate formally is the formal number, which exists in the numerable things and is a discrete quantity, whereas the efficient cause by which we numbers is the soul itself that numbers...[62]

The reply of M[2] is largely a repetition of that of Albert the Great to Aristotle's argument.[63] It makes clear that number and counting

---

170ra, lin. 43-49; G[3], IV, q. 5, f. 172va, lin. 26-36; N, IV, q. 5, f. 156rb, lin. 5-11. Rufus also specifies that in the case of time that which numerates in the extramental sense is the mobile body: "Et scire debemus quod numerans primo modo in tempore est ipsum mobile secundum quod replicat se in partibus diversis spatii secundum prius et posterius, quia ex hac replicatione est dicere quod prius et posterius in spatio est causa prioris et posterioris in motu et prius et posterius in motu est causa prioris et posterioris in tempore. Et sicut per hoc est motus actualiter distinctus per prius et posterius, ita et tempus" (*In Physicam*, IV, f. 8vb, lin. 3-8). In section 2.2 we shall explain in more detail this kind of derivation of the before and after in time from that of motion.

[62] M[2], IV, q. 2, f. 131ra, lin. 65-rb, lin. 4: "... dico quod, quando anima numerat non numerat nisi per aliquid quod est in ipsis numerabilibus quo ipsa numerat. Unde extra animam non solum sunt numerabilia, sed illud quo anima numerat ipsa. Unde quo numeramus duplex est, scilicet effective vel formaliter; quo numeramus formaliter est numerus formalis, qui est in rebus numerabilibus et est quantitas discreta; quo autem numeramus effective est ipsa anima quae numerat".

[63] Albert the Great, *In Physicam*, IV, tract. 3, cap. 16, p. 289b, lin. 63-290a, lin. 16. Albert the Great's passage on the extramental reality of number is also quoted in Maier, *Metaphysische Hintergründe*, p. 67-68.

involve three distinct ontological levels: (i) the collection of two stones, (ii) the formal number as extramental accident of this collection (a discrete quantity), and (iii) the soul, which is to say our mental activity of counting the stones (that which numbers effectively). Level (ii) cannot be eliminated, as argument (A) seems to assume, because then (iii) could not be posited. In other words, in order to be able to count the collection of two stones, it is necessary to postulate the number two as an accident inhering in this collection.

In conclusion, according to all our commentators, no objection to the extramental reality of time can be raised by relying simply on the fact that time is a sort of number of motion.

(II) The realist position of the early English commentators on number suggests the possibility of a direct refutation of Averroes' view that time is actualized by our mental process of 'distinguishing' the before and after in motion. Indeed, the before and after in motion are analogous to the collection of two stones and our discerning the before and after in motion is analogous to counting. Then time as number of the before and after in motion does not depend on our discerning the successive phases of motion. Furthermore, applying to the case of time the argument of M^2,[64] one can even argue that in order to be able to discern the successive phases of motion time as extramental accident of motion must have already distinguished these phases. These ideas, however, are not developed by our commentators, and in section 2.2 we shall also suggest why they do not develop them. In fact, their refutation of Averroes' position consists mainly in showing that it is unacceptable from a physical point of view and that it is in contrast with some of the principles assumed by Aristotle about time.

For instance, they remark that time is a quantity, but quantity is an extramental accident. Thus, our soul has no quantity, and hence time cannot actually exist in the soul.[65] Furthermore, they point out that Averroes' claim that time is actualized when the soul distinguishes the successive phases of motion deprives time of any physical and objective meaning, as the following argument of N shows:

---

[64] See above, p. 225.
[65] See S, IV, q. 2, f. 56vb, lin. 19-21; P, IV, q. 4, f. 89rb, lin. 33-35; T, IV, q. 5, f. 50va, lin. 35-40; G^3, IV, q. 5, f. 172rb, lin. 22-24; N, IV, q. 5, f. 156ra, lin. 24-25; M^2, IV, q. 2, f. 130vb, lin. 56-60. See also Bacon, *In Physicam*, IV, p. 249, lin. 2-5.

(5) The Commentator says that time exists in act only when the soul actually distinguishes the before and after in motion. One can argue against this as follows. For, if this were the case, then that which would be time for me would not be time for you unless your soul made the same distinction according to the before and after, but this is absurd.[66]

Indeed, our mental 'distinction' of the successive phases of motion seems to amount to our perceiving that this motion is taking place. Then Averroes' claim that such a mental distinction actualizes time seems to refer to the modality of our perception of time. On the other hand, this phenomenological condition cannot plausibly be taken as the ground for the actual existence of time, if time must be a structural element of the physical world, as our commentators assume.

Moreover, as we shall see in section 3, Aristotle postulates that there is just one simultaneous time and that all simultaneous motions have the same time. This postulate, however, would be violated if the actual existence of time depended on the mental distinction of the successive phases of a motion, since in this case time would be individuated by a mental act and this act in turn by the subject that performs it, as the following arguments of G[1] point out:

(6) ... if it were so, then unless mind were numerically the same in distinct men, it would happen that many times would exist simultaneously. For if my mind distinguishes the before and after in this motion and similarly your mind, since the action of my mind is numerically distinct from the action of your mind, then there would be numerically distinct times simultaneously.

Furthermore, if my mind divides the before and after in this motion and your mind in another motion, since these actions are numerically distinct, and also the agents and those who divide in the two cases numerically distinct, and similarly the patients and the recipients of the division are numerically distinct, thus there would necessarily be numerically distinct times.[67]

---

[66] N, IV, q. 5, f. 156ra, lin. 40-43: "Commentator dicit quod tempus non est in actu nisi quando anima distinguit actu prius et posterius in motu. Contra quod sic, quia, si sic, tunc illud quod esset mihi tempus non esset tibi tempus nisi anima tua faceret eandem distinctionem secundum prius et posterius, quod est inconveniens". See also G[1], IV, q. 9, f. 151ra, lin. 36-38; M[3], IV, q. 1, f. 167ra, lin. 63-rb, lin. 5; G[3], IV, q. 5, f. 172rb, lin. 50-va, lin. 3.

[67] G[1], IV, q. 9, f. 151ra, lin. 40-46: "... si sic esset, tunc nisi eadem <mens> numero esset in diversis hominibus (animalibus *ms.*), accideret multa tempora simul esse. Si enim mens mea dividat prius et posterius in hoc motu et mens tua similiter,

These kinds of arguments against Averroes will be proposed repeatedly in the later exegetical tradition.[68] Certainly, the specific type of
actualization of time through the mental act of distinguishing the successive phases of motion is not a very convincing aspect of Averroes'
position. There is, however, a more general element in Averroes'
interpretation, namely, the asymmetry between the existence of time
and that of motion, which is implied by his claim that, in the absence
of a soul, time exists only potentially, but motion can exist actually.
Like Rufus and Bacon,[69] the early English commentators maintain
that this asymmetry cannot be accepted.

For instance, S writes:

> (7) But the Commentator wants to say that time exists in potency apart
> from the soul, while receiving its actuality from the soul, because the
> comparison according to the before and after cannot be done without
> the soul. Aristotle, however, says that motion and time follow one
> another both in act and in potency. Whatever the Commentator and
> the others may say, let us say together with Aristotle that time can exist
> both in act and in potency without the soul, although it cannot be per-
> ceived without the soul.[70]

---

cum alia et alia numero sit actio mentis <meae> et actio mentis tuae, aliud et aliud
tempus numero simul erit. Item, si mens mea dividit prius et posterius in hoc motu et
mens tua in alio motu, cum actio haec et illa sit alia et alia numero, agens etiam et
dividens hinc inde aliud et aliud numero, patiens etiam (ergo *ms.*) et recipiens divisionem hinc inde aliud et aliud numero, erit tempus necessario aliud et aliud
numero". See also S, IV, q. 2, f. 56vb, lin. 39-43; P, IV, q. 5, f. 89va, lin. 7-9; T, IV, q.
5, f. 50va, lin. 32-34; G³, IV, q. 5, f. 172va, lin. 5-15; N, IV, q. 5, f. 156ra, lin. 44-50.

[68] See, for instance, Thomas Wylton's question "Utrum tempus habeat esse extra
animam", edited in C. Trifogli, "Il problema dello statuto ontologico del tempo nelle
Quaestiones super Physicam di Thomas Wylton e di Giovanni di Jandun", *Documenti e studi sulla tradizione filosofica medievale*, 1 (1990) 2, p. 515-527.

[69] Rufus, *In Physicam*, IV, f. 8va, lin. 42-45: "Et quia videtur sententiam Commentatoris esse quod tempus in potentia et non secundum actum consequitur motum,
sed eius actualitas est ab anima, contra hoc est quod dicit Aristoteles motum et tempus simul esse secundum actum et potentiam. Potest enim argui: si motus est actu;
ergo tempus". Bacon, *In Physicam*, IV, p. 249, lin. 15-16.

[70] S, IV, q. 2, f. 57ra, lin. 3-9: "Commentator autem vult quod tempus sit in potentia
praeter animam, actualitatem autem capit ab anima, quia collatio per prius et posterius talis non potest fieri sine anima. Sed dicit Aristoteles quod motus et tempus
sequuntur sibi invicem et actu et potentia. Quicquid autem dicat Commentator et
alii, dicamus tunc cum Aristotele quod tempus potest <esse> sine anima et actu et
potentia, percipi tamen non potest sine anima". See also P, IV, q. 4, f. 89rb, lin. 49-
50; q. 5, f. 89va, lin. 9-11; T, IV, q. 5, f. 50va, lin. 40-44; G¹, IV, q. 9, f. 151ra, lin.
28-33; M³, IV, q. 11, f. 169vb, lin. 12-15; G³, IV, q. 5, f. 172rb, lin. 25-36; va, lin.
15-25; N, IV, q. 5, f. 156ra, lin. 25-30; ra, lin. 50-rb, lin. 4; M², IV, q. 2, f. 131ra, lin.
54-65.

In this passage, S, like other commentators, invokes Aristotle's authority to dismiss Averroes' claim that motion can exist actually, even when time exists only potentially. It is true that, just before raising the question of the relation between time and the soul, Aristotle asserts that motion and time exist simultaneously both in act and in potency.[71] In his commentary Averroes himself explains that time actually exists in what actually moves.[72] On the other hand, as Averroes admits, motion can actually exist, even if no soul exists. However, the attempt made by our commentators to reject Averroes' position as not reflecting Aristotle's view does not have great force. In fact, Aristotle's position about the relation between the existence of motion and that of time in *Physics* IV.14 does not seem to be fully consistent. At the end of argument (A), Aristotle apparently implies that, if there were no soul, time would not exist, but motion could exist,[73] as Averroes in fact maintains. Thus, in order to reject Averroes' asymmetry independent arguments proving that the actual existence of motion implies the actual existence of time are needed. S makes his most articulate attempt in the following passage:

> (8) ... motion can exist apart from the soul, according to the Commentator. Then I argue: either it will have its duration or not. If not, this is absurd. If it has its duration and the measure of its duration, either this measure is all at once or with respect to the before and after. If all at once, therefore motion would be measured by age. But this is false. If by respect to the before and after, then this measure is together with succession, and therefore is necessarily time, and so time will exist in act and not, as the Commentator says, in potency.[74]

S here assumes that motion or its duration has measure, and that the measure must have a structure similar to that of the measured thing. In this case, the relevant structure of motion is that of being a successive entity, so that its measure is also successive. Then this measure

---

[71] Aristotle, *Physics*, IV.14, 223a16-21.
[72] Averroes, *In Physicam*, IV, t. c. 130, f. 201vbL.
[73] Aristotle, *Physics*, IV.14, 223a25-29.
[74] S, IV, q. 2, f. 56vb, lin. 31-39: "... motus potest esse praeter animam, secundum Commentatorem. Arguo tunc sic: aut ergo habebit esse suae durationis aut non. Si non, hoc est inconveniens. Si habeat suam durationem et mensurationem suae durationis, aut ergo mensuratio est tota simul aut per prius et posterius. Si tota simul, ergo motus mensuraretur aevo, quod falsum est. Si per prius et posterius, tunc cum successione, et ita de necessitate tempus est, et ita actu erit tempus et non erit potentia, sicut dicit Commentator".

can only be time. Thus, S relies on the idea that time is a property necessarily concomitant with motion, this property being the successive measure of its successive duration. This idea is also present in the other early English commentaries, since many *pro*-arguments of the question 'Whether time exists' appeal to the principle that, since motion exists, its measure must exist, but this measure is time.[75]

To evaluate the cogency of this kind of argument, it can be remarked that, like Aristotle himself, Aristotelian commentators in connection with time tend to use the terms 'measure' and 'number' interchangeably. Therefore, the claim that time is the measure of motion is taken as equivalent to the definition of time. Thus, it is not surprising that this claim is the most recurrent and also the most ambiguous formula in Aristotelian commentaries. For example, it is used by Averroes. Furthermore, from an Averroistic perspective, one might admit that if motion exists, time as its measure exists, but one would certainly deny that this measure must be something really distinct from motion itself. For instance, one might say that in order to measure the duration of a motion it is enough to establish as a unit of measurement the duration of a phase of this or another motion.[76] Accordingly, in order to reject Averroes' position, the early English commentators should specify in what sense is time the measure of motion and explain why in fact motion needs to be measured by time conceived of as something essentially distinct from motion itself. Our commentators, however, never explain very clearly these points. Next we shall examine the major obstacle they meet when they deal with this topic.

---

[75] See P, IV, q. 1, f. 89ra, lin. 2-4; T, IV, q. 1, f. 49va, lin. 22-39; G^1, IV, q. 1, f. 149vb, lin. 44-57; M^3, IV, q. 1, ff. 166vb, lin. 36-167ra, lin. 10; G^3, IV, q. 1, f. 171rb, lin. 3-11; N, IV, q. 1, f. 155rb, lin. 37-42; M^2, IV, q. 1, f. 130va, lin. 28-32.

[76] This is in fact John of Jandun's reply to an objection by Thomas Wylton to Averroes' position: "... dicendum quod tempus bene mensurabit motum secundum quod ipsum tempus est ens extra animam. Et cum dicitur quod tempus non mensurat motum nisi secundum quod differt quidditative a motu, hoc nego. Immo, ipsum tempus quod mensurat ipsum motum proprie est idem essentialiter cum motu... Hoc igitur modo tempus mensurat motum, quia accipitur aliqua pars determinata motus que est essentialiter tempus, licet differt secundum rationem, ut dies aut hora, et illa pars aliquotiens sumpta reddit quantitatem illius totius motus..." (Trifogli, "Lo statuto ontologico del tempo", p. 542-543).

2.2 *Time and Motion*

The arguments presented by the early English commentators against Averroes' position do not shed much light on the meaning of their realist reaction. To get a more definite view on this point, it is helpful to examine directly the question whether time is an extramental *res* distinct from motion, although inhering in it. It is clear that Averroes' view is committed to a negative answer to this question, since he claims that outside the soul only motion exists.[77] It is equally clear that the total rejection of Averroes' view by our commentators implies a positive answer.

Formulated in these terms, the question about the ontological status of time raised by Averroes' treatment of the relation between time and the soul certainly has some analogies with the question on the ontological status of motion. In that case the question was whether motion is really distinct from the form finally acquired by the mobile substance.[78] And again the answer of the early English commentators was positive, whereas that of Averroes was negative. In the case of motion, however, our commentators were able to produce stronger arguments against Averroes than in the case of time.[79]

There is no doubt that the case of time is more complicated. Some of the immediate grounds for a real distinction between motion and its final form can no longer be proposed for a real distinction between motion and time. For instance, in the former case our commentators used the *permanentia-successiva* distinction, arguing that motion is a successive entity, whereas a form is a permanent entity, so that motion and its final form cannot be the same thing considered in different ways, as Averroes believes.[80] Time and motion, however, are both successive entities. Accordingly, one may ask why it is necessary to posit time as a successive entity in addition to motion. This objection has an immediate realist answer, one in fact given by the later English commentators Thomas Wylton and Walter Burley. The answer is that the succession that characterizes motion is temporal in the sense that it is in virtue of time that motion is successive, in the same way that in virtue of whiteness a substance is white. Burley presents this answer in an incisive form:

---

[77] See passage (3) quoted above at p. 223.
[78] See above, p. 49-50.
[79] See above, p. 55-59.
[80] See above, p. 55-57.

(9) Therefore, in short, motion does not have by itself that something of it is past and something is future. For motion is said to be past only because it was in past time, and one of its parts is before and another after only because one part was in past time and another in future time, and similarly motion is said to be past only because it was in past time. From these remarks it is evident that the before and after in duration primarily and essentially are in time and they are in motion only in virtue of time, since, that is, motion is conjoined to time. Hence it follows that time is really different from motion.[81]

Burley's answer is present in a latent and inchoate form in some of the early English commentaries. We shall now suggest what is the main reason that prevents them from formulating it openly and neatly, as Burley does.

Burley's argument for the real distinction of time and motion basically relies on the idea that the temporal order has logical priority over the order of motion. This idea is not at all alien to our commentators, since it seems to lie behind their interpretation of the formula that time is the measure or number of motion. Indeed, they tend to expand it either in the sense that the before and after in time distinguish and divide the before and after in motion or in the sense that time is the possibility of numbering the before and after in motion. On the other

---

[81] Burley, *In Physicam*, IV, f. 127rb-va: "Unde breviter motus non habet a se ipso quod aliquid eius est praeteritum et aliquid futurum, quia motus non dicitur praeteritus nisi quia fuit in tempore praeterito, nec una pars motus est prior et alia posterior nisi quia una pars fuit in tempore praeterito et alia in tempore futuro, nec dicitur motus praeteritus nisi quia fuit in tempore praeterito. Ex quibus apparet quod prius et posterius secundum durationem primo et essentialiter sunt in tempore et non sunt in motu nisi ratione temporis, ut scilicet quia motus est coniunctus tempori. Ex quo sequitur quod tempus realiter differt a motu". In this passage Burley follows the analysis of the relation between time and motion given by Avicenna. See Avicenna, *Sufficientia*, II, cap. 10, f. 33va-b. The same point is made by Thomas Wylton in the following passage: "Ergo imaginor sic quod, sicut lignum habet partem extra partem per quantitatem inherentem sibi, quod est accidens posterius ligno, illa tamen partibilitas vel divisibilitas non est alia ligni et alia quantitatis in ligno, sed eadem partibilitas quae est quantitatis primo per essentiam est ligni participatione et per accidens, ratione quantitatis extendentis lignum, sic imaginor hic. Motus in esse suo naturali habet partem extra partem, puta partem priorem et posteriorem. Ista autem partibilitas extra eius quidditatem est et sibi inest per quantitatem inherentem sibi, puta tempus. Ideo eadem partibilitas, puta secundum prius et posterius, quae est temporis essentialiter, est motus primi participatione, in hoc quod est subiectum istius quantitatis quae est tempus" (*In Physicam*, IV, f. 65va, lin. 46-vb, lin. 10). Burley's realist position on the ontological status of time is discussed in Maier, *Metaphysische Hintergründe*, p. 86-89. On Wylton's position, see Trifogli, "Il problema dello statuto ontologico del tempo", p. 491-512.

hand, only in very rare cases, as in the following passage from G¹, they explicitly state that claiming time to be the measure of motion implies the priority of the temporal order over that of motion.

> (10) (i) That time is the measure of motion is evident. That in virtue of which the before and after in motion are first distinguished and numbered is the number of motion and its measure; (ii) but this is time, since the distinction of the before and after in the mobile body, from which the before and after in motion derives, derives from nothing other than the before and after in time. (iii) This is evident, since the mobile body cannot simultaneously be in different parts of space, but it is before in one and after in another, and in this way the before and after in time correspond to its existence here and there. Therefore, it is evident that the distinction of the before and after in the mobile body derives from the before and after in time.[82]

G¹ here considers the case of the local motion of a body along some path in space. He analyzes this case at three levels: (b) that of the moving body which occupies successively different positions in space, (m) that of the motion of this body, and (t) that of the time taken by its motion. At each of these three levels there is an order of the before and after. He establishes the following relations of derivation among them: (t)→(b)→(m), where '(x)→(y)' means that (x) is prior to (y) and (y) depends upon (x). The crucial step is (t)→(b), that, together with step (b)→(m), implies the priority of the temporal order over that of motion, that is, (t)→(m). Step (t)→(b) is proved in (iii) with an argument very similar to that proposed by Burley. It can be put more explicitly as follows. When we say that the body moving along some

---

[82] G¹, IV, q. 1, f. 149vb, lin. 49-57: "(i) Quod autem tempus sit mensura motus patet. Illud per quod distinguitur et numeratur prius et posterius in motu est numerus motus et eius mensura; (ii) sed hoc est tempus, quia distinctio prioris et posterioris in mobili, a qua est prius et posterius in motu, non est nisi a priori et posteriori in tempore. (iii) Quod sic patet, quia mobile non potest simul et semel <esse> in diversis partibus spatii (passi *ms.*), sed prius in una et posterius in alia, et sic suae existentiae hic et ibi respondet prius et posterius in tempore. Patet igitur quod distinctio prioris et posterioris in mobili est a priori et posteriori in tempore". A parallel passage is in M³, IV, q. 1, f. 167ra, lin. 1-10. The priority of the temporal order over that of motion is also suggested in the following passage in T: "In mobili enim non est sic sumere prius et posterius, quia omnes partes simul sunt. In motu autem sunt prius et posterius, sed non de se, immo per naturam temporis prioris mobilis in parte priori ipsius spatii. In tempore autem sunt per naturam temporis secundum quod condicionem mensurae habet et magis concordat cum numero quam motus..." (IV, q. 21, f. 55rb, lin. 23-29).

path in space cannot occupy distinct positions simultaneously, but first occupies one position and then another, the relation of 'first-then' or 'before-after' can only be understood in temporal terms, namely, in the sense that it occupies these positions at different and successive times.

G¹, however, is not able to maintain consistently the view that the temporal order is prior to that of motion. For instance, in his answer to the question "From what does the discretion in time derive", he declares:

> (11) (i) Therefore, it must be said that the before and after are in time insofar as motion is compared to the mobile body insofar as it traverses a space. For since the mobile body cannot be simultaneously in differ-ent parts of space, but is first in one and then in another, ... and thus it is the cause of the before and after in motion and consequently in time. (ii) This answer can be confirmed as follows: the discreteness in time is caused by the numeration of the instants of time; but different instants are numbered in virtue of the different beings of the mobile body; therefore, the before and after in time are caused by the mobile body insofar as it traverses a space.[83]

This passage considers levels (b), (m), and (t). Yet, it does not preserve the relations of derivation among the corresponding orders of the before and after. The new relations are (b)→(m)→(t). Behind these new relations there is a problematic Aristotelian doctrine that the ear-ly English commentators accept with only minor modifications. This is an important part of Aristotle's 'reductionist programme' for time, which is to say, his attempt to show that all the relevant properties of time are derivative, in the sense that they do not belong to time in its own right, but in virtue of more basic kinds of quantities, such as space and motion.[84] The doctrine in question is the application of

---

[83] G¹, IV, q. 4, f. 150rb, lin. 13-19: "(i) Ideo dicendum quod prius et posterius in tempore sunt in quantum motus comparatur ad mobile prout mobile pertransit spatium. Secundum enim hoc non potest esse simul in diversis partibus, sed prius est in una et postea in alia, et hoc est sub aliquo esse, et sic est causa prioris et posterioris in motu, et per consequens in tempore. (ii) Haec responsio potest sic confirmari: dis-cretio in tempore est per numerationem ipsorum nunc in tempore; sed diversa nunc numerantur per diversa esse translati; prius igitur et posterius in tempore causantur a mobili in quantum est pertransiens spatium". See also P, IV, q. 17, f. 91rb, lin. 22-28; M³, IV, q. 5, f. 168vb, lin. 34-42; G³, IV, q. 4, f. 172ra, lin. 29-49; N, IV, q. 4, ff. 155vb, lin. 49-156ra, lin. 8; M², IV, q. 17, f. 134rb, lin. 51-va, lin. 3.

[84] On Aristotle's reductionist programme, see Hussey, *Aristotle's Physics*, Introduc-tion, p. xlii-xliii.

Aristotle's reductionist programme to the before and after in time, that is, to the temporal order. Aristotle distinguishes three levels: (s) that of space, (m) that of motion, and (t) that of time. He states that the before and after are primarily in space, and because they are in space they are in motion, and because they are in motion they are in time. Thus, he sets the relations as (s)→(m)→(t).[85]

As some Aristotelian scholars have pointed out,[86] there are two main difficulties in Aristotle's attempted derivation of the temporal order from that of motion and space expressed by these relations:

(1) the order of the "before and after" in motion cannot be derived only from that of space, since motion is intrinsically oriented, whereas spatial magnitude is not. This means that on a line, for instance, an orientation or a direction can indeed be fixed, but the opposite orientation too can equally well be fixed, whereas the direction of motion cannot be arbitrarily chosen;

(2) the intrinsic order of the "before and after" in motion, as distinct from the spatial order, derives from the order of time. For instance, the motion from a position a in space to a position b is distinct from the motion from b to a because in the former motion the mobile is temporally prior at a and temporally posterior at b, whereas in the latter motion this temporal order is reversed.

These difficulties show that there is no linear order of derivation from space to motion and then to time, as Aristotle pretends. Rather, in this connection, motion derives from both space and time. Indeed, there are two orders of the "before and after" in motion, namely, the spatial order and the temporal order.

Among Aristotelian commentators, this point was made very neatly by Simplicius:

> But the before and after in motion seem to be of two kinds: one kind derives from place, and the other from time... Indeed, since motion is

---

[85] Aristotle, *Physics*, IV.11, 219a14-19.

[86] For some classical discussions of this topic, see Owen, "Aristotle on Time", p. 154-158; D. Corish, "Aristotle's Attempted Derivation of Temporal Order from That of Movement and Space", *Phronesis*, 21 (1976), p. 241-251. More recently, White has tried to explain Aristotle's claim of the dependence of the temporal order on the order of motion by interpreting this claim as an epistemic one, i.e., in the sense that the *recognition* of the order of motion is necessary for the *recognition* of the temporal order. See White, *The Continuous and the Discrete*, p. 76-77.

intermediate between time and place, it takes the measure, i.e., the number of the before and after, from both these quantities. But in virtue of place motion is localized and in virtue of time is temporalized.[87]

Unlike Simplicius, Averroes does not see difficulties (1) and (2) in Aristotle's derivation. The early English commentators, instead, detect only difficulty (1), which is indeed the most evident of the two. They remark that Aristotle's relations of derivation break at the first level, that of space. Although one can define prior and posterior parts in space, these parts, however, exist simultaneously, since space is a permanent entity, whereas the prior and posterior parts of motion can exist only one after the other.[88] This is the "medieval version" of difficulty (1), formulated in terms of the *successiva-permanentia* distinction rather than through the more modern concept of orientation. To avoid this difficulty, G^1 and most of the other commentators of our group, probably relying on a suggestion by Rufus,[89] replace the level of space (s) with the level (b) of the body moving along some path in space. This leads to the relations (b)→(m)→(t), stated by G^1 in passage (11). The rationale for this replacement is easily seen. Since the

---

[87] Simplicius, *In Physicam*, IV, p. 716, lin. 2-11: "ἀλλ' ἔοικε διττὸν εἶναι τὸ ἐν τῇ κινήσει πρότερον καὶ ὕστερον, τὸ μὲν ἀπὸ τοῦ τόπου, τὸ δὲ ἀπὸ τοῦ χρόνου. καὶ ὥσπερ πρότερον τοῦ τόπου τὴν ἔννοιαν ἔλεγε γίνεσθαι ἀπὸ τοῦ προτέρου καὶ ὑστέρου τοῦ ἐν τῇ κινήσει ὄντος κατὰ τὴν θέσιν, οὕτω καὶ τὸν χρόνον ἐννοεῖν ἡμᾶς βούλεται ἀπὸ τοῦ προτέρου καὶ ὑστέρου τοῦ ἐν τῇ κινήσει ὄντος κατὰ τὴν θέσιν, οὕτω καὶ τὸν χρόνον ἐννοεῖν ἡμᾶς βούλεται ἀπὸ τοῦ προτέρου καὶ ὑστέρου τοῦ ἐν τῇ κινήσει, οὐ τοῦ ἀπὸ τῆς θέσεως τοῦ μεγέθους ἐγγενομένου τῇ κινήσει, ἀλλὰ τοῦ ἀπὸ τῆς χρονικῆς παρατάσεως. μέση γὰρ οὖσα ἡ κίνησις τοῦ τε τόπου καὶ τοῦ χρόνου ἑκατέρωθεν προσλαμβάνει μέτρον ἤτοι ἀριθμὸν τοῦ προτέρου καὶ ὑστέρου. ἀλλὰ κατὰ μὲν τὸν τόπον τοπίζεται, κατὰ δὲ τὸν χρόνον χρονίζεται".

[88] Referring to that from which before and after in motion derive, M^2 remarks: "Et quod a magnitudine probatio per litteram Aristotelis. Dicit enim quod prius et posterius primo sunt in loco, et propter locum in magnitudine, et propter magnitudinem in motu, et propter motum in tempore. Sed contra: licet prius et posterius inveniantur in spatio sive magnitudine supra quam est motus, et similiter in motu et tempore, tamen in spatio simul invenitur, in motu autem et tempore non simul; ergo prius et posterius in motu et tempore non causantur a priori et posteriori in spatio" (M^2, IV, q. 17, f. 134rb, lin. 27-34). See also P, IV, q. 17, f. 91rb, lin. 9-16; G^1, IV, q. 4, f. 150ra, lin. 52-60; M^3, IV, q. 5, f. 168vb, lin. 2-10; G^3, IV, q. 4, f. 172ra, lin. 13-21; N, IV, q. 4, f. 155vb, lin. 40-44.

[89] Rufus, *In Physicam*, IV, f. 8ra, lin. 3-9: "Item, dicit quod in spatio est prius et posterius. Contra: spatium non est quiddam successivum, sed permanens; ergo ibi non est prius et posterius. Dicendum quod spatium non secundum se, sed prout comparatur ad ipsum mobile habet prius et posterius. Cum enim recipiat in suis partibus ipsum mobile, in hac receptione necesse est quod una sit pars prior et reliqua posterior, cum non possit idem mobile simul et semel esse in diversis partibus". For the other commentators, see references given in note 83 above.

moving body is a substance, then it is ontologically prior to both motion and time, which are accidents. Therefore, from this point of view it can legitimately occupy the first level. Furthermore, insofar as this body is moving, the positions in space which it comes to occupy define a 'successive' order of the before and after, and not a permanent order, like that of the parts of space considered independently from the body moving along them. In (ii) of passage (11) G¹ appeals to Aristotle's doctrine of the persistent present[90] to show that the modified version of Aristotle's relations of derivation of the temporal order does in fact reflect his own view. The doctrine of the persistent present also belongs to Aristotle's reductionist programme for time, since it is based on the assumption that the identity and diversity of the temporal instant can be understood by analogy with those of the mobile body. It is clear, however, that even the modified version of Aristotle's relations of derivation is not sound. Indeed, when we say that the moving body occupies first one position in space and then another, 'first' and 'then' can only stand for temporal determinations. In other words, we have already introduced the order of time. G¹ makes this point in passage (10), when he explains in what sense time measures motion, but neglects it in passage (11), where he comments on Aristotle's derivation of the temporal order.[91]

---

[90] See above, p. 213-214.

[91] In order to save Aristotle's relations of derivation, Burley introduces a distinction between material causality and formal causality. Aristotle's relations hold only when material causality is assumed: "Intelligendum quod prius et posterius in magnitudine sunt causa materialis prioris et posterioris in motu, et prius et posterius in motu sunt causa materialis prioris et posterioris in tempore. Unde Avicenna, secundo suae *Physicae*, tractatu de tempore, dicit quod prius et posterius in hoc intellectu, scilicet quod prius deficit esse sic quod prius non est cum posteriori, cuiusmodi sunt prius et posterius secundum durationem, primo et essentialiter sunt in tempore et non sunt in aliis rebus nisi quia coexistunt partibus priori et posteriori temporis. Unde tempus ex seipso formaliter habet prius et posterius non sic intelligendo quod tempus sit relatio prioritatis sed quod tempus propter seipsum habeat huiusmodi relationes prioris et posterioris. Unde una pars motus dicitur prior et alia posterior secundum durationem, quia una pars est in priori parte temporis et alia est in posteriori parte temporis, et non dicitur una pars temporis prior alia quia est in priori parte motus, nec etiam dicitur una pars motus prior quia est in priori motu. Quare igitur dico quod prius et posterius in motu sunt causa materialis prioris et posterioris in tempore, et prius et posterius in tempore sunt causa formalis prioris et posterioris in motu" (*In Physicam*, IV, f. 128va). See Avicenna, *Sufficientia*, II, cap. 11, f. 34ra-b. Probably before and after in motion are said to be the material cause of before and after in time simply because motion is the subject and hence the material cause of time.

3. *The Unity of Time*

In *Physics* IV.14, Aristotle briefly discusses the problem of the unity of time. He starts by stating that time is the number of every continuous motion and not of any particular motion. This leads to the question: if two different motions take place simultaneously, does this imply that there are also two simultaneous times? He replies that this is not the case. More generally, he holds that the time of all simultaneous motions whatsoever is one and the same. This claim is apparently obvious, since, as it seems, simultaneity, by definition, means being at the same time. Yet, Aristotelian commentators found it problematic. Aristotle ascribes to time the ontological status of an accident of motion, and therefore there is no obvious way in which he can refer to the same time in which different motions take place, that is, to the unity of the time of different motions. Rather, it seems to follow that, since there can be many simultaneous motions, there can be many simultaneous times as well.

The argument in favour of the unity of time that Aristotle uses suggests a way out of this difficulty. He wants us to understand the unity and multiplicity of time as analogous to those of number. A collection of seven dogs and one of seven horses have the same number seven, despite the fact that dogs are specifically different from horses. Similarly, two simultaneous motions have the same time, despite the fact that one is, say, an alteration and the other a local motion.[92] Since time is a number, Aristotle seems to assume that this analogy is sufficient to show the unity of time of simultaneous motions. In any case, he provides no other arguments for this conclusion.

In the Aristotelian tradition, Aristotle's argument was generally neglected and the unity of time was implicitly regarded as a problem left open by Aristotle. A reason for this is that Aristotle's analogy seems to lead to a single but abstract time. Indeed, if it is asked how we should understand the sameness of the number seven in a collection of seven dogs and in a collection of seven horses, the answer suggested by Aristotle's theory of number is that this is a sameness by abstraction. Similarly, time will be one only by abstraction. This means that, in correspondence to the multiplicity of motions, there is

---

[92] Aristotle, *Physics*, IV.14, 223a29-b12. The analogy between the unity of time and that of number is suggested also at IV.12, 220b5-12.

also a multiplicity of lengths of time inhering in such motions, and in this way the derivation of time from motion is preserved. Nevertheless, one can still talk about the same time of different motions, provided that this is referred to an abstract time, that is, to time conceived of as a result of a mental process of abstraction from the lengths of time attached to these motions.

Some modern readings of Aristotle's theory of time are oriented towards this kind of interpretation.[93] Furthermore, the point that the analogy between number and time leads to a single but abstract time was also made by authoritative Aristotelian commentators, such as Themistius and Averroes.[94] Yet, neither Greek nor thirteenth-century commentators regarded this point as a positive solution. The reason for this is easily seen. In the interpretation just outlined, it turns out that time can be one and the same only if it is given a weak kind of reality, i.e., a mental reality. This is a price, however, that those thirteenth-century commentators who advocate the unity of time are not willing to pay. On the contrary, they assume that a positive solution must show that time is both one and extramentally real.[95] Their attempts to find a positive solution to the problem of the unity developed in different directions, which give shape to a running debate in the thirteenth and fourteenth centuries.[96]

As in the case of the two traditional problems of Aristotle's doctrine of place, the discussion of the unity of time in the early English commentaries is a review of preexisting opinions. Three main opinions are usually considered. S introduces them as follows:

> (1) And since there are three opinions on the unity of time, therefore let us discuss them. And one of them is that the unity of time derives from the unity of the first motion. The second is that it derives from the unity of matter, since matter is a principle of numbering and time is a number, and since the same matter is in every numbered thing,

---

[93] See, for instance, Annas, "Aristotle, Number and Time", p. 97-113; Hussey, *Aristotle's Physics*, Introduction, p. xli-xlii.

[94] See below, p. 254. For an alternative interpretation of Aristotle's analogy between time and number given by some early English commentators, see below, p. 254-256.

[95] For other difficulties pointed out by medieval commentators in Aristotle's treatment of the unity of time, see Maier, *Metaphysische Hintergründe*, p. 92-93.

[96] Nevertheless, the idea that there are in fact many times also found agreement, especially in the fourteenth century. See Maier, *Metaphysische Hintergründe*, p. 123-137.

similarly time is the same. The third is that many or all simultaneous motions are just one subject with respect to time.[97]

Some exponents of these opinions are known. The first one is ascribed explicitly to Averroes by our commentators. The second opinion is traditionally associated with Bonaventure.[98] The third opinion is presented in different versions, which seem all to be inspired by ideas found in Richard Rufus and Roger Bacon. Averroes' opinion was dominant in the thirteenth century, but most of our commentators reject it. The only exception is M^2, who follows closely Albert the Great in his discussion of the unity of time. S, M^3, N, and G^3 accept some version of Rufus' and Bacon's opinion, whereas G^1 and P, while not rejecting this opinion, defend Bonaventure's idea that the unity of time is guaranteed by that of matter. In presenting the discussion of our commentators, we shall start from the opinion of Averroes, then turn to that of Rufus and Bacon, and finally to that of Bonaventure.

3.1 *Averroes' Opinion*

Averroes is well aware of the fundamental ontological problem involved in Aristotle's requirement of the unity of time. The problem can be formulated as follows:

(i)   time is an accident of every motion;
(ii) but there are many simultaneous motions;
(iii) therefore there are many simultaneous times.

If premisses (i) and (ii) are both true, then conclusion (iii) follows on the basis of the principle that the same accident cannot inhere in numerically distinct subjects. This principle is explicitly accepted by Averroes. Moreover, the fact that there are many simultaneous motions, as premise (ii) states, cannot reasonably be denied. There-

---

[97] S, IV, f. 61ra, lin. 29-36: "Et quia tres sunt opiniones circa unitatem temporis, ideo videamus de illis. Et est una quod unitas temporis est ab unitate motus primi. Secunda quod est ab unitate materiae, quia materia principium est numerationis et tempus est numerus, et quia eadem est materia in omnibus numeratis, similiter idem est tempus. Tertia quod multi sive omnes motus simul sunt unum subiectum respectu temporis".

[98] However, the connection between matter and number which appears in the passage quoted from S is not found in Bonaventure. On this point, see below p. 257-261.

fore, the only way of avoiding the conclusion of a multiplicity of times, so it seems, is to reject premise (i). This is in fact the crucial point of Averroes' solution. He maintains that time is an accident of only one motion, that is, of the first motion of the heavens. In this way the unity of time is saved, because, being an accident that inheres in only one subject, time is unique.[99] Averroes' major concern is then to explain why the restriction of the subject of time to the celestial motion does not spoil the universal character of time. Specifically, he makes clear that, although time only inheres in one motion, it functions as the non-inhering number or measure of every other motion. In other words, the celestial motion and its duration define the 'universal clock' by which we measure the duration of any other motion, which in fact commonly measured in hours, days, years etc.[100]

Averroes' basic idea of restricting the subject of time to the first motion of the heavens is not absolutely new in the Aristotelian tradition. It was considered, for instance, by Simplicius and Philoponus. Simplicius introduces it as one of the solutions to the problem of the unity of time.[101] He dismisses it quickly, however, remarking that it does not reflect Aristotle's intention. On the contrary, while not presenting this idea in connection with the unity of time, Philoponus uses

---

[99] Averroes, *In Physicam*, IV, t. c. 132, f. 203vaI-vbL: "Et si posuerimus etiam quod tempus accipitur in definitione cuiuslibet motus, sequitur ut multiplicetur per multiplicationem motuum, sicut est dispositio in albedine et aliis accidentibus, quae multiplicantur per multiplicationem subiecti. Si autem posuerimus quod dispositio eius cum motu uno est dispositio sequentis in cuius definitione accipitur illud ad quod sequitur, et cum aliis motibus sicut dispositio numeri cum numerato dissolvetur quaestio. Et iam declaravimus prius quod nos (non *ed.*) percipimus tempus quando percipimus motum per quem sentimus nos esse in transmutatione continua, et est motus circularis. Tempus igitur sequitur hunc motum et iste motus accipitur in definitione eius". The expression 'tempus sequitur hunc motum' means that time is in this motion as in its subject.

[100] Ibid., f. 203vbL: "Tempus igitur sequitur hunc motum et iste motus accipitur in definitione eius et ipsum mensurat illum non secundum quod numerus mensurat numeratum, sed secundum quod mensurat aliquid quod est forma in re, alios vero motus mensurat secundum quod numerus mensurat numeratum, scilicet quod numeratum non accipitur in definitione numeri". Averroes in also concerned with the problem of the universal perception of time. This problem is dealt with extensively in t. c. 98. Averroes' treatment of the unity of time and its reception in Albert the Great and Thomas Aquinas is analyzed in detail in the classical study by A. Mansion, "La théorie aristotélicienne du temps chez les péripatéticiens médiévaux", *Revue Néoscolastique de Philosophie*, 34 (1934), p. 275-307.

[101] Simplicius, *In Physicam*, IV, p. 721, lin. 5-11. On Simplicius' own solution to the problem of the unity of time, see below, p. 248-250.

it extensively in his interpretation of other aspects of Aristotle's doctrine of time. For instance, he maintains that in the definition of time as the number of motion, "motion" stands for the first motion.[102]

Averroes' position exerted an enormous influence, especially in the thirteenth century. It was adopted by Albert the Great, Thomas Aquinas, and Giles of Rome.[103] Some remarks may help us to understand the great popularity of Averroes' solution. First of all, it seems to have a genuinely Aristotelian air. Although the text of *Physics* IV.10-14 does not explicitly suggest the restriction of the subject of time to the first motion, it does contain positive indications for the role of "universal clock" played by the duration of the first motion in the measurement of all other motions, so that at least half of Averroes' view can be found in Aristotle.[104] Furthermore, Averroes succeeds in saving the unity of time without violating the principle according to which *accidens multiplicatur ad multiplicationem sui subiecti*, and, more generally, in proving that Aristotle's postulate of a unique time is not in contrast with its ontological status of accident of motion. Finally, he shows that, in order to be one, time needs not be relegated to the realm of abstract entities, since time turns out to be both one and extramentally real, its extramental reality being granted by the reality of its unique subject, namely, the first mobile or the first motion.

The early English commentators, however, are not convinced by Averroes' position. Some of them report some details of Averroes' complex treatment of the unity of time, but when they turn to the discussion of the cogency of his solution, they concentrate on the central move of Averroes' strategy, that is, the restriction of the subject of time to just one motion. They tacitly agree that in this way Averroes succeeds in saving the unity of time. On the other hand, they also feel that this move is in some sense *ad hoc*, and that Averroes has failed to discover the real cause of the unity of time. In their view, the inadequacy of Averroes' solution comes out when the counterfactual situation of the existence of a multiplicity of heavens is considered. The

---

[102] Philoponus, *In Physicam*, IV, p. 718, lin. 13-20.

[103] On Albert the Great and Thomas Aquinas, see the study by A. Mansion quoted in note 100. For Giles of Rome, see Maier, *Metaphysische Hintergründe*, p.106-107; C. Trifogli, "La dottrina del tempo in Egidio Romano", *Documenti e studi sulla tradizione filosofica medievale*, 1 (1990) 1, p. 265-275. In my study I have pointed out, however, that Giles introduces some modifications into Averroes' original account which are oriented towards the idea of a multiplicity of times.

[104]Aristotle, *Physics*, IV.14, 223b12-224a2.

strongest and most recurrent objection against Averroes appeals exactly to this counterfactual situation. The counterfactual objection, which Rufus, Bacon, and Bonaventure[105] also regard as decisive for dismissing Averroes' solution, is formulated by M^3 as follows:

> (2) ... it is asked whether time is one because this motion <i.e., that of the heavens> is one. And it does not seem to be so. (i) For if something in virtue of its unity and insofar as it is one is the cause of <the unity of> something else, then once it is multiplied, that other thing will also be multiplied; (ii) but even if there were many heavens, according to Aristotle, one and the same time would be their common measure. (iii) Therefore, it does not follow, if motion is one, that because of this time is one. And I concede this, whatever the Commentator may say.[106]

As the minor premise (ii) suggests, the counterfactual objection to Averroes has an Aristotelian background. In the dialectical phase of his discussion, when giving a short review of the previous opinions about time, Aristotle mentions the view that time is the motion of the heavens. He rejects it, arguing that, if there were many heavens, time would be the motion of each of them, and therefore there would be many times simultaneously.[107] Averroes himself devotes a detailed comment to this argument, in which he explains that the unacceptable consequence of a multiplicity of times does not derive from the impossibility of the counterfactual condition of a multiplicity of the heavens, but from the identification of time with the motion of the heavens.[108] As our commentators point out, however, Aristotle's argument can also be formulated against Averroes' solution.

---

[105] Rufus, *In Physicam*, IV, f. 8vb, lin. 40-44: "Dubium est de hoc quod dicit quod idem est tempus diversorum motuum. Et dicet aliquis quod hoc est quia tempus est mensura unius motus primo et accidens. Sed contra hoc est quod superius dictum est: si essent plures caeli, esset unum tempus omnium illorum motuum, et tamen non esset tunc dicere quod tempus esset unus motus primo". Bacon, *In Physicam*, IV, p. 278, lin. 17-279, lin. 2; S. Bonaventure, *Liber II. Sententiarum*, dist. II, pars I, art. I, q. II, p. 50b-51a.

[106] M^3, IV, q. 10, f. 169rb, lin. 47-53: "... quaeritur an quia hic motus est unus quod propterea tempus sit unum. Et quod non videtur. (i) Quod enim per suam unitatem et secundum quod unum est causa alicuius, ipso multiplicato, multiplicabitur et reliquum; (ii) sed etsi essent plures caeli, adhuc, secundum Aristotelem, unum et idem tempus esset mensura motus utriusque. (iii) Ergo non sequitur: si motus est unus quod propter hoc tempus sit unum. Et hoc concedo, qualitercumque dicat Commentator". See also S, IV, q. 26, f. 61ra, lin. 36-39; P, IV, q. 54, f. 95va, lin. 10-13; T, IV, q. 26, f. 56ra, lin. 14-16; G^1, IV, q. 8, f. 150vb, lin. 43-48; M^2, q. 3, f. 131ra, lin. 5-10.

[107] Aristotle, *Physics*, IV.10, 218a33-b5.

[108] Averroes, *In Physicam*, IV, t. c. 93, f. 176rbE-vaG.

M² is much in favour of Averroes' treatment of the unity of time,[109] and tries to defend it against the counterfactual objection raised by the other commentators of our group:

> (3) ... if there were many heavens, since multiplicity proceeds from unity, it would be necessary for one of them to be the first and for its motion to be the cause of and the rule for the motions of the other heavens, and for time to follow this motion as its subject, whereas it would follow the motion of the other heavens as number follows the numbered.[110]

M² here points out that Averroes' choice of the motion of the heavens as the subject of time is not at all arbitrary, but has a strong ontological foundation in the fact that this motion is the first motion and thus the cause of any other motion. He also assumes that this same foundation would still persist in the counterfactual situation of the multiplicity of the heavens, in the sense that they would be joined by a causal chain, in which the motion of one of them would be the cause of all other heavenly motions.

The reply of M² seems to reflect well both the spirit of Averroes' treatment of the unity of time and Aristotle's cosmological assumptions. Nevertheless, one may still ask what would happen if the multiplicity of the heavens and their motions were causally unrelated so that all these motions were equally first. This possibility is denied without explanation by M².[111] An obscure but very interesting attempt to deal with this case is made by T.

Like the other early English commentators, T raises this counterfactual objection against Averroes. He then reports and accepts an opinion to some extent similar to that of Averroes, but that, in his view, does not run into this objection.[112] Like Averroes, the exponents of this opinion posit that the unity of time depends on heavenly motion, but they radically depart from Averroes in denying that the unity of time is guaranteed by the unity of this motion. Rather, they

---

[109] Averroes' opinion is reported at length and defended in qq. 3 and 25.

[110] M², IV, q. 3, f. 131rb, lin. 38-42: "... si multi essent caeli, cum ab unitate multitudo procedat, necesse esset unum illorum esse primum et eius motum esse causam et regulam motuum aliorum, et tempus consequi ipsum tanquam suum subiectum, motus vero aliorum tanquam numerus consequitur numeratum".

[111] M², IV, q. 25, f. 135Avb, lin. 49-52: "Unde potest dici quod, si plures essent caeli, non essent aeque primi, sed necessario haberent unum motum primum, sicut nunc est de sphaeris motis, et illum motum consequeretur tempus ut subiectum".

[112] Given the strict relation between T and Geoffrey of Aspall, it is not unlikely that Aspall himself is an exponent of this opinion.

seem to understand the unity of time in a relational way. In this view, Aristotle's postulate that all simultaneous motions have the same time must be understood in the sense that they all have a correspondence to heavenly motion. More generally, the past, present, and future phases of any motion have a correspondence to the past, present, and future phases of heavenly motion, and in virtue of this correspondence there is just one time.[113] Then – as T remarks – the counterfactual addition of another 'copy' of heavenly motion to the actual universe would not affect the unity of time, because it would not affect this correspondence:

> (4) And it can be said that there would still be the correspondence of one motion to the other in such a way that the corrupted phase of one motion corresponds to the corrupted phase of the other, and the phase to be generated in one motion to the future phase in the other, and the present phase in one motion to the present phase in the other, and therefore there would still be only one past, one future and one <present>, and therefore there would still be the unity of time.[114]

The difference between the actual situation and counterfactual situations is that, in the former, the correspondence of each motion with the first motion also expresses a causal relation, whereas in the latter, there would be two motions, i.e., the two 'first' motions, for which this correspondence would have no causal meaning.[115]

---

[113] T, IV, q. 27, f. 56va, lin. 19-30: "Aliter dicitur quod in motu est pars generanda, et eius mensura est futurum, et pars corrupta, et eius mensura est praeteritum, et pars in fieri et in praesenti, sumendo praesens divisibile, et hoc intelligatur de parte motus caeli quam partem mensurat praesens, et unde mensurando mensurat omnes alios qui fiunt in praesenti secundum correspondentiam quam habent ad praesentem motum caeli. Et sic est de praeterito et futuro, quod res corrupta vel motus corruptus correspondet motui ibi corrupto et generandus hic ibi generando, et ideo potest esse una mensura mensurans omnes motus, et tamen causari ab uno motu singulari. Et contra hoc non est aliquod argumentum prius factum".

[114] Ibid., 56va, lin. 33-38: "Et potest dici quod adhuc esset correspondentia unius motus ad alium, ita quod corruptus motus in uno ad corruptum in alio et generandus in uno ad generandum in alio et praesens in uno ad praesens in alio; et ideo non esset adhuc nisi unum praeteritum, unum futurum, unum <praesens>, et ideo adhuc unitas temporis".

[115] Ibid., lin. 39-48: "Sed nunc est maior unitas quam tunc esset quo ad hoc quod quilibet alius motus a motu caeli est causa eius ita quod corruptus in caelo est causa motus corrupti hic et generandus in caelo causa motus generandi hic, et praesens causa praesentis. Unde nunc est correspondentia sicut effectus ad causam vel ad minus ita est correspondentia quod motus hic non fit sine motu illo. Sed si ponerentur duo caeli, esset correspondentia unius motus ad alium (aliam *ms.*), sed non secundum praedictam habitudinem, quia ab alio dependet, sicut nunc omnis motus dependet ab illo motu".

Unfortunately, the report of this position made by T is too compressed to allow a precise reconstruction. The following interpretation, however, can be suggested. Since in this view the unity of time does not seem to depend on the fact that time has only one subject, we can also assume that time is in fact an accident inhering in each motion, so that there are as many times as there are motions. Then the problem is to explain how we can refer univocally to the present phase of a motion, for instance, without specifying with respect to which of these times it is present. The answer is that this is guaranteed by a correspondence between all these times, according to which what is present with respect to the time associated with the motion of the heavens is also present with respect to any other times. Thus, when we speak of the present, we refer in fact to a class of times, this class being defined by the correspondence of each time belonging to it to the present time in the heavens.

The opinion of T is very original, but is not discussed by the other commentators. With the exception of M², they think that Averroes' solution leaves open the problem of the unity of time. In their view, his position does not explain why there would be just one time even if there were two heavenly motions. More generally, they assume that an adequate solution of this problem should explain why time is one, despite the fact that there are many actual and possible motions. The other two opinions discussed by our commentators represent different attempts to show that the unity of time is independent of the multiplicity of motions.

3.2 Richard Rufus of Cornwall's and Roger Bacon's Opinion

Like most of our commentators, Rufus and Bacon are not convinced by Averroes' solution to the problem of the unity of time.[116] They use an alternative strategy to deal with this problem, which can be introduced as follows. Simultaneous motions *qua motions* are distinct and many. For instance, a qualitative motion is distinct from a local motion, although they can occur simultaneously. To save the unity of time, however, it is not necessary to choose one of the simultaneous motions as the subject of time, as Averroes does, since all simultaneous motions, *qua simultaneous*, are indistinct and in some sense one, so

---

[116] See above, note 105.

that they form just one subject for time. In other words, since time belongs to all simultaneous motions insofar as they are simultaneous and hence one, the time of simultaneous motions is one.

Evidently, the crucial point of Rufus' and Bacon's solution is the assumption of the indistinction of simultaneous motions. These two commentators explain the meaning and the role of this assumption by appealing to an analogy between the logic of being in the same time and that of being in the same place. The analogy states that the conditions that motions (viewed as quantities) must satisfy in order to be in the same time (i. e., to have the same time) are the same as the conditions that spatial magnitudes must satisfy in order to be in the same place (i. e., in order to occupy the same place). In fact, the equivalent version of this analogy in the negative form is directly used by Rufus and Bacon, which is to say that the conditions that prevent spatial magnitudes from being in the same place are the same as those that prevent motions from having the same time. The former conditions are the dimensions of spatial magnitudes. For instance, two bodies cannot be in the same place because they have three dimensions and dimensions cannot interpenetrate, whereas two lines or two surfaces can be in some sense in the same place, i. e., they can be superimposed, because they lack dimensions in two or one direction respectively.[117] Similarly, simultaneous motions can be in the same time provided that they lack the relevant dimensions. As Rufus explains:

> (5) Therefore, since time and motion and all successive entities have dimensions only in longitude, that is, according to the before and after,

---

[117] Rufus, *In Physicam*, IV, ff. 8vb, lin. 44-9ra, lin. 9: "Propterea possumus ita dicere quod terra sit divisa in aliquas partes aequales. Intelligamus illud. Et intelligamus etiam quod illae partes possint esse simul per impossibile, scilicet quod una pars possit recipere aliam et quod sint simul circa centrum, maneant tamen corpora divisa. Hoc posito erit ubi unum non numeratum et locus unus non numeratus illorum corporum non numeratorum. Et hoc est quia ista corpora indistincta sunt et non distantia. Et propterea ubi istud inest eis ut unita sunt per naturam unitatis et non per naturam multiplicationis debetur eis, et propterea non multiplicatur ubi in eis. Simile est de motibus simul existentibus, quod indistincti sunt et indistantes, et propterea debetur eis unum quando et unum tempus. Et quod sint indistincti possumus videre hoc modo, quod aliqua duo distare vere et proportionaliter hoc est per naturam dimensionis vere vel proportionaliter. Propterea corpora duo, cum undique sint dimensionata simpliciter, necesse est ipsa distare; sed superficies vel linea, ut dictum est in capitulo, ex parte ea qua sunt non dimensionatae possunt simul esse et non distare, sed ex parte ea qua sunt dimensionatae non". See also Bacon, *In Physicam*, IV, p. 279, lin. 34-280, lin. 7.

then the motions that have no distance according to the before and after have absolutely no dimension and no distance. Therefore, the motions that have no distance according to the before and after have no distance. Therefore such motions as are not distinct and not distant have one time, and this is due to the fact that time belongs to these motions insofar as they are united rather than because they are many.[118]

Rufus and Bacon assume that the extension of motion is its successive duration, the extension according to the before and after. By definition, simultaneous motions are those that start and end together, or equivalently, are not one after the other. Therefore, since there is no before and after in these motions, they do not form a longitude according to the before and after. In other words, there is no temporal distance between them.

In the account of Rufus and Bacon, simultaneous motions are one in the relevant sense because they lack temporal distance. This means that the oneness of simultaneous motions is given a privative character. On the other hand, the two commentators sometimes claim that time inheres in simultaneous motions because of a nature common to them all. This nature, however, is never explicitly described as a positive property. Furthermore, Bacon makes clear that this common nature is to be identified with the lack of distinction among simultaneous motions as explained above.[119]

In order to appreciate the originality of the solution of Rufus and Bacon, it is important to underline the privative character of the oneness that they ascribe to simultaneous motions. In fact, if in their solution we focus simply on the idea of unifying all simultaneous motions with respect to time, then this solution has an antecedent in Simplicius. Indeed, Simplicius argues that the multiplicity of simultaneous motions does not produce a corresponding multiplicity of times as follows:

---

[118] Rufus, *In Physicam*, IV, f. 9ra, lin. 9-14: "Cum ergo tempus et motus et omnia successiva dimensionantur solum secundum longitudinem sive secundum prius et posterius, motus ergo qui non distant secundum prius et posterius non habent dimensionem simpliciter <et> non distant; motus ergo qui non distant secundum prius et posterius non distant; tales ergo motus qui indistincti sunt et indistantes habent unum tempus. Et hoc est quia tempus debetur eis <magis ut> uniuntur quam per naturam multitudinis". See also Bacon, *In Physicam*, IV, p. 280, lin. 7-12. Bacon's solution has been discussed and much appreciated by A. Maier, who did not know of the existence of Rufus' commentary. See Maier, *Metaphysische Hintergründe*, p. 100-105.

[119] Bacon, *In Physicam*, IV, p. 280, lin. 20-32.

... it is not true that, as for each particular mobile there is a particular motion, so for each particular motion time is a number, but *for all motions as if they were one*. For, the before and after as such is one and the same in all simultaneous motions. Indeed, motions do not have the before and after insofar as one motion is in a particular mobile and another in another, or insofar as one is a local motion, another an increase and another an alteration, but in virtue of *their common aspect as motions*.[120]

This passage contains two main points:

(1) the claim that all simultaneous motions can be regarded as just one motion with respect to time;
(2) the explanation of this claim by appealing to the existence of something common to all simultaneous motions.

In a later passage, Simplicius specifies that such a common aspect consists in the fact that all motions have "their being in becoming", which is to say, in the successive duration of motion. He also makes clear that successive duration is not something that exists over and above particular motions. On the contrary, it exists only in particular motions, but is not individuated by any of them, so that it can be one and the same in all of them.[121]

As we shall see later in this section,[122] there is an ontological difficulty in Simplicius' assumption of something common to all particular motions, at least if "common" here means "numerically the same", as Simplicius apparently believes. Here, however, it is important to observe that while Simplicius, on one hand, and Rufus and Bacon, on the other, agree on point (1), which claims that simultaneous motions are one, they differ radically on point (2), which concerns the explanation of this claim. For Simplicius, there is something common to all motions that explains their being one. Thus, in Simplicius' view, the oneness of simultaneous motions is given a positive charac-

---

[120] Simplicius, *In Physicam*, IV, p. 720, lin. 20-26: "οὐχ ὡς ἑκάστου κινουμένου ἰδία τίς ἐστι κίνησις, οὕτως ἑκάστης κινήσεως ἀφωρισμένης ἀριθμός ἐστιν ὁ χρόνος, ἀλλὰ πασῶν ὡς μιᾶς. ἓν γὰρ καὶ ταὐτὸν ἐν πάσαις ταῖς ἅμα γινομέναις τὸ πρότερόν τε καὶ ὕστερον καθὸ τοιοῦτον. οὐ γὰρ καθὸ ἡ μὲν ἐν τῷδέ ἐστιν ἡ δὲ ἐν τῷδε, οὐδὲ καθὸ ἡ μὲν φορά ἐστιν ἡ δὲ αὔξησις ἡ δὲ ἀλλοίωσις τὸ πρότερον καὶ ὕστερον ἔχουσιν, ἀλλὰ κατὰ τὸ κοινὸν καθὸ κίνησις".
[121] Ibid., p. 721, lin. 16-26.
[122] See below, p. 252-253.

ter. For Rufus and Bacon, instead, the oneness of these motions simply means that they lack temporal distance. This is a subtle point of
the solution of Rufus and Bacon, but is often misunderstood by later
commentators. In particular, some early English commentators tend
to follow a version of this solution more similar to that proposed by
Simplicius.

Among our commentators, the opinion of Rufus and Bacon is
reported by S, T, and M³. S and M³ accept this opinion, but modify
the negative characterization of the indistinction of simultaneous
motions. For instance, S presents the following argument in favour of
the position that all simultaneous motions are just one subject with
respect to time:

> (6) (i) All things that are not distant are one by that part from which
> they are not distant, and those things that are one can be one subject
> with respect to that which refers to them qua one. (ii) Then I argue as
> follows. All motions are not distant in latitude, and it is evident that
> they have the same longitude; therefore, they are not diversified either
> in longitude and in latitude; (iii) therefore, all motions can be one, and
> therefore one subject with respect to time, since time measures motion
> in virtue of its longitude and not in virtue of its latitude.[123]

(i) repeats the claim of Rufus and Bacon that motions are one
because they have no distance. (ii), however, gives a different explanation of their lack of distance. Motions lack latitude, but, as to longitude, it is said that, insofar as they are simultaneous, they all have the
same longitude and not that they lack longitude, as Rufus and Bacon
hold. Thus, in the report of S, the oneness of simultaneous motions
derives from the fact they have the same temporal longitude.[124]

---

[123] S, IV, q. 28, f. 61va, lin. 2-11: "(i) Omnia indistantia a parte ea qua non distant
sunt unum, et quod illa quae unum sunt possunt esse unum subiectum respectu illius
quod respicit illa prout unum sunt. (ii) Arguo tunc: omnes motus sunt indistantes
secundum latitudinem; et constat quod sunt in eadem longitudine; igitur <non>
diversificati sunt et a parte longitudinis et a parte latitudinis; (iii) ergo omnes motus
possunt esse unum; ergo unum subiectum respectu temporis, quia tempus mensurat
motum ratione longitudinis et non ratione latitudinis". The same explanation is giv-
en by S in a later passage: "... quia ex quo motus multi mensurantur secundum longitudinem, nec aliter habent dimensionem, quia non a parte latitudinis, et non cadit
distinctio nisi a parte longitudinis, et omnes motus sub una longitudine sunt, et sic
unum sunt, et ita possunt unum subiectum esse respectu temporis" (ibid., f. 61vb, lin.
18-23).

[124] The report of the opinion of Rufus and Bacon made by T is somewhat more
confused, but also seems to modify it in this sense. T, IV, q. 27, f. 56rb, lin. 46-va,
lin. 3: "Aliter dicitur subtiliori modo quod tempus est quantitas, sicut motus, et ambo

A very similar modification is introduced by M³. This commentator repeats almost verbatim the majority of Rufus' treatment of the unity of time, but expands passage (5) as follows:

> (7) Therefore, since motion or time has only one proportional dimension, that is longitude, i. e., extension according to the before and after, since therefore according to this dimension simultaneous motions are indistinct, just as two straight lines that are equally extended in longitude, it is clear that those two motions that are simultaneous are not distinguished by the nature of this dimension....[125]

The example of the two lines does not appear in the solution of Rufus and Bacon. It clearly shows that in the interpretation of M³ simultaneous motions are indistinct with respect to longitude according to the before and after in the sense that they have the same longitude and not in that they lack longitude. This interpretation comes out even more clearly in the summary that M³ gives of his own position:

> (8) And in this way, since time is the measure of some motions not insofar as they are this or that motion, but rather by the same distinction of the before and after that is in them, and since this distinction is numerically the same in all simultaneously existing motions, therefore a time that is numerically the same can follow any of the different simultaneously existing motions.[126]

In this passage, the unity of time is said to be preserved by the numerical identity of the distinction of the before and after that inheres in all simultaneous motions. This explanation, which departs significantly from the view of Rufus, is also reported by P, G¹, N, and

----

habent dimensionem linearem, quia longitudinem solum, et carent omni alia dimensione. Et ideo omnes motus quotquot possunt esse simul, cum habeant tantum illam dimensionem, et omnia indimensionata a parte qua indimensionata sunt, si (sed *ms.*) simul applicentur, non faciunt plura; ideo tantum constituitur linearis dimensio sive dimensio secundum longitudinem, et ideo potest eadem mensura, ut idem tempus, omnes istos motus mensurare".

[125] M³, IV, q. 10, f. 169va, lin. 43-48: "Cum igitur motus vel tempus unicam dimensionem habeat proportionalem, scilicet longitudinem, hoc est extensionem secundum prius et posterius, cum igitur secundum hanc dimensionem sint motus simul existentes indistincti, sicut duae lineae rectae aequaliter protensae a parte longitudinis (latitudinis *ms.*), patet quod illi duo motus qui simul sunt non distinguuntur per naturam huius dimensionis...".

[126] Ibid., f. 169vb, lin. 1-5: "Et sic quia tempus est mensura aliquorum motuum non secundum quod sunt hic motus et ille, sed per eandem distinctionem prioris et posterioris quae est in ipsis, et sic quia haec distinctio est eadem numero in omnibus motibus simul existentibus, ideo idem tempus numero poterit sequi utrumque diversorum motuum simul existentium".

G³. N and G³ accept it, whereas P and G¹ do not raise objections
against it, but seem to prefer the position that bases the unity of time
on that of matter. All these four commentators, however, omit the
analogy between the unity of time and the spatial simultaneity that
characterizes the position of Rufus and Bacon.[127] Thus, it is probable
that M³ tends to conflate the opinion of Rufus with a different one.
On the other hand, the case of S and M³ suggests that this latter opinion may originate from a simplifying interpretation of the original
solution of Rufus and Bacon.

In conclusion, S, M³, N, and G³ (and to some extent also P and G¹)
solve the problem of the unity of time by arguing that simultaneous
motions have the same time because time is ascribed to motion in
virtue of its temporal longitude or of the distinction of the before and
after, that is, the successive duration. Such a longitude is the same in
all simultaneous motions, and this explains why these motions all
have the same time.

As S, G¹, and M³ remark,[128] this solution is analogous to that
offered by most early English commentators to the problem of the
identity of place of an immobile body.[129] In that case, the point was
that place must be such that a body at rest remains in the same place.
Similarly, time must be such that simultaneous motions have the
same time. Place and time, however, do not seem to satisfy these
requirements, since they have the ontological status of an accident.
Place is an accident of the body that immediately surrounds the located body, and time is an accident of motion. Accordingly, if the body
that surrounds a body at rest is replaced by another body, the place
of the body at rest does not stay the same. Likewise, since there are
many simultaneous motions, there are also many times. In the case of
place, the solution of our commentators consists in positing that the
identity of place does not derive from that of the surrounding body in
which it inheres, but from the distance of this body from the fixed
points of the universe. In the case of time, the solution of S, M³, N,
and G³ is analogous. The temporal notion that corresponds to the
local notion of distance from the cosmological points is the longitude
according to the before and after, that is, the successive duration of

---

[127] See P, IV, q. 7, f. 90ra, lin. 21-26; G¹, IV, q. 9, f. 151rb, lin. 22-28; G³, IV, q. 7,
f. 173rb, lin. 1-12; N, IV, q. 6, f. 156va, lin. 37-43.
[128] S, IV, q. 28, f. 61va, lin. 16-21. On G¹ and M³, see below note 132.
[129] See above, p. 175-186.

motion. The identity and difference of time, in fact, derives from those of this longitude and not from those of the motions in which it inheres. This longitude is the same in all simultaneous motions just as the distance from the fixed points of the universe is the same in all bodies that surround a body at rest.

This analogy also points out that the solution of our commentators to the problem of the unity of time runs into the same ontological objection that is raised against their treatment of the immobility of place.[130] Indeed, their solution violates the principle according to which the numerical identity of an accident is determined by that of its subject, since our commentators posit that a successive longitude is numerically the same in different motions. The same objection can also be raised against the account of Rufus and Bacon, because, although simultaneous motions lack temporal distance or dimension, nevertheless they are many and time is an accident of each of them. This point is made very clearly by T with a geometric example. A point added to another point does not produce any dimension, but it does produce a multiplicity of two points.[131] Thus, although simultaneous motions can be regarded as analogous to points from a quantitative point of view, nevertheless they still form a multiplicity of motions, and therefore there is a corresponding multiplicity of simultaneous times, if the principle of the numerical identity of accidents holds. In fact, the only way of saving both this principle and the unity of time regarded as an accident of motion is to restrict the subject of time to just one motion, as Averroes does.

Except for T and M², our commentators do not seem to regard the principle of the individuation of accidents as a universal rule. For instance, G¹ asserts that it is violated in three main cases:

(9) What has just been said, namely, that the same accident in number can be in different subjects, is true especially for these three accidents, namely, for place, as was made clear before, for time, as has just been said, and for number, as will be made clear later.[132]

---

130 See above, p. 180.

131 Referring to things with no dimension, T remarks: "etsi dimensionata non faciunt per eorum coniunctionem, faciunt tamen plus, ut punctus puncto adiunctus; quare cum plures sint motus, plura erunt tempora" (T, IV, q. 27, f. 56va, lin. 4-6).

132 G¹, IV, q. 9, f. 151rb, lin. 28-31: "Quod iam dictum <est>, scilicet quod idem accidens numero possit esse in diversis, specialiter veritatem habet in his tribus accidentibus, scilicet in loco, ut prius patuit, et in tempore, ut iam dictum est, et in numero, ut postea patebit". See also M³, IV, q. 10, f. 169va, lin. 59-vb, lin. 5.

Thus, before concluding this section, we shall briefly consider the case of number.

We recall that Aristotle himself explains the unity of time by analogy with that of number. He claims that as seven dogs and seven horses have the same number seven, despite the fact that dogs are different from horses, so two simultaneous motions have the same time, despite the fact that one of them is an alteration, for instance, and the other a local motion.[133] Averroes dismisses quickly Aristotle's analogy:

> (10) But if we were to posit that the relation of time to every motion were such, that is, like the relation of number to the numbered, it would follow that time would not be a natural or mobile entity, but an imaginary one.[134]

The early English commentators do not explicitly comment on Averroes' statement. It is clear, however, from section 2 that here he is assuming a position on the ontological status of number that is in conflict with that of all our commentators, including Rufus and Bacon.[135] According to Averroes, the number seven is not an extramental accident of the collection of seven dogs, but simply reflects the mental fact that we count the members of this collection. Thus, the number seven with which we count both the collection of seven dogs and that of seven horses is the result of a mental process of abstraction from concrete collections of seven things. On the contrary, according to our commentators, the number seven is an extramental accident of the collection of seven dogs, like whiteness is an extramental accident of a white substance. Thus, in their view, for the number seven that inheres in seven dogs and for the number seven that inheres in seven horses, there are only two meaningful alternatives. These numbers are the same either (i) only in species, as whitenesses inhering in distinct substances, or (ii) also in number.[136] T

---

[133] See above, p. 238.

[134] Averroes, *In Physicam*, IV, t. c. 132, f. 203vaI: "Sed si posuerimus quod dispositio temporis cum omni motu sit talis, scilicet sicut dispositio numeri cum numerato, sequitur ut tempus non sit ens naturale neque mobile, sed imaginabile". A similar point is made by Themistius, who nevertheless accepts the consequence that time will be unique, but not real. See Themistius, *In Physicam*, IV, p. 162, lin. 22-163, lin. 7.

[135] See above, p. 222-226.

[136] In particular, Rufus quotes and rejects an opinion on the unity of number which is to some extent similar to that of Averroes: "Alius modus dicendi est quod

accepts (i) and denies (ii) on the basis of the principle of the numerical identity of accidental properties.[137] Like Bacon and Rufus, all the other commentators accept (ii) and all repeat Rufus' explanation of (ii).[138] Accordingly, in their view Aristotle correctly maintains that simultaneous motions have one and the same time as different collections of a definite number of things have the same numer, in the sense that both time and number are accidents whose numerical identity does not depend on that of their subjects.

Rufus' explanation is based on a distinction between two ways of regarding a number, namely, as a discrete quantity, and as a measure. This distinction, which is usually employed by our commentators, can be illustrated as follows. The number ten is an aggregate of ten units. Then one can focus either on the aggregate of units or on the fact that the units are in a definite amount. The aggregate of units is the number ten taken as discrete quantity, whereas the fact that these units are in a definite amount expresses the number ten as measure. More explicitly, being a discrete quantity can be seen as the material element of the number ten, in the sense that it is that which the number ten has in common with every other number, whereas measure is its formal element, the unifying principle of the aggregate of units that makes the number ten specifically different from any other number.[139] Then, Rufus maintains that the number ten taken

---

numerus est aliquod ens in anima; et sicut per eandem artem aedificandi in anima possunt fieri plura aedificia, ita per eundem numerum in anima possunt numerari plures res. Sed primum quod est contra hoc est: si ille numerus esset quantitas discreta, tunc ipsa anima esset subiectum discretae quantitatis et esset multa. Et iterum, cum ipsae res numeratae sint quantae per suum numerum, si ponamus numerum in anima, ponemus quantitatem separatam a quanto et passionem a subiecto" (Rufus, *In Physicam*, IV, f. 8vb, lin. 25-31). This opinion is reported and rejected also by Bacon, G¹, and M³. Bacon, *In Physicam*, IV, p. 276, lin. 3-16; G¹, IV, q. 11, f. 151vb, lin. 42-56; M³, IV, q. 14, f. 170va, lin. 19-30.

[137] See T, IV, q. 30, f. 57ra, lin. 48-rb, lin. 40.

[138] The exception is M². He accepts (ii), but does not repeat Rufus' explanation for it. He maintains that the formal number with which we count a collection of three men and another of three horses is numerically the same. See M², q. 33, f. 135Crb, lin. 8-17. On formal number, see above, p. 225. Nor is Bacon's explanation of the unity of number exactly the same as Rufus'. See Bacon, *In Physicam*, IV, p. 276, lin. 37-278, lin. 16.

[139] For instance, G³ replies to the question "Utrum numeri differant specie ad invicem" as follows: "Dico quod numerus potest considerari prout est discreta quantitas et prout est mensura. Si primo modo consideratur, sic non differt binarius a ternario et sic de aliis, quia sic nihil aliud est numerus nisi aggregatio unitatum, et omnes unitates secundum substantiam eiusdem speciei sunt. Si secundo modo consideratur numerus, sic specie differunt binarius et quaternarius et alii numeri, quia sic

as discrete quantity is not the same in ten dogs and in ten horses, whereas the number ten taken as measure does not differ in these two collections. The reason for this latter point is that the number ten as measure belongs to these two collections not insofar as they are collections of horses and dogs, but insofar as they have a common nature. This common nature is identified with the unit replicated ten times.[140] Rufus' intuition seems that when number is regarded as a discrete quantity, the focus is principally upon the units of the collection; but these units vary in collections of specifically different things. On the other hand, when number is regarded as measure, the focus is principally upon the unit's property of being repeatable for a definite number of times and not upon the units themselves.

It is clear, however, that the objection taken from the principle of the individuation of accidents still holds. The unit replicated ten times is an accident of the collections of ten dogs and of ten horses, and hence cannot be common to these two collections in the sense of being numerically the same in both. In next subsection, we shall see a final attempt to justify the numerical identity of time and number in different subjects, one that employs Bonaventure's idea that the unity of time derives from matter.

---

numerus non debetur ipsis numeratis ratione aggregationis unitatum, sed ratione unitatis totiens replicatae. Et quia alia est replicatio ista unitatum in binario etc., propter hoc differunt isti numeri ad invicem specie" (G³, IV, q. 31, f. 178vb, lin. 38-50). See also P, IV, q. 58, f. 96va, lin. 30-37; N, IV, q. 31, f. 160va, lin. 39-46.

[140] Rufus, *In Physicam*, IV, f. 8vb, lin. 31-40: "Propterea mihi videtur quod debeamus sic dicere quod intendit dicere quod numerus est idem numero aliquo modo diversorum, sed non sicut est discreta quantitas numeratorum – sic enim diversificatur per diversitatem numeratorum – sed secundum quod mensura. Idem enim denarius non numeratus non potest esse quantitas discreta diversorum decem, potest tamen esse mensura. Causa huius est haec: denarius mensurat haec decem non quia haec, sed quia in his est unum totiens replicatum, et illud invenitur in omnibus decem. Quia ergo omnia decem communicant illam naturam per quam mensurantur decem, id est denario, propterea ab uno denario possunt mensurari, sicut per quantitatem unius virgae vel unius alicuius mensurae possunt mensurari omnia illi aequalia". See also S, IV, q. 39, f. 63vb, lin. 26-37; P, IV, q. 56, f. 96rb, lin. 7-28; G¹, IV, q. 11, f. 151vb, lin. 56-61; M³, IV, q. 14, f. 170va, lin. 58-vb, lin. 63; G³, IV, q. 29, f. 178ra, lin. 45-rb, lin. 38; N, IV, q. 29, f. 160ra, lin. 35-rb, lin. 10. At the end of his solution to the problem of the unity of time, Rufus underlines the analogy between the case of number and that of time: "Sic ergo intelligendum est simile quod, sicut numerus in quantum est mensura est idem diversorum, quia debetur eis per naturam unam inventam in eis, sic tempus in quantum quantitas vel accidens est idem diversorum motuum, quia debetur eis per naturam unam et in quantum uniuntur" (Ibid., f. 9ra, lin. 14-17). It is possible that the simplifying interpretation of Rufus' solution of the problem of the unity of time found in S and M³ originates in part from this passage.

3.3 *Bonaventure's Opinion: Its Reception in P and G¹*

In the question of his commentary on *Sentences* II devoted to the problem of the unity of the measure of separate substances, Bonaventure deals in a preliminary with the unity of time. He presents three opinions on this topic. According to the first, the unity of time derives from that of the subject in which time first exists, i. e., the first mobile and its motion. According to the second, it derives from the unity of the subject in which time first appears, i. e., again the first motion.[141] As A. Maier remarked, these two opinions are those of Avicenna and Averroes respectively.[142] Bonaventure rejects them both.[143] Instead, he follows the third opinion, according to which the unity of time derives from that of the subject that causes time, and such a subject is matter. In Bonaventure's view, time's causal dependence on matter must be explained in the sense that time is the measure of everything subject to change, and matter is the basic element that accounts for change. Indeed, something changes because it is in potency to the final form that it acquires through change, and this potency is metaphysically grounded on the potentiality of matter with respect to form. Since time is in this sense caused by matter, Bonaventure infers that the unity of time is analogous to that of matter. As matter is one and the same in substance, although it varies in being when it receives different forms, similarly, time is one and the same in substance, but varying in being by inhering in different motions and in general in different temporal entities.[144]

Even from this summary presentation, it is clear that Bonaventure's position is strictly metaphysical and seems to be devoid of any specifically physical meaning. Thus, it is not surprising that it was commonly rejected in the second half of the thirteenth century.[145] Among our commentators, S, P, T, and G¹ report a position according to which the unity of time derives from matter and probably know that Bonaventure is one of its exponents. S proposes some

---

[141] Bonaventure, *In II Sententiarum*, dist. II, pars I, art. I, q. II (*Utrum omnium aeviternorum sit unum aevum*), p. 50a-b.

[142] Maier, *Metaphysische Hintergründe*, p. 97-98.

[143] Bonaventure, *In II Sententiarum*, dist. II, pars I, art. I, q. II, p. 50b-51a.

[144] Ibid., p. 51a-b.

[145] See Maier, *Metaphysische Hintergründe*, p. 99. It is also quoted and rejected by Bacon. See Bacon, *In Physicam*, IV, p. 279, lin. 10-33.

arguments against this position,[146] whereas T dismisses it as absolutely false without arguing against it.[147] P and G¹, however, try to defend the idea that the unity of time depends ultimately on that of matter.

G¹ proposes a very general argument in favour of this idea:

> (11) ... nothing that is numerically the same can be in different subjects except in virtue of the nature of that which is numerically the same under different forms. And this is only prime matter. Therefore, if time is one in number in different subjects, this can only be in virtue of the nature of matter itself.[148]

Here G¹ assumes that matter is numerically the same when it is characterized by different forms. This assumption does not seem sound. It is true that matter taken in itself, or, as our commentators say, in its substance, i. e., apart from any form, is one, since it has no differences, and in this sense can be said numerically the same. The matter of two distinct individual substances, however, is the principle of their numerical distinction, and hence it is not clear how it could be regarded as being numerically the same in both. Therefore, if the time that inheres in different simultaneous motions has the same kind of unity as matter under different forms, this does not seem to be numerical unity. Indeed, this is the most basic objection raised by S against Bonaventure's opinion.[149] It shows that the case of matter does not seem to be of any help for establishing the numerical identity of time in different motions. This problem is not clearly addressed by G¹ and P.

Furthermore, even if one concedes that matter is numerically the same under different forms, it cannot be inferred from this that time is numerically the same in different motions. In fact, form does not function as the subject of matter, but motion is the subject of time. Therefore, the problem remains, because, since there are many

---

[146] S, IV, q. 27, f. 61rb, lin. 34-48.

[147] T, IV, q. 27, f. 56va, lin. 12-19.

[148] G¹, IV, q. 9, f. 151rb, lin. 38-40: "... nihil quod est idem numero potest esse in diversis nisi per naturam illius quod est idem numero sub formis diversis. Et hoc solum est materia prima. Igitur, si tempus est unum numero in diversis, hoc non erit nisi per naturam ipsius materiae".

[149] S, IV, q. 27, f. 61rb, lin. 34-38: "Aut enim materia accipitur secundum esse aut secundum substantiam. Si secundum esse, ergo numeratur in diversis; ergo per hoc tempus numeraretur. Si propter substantiam, arguo tunc sic. Essentia materiae et substantia est invariabilis et intransmutabilis; sed tempus nihil mensurat nisi variabile; quare etc.".

motions, there are many times. In replying to this objection, G^1 appeals directly to Bonaventure's idea that the unity of time is determined by that of its cause and not by that of its subject:

> (12) It is said that time, because it is an accident, besides having a subject, also has a cause that is naturally prior to the subject of time, namely, to motion, and this cause is called prime matter, whose multiplication and unity time follows and not the unity and multiplication of motions.[150]

The view of G^1 in this passage can be expressed more clearly by saying that the principle according to which the unity of an accident derives from the unity of its subject holds only when this subject is also in some sense the cause of the accident. This is not the case for time, since motion is the subject of time but not its cause. Its cause is in fact matter, which is ontologically prior to motion. Then the question is in what meaningful sense can matter be the cause of time. The attempts of P and G^1 to answer this question are formulated in rather obscure terms,[151] but the basic idea can be reconstructed independently of these specific formulations. In section 2.2 we have seen that,

---

[150] G^1, IV, q. 9, f. 151rb, lin. 35-38: "Dicitur quod tempus ex quo est accidens, praeter hoc quod habet subiectum, habet causam quae est prius natura quam sit subiectum temporis, scilicet motus, et haec causa dicitur materia prima, cuius multiplicationem et unitatem sequitur tempus, et non unitatem et multiplicationem motuum".

[151] In this context, P and G^1 characterize time as motion's passive habit to be numbered according to before and after. This characterization reflects an opinion on the type of number specific to time, an opinion which is reported by the two commentators in a question devoted to Aristotle's definition of time. G^1, IV, q. 7, f. 150va, lin. 21-29: "Unde dicendum, secundum quosdam, quod, cum numerus sit forma, et omnis forma est actus, erit numerus actus. Sed actus dupliciter dicitur, scilicet primus et secundus. Verbi gratia, in anima sunt duo, scilicet actus ut habitus, qui dicitur actus primus, ut scientia, et actus ut actus, sicut actu considerare de aliquo, et dicitur actus secundus. Actus autem primus dicitur dupliciter, scilicet active et passive; similiter, et actus secundus. Unde in hoc nomine 'numerus', cum sit actus, possunt accipi quattuor intentiones, scilicet (i) numeratio, actio, actus primus; (ii) numeratio, actio, actus secundus; (iii) numeratio, passio, actus primus; (iv) numeratio, passio, actus secundus. Vult igitur Aristoteles quod numerus tertio modo dictus praedicetur de tempore, cum dicit: "tempus est numerus". Est enim tempus numeratio, passio habitualis eius quod numeratur in motu. Unde tempus potest dici possibilitas numerandi prius et posterius in partibus motus". See also P, IV, q. 16, f. 91ra, lin. 56-rb, lin. 3. The meaning of these distinctions about number and their specific application to time is not clear. On the other hand, in connection with the problem of the unity of time, the characterization of time as a passive habit of motion used by P and G^1 seems to be motivated simply by their concern for stressing the similarity between time and matter.

in dealing with Aristotle's doctrine of the derivative character of the temporal order (the before and after in time), our commentators distinguish three levels: (b) that of the moving body occupying successively different positions in space, (m) that of motion, and (t) that of time.[152] Now, since level (b) is prior not only to (t) but also to (m), the cause of time which is prior to motion should be looked for at level (b). On the other hand, level (b) can be described in terms of matter, in the sense that when the mobile body takes on different positions in space, in the case of local motion, or different formal determinations, as in the other types of motion, its matter replicates itself under different beings or forms. Thus, the passive habit of the matter of the mobile body to replicate itself under different forms ultimately causes time. This is in short the interpretation given by P and G¹ of the idea that matter is the cause of time.[153] In this way P and G¹ depart from Bonaventure's original account. Bonaventure posits a rather loose connection between time and matter, holding simply that time is essentially related to change, and matter is the basic principle of change, since change involves being in potency to a form. P and G¹ try to integrate Bonaventure's idea with some other aspects of their interpretation of the Aristotelian theory of time. Thus, for example, they adjust Bonaventure's view to take into account the derivative

---

[152] See above, p. 234-237.

[153] P, IV, q. 36, f. 93vb, lin. 42-51: "... Unde tempus nihil aliud est nisi habilitas vel aptitudo motus ut numeretur secundum prius et posterius. Habitus vero passive dictus in motu respectu numerationis causatur a parte materiae, quae est causa numeri. Ex hoc enim quod mobile in motu recipit diversa esse, replicatur materia sub istis esse diversis, quae quidem materia est una essentialiter sub omnibus formis, licet accidentaliter diversificatur. Et quia haec materia est una, ideo habitus, qui praedicatur de tempore vel qui est tempus est unus essentialiter et secundum substantiam. Ut tamen iste habitus terminatur ad diversos actus, ut ad hoc prius vel illud et similiter ad hoc posterius vel illud, in diversis partibus motus, diversificatur secundum rationem, sicut et materia secundum rationem diversificatur sub diversis actibus et formis. Est ergo tempus unum secundum substantiam omnibus motibus simul existentibus, quia eadem est habilitas vel aptitudo in quolibet motu respectu numerationis; eadem dico secundum substantiam". G¹, IV, q. 9, f. 151va, lin. 12-19: "... Tempus enim per se est passio motus et est in motu sicut in subiecto; habitus passivus materiae primae est cum motu et est causa existentiae temporis in motu; motus autem est subiectum recipiens ipsum. Unde dicitur quod tempus secundum formalem praedicationem est replicatio huius habitus sub accidentibus diversis. Et causa huiusmodi habitus in motu est mobile in actu secundum quod participat substantiam materiae primae. Et ideo, sicut substantia materiae primae quantum in se est est una numero, diversificatur tamen secundum esse sub actibus et formis diversis sive differentibus, sic idem tempus secundum substantiam et essentiam est mensura omnium motuum simul terminatorum, secundum esse tamen aliquo modo differens".

character of the temporal order as well as, since they emphasize the replicability of matter under different forms, their conception of time as a number. More generally, this interpretation can be regarded as a valuable attempt to confer some physical meaning on the original position of Bonaventure. On the other hand, as far as the problem of the unity of the time is concerned, the position of P and G^1 is not very illuminating. A basic objection to the account of G^1 is raised by N:

> (13) But it seems to me that the unity in time is not caused by the passive habit of matter, which remains one and the same essentially in different beings of the mobile body, because for the same reason this habit ought to be the cause of the numerical unity of motion in different mobile things, as it seems to me.[154]

The point of this objection is that matter's passive habit to replicate itself under different forms not only causes time, but even more immediately causes motion. Thus, if the explanation of G^1 were sound, in virtue of the unity of this habit all simultaneous motions should in fact also be just one motion, so that the problem of the unity of time would not even arise.

---

[154] N, IV, q. 6, f. 156vb, lin. 38-42: "Sed mihi videtur quod unitas in tempore non causatur ab habitu passivo materiae, manente uno et eodem essentialiter in diversis esse mobilis, quia eadem ratione deberet esse causa unitatis numeralis motus in diversis mobilibus (motibus *ms.*), ut mihi videtur". See also G^3, IV, q. 7, f. 173va, lin. 40-44. For the report made by G^3 and N of the position of G^1, see G^3, IV, q. 7, f. 173rb, lin. 34-40; N, IV, q. 6, f. 156vb, lin. 4-42.

CONCLUSION

The detailed analysis carried out in this study brings to light significant elements that make it possible to draw a comprehensive outline of the early English reception of Aristotle's theories of motion, the infinite, place, and time, and to define the position of the early English commentators in the Scholastic debate on these topics. In recapitulating these elements, we shall classify them under four main headings: (1) earliness of the tradition, (2) distinctive doctrines, (3) ontological realism, and (4) anti-Averroism.

(1) *Earliness of the tradition*

There are some significant (i) exegetical and (ii) "doxographic" aspects in our commentaries that most evidently express an early stage of the reception of Aristotle's natural philosophy. Specifically, by early exegetical aspects we mean those aspects of the interpretation of our commentators that reflect a still incomplete and immature assimilation of Aristotle's physical thought. By early doxographic aspects we mean those concerning the support of opinions that tend to disappear from later thirteenth-century commentaries on the *Physics*. In our assessment of the "early" aspects of our commentaries we implicitly assume as main points of reference the commentaries on the *Physics* by Thomas Aquinas and Giles of Rome.

(i) A major exegetical aspect that indicates the earliness of our tradition appears in the treatment of Aristotle's doctrine of the infinite. The early English commentators show an incomplete command of the logic of Aristotle's distinction between the potential and actual infinites. Their uneasiness with this technical aspect of Aristotle's theory comes out especially in connection with a controversial argument with which Aristotle rejects the possibility of a potential infinite by addition in magnitude on the grounds that this would lead to an actual infinite, i.e., to the existence of an infinitely extended magnitude. The inference from a potential infinite to an actual infinite seems faulty, and moreover conflicts with some general aspects of Aristotle's theory of the infinite. Aristotelian commentators are usually very alert to the difficulties involved in Aristotle's argument. Simplicius and Averroes, for example, devote a lengthy discussion to it. Yet, the problem is essentially overlooked by most of the early English commentators. Even those who notice the problem quickly dismiss it by repeating some parts of the complex attempt to find a solution made by Averroes. Moreover, most of them make extensive use of the same faulty inference from potentially infinite to actually infinite magnitudes on which Aristotle's controversial argument is based.[1]

Other minor instances of a still superficial insight into the technical aspects of Aristotle's discussion appear in the treatment of the structure of time and its relation to the structures of motion and the instant of time.[2] It should be remarked, however, that the limited command that our commentators have of the technical aspects of the *Physics* does not affect their understanding of the philosophical ideas with which such aspects are related. Indeed, they usually have a firm grasp of these ideas and a good intuition of the implicit assumptions that lie behind them. For example, while they fail to capture the logic of the distinction between the potential and actual infinites, they are perfectly aware of the ontological assumptions that lead Aristotle to maintain that numbers are only potentially infinite.[3] As we shall recall in next section, however, a main issue on which our commentators do not grasp Aristotle's thought is that of the ontology of spatial extension.

(ii) The "doxographic" earliness of our tradition appears especially in the discussion of the problem of the place of the heavens, which is one of the major topics of the medieval debate on Aristotle's theory of place. With respect to this problem, most of our commentators depart from Averroes' position that the place of the heavens is defined with respect to the earth, and support a twelfth-century opinion that identifies it with the external surface of the heavens themselves. While Averroes' position enjoyed good fortune, the twelfth-century opinion upheld by our commentators tends to disappear from later commentaries. A reason for this is that this opinion does not focus the intrinsic connection between place and local motion, which is the crucial physical issue involved in the problem of the

---

[1] See above, p. 100-114.
[2] See above, p. 212-219, 231-237.
[3] See above, p. 125-132.

place of the heavens. Indeed, this twelfth-century view does find a place for the heavens, but such a place is completely extraneous to the rotation of the heavens.[4] For an analogous reason the fact that some of our commentators support Bonaventure's solution to the problem of the unity of time can be classified as a sign of the earliness of this tradition. Again, Bonaventure's claim that the unity of time derives from matter is a rather vague metaphysical answer to a physical problem in which the notion of matter plays no significant role, and so was disregarded by later commentators, who tend rather to adopt Averroes' more physical solution.[5] Yet, while our commentators are still attracted by these two "archaic" opinions, they also try to render them more relevant to the physical context. For example, they adopt a modified version of the twelfth-century opinion on the place of the heavens in which they introduce some elements of Averroes' solution. Similarly, in the case of Bonaventure's opinion, they attempt to show that the notion of matter is connected with Aristotle's physical notion of time as a number of motion.

(2) *Distinctive Doctrines*

Besides the traditional problems of *Physics* III-IV that are constantly discussed by thirteenth- and fourteenth-century commentators, two main doctrinal issues that are typical of the early English tradition can be indicated: (i) the debate about the actual infinity of number, and (ii) the theory of "immersive" place (*locus profundans*).

(i) Aristotle claims that numbers (i.e., positive integers) are only potentially infinite. He argues that the infinite addition in numbers is accounted for by the infinite divisibility of a continuous magnitude. The number of parts actually divided from a continuum is always finite, but can always be increased, since a continuum can be further divided. The finiteness of the parts of a continuum resulting from each stage of its division shows that numbers are only potentially infinite. Yet, in the early English debate the main objections against Aristotle's doctrine of the potential infinity of numbers arises precisely from the relation between number and continuous magnitude. Our commentators point out that, in addition to the actually divided parts, which are always finite, a continuum has potential parts, that is, those that are not yet actually divided, and these parts are actually infinite. Then the crucial question becomes whether the actually infi-

---

[4] See above, p. 197-202.
[5] See above, p. 257-261.

nite potential parts of a continuum do have a number, despite the fact that they exist only potentially. If they have a number, then such a number is actually infinite, being the number of infinitely many things. This question is much debated by the early English commentators, who hold divergent views on it. Some of them maintain that the potential parts of a continuum, just as, more generally, potencies and non-beings, do have a number, since the actual existence of a number is independent of the actual existence of the collection of things in which it inheres. Thus, they support an infinitist position according to which numbers can be actually infinite. Other commentators maintain that number can instead be ascribed only to collections of actually existing things, so that the case of the potential parts of a continuum does not constitute a counterexample to Aristotle's theory of the potential infinity of numbers.[6]

Although a significant discussion of the infinity of numbers can be found in the Greek commentators Philoponus and Simplicius, the innovative aspect of the early English debate is that the arguments proposed in it are taken from Aristotle's theory of the continuum and its potential parts, while Aristotle's doctrine of the eternity of the world, which is the traditional source of arguments for the actual infinity of numbers, is neglected. Indeed, the "cosmological" examples of actually infinite numbers, such as the number of past human beings and of past celestial revolutions in a beginningless world, are essentially the only ones considered by Philoponus, but they hardly appear in the early English commentaries. Arguments taken from the potential parts of a continuum do appear in fourteenth-century commentaries on the *Physics*, such as those by Walter Burley and William of Ockham. Yet, the comparison with these later commentators points out another peculiarity of the early English debate. The matter of contention in this debate concerns the notion of number rather than the notion of infinity. All our commentators agree that the potential parts of a continuum are actually infinite, but the controversial issue is whether potential things actually have a number. Furthermore, as has been suggested, the infinitist position supported by those commentators who hold that the actual existence of number is independent of the actual existence of numbered things can be better understood if it is viewed as an expression of the ontological realism

---

[6] See above, p. 114-125.

about numbers that appears more explicitly in their interpretation of other topics of *Physics* IV, such as the ontological status and the unity of time.[7]

(ii) The early English commentators depart from Aristotle's view in *Physics* IV that identifies place with the limit, i.e., the surface, of the containing body, and assign to place a third dimension, depth, in virtue of which place "immerses itself" in the located body. The origin of their theory of three-dimensional place is Aristotle's short discussion in the *Categories*, where he seems to regard place as a three-dimensional extension coextensive with the located body. Aristotelian commentators are usually aware that the notion of place as surface in the *Physics* is in contrast with that of three-dimensional place in the *Categories*. Yet, the dominant tendency is to regard the description of place in the *Physics* as the only one that expresses Aristotle's definite view on this topic. In the medieval tradition, a standard way to dismiss Aristotle's account in the *Categories* is by appealing to the general principle that in this work Aristotle sometimes speaks *secundum famositatem* rather than *secundum veritatem*. On the contrary, the early English commentators take very seriously Aristotle's discussion in the *Categories* and try to modify his notion of place in the *Physics* in order to reconcile it with that of the *Categories*. Thus, in order to remove the main quantitative difference between Aristotle's two notions of place, they add a third dimension to the notion of place in the *Physics*. The resulting notion of "immersive" three-dimensional place proposed by our commentators involves deep ontological difficulties that arise from the contrasting ontologies of spatial extension underlying Aristotle's two views of place. Indeed, the notion of place in the *Categories* presupposes the existence of a spatial extension that does not inhere in material substances, whereas in the *Physics* Aristotle radically denies the existence of an incorporeal extension. The problem with the position of the early English commentators is, in short, that while it retains the three-dimensionality of place in the *Categories*, it tries to adopt the more restrictive ontology of spatial extension of the *Physics*.[8]

An earlier exponent of the theory of immersive place is Roger Bacon, who supports it in his second set of questions on the *Physics* and probably is an immediate source for our commentaries. Yet, he

---

[7] See above, p. 125-132.
[8] See above, p. 141-159.

eventually rejects it in his later work *Communia naturalium*, with which this theory seems to have come to an end.[9]

The discussion of "immersive" place shows, roughly speaking, both the ontological realism of our commentators and their still incomplete understanding of Aristotle's natural philosophy. Indeed, ontological realism seems to lie behind their acceptance of the notion of place in the *Categories*, since this matches well with the realist assumption that, if there are material bodies, there must be something else in which they are located. Yet, their attempt to combine the concept of place in the *Categories* with that in the *Physics* is an evident sign of the immature assimilation of Aristotle's different presuppositions about the ontology of spatial extension in these two works.

(3) *Ontological Realism*

The ontological assumptions that underlie the approach of the early English commentators to Aristotle's natural philosophy are realist. As we have just pointed out, the two distinctive doctrines of our tradition involve a latent form of realism concerning numbers and spatial extension. This realism comes out most evidently in the discussion of the ontological status of motion and time. In the case of motion, the fundamental question for medieval commentators is whether motion is something really distinct from both the mobile substance in which it inheres and the formal determinations acquired and lost by this substance during motion. Similarly, in the case of time, the question is whether time is really distinct from the motion in which it inheres. The answer of the early English commentators to both these questions is affirmative. Thus, in their view, the natural world, insofar as it consists of material substances that undergo temporal processes, is stratified into three distinct ontological levels: (i) substances and their permanent accidental properties, e.g., qualities and quantities, (ii) motion through which substances change with respect to permanent properties, and (iii) time as a successive quantity inhering in motion. The ontological distinctions between level (ii) and level (i), and between level (iii) and both (i) and (ii) express, in abstract terms, the realism of the early English commentators concerning motion and time.

Historically, their realist position is formulated as an attack on Averroes' interpretation of Aristotle's doctrine. In the solution to an

---

[9] See above, p. 140-141, 159-164.

exegetical problem concerning Aristotle's categorical classification of motion, Averroes introduces a distinction between two ways of "regarding" motion, according to which motion can be seen either as an incomplete form (*forma incompleta*) or as a process towards a form (*via ad formam*). In the *forma*-theory, motion is nothing other than the form acquired by the mobile substance, while this form is still incomplete. In the *via*-theory, motion is really distinct from its final form and is an *ens* in itself. Averroes claims that only the *forma*-theory is true, whereas the *via*-theory is merely well-known (*famosa*). On the contrary, the early English commentators reject the *forma*-theory and support the *via*-theory.[10] In the case of time, following some suggestions by Aristotle himself, Averroes maintains that its existence depends to some extent on the human soul. He argues for this conclusion on the basis of Aristotle's definition of time as a number of motion. Since number is not an extramental property of a collection of things, but depends on the mental process of counting those things, then so time is not an extramental property of motion, but depends on our activity of counting, in the sense of distinguishing and ordering, the successive phases of motion. Thus, in Averroes' view, while motion exists in extramental reality, time does not. The early English commentators reject Averroes' position and maintain that time is a real property of motion, not depending on any mental process, and likewise that number is a real property of a collection of things. Thus, their critique of Averroes involves a realist position about the ontological status of both time and number.[11]

The realist opposition to Averroes found in the early English commentaries enlarges our knowledge of the thirteenth-century debate about the ontological status of motion and time. Before the discovery of these commentaries and specifically at the time of Anneliese Maier's studies, some realist positions, especially on time, such as those of Roger Bacon and Albert the Great, were known. Nevertheless, it seemed that the debate was largely dominated by Averroes' view, and that a significant realist reaction against it could only be found in the fourteenth century. The study of the early English tradition shows that by the middle of the thirteenth century this reaction had already started, although it did not continue with Thomas

---

[10] See above, p. 47-59.
[11] See above, p. 221-230.

Aquinas and Giles of Rome, the two most authoritative commentators of the second half of the thirteenth century. Moreover, as far as we presently know, the commentaries considered in this book represent the large majority of the commentaries on the *Physics* written before Aquinas' commentary.[12] Thus, we can even provisionally conclude that until Aquinas' time, the thirteenth-century debate on the ontological status of motion and time was in fact dominated by a critical attitude towards Averroes arising from realist assumptions.

Finally, the position of our commentators on motion and time reflects an early phase of the history of realist interpretations of Aristotelian natural philosophy. In the case of motion, the earliness of our tradition is shown especially by the type of arguments used to reject Averroes' *forma*-theory of motion. These arguments are ontological rather than physical, in the sense that they focus on the main ontological assumption underlying this theory, namely, the real identity between motion and its final form, and then try to show that it is incompatible with other ontological properties of motion. For example, our commentators argue that motion is a successive entity, and therefore cannot differ only in degree from its final form, which is a permanent entity. On the other hand, they do not try to confront Averroes' theory with specifically physical questions, such as whether during motion its final form exists in an incomplete state and how the incompleteness of this form is to be understood in each of the four species of motion distinguished by Aristotle. In short, a systematic analysis of Averroes' *forma*-theory is absent from the early English commentaries. Such a physical analysis, however, started soon after our commentaries with Thomas Aquinas and was widely used by Thomas Wylton and Walter Burley at the beginning of the fourteenth century.[13]

In the case of time, the earliness of our tradition manifests itself as a still partial assimilation of Aristotle's theory. Our commentators realize that the major obstacle in *Physics* IV.10-14 to positing a real distinction between motion and time is Aristotle's claim that time, being a number, depends on the soul. Yet, they do not notice that a more subtle obstacle arises from the doctrine of the derivation of the order of time from the order of motion. This doctrine, as much as

---

[12] See Donati, "Per lo studio dei commenti alla Fisica", first part, p. 366.
[13] See above, p. 60-66.

that of the dependence of time on the soul, is an essential part of Aristotle's "reductionist" attitude towards the ontological status of time,
but it is accepted by our commentators. As has been suggested, this
makes it difficult for them to give a satisfactory formulation of their
realist position. If the successive order of time is seen as ontologically
and logically dependent on the successive order of motion, then it is
not easy to answer the crucial question of why it is necessary to posit
time as another successive entity in addition to motion. In fact, the
early English commentators do not succeed in answering this question, and hence in their realist position time tends to be a mere
"duplicate" of motion.[14]

(4) *Anti-Averroism*

The early English tradition is characterized by a strong and perva-
sive critical attitude towards Averroes' interpretation of Aristotle's
Physics. The anti-Averroism of this tradition appears not only in ontological issues, such as the reality of motion and time, but also extends
to topics that do not immediately involve ontological assumptions.
The most important "non-ontological" criticisms of Averroes' positions concern the two traditional problems of the place of the heavens
and the unity of time. Averroes' solutions exerted a great influence on
the thirteenth- and fourteenth-century debate. Yet, most of the early
English commentators reject them.

The problem of the place of the heavens arises from the fact that
the heavens lack an external container and hence do not have, strictly
speaking, a place. On the other hand, the heavens undergo local
motion, and therefore must in some sense be in a place. Averroes'
solution claims that the place of the heavens is to be identified with
the centre of the universe, which is the earth around which they
rotate. This solution matches very well with the idea that the place of
a body should provide a frame of reference for its local motion and
rest.[15] Such an idea is repeatedly formulated by thirteenth- and fourteenth-century commentators, and, as has been suggested, largely
determines the success of Averroes' position on the place of the heavens. Some of the early English commentators acknowledge that the
earth plays an essential role as a frame of reference for the rotation of
the heavens. Nevertheless, they reject Averroes' solution mainly on

---

[14] See above, p. 231-237.
[15] See above, p. 194-197.

the grounds that it does not respect the superiority of the heavens over the earth in Aristotle's cosmology. To save this cosmological principle, they are lead to support a twelfth-century opinion according to which the place of the heavens must be identified with the external surface of the heavens themselves, though usually modifying this opinion to accomodate some aspects of Averroes' solution.[16]

The problem of the unity of time arises from Aristotle's claim that there is just one time despite the fact that there are many motions. This is in contrast with the ontological status of time as an accident of motion, which seems to imply that there are as many times as there are motions. The idea of Averroes' solution consists in restricting the subject of time to a single motion, i.e., the motion of the heavens. Then, being an accident of just one motion, time is unique. In this way, Averroes shows that the status of time as an accident of motion can be reconciled with Aristotle's requirement of a unique time, without violating the principle that the numerical identity of accidental properties is determined by the numerical identity of their subjects of inherence. Averroes' idea of restricting the subject of time to heavenly motion is brilliant both from a conceptual and an exegetical point of view, and was repeated by authoritative thirteenth-century commentators, such as Albert the Great, Thomas Aquinas, and Giles of Rome. It is disregarded, however, by most of the early English commentators. The point of their objections is that Averroes' solution provides time with only a "weak" kind of unity. The unity of time is ultimately accounted for by the factual condition that there is just one heavenly motion, so that it cannot be saved in the counterfactual situation of a plurality of heavenly motions. Thus, our commentators assume that the unity of time is independent of the plurality of actual and possible motions, but an explanation for this assumption cannot be found in Averroes' solution. In looking for such an explanation, they turn either to the opinion of Rufus and Bacon, in which the unity of the time of simultaneous motions is guaranteed by the lack of "temporal distance" of such motions, or to that of Bonaventure, in which its unity is guaranteed by matter.[17]

While the realism of the early English commentators is clearly the common ground for their rejection of Averroes' positions on the

---

[16] See above, p. 196-202.
[17] See above, p. 240-246.

ontological status of motion and time, a similar common basis for their criticisms of Averroes' solutions to the problems of the place of the heavens and the unity of time cannot easily be indicated. It is likely that the realism about time and numbers of our commentators motivates at least partially their emphasis on the principle that the unity of time is unaffected by the multiplicity of motions. This is not, however, the motivation for their critique of Averroes' solution to the problem of the place of the heavens, although, as we have been reminded above, in other parts of their discussion of place a latent realism appears. Yet, it can be suggested that something common to these two cases can be found at a more general and methodological level. It seems that some of the early English commentators tend to consider Averroes' solutions as only partial and superficial. In the case of the place of the heavens, the "incompleteness" of Averroes' solution is given by the fact that it takes into account only the local motion of the heavens but not also their priority in the Aristoteliam cosmos. A sign of this is that the solution proposed by some of our commentators is an attempt to take into account both these features of the heavens. In the case of the unity of time, Averroes' solution is regarded as partial and not definitive because, while it does save the unity of time, it does not really find an adequate explanation for it. To achieve a more precise and articulated formulation of the relation of the early English tradition to Averroes' natural philosophy we need a still more extensive knowledge of this tradition. As a result of the present study, we can safely conclude that the early English commentators use Averroes' commentary on *Physics* III-IV mainly as an exegetical source, to understand Aristotle's text and to detect the exegetical problems posed by it, but they depart from Averroes' interpretations of the most important topics concerning motion, place, and time.

BIBLIOGRAPHY

Manuscripts

Cambridge, Gonville and Caius College, ms. 367
Cambridge, Gonville and Caius College, ms. 509
Cambridge, Peterhouse, ms. 157
Cambridge, Peterhouse, ms. 192
Cesena, Biblioteca Malatestiana, ms. Plut. VIII sin. 2
Erfurt, Wissenschaftliche Bibliothek der Stadt, ms. Ampl. Q. 312
London, Wellcome Historical Medical Library, ms. 333
Oxford, Bodleian Library, ms. lat. misc. C.69
Oxford, Merton College, ms. 272
Oxford, New College, ms. 285
Padova, Biblioteca Universitaria, ms. 2248
Siena, Biblioteca Comunale degli Intronati, ms. L. III. 21
Todi, Biblioteca Comunale, ms. 23

Greek and Latin Texts

Adam de Bocfeld, *Expositio super Physicam*, ms. Padova, Biblioteca Universitaria, 2248.
Aegidius Romanus, *Commentaria in octo libros Physicorum Aristotelis*, Venetiis 1502, repr. Frankfurt 1968.
Albertus Magnus, *Physica*, (*Opera Omnia*, Tomus IV, pars I: Libri 1-4; pars II: Libri 5-8), ed. P. Hossfeld, Aschendorff, Münster 1987, 1993.
Anonymus, *Liber Sex Principiorum* (Aristoteles Latinus, I 6-7), ed. L. Minio-Paluello, adiuvante B. G. Dod, Desclée de Brouwer, Bruges-Paris 1966.
Aristotle, *De Anima*, edited with introduction and commentary by W. D. Ross, Clarendon Press, Oxford 1961.
Aristotelis Categoriae et Liber De Interpretatione, ed. L. Minio-Paluello, Clarendon Press, Oxford 1949.
Aristotle's Metaphysics, a revised text with introduction and commentary by W. D. Ross, Clarendon Press, Oxford 1924.
Aristotle's Physics, a revised text with introduction and commentary by W. D. Ross, Clarendon Press, Oxford 1936.
Averroes Cordubensis, *Aristotelis Metaphysicorum libri XIIII (Aristotelis Opera cum Averrois Commentariis,* VIII), Venetiis apud Junctas 1562, repr. Minerva, Frankfurt 1962.
Averroes Cordubensis, *Aristotelis de Physico Auditu (Aristotelis Opera cum Averrois Commentariis,* IV), Venetiis apud Junctas 1562, repr. Minerva, Frankfurt 1962.
Avicenna, *Sufficientia*, Venetiis 1508, repr. Edition de la bibliothèque S. J., Louvain 1961.
S. Bonaventurae Liber II. Sententiarum (Opera theologica selecta, Tomus II), Editio minor, Quaracchi-Firenze 1938.
Gualterus de Burley, *In Physicam Aristotelis Expositio et Quaestiones*, Venetiis 1501, repr. Hildesheim-New York 1972.

Guillelmus de Bonkes, *Quaestiones super Physicam*, ms. Cambridge, Peterhouse, 192, I, ff. 37ra-119vb.

Guillelmi de Ockham Expositio in libros Physicorum Aristotelis, (*Guillelmi de Ockham Opera Philosophica*, IV), ed. V. Richter and G. Leibold, St. Bonaventure 1985.

The Tractatus de successivis attributed to William Ockham, ed. P. Boehner, St. Bonaventure 1944.

Ioannis Philoponi in Aristotelis Physicorum libros tres priores commentaria (*Commentaria in Aristotelem Graeca*, XVI), ed. H. Vitelli, Berlin 1887.

Ioannis Philoponi in Aristotelis Physicorum libros quinque posteriores commentaria (*Commentaria in Aristotelem Graeca*, XVII), ed. H. Vitelli, Berlin 1888.

Johannes Duns Scotus, *Ordinatio*, liber II (*Opera Omnia*, VII), Vatican City 1973.

Richardus Rufus de Cornubia, *Quaestiones super Physicam*, ms. Erfurt, Wissenschaftliche Bibliothek der Stadt, Ampl. Q. 312, ff. 1ra-14ra.

Roberti Grosseteste Episcopi Lincolniensis Commentarius in VIII libros Physicorum Aristotelis, ed. R. C. Dales, University of Colorado Press, Boulder (Colorado) 1963.

Rogerus Bacon, *Communia Naturalium*, I (*Opera hactenus inedita Rogeri Baconi*, Fasc. III), ed. R. Steele, Clarendon Press, Oxford 1911.

Rogerus Bacon, *Questiones supra libros quatuor Physicorum Aristotelis* (*Questiones prime*) (*Opera hactenus inedita Rogeri Baconi*, Fasc. VIII), ed. F.M. Delorme with the collaboration of R. Steele, Clarendon Press, Oxford 1928.

Rogerus Bacon, *Questiones supra libros octo Physicorum Aristotelis* (*Questiones altere*) (*Opera hactenus inedita Rogeri Baconi*, Fasc. XIII), ed. F.M. Delorme with the collaboration of R. Steele, Clarendon Press, Oxford 1935.

Simplicii in Aristotelis Physicorum libros quattuor priores commentaria (*Commentaria in Aristotelem Graeca*, IX), ed. H. Diels, Berlin 1882.

Simplicii in Aristotelis Physicorum libros quattuor posteriores commentaria (*Commentaria in Aristotelem Graeca*, X), ed. H. Diels, Berlin 1895.

Themistii in Aristotelis Physica Paraphrasis (*Commentaria in Aristotelem Graeca*, V, 2), ed. H. Schenkl, Berlin 1900.

S. Thomae Aquinatis In octo libros Physicorum Aristotelis Expositio, ed. P. M. Maggiolo, Marietti, Torino-Roma 1965.

Thomas de Wylton, *Quaestiones libri Physicorum*, ms. Cesena, Biblioteca Malatestiana, Plut. VIII sin. 2, ff. 1ra-141vb.

Translations

Aristotle's Categories and De Interpretatione, Translated with Notes by J. L. Ackrill, Clarendon Press, Oxford 1963.

Aristotle, *Physics*, Books I and II, Translated with Introduction, Commentary, Note on Recent Work, and Revised Bibliography by W. Charlton, Clarendon Press, Oxford 1970.

Aristotle's Physics, Books III and IV, Translated with Notes by Edward Hussey, Clarendon Press, Oxford 1983.

Aristotle, *Physics*, translated by Robin Waterfield, Introduction and notes by David Bostock, Oxford University Press, Oxford 1996.

Secondary Literature

Algra, K., *Concepts of Space in Greek Thought*, Brill, Leiden-New York-Köln 1995.

Annas, J., "Aristotle, Number and Time", *Philosophical Quarterly*, 25 (1975), p. 97-113.

Bostock, D. "Aristotle, Zeno, and the Potential Infinite", *Proceedings of the Aristotelian Society*, 73 (1972-73), p. 37-51.

Callus, D. A., "Introduction of Aristotelian Learning to Oxford", *Proceedings of the British Academy*, 29 (1943), p. 229-281.

Caroti, S., "Oresme on Motion (*Questiones super Physicam*, III, 1-8)", *Vivarium*, 31 (1993) 1, p. 8-36.

Charlton, W., "Aristotle's Potential Infinites", in L. Judson (ed.), *Aristotle's Physics: A Collection of Essays*, Clarendon Press, Oxford 1991, p. 129-149.

Corish, D., "Aristotle's Attempted Derivation of Temporal Order from That of Movement and Space", *Phronesis*, 21 (1976), p. 241-251.

Croese, I., *Simplicius on Continuous and Instantaneous Change*, Zeno Institute of Philosophy, The Leiden-Utrecht Research Institute, Utrecht 1998.

Cross, R., *The Physics of Duns Scotus. The Scientific Context of a Theological Vision*, Clarendon Press, Oxford 1998.

Del Punta, F. – Donati, S., – Trifogli, C., "Commentaries on Aristotle's *Physics* in Britain, ca. 1250-1270", in J. Marenbon (ed.), *Aristotle in Britain during the Middle Ages*, Proceedings of the international conference at Cambridge 8-11 April 1994 organized by the Société Internationale pour l'Etude de la Philosophie Médiévale, Brepols, Turnhout 1996, p. 265-283.

Donati, S., "Per lo studio dei commenti alla *Fisica* del XIII secolo. I: Commenti di probabile origine inglese degli anni 1250-1270 ca.", first part, *Documenti e studi sulla tradizione filosofica medievale*, 2 (1991), p. 361-441; second part, ibid., 4 (1993), p. 25-133.

Ead., "*Physica* I, 1: L'interpretazione dei commentatori inglesi della *Translatio Vetus* e la loro recezione del commento di Averroè", *Medioevo*, 21 (1995), p. 75-255.

Ead., "Commenti parigini alla *Fisica* degli anni 1270-1300 ca.", in A. Speer (ed.), *Die Bibliotheca Amploniana im Spannungsfeld von Aristotelismus, Nominalismus und Humanismus* (*Miscellanea Mediaevalia*, Bd. 23), De Gruyter, Berlin-New York 1995, p. 136-256.

Ead., "Materie und räumliche Ausdehnung in einigen ungedruckten englischen Physikkommentaren aus der Zeit von etwa 1250-1270", in J. Aertsen, A. Speer (eds.), *Raum und Raumvorstellungen im Mittelalter* (*Miscellanea Mediaevalia*, Bd. 25), De Gruyter, Berlin-New York 1998, p. 17-51.

Ead., "Il commento alla *Fisica* di Adamo di Bocfeld e un commento anonimo della sua scuola", *Documenti e studi sulla tradizione filosofica medievale*, 9 (1998), p. 111-178; 10 (1999), p. 1-65.

Duhem, P., *Le Système du Monde. Histoire des doctrines cosmologiques de Platon a Copernic*, 10 vols., Hermann, Paris 1913-1959.

Furley, D. J., "The Greek Commentators' Treatment of Aristotle's Theory of the Continuous", in N. Kretzmann (ed.), *Infinity and Continuity in Ancient and Medieval Thought*, Cornell University Press, Ithaca and London 1982, p. 17-36.

Gill, M. L., "Aristotle's Theory of Causal Action in *Physics* III 3", *Phronesis*, 25 (1980), p. 129-147.

Graham, D. W., "Aristotle's Definition of Motion", *Ancient Philosophy*, 8 (1988), p. 209-215.

Grant, E., "Place and Space in Medieval Physical Thought", in P. K. Machamer, R. G. Turnbull (eds.), *Motion and Time, Space and Matter. Interrelations in the History of Philosophy and Science*, Ohio State University Press, Columbus 1976, p. 137-167.

Id., "The Medieval Doctrine of Place: Some Fundamental Problems and Solutions", in A. Maierù, A. Paravicini-Bagliani (eds.), *Studi sul XIV secolo in memoria di Anneliese Maier*, Edizioni di storia e letteratura, Roma 1981, p. 57-79.

Id., *Much Ado about Nothing, Theories of space and vacuum from the Middle Ages to the Scientific Revolution*, Cambridge University Press, Cambridge 1981.

Hasnawi, A., "Alexandre d'Aphrodise vs Jean Philopon: Notes sur quelques traités d'Alexandre "perdus" en Grec, conservés en Arabe", *Arabic Sciences and Philosophy*, 4 (1994), p. 53-109.

Hintikka, J., "Aristotelian Infinity", *Philosophical Review*, 75 (1966), p. 197-218.

Inwood, M., "Aristotle on the Reality of Time", in L. Judson (ed.), *Aristotle's Physics: A Collection of Essays*, Clarendon Press, Oxford 1991, p. 151-178.

Jeck, U. R., *Aristoteles contra Augustinum. Zur Frage nach dem Verhältnis von Zeit und Seele bei den antiken Aristoteleskommentatoren, im arabischen Aristotelismus und im 13. Jahrhundert*, Grüner, Amsterdam-Philadelphia 1994.

King, H., "Aristotle's Theory of TOPOS", *Classical Quarterly*, 44 (1950), p. 76-96

Kosman, L. A., "Aristotle's definition of motion", *Phronesis*, 14 (1969), p. 40-62.

Kostman, J., "Aristotle's Definition of Change", *History of Philosophy Quarterly*, 4 (1987) 1, p. 3-16.

Kretzmann, N., "Aristotle on the Instant of Change", *Proceedings of the Aristotelian Society*, Suppl. vol. 50 (1976), p. 91-114.

Lang, H. S., *Aristotle's Physics and Its Medieval Varieties*, State University of New York Press, Albany 1992.

Lear, J., "Aristotelian Infinity", *Proceedings of the Aristotelian Society*, 80 (1979-80), p. 187-210.

Luna, C., "La relation chez Simplicius", in I. Hadot (ed.), *Simplicius. Sa vie, son oeuvre, sa survie*. Actes du colloque international de Paris (28 Sept.-1er Oct. 1985), De Gruyter, Berlin-New York 1987, p. 113-147.

MacDonald, S., "Aquinas's Parasitic Cosmological Argument", *Medieval Philosophy and Theology*, 1 (1991), p. 119-155.

Macrae, E., "Geoffrey of Aspall's Commentaries on Aristotle", *Mediaeval and Renaissance Studies*, 6 (1968), p. 94-134.

Maier, A., *Die Vorläufer Galileis im 14. Jahrhundert* (*Studien zur Naturphilosophie der Spätscholastik*, Bd. 1), Edizioni di storia e letteratura, Roma 1949.

Ead., *Zwei Grundprobleme der scholastischen Naturphilosophie* (*Studien zur Naturphilosophie der Spätscholastik*, Bd. 2), Edizioni di storia e letteratura, Roma 1951.

Ead., *An der Grenze von Scholastik und Naturwissenschaft* (*Studien zur Naturphilosophie der Spätscholastik*, Bd. 3), Edizioni di storia e letteratura, Roma 1952.

Ead., *Metaphysische Hintergründe der Spätscholastischen Naturphilosophie* (*Studien zur Naturphilosophie der Spätscholastik*, Bd. 4), Edizioni di storia e letteratura, Roma 1955.

Ead., *Zwischen Philosophie und Mechanik*, (*Studien zur Naturphilosophie der Spätscholastik*, Bd. 5), Edizioni di storia e letteratura, Roma 1958.

Mansion, A., "La théorie aristotélicienne du temps chez les péripatéticiens médiévaux", *Revue Néoscolastique de Philosophie*, 36 (1934), p. 275-307.

McCord Adams, M., *William Ockham*, University of Notre Dame Press, Notre Dame, Indiana 1987.

McCullough, E. J., "St. Albert on Motion as *Forma fluens* and *Fluxus formae*", in J. A. Weisheipl (ed.), *Albertus Magnus and the Sciences. Commemorative Essays 1980*, Pontifical Institute of Medieval Studies, Toronto 1980, p. 129-153.

Mendell, H., "Topoi on Topos: The Development of Aristotle's Concept of Place", *Phronesis*, 32 (1987), p. 206-231

Meyer, G., "Die Bewegungslehre des Thomas von Aquin im Kommentar zum 3. Buch der Aristotelischen *Physik*", in L. Elders (ed.), *La philosophie de la nature de Saint Thomas d'Aquin*, Actes du Symposium sur la pensée de Saint Thomas tenu à Rolduc, les 7 et 8 Nov. 1981, Libreria editrice vaticana, Città del Vaticano 1982, p. 45-65.

Miller, F. D., "Aristotle on the Reality of Time", *Archiv für Geschichte der Philosophie*, 56 (1974), p. 132-155.

Murdoch, J. E., "Propositional Analysis in Fourteenth-Century Natural Philosophy", *Synthese*, 40 (1979), p. 117-146.

Id., "William of Ockham and the Logic of Infinity and Continuity", in N. Kretzmann (ed.), *Infinity and Continuity in Ancient and Medieval Thought*, Cornell University Press, Ithaca and London 1982, p. 165-206.

Id., "Infinity and Continuity", in N. Kretzmann, A. Kenny, J. Pinborg (eds.), *The Cambridge History of Later Medieval Philosophy*, Cambridge University Press, Cambridge 1982, p. 564-591.

Owen, G. E. L., "Inherence", *Phronesis*, 10 (1965), p. 97-105.

Id., "Aristotle on Time", in J. Barnes, M. Schofield, R. Sorabji (eds.), *Articles on Aristotle*, vol. 3 (*Metaphysics*), Duckworth, London 1979, p. 140-158.

Plevano, R., "Richard Rufus of Cornwall and Geoffrey of Aspall. Two Questions on the Instant of Change", *Medioevo*, 19 (1993), p. 167-232.

Porro, P., *Forme e modelli di durata nel pensiero medievale. L'aevum, il tempo discreto, la categoria "quando"*, Leuven University Press, Leuven 1996.

Riggert, H., "Vier Fragen über die Zahl. Ein ungedruckter Text des Wilhelm von Clifford zu Arist. Phys. IV 14", in A. Zimmermann (ed.), *Aristotelisches Erbe im arabisch-lateinischen Mittelalter. Uebersetzungen, Kommentare, Interpretationen* (*Miscellanea Mediaevalia*, Bd. 18), De Gruyter, Berlin-New York 1986, p. 81-95.

Sedley, D., "Philoponus' Conception of Space", in R. Sorabji (ed.), *Philoponus and the Rejection of Aristotelian Science*, Duckworth, London 1987, p. 140-153.

Solmsen, F., *Aristotle's System of the Physical World. A comparison with his predecessors*, Cornell University Press, Ithaca (N. Y.) 1960.

Sorabji, R., *Time, Creation and the Continuum. Theories in antiquity and the early middle ages*, Duckworth, London 1983.

Id., *Matter, Space and Motion, Theories in Antiquity and Their Sequel*, Duckworth, London 1988.

Id., "Infinity and the Creation", in R. Sorabji (ed.), *Philoponus and the Rejection of Aristotelian Science*, Duckworth, London 1987, p. 164-178.

Taylor, A. E., *A Commentary on Plato's Timaeus*, Clarendon Press, Oxford 1928.

Trifogli, C., "La dottrina del luogo in Egidio Romano", *Medioevo* 14 (1988), p. 254-290.

Ead., "Il luogo dell'ultima sfera nei commenti tardo-antichi e medievali a *Physica* IV.5", *Giornale critico della filosofia italiana*, 68 (1989), p. 144-152.

Ead., "La dottrina del tempo in Egidio Romano", *Documenti e studi sulla tradizione filosofica medievale*, 1 (1990) 1, p. 265-275.

Ead., "Il problema dello statuto ontologico del tempo nelle *Quaestiones super Physicam* di Thomas Wylton e di Giovanni di Jandun", *Documenti e studi sulla tradizione filosofica medievale*, 1 (1990) 2, p. 515-527.

Ead., "Thomas Wylton on the Instant of Time", in A. Zimmermann (ed.), *Mensch und Natur im Mittelalter* (*Miscellanea Mediaevalia*, Bd. 21/1), De Gruyter, Berlin-New York 1991, p. 308-318.

Ead., "Le questioni sul libro III della *Fisica* in alcuni commenti inglesi intorno alla metà del sec. XIII", first part in *Documenti e studi sulla tradizione filosofica medievale*, 2 (1991) 2, p. 443-501; second part ibid., 4 (1993), p. 135-178.

Ead., "Thomas Wylton on Motion", *Archiv für Geschichte der Philosophie*, 77 (1995), p. 135-154.

Ead., "Due questioni sul movimento nel Commento alla *Physica* di Thomas Wylton", *Medioevo*, 21 (1995), p. 31-73.

Ead., "Le questioni sul libro IV della *Fisica* in alcuni commenti inglesi intorno alla metà del sec. XIII. Parte I", *Documenti e studi sulla tradizione filosofica medievale*, 7 (1996), p. 39-114.

Ead., "Le questioni sul libro IV della *Fisica* in alcuni commenti inglesi intorno alla metà del sec. XIII. Parte II", *Documenti e studi sulla tradizione filosofica medievale*, 9 (1998), p. 179-260.

Ead., "An Anonymous Question on the Immobility of Place from the End of the XIIIth Century", in A. Speer (ed.), *Raum und Raumvorstellungen im Mittelalter* (*Miscellanea Mediaevalia*, Bd. 25), De Gruyter, Berlin-New York 1998, p. 147-167.

Ead., "Roger Bacon and Aristotle's Doctrine of Place", *Vivarium*, 35 (1997), 2, p. 155-176.

Ead., "Thomas Wylton on the Immobility of Place", *Recherches de Théologie et Philosophie médiévales*, 65 (1998) 1, p. 1-39.

Waterlow, S., *Nature, Change and Agency in Aristotle's Physics, A philosophical study*, Clarendon Press, Oxford 1982.

White, M. J., *The Continuous and the Discrete. Ancient Physical Theories from a Contemporary Perspective*, Clarendon Press, Oxford 1992.

Wood, R., "Richard Rufus of Cornwall on Creation: The Reception of Aristotelian Physics in the West", *Medieval Philosophy and Theology*, 2 (1992), p. 1-30.

Ead., "Richard Rufus of Cornwall and Aristotle's Physics", *Franciscan Studies*, 52 (1992), p. 247-279.

Ead., "Richard Rufus: Physics at Paris before 1240", *Documenti e studi sulla tradizione filosofica medievale*, 5 (1994), p. 87-127.

Zimmermann, A., *Verzeichnis ungedruckter Kommentare zur Metaphysik und Physik des Aristoteles aus der Zeit von etwa 1250-1350*, Brill, Leiden-Köln 1971.

INDEX OF NAMES

INDEX OF MANUSCRIPTS

INDEX OF SUBJECTS

STUDIEN UND TEXTE
ZUR GEISTESGESCHICHTE
DES MITTELALTERS

25. Livesey, S. J. *Theology and Science in the Fourteenth Century.* Three Questions on the Unity and Subalternation of the Sciences from John of Reading's Commentary on the *Sentences.* Introduction and Critical Edition. 1989. ISBN 90 04 09023 1

26. Elders, L. J. *The Philosophical Theology of St Thomas Aquinas.* 1990. ISBN 90 04 09156 4

27. Wissink, J. B. (Ed.). *The Eternity of the World in the Thought of Thomas Aquinas and his Contemporaries.* 1990. ISBN 90 04 09183 1

28. Schneider, N. *Die Kosmologie des Franciscus de Marchia.* Texte, Quellen und Untersuchungen zur Naturphilosophie des 14. Jahrhunderts. 1991. ISBN 90 04 09280 3

29. Langholm, O. *Economics in the Medieval Schools.* Wealth, Exchange, Value, Money and Usury according to the Paris Theological Tradition, 1200-1350. 1992. ISBN 90 04 09422 9

30. Rijk, L. M. de. *Peter of Spain (Petrus Hispanus Portugalensis): Syncategoreumata.* First Critical Edition with an Introduction and Indexes. With an English Translation by Joke Spruyt. 1992. ISBN 90 04 09434 2

31. Resnick, I. M. *Divine Power and Possibility in St. Peter Damian's* De Divina Omnipotentia. 1992. ISBN 90 04 09572 1

32. O'Rourke, F. *Pseudo-Dionysius and the Metaphysics of Aquinas.* 1992. ISBN 90 04 09466 0

33. Hall, D. C. *The Trinity.* An Analysis of St. Thomas Aquinas' *Expositio* of the *De Trinitate* of Boethius. 1992. ISBN 90 04 09631 0

34. Elders, L. J. *The Metaphysics of Being of St. Thomas Aquinas in a Historical Perspective.* 1992. ISBN 90 04 09645 0

35. Westra, H. J. (Ed.). *From Athens to Chartres.* Neoplatonism and Medieval Thought. Studies in Honour of Edouard Jeauneau. 1992. ISBN 90 04 09649 3

36. Schulz, G. *Veritas est adæquatio intellectus et rei.* Untersuchungen zur Wahrheitslehre des Thomas von Aquin und zur Kritik Kants an einem überlieferten Wahrheitsbegriff. 1993. ISBN 90 04 09655 8

37. Kann, Ch. *Die Eigenschaften der Termini.* Eine Untersuchung zur *Perutilis logica* Alberts von Sachsen. 1994. ISBN 90 04 09619 1

38. Jacobi, K. (Hrsg.). *Argumentationstheorie.* Scholastische Forschungen zu den logischen und semantischen Regeln korrekten Folgerns. 1993. ISBN 90 04 09822 4

39. Butterworth, C. E., and B. A. Kessel (Eds.). *The Introduction of Arabic Philosophy into Europe.* 1994. ISBN 90 04 09842 9

40. Kaufmann, M. *Begriffe, Sätze, Dinge.* Referenz und Wahrheit bei Wilhelm von Ockham. 1994. ISBN 90 04 09889 5

41. Hülsen, C. R. *Zur Semantik anaphorischer Pronomina.* Untersuchungen scholastischer und moderner Theorien. 1994. ISBN 90 04 09832 1

42. Rijk, L. M. de (Ed. & Tr.). *Nicholas of Autrecourt.* His Correspondence with Master Giles and Bernard of Arezzo. A Critical Edition from the Two Parisian Manuscripts with an Introduction, English Translation, Explanatory Notes and Indexes. 1994. ISBN 90 04 09988 3

43. Schönberger, R. *Relation als Vergleich.* Die Relationstheorie des Johannes Buridan im Kontext seines Denkens und der Scholastik. 1994. ISBN 90 04 09854 2

44. Saarinen, R. *Weakness of the Will in Medieval Thought.* From Augustine to Buridan. 1994. ISBN 90 04 09994 8

45. Speer, A. *Die entdeckte Natur.* Untersuchungen zu Begründungsversuchen einer „scientia naturalis" im 12. Jahrhundert. 1995. ISBN 90 04 10345 7

46. Te Velde, R. A. *Participation and Substantiality in Thomas Aquinas.* 1995. ISBN 90 04 10381 3

47. Tuninetti, L. F. „*Per Se Notum*". Die logische Beschaffenheit des Selbstverständlichen im Denken des Thomas von Aquin. 1996. ISBN 90 04 10368 6

48. Hoenen, M.J.F.M. und De Libera, A. (Hrsg.). *Albertus Magnus und der Albertismus.* Deutsche philosophische Kultur des Mittelalters. 1995. ISBN 90 04 10439 9

49. Bäck, A. *On Reduplication.* Logical Theories of Qualification. 1996. ISBN 90 04 10539 5

50. Etzkorn, G. J. *Iter Vaticanum Franciscanum*. A Description of Some One Hundred Manuscripts of the Vaticanus Latinus Collection. 1996. ISBN 90 04 10561 1
51. Sylwanowicz, M. *Contingent Causality and the Foundations of Duns Scotus' Metaphysics*. 1996. ISBN 90 04 10535 2
52. Aertsen, J.A. *Medieval Philosophy and the Transcendentals*. The Case of Thomas Aquinas. 1996. ISBN 90 04 10585 9
53. Honnefelder, L., R. Wood, M. Dreyer (Eds.). *John Duns Scotus*. Metaphysics and Ethics. 1996. ISBN 90 04 10357 0
54. Holopainen, T. J. *Dialectic and Theology in the Eleventh Century*. 1996. ISBN 90 04 10577 8
55. Synan, E.A. (Ed.). *Questions on the* De Anima *of Aristotle by Magister Adam Burley and Dominus Walter Burley* 1997. ISBN 90 04 10655 3
56. Schupp, F. (Hrsg.). *Abbo von Fleury:* De syllogismis hypotheticis. Textkritisch herausgegeben, übersetzt, eingeleitet und kommentiert. 1997. ISBN 90 04 10748 7
57. Hackett, J. (Ed.). *Roger Bacon and the Sciences*. Commemorative Essays. 1997. ISBN 90 04 10015 6
58. Hoenen, M.J.F.M. and Nauta, L. (Eds.). *Boethius in the Middle Ages*. Latin and Vernacular Traditions of the *Consolatio philosophiae*. 1997. ISBN 90 04 10831 9
59. Goris, W. *Einheit als Prinzip und Ziel*. Versuch über die Einheitsmetaphysik des *Opus tripartitum* Meister Eckharts. 1997. ISBN 90 04 10905 6
60. Rijk, L.M. de (Ed.). *Giraldus Odonis O.F.M.:* Opera Philosophica. *Vol. 1.: Logica.* Critical Edition from the Manuscripts. 1997. ISBN 90 04 10950 1
61. Kapriev, G. *...ipsa vita et veritas*. Der "ontologische Gottesbeweis" und die Ideenwelt Anselms von Canterbury. 1998. ISBN 90 04 11097 6
62. Hentschel, F. (Hrsg.). *Musik – und die Geschichte der Philosophie und Naturwissenschaften im Mittelalter.*Fragen zur Wechselwirkung von 'musica' und 'philosophia' im Mittelalter. 1998. ISBN 90 04 11093 3
63. Evans, G.R. *Getting it wrong*. The Medieval Epistemology of Error. 1998. ISBN 90 04 11240 5
64. Enders, M. *Wahrheit und Notwendigkeit*. Die Theorie der Wahrheit bei Anselm von Canterbury im Gesamtzusammenhang seines Denkens und unter besonderer Berücksichtigung seiner Antiken Quellen (Aristoteles, Cicero, Augustinus, Boethius). 1999. ISBN 90 04 11264 2
65. Park, S.C. *Die Rezeption der mittelalterlichen Sprachphilosophie in der Theologie des Thomas von Aquin*. Mit besonderer Berücksichtigung der Analogie. 1999. ISBN 90 04 11272 3
66. Tellkamp, J.A. *Sinne, Gegenstände und Sensibilia*. Zur Wahrnehmungslehre des Thomas von Aquin. 1999. ISBN 90 04 11410 6
67. Davenport, A.A. *Measure of a Different Greatness*. The Intensive Infinite, 1250-1650. 1999. ISBN 90 04 11481 5
68. Kaldellis, A. *The Argument of Psellos'* Chronographia. 1999. ISBN 90 04 11494 7
69. Reynolds, P.L. *Food and the Body*. Some Peculiar Questions in High Medieval Theology. 1999. ISBN 90 04 11532 3
70. Lagerlund, H. *Modal Syllogistics in the Middle Ages*. 2000. ISBN 90 04 11626 5
71. Köhler, T.W. *Grundlagen des philosophisch-anthropologischen Diskurses im dreizehnten Jahrhundert*. Die Erkenntnisbemühung um den Menschen im zeitgenössischen Verständnis. 2000. ISBN 90 04 11623 0
72. Trifogli, C. *Oxford Physics in the Thirteenth Century (ca. 1250-1270)*. Motion, Infinity, Place and Time. 2000. ISBN 90 04 11657 5